CARNAL COMMERCE IN COUNTER-REFORMATION ROME

Focusing on the period 1566–1656, this original and lively study sheds new light on the daily lives and material culture of ordinary prostitutes and their clients in Rome after the Counter-Reformation. Tessa Storey uses a range of archival sources, including criminal records, letters, courtroom testimonies, images and popular and elite literature, to reveal issues of especial concern to contemporaries. In particular, she explores how and why women became prostitutes, the relationships between prostitutes and clients, and the wealth which potentially could be accumulated. Notarial documents provide a unique perspective on the economics and material culture of prostitution, showing what could be earned and how prostitutes dressed and furnished their homes. The book challenges traditional assumptions about the effect of post-Tridentine reforms on Roman prostitution, revealing that, despite energetic attempts at social disciplining by the Counter-Reformation popes, prostitution continued to flourish, and to provide a lucrative living for many women.

TESSA STOREY is a Research Associate at the Department of History, University of Leicester.

NEW STUDIES IN EUROPEAN HISTORY

Edited by

PETER BALDWIN, University of California, Los Angeles
CHRISTOPHER CLARK, University of Cambridge
JAMES B. COLLINS, Georgetown University
MIA RODRÍGUEZ-SALGADO, London School of Economics
and Political Science
LYNDAL ROPER, University of Oxford

The aim of this series in early modern and modern European history is to publish outstanding works of research, addressed to important themes across a wide geographical range, from southern and central Europe, to Scandinavia and Russia, from the time of the Renaissance to the Second World War. As it develops the series will comprise focused works of wide contextual range and intellectual ambition.

For a full list of titles published in the series, please see the end of the book.

CARNAL COMMERCE IN COUNTER-REFORMATION ROME

TESSA STOREY
University of Leicester

CAMBRIDGE
UNIVERSITY PRESS

CAMBRIDGE UNIVERSITY PRESS

Cambridge, New York, Melbourne, Madrid, Cape Town, Singapore, São Paulo, Delhi

Cambridge University Press
The Edinburgh Building, Cambridge CB2 8RU, UK

Published in the United States of America by Cambridge University Press, New York

www.cambridge.org
Information on this title: www.cambridge.org/9780521844338

© Tessa Storey 2008

First published 2008

Printed in the United Kingdom at the University Press, Cambridge

A catalogue record for this publication is available from the British Library

ISBN 978-0-521-84433-8 hardback

For Mum and Dad

Contents

Contents

Figures

Maps

Tables

Acknowledgements

Like so many others, this book started out as a PhD thesis. Later, some things were added and some things were taken away and the result has been a long time in the making. Accordingly, the list of those who have been involved is long, and some will barely remember me; others are still very present in my life, but the debt of gratitude remains.

I would like to give a heartfelt thank you first to those historians who have advised, supported and encouraged me along the way. Sandra Cavallo's teaching of gender history inspired me to do an MA and then a PhD, and she has been teacher, colleague and friend, reading endless drafts, helping me think about masculinity and material culture, and supporting me from the wings. Olwen Hufton taught me to think about which questions to ask, about the practicalities of women's lives, and her incisive comments as supervisor helped me lay the foundations of the book. Laurence Fontaine also supervised me, giving an enormous amount of her time and energy, and setting me thinking in unexpected directions about economics and material goods. More recently Lyndal Roper, first as examiner, then as colleague, finally as reader and editor, has read and re-read the drafts of this book, combining tough criticism, insights and encouragement in equal parts, whilst teaching me a great deal about early modern Europe, gender and how to write! My thanks also to Mary Laven and the other anonymous readers at Cambridge University Press for their comments and suggestions as to how to improve the text, and to Michael Watson the editor, Helen Waterhouse, Carol Fellingham Webb, my copy editor, and the rest of the production team at the Press.

I am very grateful to the many others who have read different versions of this book and assisted in many ways: Renata Ago, who helped me with documents and thinking about Rome; Michèle Cohen, who has read, commented and been a friend; Sara Matthews-Grieco and Simon Ditchfield, who have read much of this, at one stage or another, made many suggestions and urged me on. Lotte Van de Pol has shared her wonderful work on Amsterdam with me and Angelica Pediconi has helped me with hygiene in Rome. Attending seminars held by the Centre for the Domestic Interior project at the Victoria and Albert Museum was stimulating and several of those involved – Marta Ajmar, Flora Dennis and Ann Machette – have helped me think about material culture and music. Patrizia Cavazzini and Helen Langdon have at very short notice been extremely helpful with their expertise on Baroque paintings.

A project like this, undertaken in the seemingly impenetrable archives of Italy, requires a great deal of help from the natives. My heartfelt thanks go to those Italians, friends and acquaintances, who have been involved along the way: Riccardo Bassani for showing me how to use the archives in Rome and how to find my *cortigiane* in the first place, as well as providing me with a floor to sleep on; Federica Favino, who helped with Latin, palaeography and much much more; and Maria Pia di Donato, who has likewise helped with Latin and translations. I should also like to thank all those archivists who have helped me in the Archivio Capitolino, Archivio del Vicariato di Roma, the Vatican Archives and Vatican Library, but above all in the Archivio di Stato di Roma, particularly Anna Lia Bonella, Augusto Pompeo and Michele di Sivo.

Along the way a great deal of money has been spent and much pasta and wine consumed. I gratefully acknowledge the financial support of the Department of Education and Science and the European University Institute for the four years in Florence, and the École Française de Rome for its several grants to stay in Rome and the use of its marvellous library and accommodation, particularly Dr Catherine Brice for assisting me and encouraging this project. After my PhD the Leverhulme Trust stepped in with a generous special research fellowship which enabled me to start writing up and teaching.

Particular thanks are owed for the support from friends at the European University Institute: Cristina Espinoza, Mette Zolner, Veronique Pujas, Mario Drago, Silvain Rivet, Mirabelle Madigner, Cathy Richmond, Cathy Woolf and Sergio Amadeo. A huge thank you must go to Mai, Mimmo and Lidia Cinga Cozzupoli, who were tireless in their much needed offers of hospitality and company when I went to research in Rome. Thanks also must go to Paul Ginsborg, who unwittingly inspired me to go back to university to study Italian and history, to Patrick Guilfoyle for helping with my first computer, and to all those old and new friends who have egged me on, refraining from raising an eyebrow when all enquiries were met with the same old reply, 'still finishing the book'. A special thank you to Magda and Petra, who in turn have made it possible to work without worrying about my children.

Finally my deepest thanks must go to my family, both Storeys and Dows, for their unfailing moral support. To Emily and Edward, who were not consulted, and around whose young lives I have tried to balance the claims of motherhood and academe, and who have given up much time with me for the sake of this book. To Abigail, Kazi and to James, who in the course of all this became my husband. He has fallen asleep over endless drafts, pointed out the racy double entendres, helped with the statistics, dried tears, picked up the pieces and lent his unswerving dedication, emotional and intellectual support throughout. Last but not least, to my parents who, in one way or another, over all the years, in so many different ways, have made all this possible, and to whom I dedicate this book.

Notes on the text

MONEY

There were ten *baiocchi* to a *giulio*, and ten *giulii* to one silver *scudo*.

Wages in the Roman construction industry at this time were forty or fifty *baiocchi* a day for builders and twenty-five to thirty *baiocchi* for their assistants, but they may not have found work every day. An artisan might earn about three *scudi* a month, and a very good one five or six.[1] One of the Bargello of Rome's policemen earned four *scudi* a month, plus bed and board.[2] Women were paid far less. A washerwoman or female servant might earn about one *scudo* a month, and a wet nurse two *scudi*, although they would have received board and lodging as well. As for what that could buy, in 1628 the legal price of an eight-ounce loaf of bread was one *baiocco* and dinner in an *osteria* could cost between eight and twelve *baiocchi*.[3]

TIME

The time was calculated from sundown. For convenience I have estimated the times myself.

All translations are mine, with help from Maria Pia di Donato and Federica Favino unless otherwise mentioned.

Spellings and punctuation of quotations from the archives have been modernised.

---

[1] The second figure is for a leather-worker, aged forty-one, cited in Renata Ago, *Economia barocca. Mercato e istituzioni nella Roma del seicento* (Rome: Donzelli, 1998), 14.
[2] ASR, TCG, Testimoni per la Difesa, vol. 190, c18r, 19 March 1603.
[3] Mario Romani, *Pellegrini e Viaggiatori nell'economia di Roma dal XIV al XVII secolo* (Milan: Vita e Pensiero, 1948).

Abbreviations

ARSI	Archivum Romanum Societatis Iesu
ARSRSP	*Archivio Romana della Società Reale per Storia Patria* (a journal)
AS	Archivio di Stato, Sezione Orvieto
ASF	Archivio di Stato di Firenze
ASR	Archivio di Stato di Roma
ASV	Archivio Segreto Vaticano
AVIC	Archivio del Vicariato di Roma
BAV	Biblioteca Apostolica Vaticana
BNF	Biblioteca Nazionale di Firenze
RB	*Relazioni dei Birri*
SA	*Stati delle Anime*
SAF	Sant'Andrea delle Fratte
SLL	San Lorenzo in Lucina
SMP	Santa Maria del Popolo
TCG	Tribunale Criminale del Governatore
TD	Testimoni per la Difesa
TNC	Trenta Notai Capitolini
U19	Ufficio 19
Urb. Lat.	Urbinati Latini

Introduction

> It seemed a harsh and monstrous thing that in holy Rome there should be so many prostitutes, and that they should be held in such high esteem, that they seemed to be queens (thanks to human incontinence and intemperance).[1]

On the night before Palm Sunday in 1559, the Bishop of Polignano was enjoying the delights of the flesh in the arms of a Jewish courtesan named Porzia. Sadly for him, his pleasures were to be short lived. A servant had informed on him and the couple were arrested the same night. The Bishop was sentenced to perpetual imprisonment whilst Porzia was exiled from Rome, having been publicly whipped, had her goods confiscated and her house ransacked. In the following days, diplomatic reports known as *avvisi*[2] circulated with details of the case, expressing the public's astonishment at these events. It was not so much the Bishop's punishment which was shocking. He had 'acted against the law' (sex between Jews and Christians was forbidden by canon law) and priests were expected to live chastely.[3] On the contrary, the outcry was occasioned 'by the sentence handed out to Porzia because she was a public courtesan and paid her tribute every year', and was therefore 'guilty of nothing'.[4]

Porzia and the unfortunate Bishop were amongst the first high-profile victims to fall foul of the Counter-Reformation papacy's rapid shift in

[1] Ortensio Lando, *Commentario delle più notabili et mostruose cose d'Italia, e altri luoghi* (Venice, 1548), 15.

[2] Daily reports which informed courts and merchants of important political, economic and social events – often written by diplomatic correspondents. See Jean Delumeau, *Vie économique et sociale de Rome dans la seconde moitié du XVIe siècle* (2 vols.) (Paris: De Boccard, 1957), 25–36. And Tullio Bulgarelli, *Gli avvisi a stampa in Roma nel Cinquecento* (Rome: Istituto di Studi Romani Editore, 1967).

[3] Clearly fornication by priests was also frowned upon, especially given the religious climate. On Jews and Christians see James A. Brundage, *Sex, Law and Marriage in the Middle Ages* (Aldershot: Variorum, 1993), 25–40, 30. More generally see Merry E. Wiesner-Hanks, *Christianity and Sexuality in the Early Modern World: Regulating Desire, Reforming Practice* (London: Routledge, 2000), 107.

[4] BAV, Urbinati Latini, vol. 1039, c20r, 25 March 1559; c24r, 8 April 1559; c28v, 22 April 1559.

attitudes towards sexual immorality in Rome. Hitherto, the city had been remarkable for its leniency towards prostitution and any woman who had registered herself as a prostitute could practise her profession virtually unhindered. Furthermore, as the shock and pity which accompanied Porzia's punishment demonstrated, the immorality of her actions did not trouble the average bystander. Indeed, sympathy for prostitutes ensnared by the new laws would be expressed on many other occasions in the *avvisi* over the following decades, until the Romans eventually became used to this new approach to the policing of sexual morality.

I

Prostitutes had long been tolerated in Rome, as in other towns and cities across Europe, their place in society underpinned by a celebration of male virility and medical understandings of the body. They served to protect wives and 'honest' virgins from the lusts of males, who were thereby able to have extra-marital sex without disturbing the social order.[5] Prostitution was regulated more closely in some cities than in others, but by the fourteenth century many municipalities had at the very least attempted to separate prostitutes from other women. In cities such as Castile, Dijon, Amsterdam and across the Italian peninsula, brothels or 'red-light' areas were established; prostitutes were often ordered to wear distinctive attire. In many places, such as Venice, Bologna and Florence, government offices were set up specifically to control prostitution. Prostitutes had to register with them and pay taxes, which generated a significant income for local governments, whilst a panoply of laws restricted their activities.[6] Despite

[5] Jacques Rossiaud, *Medieval Prostitution* (Oxford: Basil Blackwell, 1988), chapter 6. Linda L. Otis, *Prostitution in Medieval Society: the History of an Urban Institution in Languedoc* (London: University of Chicago Press, 1985). Rinaldo Comba, '"Apetitus libidinis Coherceatur"': Strutture demografiche, reati sessuali e disciplina dei comportamenti nel Piemonte tardo-medievale', *Studi Storici* 27:3 (1986), 529–76, 552. For analyses which stress this idea of the role of prostitution in upholding the social order see Carol Lansing, 'Gender and Civic Authority: Sexual Control in a Medieval Italian Town', *Journal of Social History* 31:1 (1997), 33–59. Mary Elizabeth Perry, *Gender and Disorder in Early Modern Seville* (Princeton: Princeton University Press, 1990), 46. And Guido Ruggiero, *The Boundaries of Eros: Sex, Crime and Sexuality in Renaissance Venice* (London and New York: Oxford University Press, 1995), esp. 146–68.

[6] Otis, *Prostitution in Medieval Society*. Rossiaud, *Medieval Prostitution*. Elisabeth Pavan, 'Police des moeurs, société et politique à Venise à la fin du Moyen Age', *Revue Historique* 36:5 (1980), 241–88. Richard Trexler, 'La prostitution florentine au XVe siècle: patronages et clientèles', *Annales ESC* 36 (1981), 985–1015. Maria Serena Mazzi, *Prostitute e Lenoni nella Firenze del Quattrocento* (Milan: Mondadori, 1991). John Brackett, 'The Florentine Onestà and the Control of Prostitution, 1403–1680', *Sixteenth Century Journal* 24:2 (1993), 273–300. For a general overview of several Italian cities see Romano Canosa and Isabella Colonnello, *Storia della prostituzione in Italia* (Rome: Sapere 2000, 1989).

its position at the centre of Catholic Christendom, Rome had exercised very little control over its prostitutes prior to the mid-sixteenth century. They were required to register with the Curia Savelli, one of the city's many tribunals, which collected a yearly tax, but apart from this there was little legislation. At the lower end of the social hierarchy the profession was focused around a few brothels and *stufe* (bath-houses), the first of which opened in 1422.[7] At the other end of the social spectrum elite courtesans received clients in their famously splendid apartments.

Change came in the sixteenth century as a wave of official intolerance towards prostitution swept across Europe. Some scholars have attributed this to the sudden and appalling consequences of syphilis which first appeared in the last decade of the fifteenth century. However, sexual contact was only one of the many ways the disease was believed to be transmitted and the timing is incorrect, since the brothels closed down several decades after the appearance of syphilis.[8] Others have linked the change to the long-standing association between prostitution and disease, to the newly apparent dovetailing of prostitution and crime and a general desire for improved social order, and in particular to the impact of Protestantism.[9] The results were the closure of brothels, the rejection of 'official' prostitution and the promulgation of harsh legislation against prostitutes. This occurred first in Protestant areas: in 1526 in Zwickau, in Augsburg in 1532 and in London in 1546. Most of the brothels in Languedoc closed in the 1550s, a decade before they were prohibited by the Decree of Orleans (1561), and prostitution was criminalised in Amsterdam in 1578, when the Protestants came

For developments in Germany see Lyndal Roper, 'Discipline and Respectability: Prostitution and the Reformation in Augsburg', *History Workshop Journal* 19 (1985), 3–28. Roper, 'Madri di depravazione: le mezzane nel Cinquecento', *Memoria* 2 (1986), 7–23. For Spain see Mary Elizabeth Perry, 'Deviant Insiders: Legalized Prostitutes and a Consciousness of Women in Early Modern Seville', *Comparative Studies in Society and History* 27 (1985), 138–58. And Perry, *Gender and Disorder*. Denis Menjot, 'Prostitution et ruffianage dans les villes de Castille à la fin du Moyen Age', *IAHCCJ Bulletin* 19 (1994), 21–38. Iñaki Bazán Díaz, Francisco Vázquez García and Andrés Moreno Mengibar, 'La prostitution au pays Basque entre XIVe et XVIIe siècles', *Annales HSS* 55:6 (2000), 1283–302. For England see Ruth Mazo Karras, *Common Women: Prostitution and Sexuality in Medieval England* (Oxford and New York; Oxford University Press, 1996). In Florence in 1569 prostitutes paid between 38 *soldi* and 1–2 *scudi* per annum according to their income as a licence to practise. Canosa and Colonnello, *Storia della prostituzione*, 107–8. Venetian prostitutes who paid more than 40 ducats rent were taxed to help build the Arsenal. Pavan, 'Police des moeurs', 280. In 1501 25 per cent of Carmona's normal income was derived from the brothel. Menjot, 'Prostitution et ruffianage', 29, 31.

[7] There were at least five *stufe* operating in the Ponte-Parione area in the early sixteenth century. Angelica Pediconi, 'The Art and Culture of Bathing in Renaissance Rome', MA dissertation, History of Design, Victoria and Albert Museum/Royal College of Art, 2004, 121, 142. Also Canosa and Colonnello, *Storia della prostituzione*, 49.

[8] Otis, *Prostitution in Medieval Society*, 40–5.

[9] Ibid. Roussiaud, *Medieval Prostitution*, 51. And Roper, 'Discipline and Respectability', 13.

to power.[10] In Catholic areas the legislative response was slower and less dramatic. In Spain municipal brothels remained open for another hundred years, until 1626. In Italian cities prostitution continued to be tolerated, but municipalities sought to hem it in with restrictions.[11]

II

The arrests of Porzia and the Bishop took place as the movement for Catholic renewal gathered pace in the mid to late sixteenth century. Under the auspices of several particularly zealous popes – Paul IV, Pius IV, Pius V and Sixtus V – Rome, seat of the papacy and a place of pilgrimage for hundreds of thousands of Catholics from across Europe, was in the public eye. Its reputation was tarnished by its many prostitutes and the wealthy courtesans who had flourished in the tolerant atmosphere of the Holy City, a fact echoed in Protestant propaganda, which portrayed the city as Babylon and the Pope as a whore.[12] As part of a general phase of renewal in the city, it was important therefore that the papacy be seen to act against prostitution and establish a new reputation for moral rectitude.

Prostitution lay at the heart of Protestant and Catholic concerns about female sexuality and wider social discipline. It was not just a problem of individual immorality. Prostitutes were emblematic of female 'disorderliness', and 'waywardness' in general, illustrating the dangers of allowing women to escape from male control. They epitomised everything that women should not be, or do. Furthermore, prostitution was seen as a 'canker', a symptom of moral degeneracy which could spread like a disease throughout society, multiplying what Borromeo referred to as the 'occasions to sin.'[13] Prostitutes promoted the ruin of others by seducing young men and setting a bad example to other young women. Sociability around prostitutes was associated with general indiscipline and a range of other vices: drinking, gambling, dancing, vanity and greed. By eliminating or restricting prostitution, city fathers hoped to increase their control over female immorality, to

---

[10] See Roper, 'Discipline and Respectability' for timings in German states; Otis, *Prostitution in Medieval Society*, for France; Mazo Karras, *Common Women*, for England; and for Amsterdam, Lotte Van de Pol, *Het Amsterdams Hoerdom. Prostitutie in de Zeventiende en Achtiende Eeuw* (Amsterdam: Wereldbibliotheek, 1996) (translation forthcoming from Oxford University Press).

[11] For Spain see Perry, 'Deviant Insiders', and for Italy, Canosa and Colonnello, *Storia della prostituzione*.

[12] On courtesans as one of the 'sights' of the city see Elizabeth S. Cohen, 'Seen and Known: Prostitutes in the Cityscape of Late Sixteenth-Century Rome', *Renaissance Studies* 12:3 (1998), 392–409. On such propaganda see Robert Scribner, *For the Sake of Simple Folk: Popular Propaganda for the German Reformation* (Cambridge: Cambridge University Press, 1981).

[13] Wietse de Boer, *The Conquest of the Soul: Confession, Discipline and Public Order in Counter-Reformation Milan* (Leiden, Boston and Cologne: Brill, 2001), 70.

punish, reform and redeem the women involved in it, and more generally to purify the social arena.[14]

The Counter-Reformation has been identified by gender historians as a period in which civic and ecclesiastic authorities strengthened patriarchal control over women: limiting their autonomy of action in both public and religious spheres; bringing them further under male control; attempting to inculcate a stricter sexual morality; and imposing new behavioural norms. The reforms of prostitution were just one facet of this broader campaign. As a result of recent scholarly interest, particularly by gender historians, we now know a great deal about the nature of these ideals and the ways in which they were disseminated: models of perfect womanhood were preached from pulpits, enshrined in imagery and codified in conduct books.[15] We know far less about responses to these measures and the extent to which the new morality and norms permeated the consciousness of ordinary citizens, although what research there is suggests that women did not accept the loss of their autonomy meekly.[16] This book considers the impact of this phase of 'social disciplining' on the lives of the women – and men – involved in prostitution, at the heart of the Catholic world in the century following the Tridentine reforms. It explores the effects of the discipline ordinances on the daily lives and practices of prostitutes and their clients, it examines whether the number of wealthy prostitutes was visibly reduced, and it asks whether the new morality affected the way prostitutes viewed themselves, were viewed by their clients and were viewed within their communities.

Although generally considered to affect only a 'marginal' social group, prostitution in this society was something to which many thousands of women turned, at some point in their lives, whether on a long-term basis or to tide them briefly over a crisis. In looking at the impact of the Counter-Reformation on prostitutes and prostitution we are examining just one facet of a much broader campaign to restrict women's sexuality, social autonomy and economic activities. This was achieved by reinscribing them within the ever narrowing confines of marriage, claustration, or regulated and policed prostitution, bringing women increasingly under male control, whichever sphere they moved through. Furthermore, although the three separate paths

[14] See also Jennifer Selwyn's discussion of Jesuit attitudes towards prostitutes in *A Paradise Inhabited by Devils: the Jesuits' Civilizing Mission in Early Modern Naples* (Aldershot: Ashgate, 2004), 174–5.

[15] Many of the essays in the following collections discuss early modern constructions of gender. Geraldine A. Johnson and Sara F. Matthews Grieco, eds., *Picturing Women in Renaissance and Baroque Italy* (Cambridge: Cambridge University Press, 1997). Letizia Panizza, ed., *Women in Italian Renaissance Culture and Society* (Oxford: Legenda, 2000). And M. Migiel and J. Schiesari, eds., *Refiguring Woman: Perspectives on Gender and the Italian Renaissance* (New York: Cornell University Press, 1991).

[16] This will be discussed further in the conclusion.

mapped out for women appear to have been radically divergent, bounded by the impenetrable walls of law and normative discourse, symbolically and practically they were interwoven and interpenetrating.[17] Prostitution shored up marriage by 'protecting' wives and virgins from the attentions of other men, providing a legitimate space outside it which catered to those men whose sexual and affective needs could not be met by marriage. Likewise the status and praise accorded to the purity of nuns were intensified by the contrast with the unbridled sexuality and corruption of 'whores'.

Although those women who became nuns generally remained within a convent, many other women might experience all three states of womanhood in their life-time: marriage, prostitution and the taking of religious orders. The majority of women lived in poverty and the two ideal states of womanhood, marriage and the convent, both came at a price. A dowry was required for both institutions and it was a price which many women could not afford, or at least, not immediately. Many earned a dowry through prostitution itself; others prostituted themselves when the material advantages associated with marriage failed to appear, or when they found themselves widowed or abandoned, perhaps with children to raise. When prostitution failed to deliver the hoped-for material benefits, when it proved too unpleasant or perhaps dangerous, women could always 'repent', and for a small price, end their days as a nun in a convent for the *convertite*.

III

The historiography of prostitution in pre-modern Italy and Europe has been weighted in favour of studies of the later middle ages and Renaissance. The fourteenth and fifteenth centuries in southern France, Florence, Venice and England in particular have been well documented. Until very recently, studies of the phenomenon in Rome were limited to the early sixteenth century, driven by curiosity about the so-called 'golden age' of the elite courtesans. This produced an extensive, if rather uniform, bibliography on the lives and loves of courtesans in the context of High Renaissance Rome.[18] However, such was the apparent vigour with which the Counter-Reformation papacy sought to tackle prostitution, it has often

---

[17] See Silvia Evangelisti's comments on the intersections and overlaps between marriage and the convent in 'Wives, Widows and Brides of Christ: Marriage and the Convent in the Historiography of Early Modern Italy', *Historical Journal* 43: 1 (2000), 233–47, 241.

[18] Prior to the mid-twentieth century these works were based on a combination of extensive archival research and use of literary sources. Salvatore Bonghi, *Il Velo Giallo di Tullia D'Aragona* (Florence: G. Carnesecchi e Figli, 1886). A. Bertolotti, *Repressioni straordinarie alla prostituzione in Roma nel secolo XVI* (Rome: Tipografia delle Mantellate, 1887). Guido Biagi, *Un' etèra romana: Tullia d'Aragona*,

been assumed that practices of prostitution in the city were profoundly modified, and that the well-to-do courtesans, in particular, disappeared.[19] As a reflection of this, histories of prostitution in Rome came to an abrupt end in the mid to late sixteenth century; the same was true for the rest of Europe. The seventeenth and eighteenth centuries were largely shrouded in silence, as if the Reformations had resulted in the 'disappearance' of prostitution from the social scene.

This silence has gradually been broken, by Roper's essay on post-Reformation Augsburg, and particularly for the eighteenth century by Benabou's study of Paris, Henderson's work on London and Van de Pol's extensive survey of prostitution in Amsterdam in the seventeenth and eighteenth centuries.[20] For Rome, Cohen and Camerano have shifted the focus away from the elite courtesan of the early Cinquecento and on to the 'ordinary' prostitutes and courtesans of the late sixteenth and early seventeenth century.[21]

This book challenges the traditional chronology and perceptions of prostitution in post-Tridentine Rome. It examines in detail the debate which

---

(Florence: Roberto Paggi, 1897). Arturo Graf, *Attraverso il cinquecento* (Turin: Ermanno Loescher, 1888), 257–9. Alessandro Ferrajoli, 'Il ruolo della corte di Leone X', *ARSRSP*, vols. 35–9 (1912–16). Emmanuel Rodocanachi, *La femme italienne à l'époque de la Renaissance* (Paris: Hachette, 1907). And Rodocanachi, *Cortigiane e buffoni di Roma* (Milan: Edizioni Pervinca, 1927). From the 1940s until the 1990s histories of prostitution were based on those cited above. Umberto Gnoli, *Cortigiane romane* (Arezzo: Il Vasari, 1941). Paul Larivaille, *La vita quotidiana delle cortigiane nell'Italia del Rinascimento* (Milan: Rizzoli, 1975). Georgina Masson, *Courtesans of the Italian Renaissance* (London: Secker and Warburg, 1975). Lynne Lawner, *Lives of the Courtesans* (New York: Rizzoli, 1986). For a recent monograph on early sixteenth-century Roman courtesans based on entirely new research and focusing on their financial arrangements with bankers, see Monica Kurzel-Runtscheiner, *Töchter der Venus: Die Kurtisanen Roms im 16. Jahrhundert* (Munich: Beck, 1995).

[19] This is the general impression which emerges from this literature, with the reforms made by Pius V cited as marking the closure of this period.

[20] Roper, 'Discipline and Respectability' and 'Madri di depravazione'. Van de Pol, *Het Amsterdams Hoerdom*. Tony Henderson, *Disorderly Women in Eighteenth-Century London: Prostitution and Control in the Metropolis, 1730–1830* (London and New York: Longman, 1999). Faramerz Dabhoiwala, 'The Pattern of Sexual Immorality in Seventeenth and Eighteenth Century London', in Paul Griffiths and Mark S. R. Jenner, eds., *Londinopolis: Essays in the Cultural and Social History of Early Modern London* (Manchester and New York: Manchester University Press, 2000), 86–106. Erica Marie Benabou, *La prostitution et la police des moeurs au XVIIIe siècle* (Paris: Perrin, 1987). Alain Corbin, *Les filles de noce*, 2nd edn (Paris: Flammarion, 1982).

[21] See Elizabeth and Thomas Cohen, *Words and Deeds in Renaissance Rome: Trials before the Papal Magistrates* (Toronto: University of Toronto Press, 1993). Also Elizabeth S. Cohen, 'Open and Shut: the Social Meanings of the Cinquecento Roman House', *Studies in the Decorative Arts*, Fall–Winter (2001–2), 61–84. And Elizabeth S. Cohen, 'Seen and Known', 'Camilla the Go-Between', 'The Politics of Gender in a Roman Household (1559)', *Continuity and Change* 4 (1989), 53–77. 'Honour and Gender in the Streets of Early Modern Rome', *Journal of Interdisciplinary History* 22:4 (1992), 597–625. Alessandra Camerano 'Assistenza richiesta ed assistenza imposta: il Conservatorio di S. Caterina della Rosa di Roma', *Quaderni Storici* 82 (1993), 227–60. And Camerano, 'Donne oneste o meretrici?', *Quaderni Storici* 99:3 (1998), 637–75.

took place between Pius V and the lay city government, suggesting that the aims of papal legislation were not as repressive as has often been believed, and demonstrating the extent to which papal policy was contested and obstructed by the laity. Relying on a range of sources, it argues that prostitution continued to flourish well into the late seventeenth century, finding that the norms and values of lay people were resistant to the imposition of new behavioural mores. It also questions the 'myth' put about in Counter-Reformation rhetoric, that the wealthy courtesans disappeared and that Roman prostitution became a miserable and impoverished affair. It finds, on the contrary, that the profession was characterised by large numbers of 'comfortably-off' courtesans who were frequented openly, as ever, by the city's large numbers of wealthy men.

IV

Like several other recent studies of prostitution, this one draws extensively on records from the archives of criminal tribunals.[22] With one or two exceptions the criminal sources used here are drawn from the archives of the *Governatore di Roma*, the head of justice in the city and its province.[23] A prelate, the Governor had jurisdiction over both civil and criminal matters, laymen and clergy, and could issue edicts and decrees. He also had authority over two prisons and had a body of policemen (*birri* or *sbirri*) at his command. His power, however, was undermined by the plethora of different tribunals and courts within Rome, the jurisdictions of which overlapped and undercut his. In particular there were the *Tribunale del Senatore*, the court of the Capitoline Administration, the *Tribunale della Curia del Borgo*, created in the 1550s to take over criminal responsibility for the Borgo, and the *Corte Savella*. In addition the *Tribunale del Vicariato*, run by the Vicar General of the city, had jurisdiction over spiritual, marital and moral affairs and a great many cases regarding prostitutes would have been brought before these courts.[24]

---

[22] Van de Pol, *Het Amsterdams hoerdom*. The work of Thomas and Elizabeth Cohen is based on the criminal tribunals in Rome, that of Guido Ruggiero on trials from Venice.

[23] Augusto Pompeo, 'Procedure usuali e "iura specialia in criminalibus" nei tribunali romani di antico regime', *Archivi per la Storia* 1–2 (1991), 111–24. Niccolò Del Re, *Monsignor Governatore di Roma* (Rome: Istituto di Studi Romani, 1972). Carlo Cirillo Fornili, *Delinquenti e carcerati a Roma alla metà del '600: opera dei papi nella riforma carceraria* (Rome: Editrice Pontificia Università Gregoriana, 1991).

[24] Pompeo, 'Procedure usuali', 111, 115–16. Luigi Londei, 'La funzione giudiziaria nello Stato pontificio di antico regime', *Archivi per la Storia* 1–2 (1991), 13–31. Irene Polverini Fosi, 'Fonti giudiziarie e tribunali nella Roma del cinquecento. Problemi metodologici per una ricerca di demografia storica',

The criminal justice system was based on an inquisitorial procedure and cases were started largely through direct accusation by a third party; increasingly this was the public prosecutor himself. Once the complaint had been filed the accused was cited to appear in court, and kept in prison in isolation until after the initial interrogation. Subsequently there would be an opportunity for him or her to prepare a defence, witnesses would be called and there might be a confrontation between them. Sometimes only a notary was present in court, at others the public prosecutor or judge was there too. In serious cases, in the absence of a confession, torture was commonly used.

Three archival series from the Governor's tribunal have provided the bulk of the sources used. The *Processi per informazione* were the initial interrogations of the accused and witnesses, the most complete forms of trials surviving, which can run to hundreds of pages.[25] One of the difficulties with using the *Processi* is that we cannot be sure that all the documents pertaining to the trial are in the volume; they can be distributed in other archival series, such as the *Interrogazioni*, or *Testimonii per la difesa*. In particular the series of sentences is incomplete, so it is often impossible to know the outcome of the trial. The reader must therefore forgive the abrupt way in which these stories end.

The *Costituti* record the moment when the court interrogated the accused in some detail about his or her past, social condition, wealth and profession in order to ascertain their character and social circumstances, thereby providing much biographical detail. The *Relazioni dei birri* are the reports drawn up daily by the *birri* describing whom they had arrested the previous night during their rounds of the city and why.[26]

Criminal records have been found to provide an extraordinarily rich source for accounts of the social practices, personal biographies, relationships and daily lives of the poor, material otherwise hidden to the eyes of the historian. But many caveats must be attached to their use. One of these relates to how representative they are, particularly when much of the

---

in Eugenio Sonnino, ed., *Popolazione e società a Roma dal medioevo all'età contemporanea* (Rome: Il Calamo, 1998), 591–6. Sadly, trial documents from the *Vicariato* were destroyed during the French occupation in the late eighteenth century.

[25] Thomas and Elizabeth Cohen have worked extensively on the *Processi per informazione* and have transcribed and analysed several cases related to prostitutes. See their *Words and Deeds in Renaissance Rome*. See also Fornili, *Delinquenti e carcerati*, 155–66. And Thomas V. Cohen, *Love and Death in Renaissance Italy* (Chicago and London: University of Chicago Press, 2004).

[26] ASR, TCG, *Relazioni dei birri*, Buste, 1–8. The period covers the pontificate of Clement VIII, and is particularly interesting since it includes the preparation for and aftermath of the Jubilee of 1600.

discussion is based on case studies.[27] To mitigate this I have drawn here on some five hundred criminal records, which, even if not all discussed, have helped to contextualise findings against a broader background. Another criticism is that criminal records in many countries do not record the voice of the accused, only those of the interrogators and court scribes. In Italy, however, one of the characteristics of court records is that the notary was required to transcribe the questions of the interrogator and the replies of those being investigated in Italian, ad verbatim, not as a summary, and also to note any physical gestures, cries or reactions he or she might make. Depositions vary from curt or repetitive accounts, to highly articulate, sophisticated narrations. Overall they are remarkable for the amount of incidental detail and biographical narrative they provide, and it is this information which is used as the basis for this study.[28]

We clearly cannot consider these interrogations as transparent records of events, nor are they an 'early modern version of the oral history interview', as Roper pointedly reminds us: 'They are the constructed record of a conversation where the differences of power are highly visible, and the distance of the record from "memory" cannot be overlooked.'[29] As a result these records are difficult to interpret. Many different solutions to these problems have been adopted by historians working with criminal records.[30] The analysis here draws on concepts developed by historians of social science who have explored the role played by narratives in the formation and articulation of social identities. This approach is premised on the belief that 'It is through narrativity that we come to know, understand, and make sense of the social world, and it is through narratives and narrativity

---

[27] See Samuel K. Cohn's observations in *Women in the Streets: Essays on Sex and Power in Renaissance Italy* (Baltimore and London: The Johns Hopkins University Press, 1996), 105. The debate over quantitative versus qualitative use of criminal sources has been particularly lively in Italy. Eduardo Grendi, 'Premessa', *Quaderni Storici* 66 (1987), 695–700, 695. Mario Sbriccoli, 'Fonti giudiziarie e fonti giuridiche. Riflessioni sulla fase attuale degli studi di storia del crimine e della giustizia criminale', *Studi Storici* 29 (1988), 491–501, 494.

[28] This is similar to the kind of detail to which Carlo Ginzburg refers in his essay 'Clues: Roots of an Evidential Paradigm', in his *Myths, Emblems, Clues* (London: Hutchinson Radius, 1990), 96–125.

[29] Lyndal Roper, *Oedipus and the Devil: Witchcraft, Sexuality and Religion in Early Modern Europe* (London and New York: Routledge, 1994), 55. Also Jim Sharpe, 'Human Relations and the History of Crime', *IAHCCJ Bulletin* 14 (1991), 10–32, 12. And Pieter Spierenburg, 'Justice and the Mental World', *IAHCCJ Bulletin* 14 (1991), 38–77.

[30] See Natalie Zemon Davis in *The Return of Martin Guerre* (Cambridge, Mass. and London: Harvard University Press, 1983) and *Fiction in the Archives: Pardon Tales and their Tellers in Sixteenth-Century France* (Stanford: Stanford University Press, 1987), 48. Carlo Ginzburg, *The Cheese and the Worms: the Cosmos of a Sixteenth Century Miller*, trans. John and Anne Tedeschi (London: Penguin, 1992). Edward Muir and Guido Ruggiero, *History from Crime*, trans. Corrada Biazz Curry, Margaret A. Gallucci and Mary M. Gallucci (Baltimore: The Johns Hopkins University Press, 1994).

that we constitute our social identities.'[31] Narratives serve to link otherwise isolated events into coherent episodes, helping individuals to understand and explain to others who they are, and to create and maintain a personal identity.[32] Discussing people's depositions in terms of narrative identities leaves space to speculate on elements of self-conscious presentation of the self and manipulation of the truth. At the same time, people's narrations of themselves are viewed here as being relatively spontaneous, compared with approaches which perceive court-room narratives as being inevitably highly stylised and formulaic.

An important postulate of this approach is that the narratives which historical actors use to represent themselves are not 'invented' by individuals, but are appropriated from a limited pool of narratives available within a given society. This premise enables historians to look beyond the veracity of the individual's account, and focus instead on the pre-existing narratives which shaped personal narrative identities. It facilitates speculation about the relationship which existed between 'personal' narratives of prostitution and contemporary stereotypes of prostitution, such as those discussed in chapter 1.[33]

v

Prostitutes and courtesans feature in a surprising number of early modern narrative genres. Some, such as Aretino's dialogues, circulated only amongst a narrow male elite, although they are by far the best known to modern scholars.[34] Others were destined for a broader public, such as the comedies by the Venetian playwright Ruzzante or the moralising verses discussed

---

[31] Margaret Somers, 'The Narrative Constitution of Identity: a Relational and Network Approach', *Theory and Society* 23 (1994), 605–49, 606, 614.

[32] Charlotte Linde, *Life Stories: the Creation of Coherence* (New York and Oxford: Oxford University Press, 1993), 98. And Linde 'Explanatory Systems in Oral Life Stories', in D. Holland and N. Quinn, eds., *Cultural Models in Language and Thought* (New York: Cambridge University Press, 1987).

[33] Somers also suggests that public narratives affect how people act. Somers, 'The Narrative Constitution of Identity', 614. I discuss this issue in detail in 'Storie di prostituzione nella Roma della Controriforma', *Quaderni Storici* 106:1 (2001), 261–95. On circulation, reception and appropriation see Roger Chartier, *The Cultural Uses of Print in Early Modern France*, trans. Lydia G. Cochrane (Princeton: Princeton University Press, 1987).

[34] Francisco Delicado, *La Lozana Andalusa*, ed. Luisa Orioli (Milan: Adelphi, 1970). [Anon.] *Ragionamento del Zoppino: Fatto frate, e Lodovico, puttaniere, dove contiensi la vita e genealogia di tutte le cortigiane di Roma*, attributed to Francisco Delicado (Milan: Longanesi, 1969) (orig. 1539, Venice). Pietro Aretino, 'Ragionamento della Antonia' (orig. 1534) and 'Dialogo nel quale a Nanna insegna a la Pippa' (orig. 1536) ed. Paolo Procaccioli, intro. Nino Borsellino, in Aretino, *Ragionamento, Dialogo* (Milan: Garzanti, 1984). Also Aretino, *Il Piacevol Ragionamento de l'Aretino: Dialogo di Giulia e di Madalena*, ed. Claudio Galderisi (Rome: Salerno Editrice, 1987).

below. These genres were by no means hermetically sealed from one another, and although destined for different publics, shared many themes, concerns and stereotypes about prostitution. Indeed, some were penned by the same authors.[35] The 'popular' songs and illustrated broadsheets which form the basis of this study were mostly intended to dissuade men from frequenting prostitutes and women from practising prostitution.[36]

The moralising verses and broadsheets considered here were printed in cities across Italy between 1520 and 1680.[37] The earliest surviving examples appeared with the first wave of syphilis in Europe. This spread in a particularly rapid and virulent form across the continent and was soon linked – though not exclusively – to prostitutes. These texts warned of the dangers of prostitution in the context of this frightening new disease. There were three typical formats. Some, written in verse with a refrain, often in dialect, were printed on rough cheap paper in small, octavo-sized booklets, perhaps with a woodcut on the front. A second type took the form of a single illustrated 'broadsheet', with images placed at the centre of the page and the text below. A third type appeared towards the end of the sixteenth century, composed of a number of small, sequentially placed images which told a story, with the text placed below (as David Kunzle points out, rather like an early comic strip[38]). Evidence that these images were destined to circulate throughout the social spectrum comes from the different formats in which the images could be produced. *La vita et miseranda fine della puttana* started life as a series of full-size paintings by Giacomo Piccini in Venice. They were copied as engravings and produced as a series of prints by Giuseppe Longhi in Bologna around 1675, in two sizes.[39]

---

[35] On the heterogeneity of early modern print culture see Chartier, *The Cultural Uses of Print*, 3–4.

[36] I have found one exception to this, an unlicensed pamphlet in which a mother encourages her daughter to enter prostitution, which is discussed in chapter 1. *Opera Nova dove si Contiene un esordio che da una donna a una sua figliuola, nella quale l'insegna con quante sorte di gente ha da fare l'amore, cosa ridiculosa e bella. Con un lamento che fa una figliuola con la madre che è mal maritata* (Perugia, 1584).

[37] David Kunzle reproduces and comments on most of the images discussed here in *The Early Comic Strip: Narrative Strips and Picture Stories in the European Broadsheet from c.1450 to 1825* (Berkeley: University of California Press, 1973), 3. See also Alberto Milano, 'Stampe e stampatori nel fondo di stampe P. P. della raccolta Bertarelli,' in Annamaria Amitrano Savarese and Aurelio Rigoli, eds., *Stampe popolari profani della civica raccolta Achille Bertarelli* (Vigevano: Diakronia, 1995), 72–80. More recently Sara F. Matthews Grieco has discussed some of them in 'Pedagogical Prints: Moralizing Broadsheets and Wayward Women in Counter Reformation Italy,' in Johnson and Matthews Grieco, *Picturing Women*, 61–88, 77.

[38] Kunzle, *The Early Comic Strip*, 4. See the illustrations.

[39] Milano, 'Stampe e stampatori'. One size is 322 by 393 mm, the other 133 by 175 mm.

More than thirty pamphlets and seven broadsheets belonging to this genre have survived, mostly falling into four broad categories.[40] The earliest portray the courtesan's life as a simple alternation between her pride and fall.[41] In the later Cinquecento the plot is structured around the courtesan's life-cycle, focusing on key moments in her life: how she became a prostitute, her brief moment of professional success, the causes of her demise and her ignominious death. A third plot evolved in the seventeenth century, warning prostitutes not to trust their clients, who might rob and even murder them. A fourth type is directed at men, as potential clients, warning them of the many dangers of becoming involved with prostitutes.

Written or commissioned by the *cantastorie* and *cantimbanchi*, (professional storytellers), they were intended first to be sung or recited in piazzas and markets, acted out by troupes of actors, and then sold.[42] Even so, their purchase was probably restricted to wealthier artisans, merchants, professional men and gentlemen. A copy of the *Lamento della cortigiana ferrarese* was purchased in Perugia in September 1530 at the cost of a *quattrino*, quarter of a gold ducat.[43] Despite this, the images would then have been hung in taverns (*osterie*) or homes, the songs repeated and learned by others, so they would have been seen and heard by a far greater audience than were actually able to purchase them.[44] Economics dictated that the verses be entertaining and popular with the public.[45] Furthermore, the fact that they were light, small and cheap meant that they could easily be carried by pedlars. Prints made in northern Italy (where the presses were concentrated) certainly reached Rome, where by the seventeenth century there were eighty-nine booksellers licensed to sell such publications.[46] These were 'popular'

[40] Those which don't tend to be isolated examples written in local dialect, clearly addressing specific public and local issues.

[41] See *Il vanto e lamento della cortigiana ferrarese* (*The Boast and Lament of the Courtesan from Ferrara*). The theme is starkly illustrated in *Ecco il miserabile fine della Sig. Anzola* (late sixteenth-century), Civica Raccolta Stampe Achille Bertarelli, Popolari Profane, IIF-I.

[42] For accounts of *cantastorie* placing their orders with printers, see Ottavia Niccoli, *Profeti e popolo nell'Italia del Rinascimento* (Rome: Laterza, 1987), 15–16.

[43] From Cuovanni, Aquilecchia, 'Per l'attribuzione e il testo del "Lamento di una cortigiana ferrarese"' *Tra latino e volgare per Carlo Dionisotti*, ed. Gabriella Bernardoni Trezzini (Padua: Anteore, 1975). Sean Shesgreen also comes to this conclusion in *Images of the Outcast: the Urban Poor in the Cries of London* (Manchester: Manchester University Press, 2002), 22–3.

[44] See Maria Pia Fantini's research into a prostitute in Modena who read printed 'orations' which she then taught to other prostitutes. 'La circolazione clandestina dell'orazione di Santa Marta: un episodio modenese', in Gabriella Zarri, ed., *Donna, disciplina, creanza cristiana dal XV al XVII secolo. Studi e testi a stampa* (Rome: Edizioni di Storia e Letteratura, 1996), 45–65.

[45] Matthews Grieco, 'Pedagogical Prints', 62.

[46] On the networks of pedlars see Laurence Fontaine, *History of Pedlars in Europe*, trans. Vicki Whittaker (Oxford: Polity Press, 1996). On print shops in Rome see Alberta Bertone Pannain, Sandro Bulgarelli and Ludovica Mazzola, *Il giornalismo romano, delle origini, sec. XVI–XVII*, Mostra Bibliografica

texts, in the sense that they travelled widely and were destined for a broad public, although the majority of them were essentially vehicles of social control.[47]

VI

Chapter 1 introduces the reader to these texts and images, identifying the central themes around which the narratives were structured. They were aimed at a mass market, so we can assume that they reflected those concerns and beliefs about prostitution which were most 'pressing' and would appeal to a broad public. Four themes are particularly striking: the problem of recruitment into prostitution, especially the roles played by mother and father; the belief that it was possible to amass considerable, albeit transitory wealth through prostitution; the portrayal of relationships between prostitutes and clients; and the changing nature of the warnings issued about prostitution.

Chapter 2 introduces the social, demographic and cultural background to prostitution in sixteenth-century Rome. It considers a range of factors governing tolerance, such as traditional medical beliefs about male sexuality, fears for female honour in a city populated largely by men and the financial benefits accruing to the city from prostitution. It moves on to discuss perceptions that prostitutes were increasingly numerous, unacceptably free and inappropriately wealthy. This was dangerous because if there were no way of distinguishing between honest and dishonest women, it would be impossible to categorise and control women according to their sexuality.

Chapter 3 documents the struggle for power which ensued after Pius V tried to take control of prostitution in the city in 1566. Power had traditionally been shared between the papacy and the lay civic government, known as the *Popolo Romano*. By the late sixteenth century these two bodies were embroiled in a battle for supremacy. As a result, the *Popolo Romano* resisted Pius V's demands vigorously, making one of its last major stands against the encroaching power of the papacy. Two letters connected to the disagreement reveal the religious, social and economic concerns of the elite laymen who were represented in the *Popolo Romano*. They reveal the terms

---

(Rome: Biblioteca Nazionale Centrale, 1979), 17. At least two of these broadsheets were available in Rome. See Francesco Ehrle, *Roma prima di Sisto V: la pianta di Roma du Perac-Lafrery* (Rome: Danesi, 1908).

47 On circulation and publics, see Scribner, *For the Sake of Simple Folk*. And Niccoli, *Profeti e popolo*. On prints and social control see B. E. Maidment, *Reading Popular Prints, 1790–1870* (Manchester and New York: Manchester University Press, 1996), 19.

of the debate and demonstrate the diversity of contemporary viewpoints on the correct role of the church with regards to prostitution. The second part of the chapter looks at what this legislation achieved in practice, using the parish records as evidence of the residence patterns of prostitutes, and discussing evidence relating to toleration of prostitutes within the neighbourhoods in which they lived.

Given the intensely negative treatment of prostitutes in much church discourse, and the frequent criminalisation of prostitution, it has often been presumed that prostitutes were always conceived of as stigmatised members of society, living ostracised lives on the margins of communities.[48] Mazo Karras's recent study of prostitution in medieval England finds much evidence which supports this view. She cites the frequency with which derogatory terms such as 'common whore' were used against women, points out that although individuals were tolerated there was a generalised resentment of prostitutes as a group, since they were seen as fomentors of social disorder, and notes that the broader community frequently reported them to the church courts.[49] Yet such findings cannot necessarily be applied elsewhere or to the whole period. Other historians have found many signs that prior to the Reformation, prostitutes were considered to have a central role in community life, defending the 'collective public order',[50] 'underpinning the community ethic',[51] 'symbolically marginal and yet symbolically central to their communities'.[52] Furthermore, Otis, Pavan and Roper have found that prior to the early sixteenth century, prostitutes were spoken of in neutral terms, as 'public' or 'common women', and prostitution referred to as a 'trade' or categorised broadly with other forms of misdemeanour. It was only after the Reformation that a linguistic shift took place, with pejorative terms such as 'whore' and 'sinner' being applied to prostitutes as a matter of course.[53] Hébert's study of eighteenth-century Montpellier goes even further, focusing specifically on relations between prostitutes and their local community and identifying several reasons why prostitutes were neither stigmatised nor marginalised by that community. She finds that these women were integrated by virtue of their close family or of more

---

[48] See Shannon Bell's discussion of the 'othering' of prostitutes in *Reading, Writing and Rewriting the Prostitute Body* (Bloomington and Indianapolis: Indiana University Press, 1994). As an example prostitution is dealt with in a chapter entitled 'Forms of Deviance' in Robert Jütte, *Poverty and Deviance in Early Modern Europe* (Cambridge: Cambridge University Press, 1994).

[49] Mazo Karras, *Common Women*, 86. For her lengthy discussion of this subject see esp. 84, 95, 96–101.

[50] Jacques Rossiaud, 'Prostitution, jeunesse et société dans les villes du sud-est au XVe siècle', *Annales ESC* 31:2 (1976), 289–325, 307–8, 324.

[51] Trexler, 'La prostitution florentine', 984.   [52] Roper, 'Discipline and Respectability', 19.

[53] Pavan, 'Police des moeurs', 265. Roper, 'Discipline and Respectability', 17. Otis, *Prostitution in Medieval Society*, 40–5.

distant relatives, by any 'honest' work they had done, as well as by the networks established through prostitution. They also participated in the exchange of services common to neighbourhoods, sharing meals, drinks and confidences with their neighbours. Provided prostitutes adhered to communal morality, their presence went undisturbed by neighbours, although newcomers to the city were more likely to be regarded with suspicion. Prostitutes were denounced by neighbours only when they had caused a scandal, whether procuring their daughters, abandoning children, taking in unknown men – particularly soldiers – or disturbing the sleep of others. Even then it was only when a woman ignored the pressure applied by the community that she was reported to the police.[54] The evidence from Rome which is discussed in chapter 3 points in a very similar direction. It suggests that prostitutes were often firmly rooted within their neigbourhoods through financial and kin networks, and that attitudes towards them were generally tolerant, provided certain norms were respected.

Chapter 4 considers the legislation issued in the decades after the Council of Trent, and its effects on practices. The records of police arrests and depositions from criminal trials indicate policing policies, but above all allow us to explore the nature of sociability with prostitutes and the attempts by the police to control it. It finds that policing was largely directed at breaking up parties and subduing the violent fights and brawls which broke out amongst men, much of whose social life revolved around prostitutes, but had little impact on practices of prostitution overall. There were too few policemen, with too little power, and attempts to discipline courtesans associated with the social elite were particularly unsuccessful in the longer term. Profound power struggles were at work within Roman society, as elite men often refused to acknowledge the authority of the Governor of Rome and his policemen.

Chapter 5 draws a profile of the 'typical' prostitute in the city, starting with a discussion of the categories and identities assigned to prostitutes. As a reflection of the stigmatising terms applied to prostitutes by the church and the law there is often an assumption that such stigma was interiorised by prostitutes themselves.[55] However, several historians would

---

[54] Geneviève Hébert, 'Les "femmes de mauvaise vie" dans la communauté (Montpellier, 1713–1742)', *Histoire Sociale* 36:72 (2003), 497–517, 509–13.

[55] 'Women who became licensed prostitutes accepted what many sociologists consider a label of secondary deviance . . . Then through the ritual of licensing, they acknowledged their deviance . . . Entry into the brothel brought them into a deviant group whose members shared a common identity and a similar isolation within respectable society.' Perry, 'Deviant Insiders', 146.

dispute this view. Ferrante has shown that in post-Tridentine Bologna unmarried women who prostituted themselves considered themselves simply as 'free women', and that although stigmatised by the tribunals, prostitution did not necessarily represent an 'irreversible and marginalised destiny'[56]. Benabou likewise finds 'resistance' to the stigmatised identities in eighteenth-century Paris.[57] In order to explore this issue, the chapter examines the different ways in which women who prostituted themselves described their identities and activities, arguing that the simple binary categories of 'honesty' and 'dishonesty' did not have much meaning for these women in post-Tridentine Rome.

This chapter also aims to answer some of the socio-economic and biographical questions about prostitutes which have intrigued many other historians of prostitution. Despite differing social, cultural and economic contexts across early modern and even nineteenth-century Europe, there are some factors which seem to have been relatively constant. The majority of prostitutes were aged between sixteen and twenty-five, with little evidence of the kind of child prostitution of which civic and religious authorities have been so afraid.[58] Although it is often assumed that prostitutes were always 'outsiders', the extent to which this was true has been shown to depend on local factors such as rates of immigration and community attitudes towards prostitutes. Thus in fifteenth-century Florence prostitutes were specifically recruited from abroad; most prostitutes working in Malaga in 1500 were from Andalusia, but not from the city itself; in eighteenth-century Montpellier only one-third were immigrants, and in sixteenth-century Augsburg the majority were local women.[59] A significant degree of social dislocation tends to be the rule, be it the result of migration, loss of a spouse or losing a parent.[60] Yet prostitutes were not necessarily recruited from the

---

[56] Lucia Ferrante, 'Pro mercede carnali. Il giusto prezzo rivendicato in tribunale', *Memoria* 17 (1986), 42–58, and 'Il valore del corpo' in Angela Groppi, ed., *Il lavoro delle donne* (Rome and Bari: Laterza, 1996), 219, 228.

[57] Benabou, *La prostitution*, 307, 317–18.

[58] Data from later periods is much more comprehensive and can provide interesting comparisons with the early modern period. See particularly Judith Walkowitz, *Prostitution and Victorian Society: Women, Class and the State* (Cambridge: Cambridge University Press, 1980), 19; Frances Finnegan, *Poverty and Prostitution: a Study of Victorian Prostitutes in York* (Cambridge: Cambridge University Press, 1979), 81, 85. Rossiaud, *Medieval Prostitution*, 33. Also Colin Jones, 'Prostitution and the Ruling Class in Eighteenth Century Montpellier', *History Workshop Journal* 6 (1978), 7–28.

[59] Trexler, 'La prostitution florentine'. Although Rossiaud says that the majority were not 'foreigners', by this he means they were from the Rhone valley. In terms of early modern community, anyone from anywhere outside a given village, town or city was effectively a 'foreigner'. *Medieval Prostitution*, 32. Menjot, 'Prostitution et ruffianage', 32. The exception is Roper who finds that, of those whose origins were known, slightly more came from Augsburg than not. 'Madri di depravazione', 13. Hébert, 'Les "femme de mauvaise vie"', 503.

[60] Hébert, 'Les "femme de mauvaise vie"', 502.

lowest echelons of society – the destitute and vagabonds. Evidence from France and Germany suggests that prostitutes were usually daughters of the artisans, working men or former servants.[61] Only Henderson's study of eighteenth-century London shows a more desperate picture: of his sample most prostitutes' parents had been paupers, and nearly all the women were orphans.[62]

The answers to these questions for Rome are sought in the parish records. These reveal that at least two-thirds of prostitutes had come from outside Rome (a similar proportion to the population at large), which prompts a look at migration and the extent to which women had kin or networks in place in the city on arrival. Parish records also permit an analysis of household composition. Since the majority of prostitutes in Rome were heads of households, nearly half of them living alone, many supporting family, we are reminded of the economic imperatives these women faced. The remainder of the chapter therefore contextualises women's recourse to prostitution in the light of the economic opportunities and alternatives available in early modern Rome. Influenced by Ferrante's study of Bologna, prostitution is framed as a form of woman's work, to which they turned as and when necessary: before marriage, between marriages, on abandonment or widowhood.[63] This leads to a discussion about agency, and whether it can ever be said that women have a 'choice' about becoming prostitutes, concluding that in early modern Rome, at least, they often did.

Chapter 6 explores accounts of how and why women became prostitutes. It is often assumed that prostitutes were 'victims': former slaves, pregnant servants, women who had been raped, or debtors.[64] Sometimes there is evidence to support this, as in Rossiaud's study of prostitutes in brothels in south-eastern France during the fifteenth century. He finds that 50 per cent of the women were recruited by force (such as by brothel farmers) and 27 per cent through rape.[65] Yet other research, such as Benabou's study of eighteenth-century Paris and Walkowitz's findings for nineteenth-century London, reveals that women mostly 'slipped' into prostitution after spending some time trying to find work, and that they often alternated between prostitution and a regular job.[66] Contemporaries tended to point an accusing finger at mothers, who were widely blamed for leading daughters astray

---

[61] Rossiaud, *Medieval Prostitution*, 32–3. Benabou, *La prostitution*, 18. Also Roper, 'Madri di depravazione,' 13.

[62] Henderson, *Disorderly Women*, 14.   [63] Ferrante, 'Pro mercede carnali', and 'Il valore del corpo'.

[64] Though they offer little evidence to support these assumptions this is the general tone of Mazzi, *Prostitute e lenoni*, 315–16, 261, and Pavan, 'Police des moeurs', 260.

[65] Rossiaud, *Medieval prostitution*, 33.

[66] Benabou, *La prostitution*, 267. Walkowitz, *Prostitution and Victorian Society*, 19.

(as has been shown for sixteenth-century Augsburg).[67] This was certainly true of Italy where literary and moralising texts focused on the maternal role in recruitment. Legislation spread the blame more evenly, suspecting both parents and husbands of forcing women to prostitute themselves. The Roman criminal records allow us glimpses of the range of circumstances which resulted in women turning to prostitution. Although no single 'method' of recruitment emerges from the Roman criminal records as having predominated, there were numerous investigations into accusations of forced prostitution, which draw attention to the roles played by fathers, mothers and husbands. We find striking similarities between the roles attributed to men and women in moralising narratives and those attributed to them in court-room depositions, although in practice men played far more significant roles than is suggested in literature. The pedestrian explanation for this lies in an unwillingness to portray husbands/fathers as villains in literature, but it raises questions about the relative importance of economic solvency over female chastity in the construction of male honour. What emerges with clarity is the expectation that a great deal of money could be gained by 'putting a woman out to earn'.

Chapter 7 addresses the economics of prostitution. This is a subject rarely considered in depth, partly owing to lack of sources. It may also be a reflection of the fact that in Protestant countries prostitution as a 'profession' was outlawed, becoming a moral category, with the result that 'prostitutes [were] considered either as fornicators or adulteresses like other women'.[68] It has been argued that as a result of the stigmatising attitudes towards prostitution, prostitution cannot be viewed principally as a commercial activity nor regarded as a neutral form of work.[69] There is a risk, however, that an emphasis on immorality, dishonour and marginality may obscure the fundamental fact that prostitution is ultimately a commercial relationship. Lotte Van de Pol reverses this bias in her huge study of prostitution in Amsterdam between 1650 and 1750. She argues that, although illegal, prostitution was 'just like any other pre-industrial trade in the small scale of its operations, its clearly defined roles for both sexes, and the importance of negotiations, credit and debt'.[70]

Precisely how lucrative prostitution was varied greatly according to time and place. Van de Pol observes that despite the appearance of glamour, 'the world of prostitution was generally characterized by poverty'. She finds

---

[67] Roper, 'Madri di depravazione'.   [68] Ibid., 15, 21.   [69] Mazo Karras, *Common Women*, 8, 84.
[70] Lotte Van de Pol analyses the confessions of some 9,000 prostitutes over a hundred-year span in *Het Amsterdams Hoerdom*. As yet unpublished in English, this is from an unpublished translation of chapter 7, 'Sex for money and money for sex: prostitution as a pre-industrial trade', 31.

that most of the earnings were swallowed up catering for primary needs and payments to the brothel owners and music hall owners where prostitutes worked.[71] On the other hand Rossiaud finds that a woman working in a public brothel in late medieval southern France earned for one half-hour with a client about the equivalent of half a day's work in the vineyards, and three to six times that much for spending the night with him.[72] Otis likewise finds documents from fifteenth-century Languedoc indicating that prostitution could pay well.[73] Detailed research into the economics of Italian prostitution so far has focused on early sixteenth-century elite courtesans, confirming the impression of a few very affluent women at the top of the profession. Cathy Santore analyses the inventory of an extremely successful Venetian courtesan, describing her possessions and wealth. Monica Kurzel-Runtscheiner researches the finances of some mid-sixteenth-century Roman courtesans, revealing their networks of relationships with bankers and merchants.[74] The economic world of the ordinary Italian prostitute has not as yet been studied, although Stefano D'Amico has recently suggested that common prostitutes in seventeenth-century Milan were attracted by the potential earnings to be made.[75]

We can build a picture of the financial arrangements of prostitutes in Rome by referring to criminal records and notarial documents. The chapter opens by looking at how the commercial aspects of relationships were managed, how prices were agreed and what women could do to ensure they were paid. What emerges is the importance of having one or more long-term 'friendships' with clients, which provided women with some economic stability. The daily earning potential of the average prostitute is explored and set against the expenses sustained: paying rent, buying clothes, paying for food. Wills reveal how much prostitutes were able to leave as cash bequests, and the extent to which they were indebted. Notarial documents refer to investments, loans and property; criminal records show the amounts of money needed to be raised to pay bails. In order to understand what a prostitute's earnings meant, these findings are contextualised in the broader economic environment with reference to a census drawn up in 1656. This permits us to understand contemporary classifications of poverty and wealth, and to locate the city's prostitutes within these categories.

Notarial records have been a particularly valuable source in the quest to document the poverty, wealth and material possessions of prostitutes.

---

[71] Ibid., 33.   [72] Rossiaud, *Medieval Prostitution*, 35, fn. 17.

[73] Otis, *Prostitution in Medieval Society*, 65–6.

[74] Cathy Santore, 'Julia Lombardo "sotuosa meretrize": a Portrait by Property', *Renaissance Quarterly* 41:1 (1988), 44–83. Kurzel-Runtscheiner, *Töchter der Venus*.

[75] Stefano D'Amico, 'Shameful Mother: Poverty and Prostitution in Seventeenth-Century Milan', *Journal of Family History* 30:1 (2005), 69.

Sales, purchases, rentals, loans and such like were usually certified before a notary, particularly if significant sums of money were involved. Women who had prostituted themselves, however briefly, were legally obliged to draw up a will in a notary's presence, bequeathing one-fifth (later one-third) of their estate to the Monastery of the Convertite, at the risk of having everything confiscated.[76] This included any woman who had ever been known to have prostituted herself, whatever her status and condition at the time of her death. Parish priests, rectors, curates and notaries were also charged with the responsibility of ensuring that such women were identified, so that their estate could duly be taxed. This has resulted in a wealth of documents which reflect different aspects of the economic status of prostitutes from across the economic spectrum. The range in prices, and the quality and quantity of objects in the documents indicate that even quite modest prostitutes sometimes used the notarial office – whilst all kinds drew up wills. This study is based on 124 of these, selected at random, drawn up between the years 1594 and 1609 in the office of a notary based in Campo Marzio, the district where most prostitutes lived.[77] Taken as a whole these documents therefore represent a broad spectrum of women involved in prostitution.

Although this documentation is very rich, it presents numerous problems. Very few of the wills have inventories attached, mentioning only those few items included in bequests; only rarely is there any mention of the value of the testator's goods, whether of individual items or her total assets. What can be said about these objects, other than to describe their appearance and value? Three broad interpretative paradigms have evolved in historical scholarship as ways of approaching early modern material culture and traces of 'the world of goods'. Firstly, we can view a person's material goods in relation to overall practices of consumption, looking for the accumulation of objects, the spread of luxury goods and the presence of innovative or fashionable items in an attempt to document their owner's relationship to broader social and economic trends. Secondly, we can view their possessions in relation to their function as status symbols, acquired with a view

---

[76] The proportion was augmented by Pope Innocent X, who ruled between 1644 and 1655. JoBaptista Scanaroli, *De visitatione carceratorum, libri tres* (Rome, 1655), 37. Alessandra Camerano discusses the problems of identifying prostitutes in these documents. 'Donne oneste o meretrici?'

[77] Fifty are wills and sixty-nine are various kinds of contract stipulating the conditions of a sale, loans of money, debt repayments and the rental of furnishings or apartments. Prostitutes are identified in the documents as a *curiale*, or the specific legacy to the *Monasterio delle Convertite* is the tell-tale sign that they were prostitutes. A database of more than a thousand prostitutes which I have compiled from the parish and criminal records has enabled me to cross-reference and identify prostitutes. For a comprehensive analysis of notarial documents in Rome see Renata Ago, *Economia barocca. Mercato e istituzioni nella Roma del seicento* (Rome: Donzelli, 1998).

to conspicuous consumption.[78] Prostitutes who aspired to ascend the professional hierarchy in early modern Rome were obliged to provide the kind of domestic interior expected by elite men if they were to attract patronage. Their homes were sites of intense sociability, places where objects were seen, commented on and compared with other people's. As Peter Thornton has pointed out, reports and letters stressed that courtesans owned 'the best' things; their possessions were compared to those of cardinals and even popes. Clearly, status, display and emulation would have been amongst their motives for acquiring goods.[79] A third approach to material culture has developed more recently. This emphasises the meanings attached to objects within the specific social and cultural context of their ownership and consumption. It encourages us to perceive the functions of objects within relationships and in relation to everyday behaviour.[80] This study will adopt this perspective. Using circumstantial evidence provided by criminal records it attempts to get closer to the uses, meanings and memories attached to domestic objects, and to explore their role in the daily life of prostitutes and their clients.[81]

Chapter 8 explores the material world of prostitution through the lens of the courtesan's domestic interior. Unlike Paris, London or Amsterdam where prostitution revolved mainly around brothels, taverns, music halls or brief rentals in lodging houses, prostitution in Rome was largely a domestic affair. Certainly, prostitutes and courtesans also met men in taverns and on

---

[78] For conspicuous consumption see Thorstein Veblen, *The Theory of the Leisure Class: an Economic Study of Institutions* (New York: Macmillan, 1912 (original edn, 1899)). There is, however, considerable overlap between these areas of inquiry. For an overview see Daniel Miller, *Acknowledging Consumption: a Review of New Studies* (London and New York: Routledge, 1995). With particular reference to Italy, Richard A. Goldthwaite, *Wealth and the Demand for Art in Italy 1300–1600* (Baltimore and London: The Johns Hopkins University Press 1993). And Lisa Jardine, *Worldly Goods: a New History of the Renaissance* (London: Macmillan, 1996).

[79] Peter Thornton, *The Italian Renaissance Interior, 1400–1600* (London: Weidenfeld and Nicolson, 1991), 354–5.

[80] Amanda Vickery, 'Women and the World of Goods: a Lancashire Consumer and her Possessions', in John Brewer and Roy Porter, eds., *Consumption and the World of Goods* (London and New York: Routledge, 1993), 274–81. Lorna Weatherill, 'The Meanings of Consumer Behaviour,' in Brewer and Porter, *Consumption and the World of Goods*, 206–27. Arjun Appadurai, 'Introduction: Commodities and the Politics of Value', in A. Appadurai, ed., *The Social Life of Things: Commodities in Cultural Perspective* (Cambridge: Cambridge University Press, 1986), 3–63. Sara Pennell, 'Consumption and Consumerism in Early Modern England', *The Historical Journal* 42:2 (1999), 549–64.

[81] For a fuller discussion of the meanings and uses attached to clothes, jewellery and small objects see my 'Fragments from the "Life Histories" of Jewellery Belonging to Prostitutes in Early Modern Rome', *Renaissance Quarterly* 19:5 (2005), 647–57 and 'The Clothing of Courtesans in Seventeenth Century Rome', in Catherine Richardson, ed., *Clothing Culture, 1350–1650* (Aldershot: Ashgate, 2004), 95–108. I consider the economic functions of objects more fully in 'Prostitution and the Circulation of Second-Hand Goods in Seventeenth Century Rome', in Laurence Fontaine, ed., *Alternative Exchanges: Second-Hand Circulations from the Sixteenth Century to the present* (Oxford: Berghahn, 2007).

the streets, but it was in their rooms that they entertained clients and their friends; this was true even for relatively poor prostitutes. Their domestic interior and its contents lay at the heart of their professional life, particularly since their homes were furnished with objects they had purchased with their earnings or been given by clients. These objects were therefore central to their relationships with men, as well as being crucial to their economic survival. This chapter examines what they owned, how they acquired these objects and what they were used for, with an emphasis on the role played by these objects within prostitute/client relationships.

The men who frequented prostitutes have often been left in the shadows of historical accounts, partly because much documentation has pertained to brothels, which recorded details about the women, but not the clients. This trend has been bucked in recent work on early modern Italy. Ferrante shows that long-term relationships with clients were the norm, revealing the extent to which prostitutes hoped that they might eventually marry their clients – and the legal structures in place through which they could try to pursue this goal.[82] Using approaches based on historical anthropology and micro-history,[83] Guido Ruggiero and Elizabeth and Tom Cohen have explored the inner dynamics and structures of prostitute/client relationships in Venice and Rome respectively. Ruggiero has looked particularly at love magic, and beliefs that prostitutes could 'bind' men into relationships against their will.[84] Elizabeth Cohen has studied the importance of honour within prostitute/client relationships and the position of prostitutes within their neighbourhoods.[85]

This book tries to keep clients in view throughout, particularly in the discussions on financial arrangements and practices of sociability. In the final chapter the focus shifts entirely to the clients and their relationships with prostitutes, using case studies to explore how men and women

[82] Ferrante, 'Pro mercede carnali' and 'Il valore del corpo'.

[83] For some interesting explanations and defences of micro-history see Giovanni Levi, 'On Microhistory', in Peter Burke, ed., *New Perspectives on Historical Writing* (Cambridge: Polity Press, 1991), 93–113. Jacques Revel, 'Micro-analyse et construction du social', in Revel, ed., *Jeux d'echelles: la micro-analyse à l'expérience* (Paris: Gallimard-Le Seuil, 1996), 15–36. Grendi, 'Ripensare la microstoria'.

[84] The term 'binding' particularly used in Ruggiero, *Binding Passions: Tales of Magic, Marriage and Power at the End of the Renaissance* (Oxford: Oxford University Press, 1993), 41, 37, and 'Re-reading the Renaissance: Civic Morality and the World of Marriage, Love and Sex', in J. G. Turner, ed., *Sexuality and Gender in Early Modern Europe: Institutions, Texts, Images* (Cambridge: Cambridge University Press, 1993), 10–30. Also the essay 'Lucretia's Magic', in Elizabeth and Tom Cohen, *Words and Deeds in Renaissance Rome*. And Fantini, 'La circolazione clandestina dell'orazione di Santa Marta'.

[85] See the essay 'Paolo di Grassi and his Courtesans', in Thomas V. and Elizabeth S. Cohen, *Words and Deeds in Renaissance Rome*. Also Elizabeth S. Cohen, 'Open and Shut: the Social Meanings of the Cinquecento Roman House', *Studies in the Decorative Arts*, Fall–Winter (2001–2), 61–84. And Elizabeth S. Cohen, 'Camilla the Go-Between', Elizabeth S. Cohen, 'Honour and Gender'.

in prostitution talked about their relationships in the early seventeenth century. The emphasis is particularly on what was revealed about the feelings of love, rivalry and anger which accompanied these 'commercial' relationships. It closes with a discussion of evidence that relationships seem to have been affected by the negative attitudes towards prostitution which were expounded by the Counter-Reformation.

The term 'carnal commerce' used in the title of this book was not just an 'official' term for prostitution, but was one used in everyday spoken language, by court officials, prostitutes and clients alike. It is adopted here not only as a less derogatory term for the profession, but because it draws attention to the commercial component of prostitution which is emphasised in this study. The other half of the transaction in this commerce, that relating to the body and sexuality, will, however, barely be touched upon. This is not a casual oversight, or due to the author's prudery, but a reflection of the nature of the historical sources which have been studied. Certain forms of literature and art from the period have long been famed – indeed, infamous – for their voyeuristic and pornographic approach to prostitution, and much has been written about them. On the contrary, the popular prints discussed here make absolutely no reference to sexuality or the body. They concern themseves with matters such as recruitment, wealth, syphilis and relationships. The same could be said of the criminal records which form the base of this research. In the eyes of the modern reader or scholar, an extraordinary lack of interest was shown by the criminal tribunal in the ordinary sexual relationships between prostitute and client. This may have been because sexuality had not yet been 'constituted as an area of investigation', as Foucault describes it.[86] It may also have been because this was not the main area of competence for the criminal courts, and the records of the Vicars' court have been lost. The result is that questions about sexual encounters only arose when 'unnatural' practices (i.e., anal intercourse) were suspected, when there were accusations of rape, or when de-flowering of virgins occurred. Likewise there is very little material relating to the 'arts of love', to contraceptive methods, abortion and birth experiences, all of which were surely central to the lives of these women. What little I have found pertaining to the body, sexuality and sensuality did not find its way easily into the framework governing this book. As a result, the sexual and bodily history of prostitution in Rome awaits its turn to be written.

---

[86] Michel Foucault, *History of Sexuality, vol. I*, trans. Robert Hurley (New York: Random House, 1990), 98.

CHAPTER I

Themes and issues in literature and image

PRIDE COMES BEFORE A FALL

On 10 February 1525, Carnival was in full swing in Renaissance Rome. Down by the Tiber a large crowd had gathered around Mastro Andrea, a well-known poet, painter and satirist at the papal court. Dressed in pauper's rags and ringing a hand bell he pulled a cart through the streets. In it stood 'paper effigies . . . of all the old courtesans of Rome, each inscribed with her name'. When he reached the river he stopped and threw in the effigies, one by one.[1] Pope Clement VII was there, along with his court, and we can imagine the riverbank lined with onlookers on a clear winter's morning: the Pope in red, as was then customary; the wealthy perhaps with fur-lined cloaks with huge bell-like sleeves; the courtiers and guards in brightly coloured, tight hose; the poor in drab rough wool. Amongst them may even have been some of the famous courtesans: escorted by their servants, heavily veiled and wearing cloth of gold, slashed velvets, pearls and rings.[2] The performance was accompanied by the recitation or singing of a verse entitled *Purgatorio delle cortigiane di Roma*. Mastro Andrea may have parodied the affectations, airs and graces often attributed to these high-class prostitutes, before mimicking their anguished downfall. We cannot tell whether this first performance was intended to be taken seriously, as a meditation on the vanity of these women, or whether it was intended to mock and taunt the city's courtesans. Perhaps both, for Bakhtin describes carnival laughter as 'ambivalent: gay, triumphant, and at the same time

[1] Archivio di Stato di Firenze, Carte Strozziane, serie I, c409. Written by an anonymous correspondent to Paolo Vettori, in Civitavecchia. For his clothing, see the frontispiece of *Purgatorio delle cortigiane, recitato in Roma per Andrea Pittore, nella festa di Carnovale, vestito di povero con le croccie et uno campanello in mano* (Siena, 1546). Cited in Graf, *Attraverso il cinquecento*, 256. Also cited and discussed in Hilde Kurz, 'Italian Models of Hogarth's Picture Stories', *Journal of the Warburg and Courtauld Institutes* 15 (1952), 136–68, 136–7. See also Aquilecchia, 'Per l'attribuzione e il testo del "Lamento d' una cortigiana ferrarese"', 11.

[2] Drawn from a description of a courtesan entering the church of Sant'Agostino. Pietro Aretino, *Il piacevol ragionamento del' Aretino*, 51.

mocking, deriding'.[3] Nor was it recorded whether the crowd laughed or cried as he took more than a hundred lines of verse to describe the 'pain, cries, sighs and troubles of those afflicted' in the hospital for incurables, San Giacomo, 'filling the beds from wall to wall', disfigured by syphilis, 'which eats the flesh to the bone . . . so that she who had noble, divine features, the incurable illness has turned into a monster'.[4] We do know that he was addressing the young, carefree courtesans who were the implied listeners of the tale:

You who are in joy, singing and laughing in beautiful palaces and are favoured in court, your face will not always be so lovely . . . Do not trust your beauty, which is brief and fragile like the smoke and wind . . . Think instead of the acute torments and the miseries of this hospital, which beats purgatory, and every lament.[5]

We also know that the courtesans who were named in the verse were not amused by the ritualised humiliation acted out that day before the eyes of the city. Mastro Andrea had taken care that they should know of his verses, 'sending the sonnet and the song that was sung to Orsolina'. Matrema non vole, Lorenzina, Angela, Cecilia and Beatrice were alive and well, since the next day they pursued Mastro Andrea 'to get their revenge, whipping him through the streets'.[6]

The account of the events surrounding the first performance of the *Purgatorio*, which went on to be published in Bologna in 1529 and Siena in 1546, points to some of the key characteristics of these and many other similar texts published about prostitution in this period.[7] They were penned by educated men who, if not noble themselves, lived and worked in a courtly, humanist milieu. As a result some of the literary features and concerns of these verses can be linked to various forms of elite literature, such as Aretino's dialogues and Petrarchan love poetry.[8] On the other hand the verses were printed on rough paper, in heavy ink, to be heard and read by people from all walks of life. They were destined for a broad, usually local

---

[3] Mikhail Bakhtin, *Rabelais and his World*, trans. Hélène Iswolsky (Bloomington: Indiana University Press, 1984), 11–12.

[4] Ibid., 19, 21, 46–7.

[5] *Purgatorio delle cortigiane. Sonnetti sopra el detto purgatorio* (Bologna, 1529), lines 28–35.

[6] Graf, *Attraverso il cinquecento*, 256.

[7] The 1546 edition is the *Purgatorio delle cortigiane*; see note 1 above.

[8] Paul F. Grendler, *Critics of the Italian World, 1530–1560* (Madison and London: University of Wisconsin Press, 1969). Vincenzo de Caprio, 'Intellettuali e mercato del lavoro nella Roma medicea', *Studi Romani* 29:1 (1981), 26–46. Paul Larivaille, 'L'Orazia de l'Aretin, tragédie des ambitions déçues', in *Les écrivains et le pouvoir en Italie à l'époque de la Renaissance*, Centre de Recherche sur la Renaissance Italienne (Paris: Université de la Sorbonne Nouvelle, 1973), 283–93.

public, who knew and could respond to these tales because they knew the protagonists (or others very like them) and presumably shared some of the concerns voiced in the text. They were also intended to be heard and read by prostitutes and courtesans themselves. The early sixteenth-century courtesans were famed for being not just literate, but highly educated companions as well as lovers. There is evidence to suggest that this link between courtesans and literacy continued well into the seventeenth century. Although there would have been widely differing levels of competence, some could certainly write, some could read, and as Maria Pia Fantini has shown, these were skills which could be shared, taught and delegated to others.[9]

THE FORTUNATE UNFORTUNATE COURTESAN

The earliest moralising narratives were built around the alternation between the pleasures and riches enjoyed by courtesans at the peak of their careers, and the desperate poverty and pain of syphilis which were threatened as the inevitable aftermath. The aim was to drive home the point that whilst the immediate rewards might be very attractive, the wheel of fortune would turn and the courtesan would reap her bitter harvest. This bi-partite structure is most evident in a text from the 1540s which went through many editions and was much copied, called 'The Boast and Lament of the Courtesan from Ferrara'. The first part was her boast, and in thirty-eight *terzine* it dwelt on her fame and bewitching beauty.

> I am that famous woman from Ferrara
> who carries the boast, the sceptre and the honour
> Of beauty and pomp, gentility and courtesy.
> . . . I have two eyes blacker than a raven
> So that who looks into them is stupefied
> and willingly becomes my prisoner.

In what was to become a stock topos, it exhaustively describes her wealth in terms of her possessions, ranging from her clothes to her well-stocked larder.

Many dresses of gold, velvet and silk, worked with fine stones and pearls . . . with stockings and shoes cut in various styles. And to show my pomp and my worth,

---

[9] See Fantini, 'La circolazione clandestina dell'orazione di Santa Marta'. For a more detailed discussion of the literacy of prostitutes, see her 'Les mots secrets des prostituées (Modène, 1580–1620)', *Clio: Histoire, Femmes, et Sociétés* (*Parler, Chanter, Lire, Écrire*) 11 (2000), 21–47. There is a lengthy letter penned by a Sicilian courtesan to the Governor's Tribunal in Rome. ASR, TCG, Processi vol. 23 (1602), fols. 1–340 (final pages).

at my neck I wear a chain worth at least two-hundred ducats[10] . . . I don't know anyone who can match me, who has the house so well supplied with bread, wood, wine, oil and salt . . . I have a cupboard full of silver, the tables, walls and chests full of carpets and tapestries.[11]

The second part is her lament: a pitiful description of how she has caught syphilis and is no longer the darling of society. She has lost everything, and her desire for delicacies and fine wines has been replaced by the most basic of needs: hunger and thirst.

I wore [cloth of] gold . . . now rough sackcloth. I hated Partridge, now I long [to eat]roots . . . I slept on silken sheets, now out in the wind underneath the benches, when I used to disdain golden rooms. Wines from Corsica, Greece, Trebbiano and Malvagia never pleased me, and now I realise that I'm thirsting for river water.[12]

There is particular emphasis in the 'downfall' on the courtesan's ravaged body, which contrasts with the lovely, smooth, 'closed' body of which she boasted in her prime. Once she had 'a throat of alabaster, whiter than the snow', a perfect example of the Renaissance 'aesthetic of the beautiful'.[13] The decay which follows is the more horrifying, stressing the 'openness' of her body, a process described by Bakhtin as 'grotesque realism'.[14] Her flesh even fuses with the material objects which earlier symbolised her success, thus involving her worldly goods in the same process of physical and social degradation. 'Her beautiful lace has turned into cabbage leaves and her pearls have become boils and pains.'[15] This trope draws upon a contrast between her inner, hidden moral corruption and her exterior beauty. This reverses and implicitly attacks the neo-Platonic idea that outer beauty was an expression of inner virtue, a concept which was fundamental to the justification and acceptance of the 'honest courtesan' in Renaissance society.

These dichotomies are also expressed visually in the illustrated broadsheets. 'Here is the Miserable End of the Signora Anzola' is a long lament by the courtesan who describes how she has lost her youth, beauty and riches, and lies bewailing her corrupted and painful body (see Figure 1).[16] It is dominated by the image of her lying in bed, revealing her young body

---

[10] *Il vanto e lamento della cortigiana ferrarese, per esempio a tutte le donne di mala vita* (Siena, 1540) (hereafter *Il Vanto*), lines 43–53.

[11] Ibid., lines 55–60.

[12] *Il lamento di una cortigiana ferrarese quale per aver il mal franzese si condussi andare in carretta. Mastro Andrea Veneziano* (Siena, 1540), lines 11–12, 28–33.

[13] Bakhtin, *Rabelais and his World*, 29.   [14] Ibid., chapter 5.

[15] *Il lamento di una cortigiana ferrarese* (1540), lines 16–17.

[16] *Ecco il miserabile fine della Signora Anzola* (late sixteenth century), Civica Raccolta Stampe Bertarelli.

horribly marked by the sores and boils of syphilis. However, there are elements of the picture which echo the text's references to the pleasures of her early career, and which indicate that she had been a successful courtesan. She is propped up on cushions on a comfortable chaise longue, wearing a large necklace, with two female servants and a well-dressed barber-surgeon in attendance on her. Her posture assumes more than a passing resemblance to Renaissance paintings of female nudes, such as Titian's *Venus of Urbino*, and is presumably meant to echo such images, given that portraits of courtesans were often painted for their lovers, and that they posed as artists' models.[17]

THE CINQUECENTO: COURTESANS, CLIENTS AND GREED

The courtesan's downfall and illness are implicitly a punishment for a life of sin, as well as a reminder to women that beauty is no protection against the inevitability of ageing, decay and illness.[18] This was the obvious moral message behind these texts. Yet, surprisingly perhaps, in several early Cinquecento texts, including the very popular *Lament of a Courtesan from Ferrara*, the explicitly stated moral of the story is different. It is a critique of the way in which relationships between courtesan and client were conducted. The model upon which relationships between the 'honest courtesans' and their 'lovers' were based in this period was that of courtly love.[19] The prospective or current lover (*amante*, never *cliente*) was the humble servant, bowing to his beloved who may or may not bestow her favours upon him. This is illustrated in the broadsheet *Questo si è il manco mal di n'altre meretrize morir in l'ospeal* (see Figure 2), dominated by the central image of the two lovers paying homage to their courtesan, one on bended knee offering flowers, the other making a gesture of his loyalty. There were advantages to this system. In conferring an aura of 'distinction' on the women, it created and sustained both a form of prostitution and a type of prostitute reserved for men of the elite. The unwelcome consequences of this arrangement, as

---

[17] For the debate on paintings of courtesans in the Renaissance see Elizabeth Cropper, 'On Beautiful Women: Parmigianino, Petrarchismo and the Vernacular Style,' *Art Bulletin* 58:3 (1976), 374–94. Cathy Santore, 'The Tools of Venus', *The Society for Renaissance Studies*, 11:3 (1997), 179–208. Patricia Simons, 'Portraiture, Portrayal and Idealization: Ambiguous Individualism in Representations of Renaissance Women', in Alison Brown, ed., *Languages and Images of Renaissance Italy* (Oxford: Clarendon Press, 1995), 271–85. Paola Tinagli, *Women in Italian Renaissance Art: Gender, Representation, Identity* (Manchester and New York: Manchester University Press, 1997).

[18] *Purgatorio delle cortigiane* (1529).

[19] For examples see Graf, *Attraverso il cinquecento* and Vittorio Cian, *Galanterie italiane del secolo XVI* (Turin: La Letteratura, 1888).

far as some men were concerned, was that it gave the courtesan the upper hand, allowing her to wield power and to decide whether to accept or reject 'lovers', picking and choosing amongst her prospective clientele.

Critiques of these relationships abounded. Dissatisfaction was voiced in the many satires and vituperative verses about courtesans which circulated at the time, alongside the Petrarchan-style love poems in which adoration for their mistresses scaled the heights of hyperbole.[20] Most famously, in Aretino's *Dialogues* the paradigm of disinterested, idealising love which informed these relationships is mocked. The adored courtesans are portrayed as cunning greedy whores, extorting money and objects from naive young men. In the moralising popular texts under consideration here, courtesans are warned not to reject poor, lower-status clients in favour of noblemen and gentlemen. It is implied that to do so is to aim above their station, an arrogance they called 'superbia': 'If you do not learn the lesson I am teaching you, arrogant courtesans *(superbe cortigiane)*, either Ponte-Sisto [the bridge where the beggars and the destitute begged] or the hospital [San Giacomo, the syphilis hospital] will await you'. Thus warns the repentant courtesan.[21] And what was the lesson she had to impart?

Earn what you can today and tomorrow, a *scudo*, a *giulio*, whatever you can get, otherwise you will go begging for your bread . . . willingly serve all comers, make those who come along happy, because it is better to have something than nothing . . . Always deign to give your self at any time, to everyone who comes, do not playact the great lady.[22]

Kurz suggests that this is just a bit of light-hearted 'Carnival humour'. It was certainly mocking, but to minimise the importance of this warning and these attacks on the 'arrogant courtesan' is to fail to see that this is the central message of these early texts. The words 'arrogant', 'haughty' and 'boastful' *(superbe, altiere, vanagloria)* are all employed to describe courtesans in three sonnets on the *Purgatory of the Courtesans*. The same warning emerges in Aretino's *Sei Giornate*, as Nanna advises her daughter how to remain at the top of the profession.

Tough luck for those who don't use their head: you need to know how to look after yourself in this world, and not act like a queen, never opening the door except to bishops and gentlemen . . . and those who don't deign to open the door except to those in velvet are mad. Because those dressed in woollen cloth can have

---

[20] Many examples and references to both types of verse can be found in the nineteenth-century literature on the courtesans, for example, Graf, *Attraverso il cinquecento*, Gnoli, *Cortigiane romane* and Rodocanachi, *Cortigiane e buffoni di Roma*.

[21] *Il lamento di una cortigiana ferrarese*, lines 55–7.   [22] Ibid., lines 71–2.

Fig. 1 *Ecco il miserabile fine della Signora Anzola* (Here you see the Miserable Death of Signora Anzola) (*c.* late sixteenth century)

Fig. 2 *Questo Sié il manco mal di n'altre meretrize morir in l'ospeal* (This is the Least of the Sufferings of us Prostitutes, Dying in a Hospital) (early seventeenth century)

Fig. 3.1–12 *La vita et miseranda fine della puttana* (The Life and Miserable Death of the Prostitute) (*c.* 1650)

Fig. 3.1 She goes to parties

Fig. 3.2 The old procuress visits

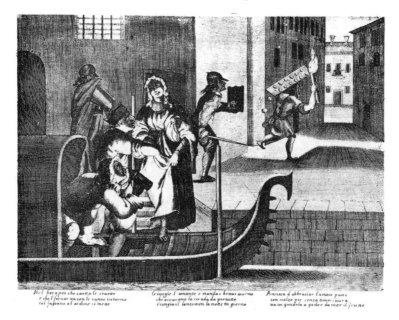

Fig. 3.3 She runs away with her lover by night

Fig. 3.4 She lives the life of a duchess

Fig. 3.5 With her lovers in Piazza San Marco

Fig. 3.6 She has her portrait painted as an Amazon

Fig. 3.7 Her lover finds a rival under the bed

Fig. 3.8 The second-hand dealer takes everything away

Fig. 3.9 She picks up English sailors in taverns

Fig. 3.10 She becomes a spy and a ruffian

Fig. 3.11 Sick with syphilis she begs for money

Fig. 3.12 Her miserable life ends in hospital

Fig. 4.1–12 *Vita del lascivo* (The Life of the Rake) (Venice, *c.* 1660s)

Fig. 4.1 The youth starts courting prostitutes

Fig. 4.2 He buys her a gift of English stockings

La scalta che diuora più del Tarlo   Il fà con larga, e lusinghiera offerta
De progressi col pazzo non incerta,   Padron di casa, sol per ispogliarlo

Fig. 4.3 The courtesan invites him to enter her home

Mentre il figlio frequenta la non casta,   Il padre, della propria casa il caccia,
Casa, quasi dal padre in giù la faccia,   Poichè una casa ad un sol huomo basta

Fig. 4.4 His father throws him out of his house

Qui la pietosa madre da nascosto
Del padre lo soccorre e lo ruina,

E del soccorso la celata mina
A commun danno scoppiarà ben tosto

Fig. 4.5 His mother pities him and gives him money

Ecco a dispetto dell' auaro padre,
Col cestarol, al fianco puttaneggia·

Voi godrei (dice) finch' april uerdeggia,
Honorando il dinaro di mia madre·

Fig. 4.6 The youth goes whoring with his mother's money

Fig. 4.7 Food and music sharpen his libido

Fig. 4.8 Made a German baron, they go to live in the country

Fig. 4.9 He starts gambling and loses large sums of money

Fig. 4.10 Abandoned by his woman, he takes to stealing and is arrested

Dall' esempi lar bonta d' amico uero
Vien tratto fuor della penosa gabbia

Hor ghe uenga la rogna anzi la rabia
Se non attende à qualche util mestiero.

Fig. 4.11 A true friend helps him leave prison

Ma ecco il nosstro gran baron todesco
Al sontico à sfamarsi di panada

Con una uitta tutta magagnada
Va all' hospidal che piu seco non tresca

Fig. 4.12 Our German baron eats at the refuge for the destitute

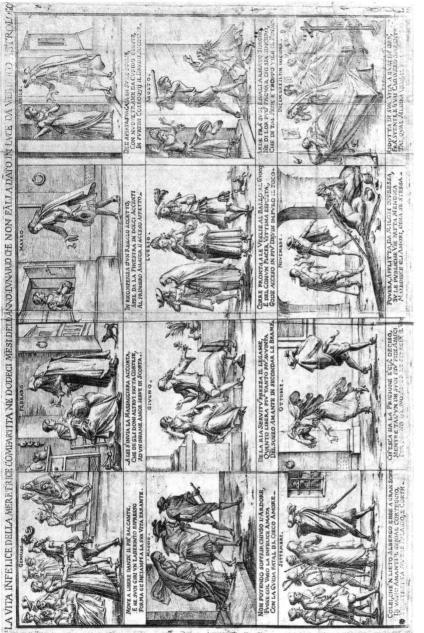

Fig. 5 *La vita infelice della meretrice comparata ne dodeci mesi dell'anno lunario che non falla dato in luce da Verriero astrologo* (The Unhappy Life of the Prostitute Compared to the Twelve Months of the Lunar Year) (1692).

stacks of ducats underneath, and I know well that tavern keepers, chicken-sellers, water-sellers, spenders and Jews give a good tip.[23]

We find the same theme in the poem by the Venetian nobleman Veniero, about the courtesan *La Zaffetta*. This poem describes how Zaffetta, who had refused to continue seeing her former lover, was punished with a mass rape, orchestrated by him. After some seventy verses of graphic, voyeuristic description, the narrator concludes with a 'moral lesson'. This states that courtesans should forget their airs and graces, be humble, obedient and submissive towards their clients.

If someone loves you, proud courtesans, find it in yourselves to be courteous and discreet, so that it would be a pleasure for men to say 'I love a woman who wishes to serve me, who comes quickly when I call her, doesn't want to trick me, and never argues. She takes whatever I give her, and doesn't dare to say "give me this, give me that."'[24]

What all these texts have in common is their attack on the ambition of the courtesan, who uses her 'power' and position to pick and choose her clientele so as to advance her social position. As one narrator says, after describing her sorrowful downfall, 'let this be an example to those mothers who are ambitious to take their daughters to parties, to dances . . . looking for something better than wheaten bread, because often the opposite happens'.[25] This characterisation was derived from long-standing associations between women and the sin of *lussuria*, considered to be the 'pre-eminent female sin' in Renaissance Italy.[26] The link to women can be traced back to Eve giving into the temptation for unnecessary things, and its connotations encompassed both 'sins of the body' – sensuality, self-indulgence and lechery – and 'sins of the mind' – greed for superfluities and for things to which one had no title. It was also a primary, 'generative' sin, linked to pride and social ambition, vanity and, particularly, *superbia*.[27] This condemnation of ambition was also part of the central theme of ecclesiastical literature on

---

[23] Pietro Aretino, *Sei giornate*, ed. Giovanni Aquilecchia (Rome and Bari: Laterza, 1975), 104.

[24] Lorenzo Veniero, *La Zaffetta* (orig. 531, Venice), reprint (Paris: 1861), verses 70–1.

[25] *La fortunata cortigiana sfortunata: dove s'intende principio, mezo e fine della vita cortigianesca* (Venice, 1668). *La vita et miseranda fine della puttana* (Venice, 1650), lines 192–3, 202–3.

[26] Ruth Mazo Karras discusses medieval English literature on the theme of prostitutes and greed in her *Common Women*, 88–95. For *lussuria* see Sara F. Matthews Grieco, *Ange ou diablesse: la représentation de la femme au XVIe siècle* (Paris: Flammarion, 1991). H. Diane Russell, with Bernadine Barnes, *Eva/Ave: Woman in Renaissance and Baroque Prints* (Washington, D.C., National Gallery of Art; New York: The Feminist Press at the City University of New York, 1990).

[27] For a very rich analysis of the derivations and meanings of the term see John Sekora, *Luxury: the Concept in Western Thought, Eden to Smollett* (Baltimore: The Johns Hopkins University Press, 1977), 23–62.

poverty, which was that the poor should accept their condition as part of God's order.[28] However, the vehemence with which these attacks were made on the 'inappropriate' social ambitions of prostitutes points to more than just the operation of a literary tradition. This raises questions about the extent to which such criticisms of prostitutes were grounded not in moral outrage, but in widespread perceptions, possibly resentment, that wealth and possessions came too easily to those women who lived a 'dishonest' way of life.

WARNINGS TO COURTESANS IN
COUNTER-REFORMATION TEXTS

Towards the end of the sixteenth century the simple bi-partite scheme was dropped and new plot structures emerged. A very popular one describes the 'career' path of the courtesan as a cycle, moving from poverty to wealth and back again, probably based on the traditional theme of the 'wheel of fortune'. An example is the illustrated broadsheet *La vita et miseranda fine della puttana* (The Life and Miserable End of the Prostitute) printed in Venice in 1650 (see Figures 3.1–12), which also appeared in a longer narrative version in 1668 as *La fortunata cortigiana sfortunata* (The Fortunate Unfortunate Courtesan).[29] The latter is narrated by a courtesan dying from syphilis who looks back over her life, holding herself up as a 'mirror to all', warning others not to follow in her footsteps. As a poor young woman her mother 'had so little care of me, that I am nearly in my grave'. She let her go to parties (see Figure 3.1) and allowed a procuress to seduce her with dreams of 'becoming a queen' (see Figure 3.2). The procuress encouraged her to run away by night and she found herself in a gondola, embraced by a gentleman 'all in velvet' (see Figure 3.3). She was taken to a villa, and her life was transformed: wearing 'earrings, rings, bracelets and necklaces of heavy gold, looking so proud and magnificently dressed . . . treated like a Duchess' (see Figure 3.4). However, true to her feminine nature, 'eventually living in a villa bored me, and it all seemed as nothing, for all that I had, I was not content'. So during Carnival she arranged through a procuress to take other lovers, 'Armenians . . . and Slavs, even some Moors' (see Figure 3.5). At the height of her career she had her portrait painted 'in the form of

---

[28] For a discussion of attitudes towards poverty and an analysis of this theme in popular pamphlets, see Giorgio Caravale, 'Censura e pauperismo tra cinque e seicento', *Rivista di Storia e Letteratura Religiosa* 38:1 (2002), 39–77, esp. 67.

[29] *La vita et miseranda fine della puttana* (Venice, 1650). In the following section I refer to the images of the former version, whilst citing from the latter because the text is richer.

Minerva, so my beauty could be seen', and had hung 'it so that it could even be seen from the street' (see Figure 3.6). But one day the lover who had been 'paying my bills' found his rival in her house, hidden under the bed (see Figure 3.7). 'My lover, and all the affection he had for me turned to hate and disdain' and he abandoned her. She decided 'to call the Jew' (the second-hand dealer) and she wept, as the leather wall-hangings were stripped away and her precious possessions were removed: 'And I can tell you, it all went for the price of a piece of bread' (see Figure 3.8). After this 'I was reduced to working outlying districts', and as an indication of how low she had fallen she specifies that it was an area 'frequented by English sailors' (see Figure 3.9). After working as a spy and procuress (see Figure 3.10), she then turned to begging on the bridges (see Figure 3.11) and finally she laments, 'I find myself here in hospital, lying almost dead and buried in this bed, covered in scabs and full of illness' (see Figure 3.12).[30]

This new plot structure had several advantages. Whilst her rise to success gives a focus to the first half of the narrative, the details about the different phases of her career make her wealth a less dominant theme. This provides an opportunity to address other issues, such as the role played by the mother in recruitment and the importance of the client in triggering the courtesan's downfall.

By the seventeenth century the warnings voiced in these narratives had also shifted towards a greater emphasis on the spiritual dangers faced by prostitutes. Syphilis still featured as one of the many dangers, but it was no longer the central threat. Perhaps this was because the disease was no longer a novelty, was less virulent, was widespread in the population at large and had lost its power to scare. Or it may have reflected the general thrust of Counter-Reform teachings, as syphilis was replaced by the threat of hell-fire and purgatory for those who failed to turn away from their sinful lives. In *The Life and Miserable End of Prostitutes*, an illustrated broadsheet from about 1600, two forms of punishment are shown: worldly punishment involves prison and exile, whilst spiritual punishment means the burning fires of hell. But between these two the hope of penitence and reform are offered. A former courtesan ministers to the sick, reminding them that it is always possible to leave their wicked lives behind.[31]

The importance of repenting before it is too late is the message of another group of seventeenth-century Venetian texts which tell the tale of a successful courtesan who, naively, gives her heart to a thief posing as a lover. Once

---

[30] *La fortunata cortegiana sfortunata*, lines 6–7, 17–18, 25, 37, 44–50, 67.

[31] *Il miserabile fine di quelli che seguono le meretrici* (Rome, 1611), reproduced in Kunzle, *The Early Comic Strip*, 276–7.

he has gained her trust he steals all her possessions, and in three versions of this tale he murders her. The message is that no matter how beautiful and successful a courtesan may be, she is exposed daily to the danger of 'treacherous' clients and death may come suddenly. The most sombre of these is *The Lament Made by a Courtesan on the Loss of the Good Times*, in which twenty-seven verses of pious warnings and judgements play on the contrast between spiritual and earthly love and riches. The courtesan loves and gives her heart to a lover rather than to God, and seeks only to acquire material wealth, rather than storing up spiritual treasure in heaven, finally dying a 'bad death'.[32] In *A Tearful and Lamentable Case: Cecilia Bruni Muranese Courtesan*, from 1621, the heroine expresses her dread of being buried in the sand, implicitly making reference to the fact that sinners were denied burial in consecrated ground. This was perhaps the most meaningful way to communicate to the average prostitute the consequences of failing to repent. 'Oh misery, I am dead, ohhh! in sin, I have died in sin, ohhh!, poor me, if only I had at least confessed my errors I would not have to be buried by the sea'.[33]

In *The Girl from Verona: a Compassionate Case*, the courtesan only just has time to beg forgiveness before she dies. As if reminding the listener that it is never too late (and perhaps intending to teach the listening public the appropriate words), she cries out:

I beg you, o Lord, to forgive me, my past errors, Oh God, do not look at my sins, because I have repented . . . Jesus, my saviour, have pity upon me, lord God, do not leave my soul to stray damned and abandoned in hell. I beseech thee lord, pardon me my past errors.[34]

These last two texts, *Cecilia Bruni* and *The Girl from Verona*, represent a striking departure from the Cinquecento texts, in particular in their characterisation of the courtesan. In Aretino's dialogues it was the courtesan who was the thief and trickster, whereas here the courtesan is cast in a positive and sympathetic light. She is the betrayed 'heroine' of the story; at the time of her death she is rich and beautiful, 'kindly and courteous',

---

[32] *Il lamento che fa una cortesana per esser li mancato il suo bon tempo*, Novamente composta da me Paolo Britti (Macerata, 1632).

[33] *Caso lacrimoso e lamentevole. Di Cecilia Bruni Muranese cortegiana in Venetia à San Paterniano. Occisa nella propria sua casa, dal suo amante, portandogli via Ori, e Gioie alli 8 Agosto, 1618* (Macerata and Ronciglione, 1621).

[34] *La Veronese. Caso compassionevole: Dove s'intende la inusitata morte data da un giovane Parmesano ad Elisabetta cortegiana Veronese. La quale sotto colore di benevolenza è stata condotta da lui fuori di Verona nella bassa di Caldiero, dove l'hà uccisa, rubbata, e sepolta il di 18 del mese di Luglio 1605* (Macerata, 1619). There is another text on this theme: *Risposta sotterranea della Signora Margarita Francese, Famossissima Cortegiana di Venetia, uccisa a tradimento da un suo amante* (Venice, 1614).

a trusting victim of the man's greed, 'all lost . . . poor thing'. It is the client-lover who is the villain, a wicked and dangerous figure, referred to as 'treacherous and astute . . . a traitor . . . a fraud'.[35]

On the one hand these tales bear the hallmarks of the influence of the Jesuits on contemporary culture. From the late sixteenth-century onwards the plot of the 'unrepentant female sinner who met with a violent end' was commonly given in instruction manuals for Jesuit missionaries, as a tale to be told in the fight against illicit sexuality.[36] On the other hand, these were not all crude 'scare-mongering' tales. They seem to have been written with a view to creating a less judgemental narrative, one which would communicate the religious message to the target public more effectively. Here are heroines with whom prostitutes could actually identify, while the danger of being murdered by a client was probably a commonly held fear. Another indication that printers were seeking to make these texts seem more relevant was reference to a 'real', apparently local event. Thus the title page of the *Lament of Cecilia Bruni Muranese* tells us that she was 'killed in her own house, by her lover, who took away her gold and jewels, on the eighth of August, 1618'.

It is also interesting how these texts deal with the practical moral of the story, for although the final verses warn women to repent before it is too late, the story's moral is left ambiguous. In *La Veronese*, it is the man's sinfulness which is stressed, since he broke the bonds of trust by killing a woman who loved him. Indeed, there is no mention of *her* sinfulness until the moment after he has struck the mortal blow.[37] In *La Veronese* and *Cecilia Bruni* the narrator both admonishes courtesans to amend their sinful lives, and warns them never to trust men and their promises. This rather compromises the moral message, since it could be read as implying that if they do not leave their wicked life, they should at least be less naive and trusting of their clients in future.

Take my example, women, all of you, and never trust your many lovers, who with their false words and clever talk, are laying traps for you, death and tears.[38]

WARNINGS TO CLIENTS

Prostitution narratives were also directed at men, and in them we encounter a variety of dangers which lie in wait for hapless youths seduced by the

---

[35] *Cecilia Bruni Muranese cortegiana* and *La Veronese.*   [36] Selwyn, *A Paradise*, 168.
[37] Ibid.   [38] *Cecilia Bruni Muranese cortegiana.*

attractions of a dissolute life. The threat of contracting syphilis hangs like a shadow over the majority of these texts, and, unlike those directed at prostitutes, this does not change in the seventeenth century.

Comrade, comrade / . . . I went to Carampane / only a month ago / but I am already full of the French disease / of boils and sores / I can say without a doubt / that I am well supplied with . . . (?) The reason, the reason / is that a procuress led me / to a dirty whore.[39]

As if in a mirror image of those texts directed at prostitutes, the other key warning to men was the danger of squandering their wealth on courtesans – enriching them at the risk of impoverishing themselves.

Poor men, we have been led into a vile and lowly state . . . We were continually forced to satisfy their dishonest desires, to buy rings, chains and clothes. We also had to see to the house, and to sate their incredible hunger.[40]

Many were directed at sons of the elite. This is sometimes evident just from the 'literary' vocabulary used in the text: 'Never did the people of Carthage feel such hate against the Romans, as is born in you against she whom once you praised in your pages.' These place considerable emphasis on the social consequences attendant on associating with courtesans: the loss of family, wealth and social status. 'He was once rich with silver, lived contented and happily, owning fields, houses and palaces, had pleasures and entertainment'.[41] In *The Miserable End of Those who Follow Prostitutes*, published in Rome in 1611, the client is shown borrowing money so as to 'pay for his desires', then being taken to prison for not paying his debts; finally there is the ultimate shame of having to sell his lands and patrimony in order to pay off his creditors.[42]

The illustrated broadsheet *Vita del lascivo*, from later seventeenth-century Venice, is a veritable compendium of the various misfortunes to befall clients, illustrating particularly well the dangers that lie in the courtesan's apartments (see Figures 4.1–12). It opens by showing four men flirting with courtesans who stand enticingly at their windows and doors: thresholds

[39] *Nuova canzonetta: Nella quale s'intende il lamento che fa un povero giovane con un suo compagno per esser stato gabbato da una cortegiana sopra l'aria della Nave* (Treviso, seventeenth century).

[40] 'Nuova Canzonetta, Di giovani impoveriti per le meretrici', in Carlo Verzone, ed., *Le Rime Burlesche di A. F. Antonfrancesco Grazzini, detto il Lasca, Le Rime Burlesche. Edite e Inedite* (Florence: Sansoni, 1882), 180. This is also the theme in *Ridicolosa canzonetta nella qual s'intende un suggetto occorso sopra d'un contadino gabato da una meretrice, comme leggendo intenderete il tutto* (Macerata, 162?).

[41] *Canzonetta nuova nella quale s'intende un giovane caduto in precipitio, per amare una meretrice* (Macerata: Pietro Salvioni, 1627).

[42] *Il miserabile fine di quelli che seguono le meretrici*, in Kunzle, *The Early Comic Strip*, 276–7.

to sin (see Figure 4.1).[43] One youth then purchases a gift (flame-coloured English stockings) (see Figure 4.2), which gains him entry to their villa. The door to the courtyard is opened and he walks naively towards her apartments. Meanwhile the courtesan's servant locks the door behind him, suggesting metaphorically that there will be no escape, which is echoed by the image of a large bird cage at the window of her rooms (see Figure 4.3). Once inside the courtesan's apartments he gives himself up to the pleasures of the appetites: music, food, wine and a comfortable bed (see Figure 4.7). He is made a baron, and becomes even more profligate, moving to the country (see Figure 4.8). By now he is trapped in his life of luxury and he is soon set on an inexorable social decline. He starts gambling (see Figure 4.9), is jilted by the courtesan, then arrested and imprisoned for brawling over her with his rivals (see Figure 4.10). Finally released, he falls ill with syphilis and, having lost his honour and friends, ends up at the hospital in search of food (see Figure 4.12).

Just as the courtesan's rooms are the site of his downfall, we observe interesting uses made of pictorial space to illustrate the client's gradual loss of social status. The streets should be spaces associated with the lives of honourable men conducting their business or enjoying the company of their friends. They are properly the theatre of man's civic role and public honour. However, to the man who has strayed from an 'honourable' life, the streets acquire new meanings. They become the site of his public humiliation as he is handcuffed by the police (see Figure 4.10) and led to prison. In a contemporary broadsheet *Il miserabile fine di quelli che seguono le meretrici*, 'fallen' men are led through the streets to the galleys; one is shown being carried through the streets on a chair to take the cure for syphilis which he has picked up from prostitutes and when he finally dies *miseramente,* his body is laid out in the streets for all to see.[44]

There are, however, frequent indications of ways in which men can exact their revenge against prostitutes. In *La Vita infelice della meretrice comparata ne dodeci mesi* (see Figure 5) a former client, having been imprisoned on account of a fight over his courtesan, slashes her face once he is freed. In the following image the courtesan is insulted by former lovers as she lies begging in the streets. Although there was nothing new in exorting men to be wary of prostitutes, by setting these examples Counter-Reformation texts seem to have stressed the ways in

---

[43] *Vita del lascivo* (Venice, *c.* 1660).

[44] *Il miserabile fine di quelli che seguono le meretrici* (Rome, 1611). Source, David Kunzle, *The Early Comic Strip,* 276–7.

which men could reassert their dominance and power over courtesans, disdaining rather than adoring them, as had been demanded by the etiquette of Renaissance courtly-love culture. Women were warned, on the other hand, not to trust their clients, not to 'love' them, to be wary. Although this may have been practical advice, it seems more likely it was intended to strike at the unwritten 'code' of reciprocity, even respect, which had been the ideal and foundation of long-term friendships within prostitution.

BECOMING A PROSTITUTE

In classical literature prostitution was presented as a female world. In Renaissance reworkings of the genre this point was emphasised, particularly in Aretino's dialogues in which mothers encourage their daughters to become prostitutes, and instruct them in the arts of love.[45] The humour of this topos in the Cinquecento derived partly from the subversion of the principles underlying the ideal mother–daughter relationship, and partly from its parody of the master–pupil relationship, so dear to humanists. Given that the famous courtesans of the Renaissance prided themselves on their education and their mastery of the 'arts' of love, these texts also deliberately attacked their claims to professionalism. Nana asserts that a courtesan can learn her trade in no time at all: 'I learnt in three months, no two, no one, everything you need to know about screwing men.'[46]

This light-hearted view of prostitution was evidently not restricted to elite circles. In 1584 a pamphlet printed illegally in Perugia dealt with the same theme. Entitled *Advice which a woman gives her daughter, in which she teaches her about the many types of people she will have to make love with*, the text opens with the mother's advice to her daughter. 'Daughter, while you are in the bloom of youth, take my advice, take as many lovers as you can and open to everyone, and anyone, as long as you bring in some money, as everyone will do for us'.[47]

She describes each category of man, listing them according to how much money they will pay her or what they will give her, pointing out which men to avoid and concluding with the advice never to fall in love with them. The text was intended to amuse (it is subtitled 'something ridiculous and

---

[45] See Lucian's dialogues from the second century AD. *Chattering Courtesans and Other Sardonic Sketches,* ed. and trans. Keith Sidwell (London: Penguin, 2004). Aretino's *Ragionamento, Dialogo and Dialogo di Giulia e di Madalena* and Anon., *Il Ragionamento dello Zoppino.*

[46] Aretino, *Ragionamento*, 148–9.   [47] *Opera Nova dove si Contiene un esordio* etc. (Perugia, 1584).

pretty') and prostitution is shown in this text as an easy way for a girl to get by in the world.

With cooks and tavern keepers know how to behave, since they will give you money and you can order them about . . . be polite with policemen, more than any others, as they spend freely . . . don't have anything to do with students, but if you really want to give them something, make sure you are paid first, and under no circumstances go to their homes.[48]

This pamphlet is an unusual survival, however, and in the majority of narratives dating from after the Counter-Reformation the humour disappears, as does any reference to prostitution as a 'trade'. Some mothers are guilty of having encouraged their daughters' latent vanity and frivolity in their eagerness to find them husbands. 'Look at her cunning mother, now her daughter is growing up, although she is poor, she wants her to be well-dressed'.[49] Others are careless: 'The person who neglected to look after me was my mother, who took so little care of me that I am almost in my grave, because she took me to each party, even though she saw there were lovers'.[50]

In *The Unhappy Life of the Prostitute in the Twelve Months of the Year*, the honest young protagonist is tempted from her lace-making in the security of her home by the courteous advances of a handsome youth (see Figure 5). Once her passions have been aroused all is lost: 'Not able to suppress her ardour any longer she flees . . . guided by blind passion.' According to contemporary beliefs, it is women's constitutional propensity towards sensuality and lust which puts young women in such danger and against which a mother should guard her daughter.

ABSENT FATHERS

Fathers, on the contrary, are barely mentioned. One appears in a verse written in Venetian dialect which describes the misfortunes which befall a poor family when a daughter is born. However, the father is quickly exonerated from responsibility. 'Truly, the poor father is without fault, but what is true is that mothers are to blame when girls fall'.[51] Whilst he, naive and trusting, had been worrying about how to save money for the daughter's dowry, the mother had been secretly spending all the family

---

[48] Ibid.
[49] *La putta che diventa corteggiana, per il mal governo di sua madre, per volerghe far metter troppo presto il para su* (Venice, 1668).
[50] *La fortunata cortegiana sfortunata.*   [51] *La putta che diventa corteggiana.*

savings on adorning their daughter: buying her mirrors, earrings and new clothes. When the father finally discovers the truth, he 'dies of shame'.[52] The family dynamics are little different from those in *The Life of the Rake*, which portrays the drama played out in an elite family when the father discovers that his son is frequenting courtesans. Furious, he chases his son from the house (see Figure 4.4), but whilst he sleeps the mother slips her son money, which he then uses to finance his relationship with a courtesan. 'Here the pitying mother, in secret and without the father knowing, helps him and ruins him' (see Figure 4.5).[53]

The members of the family, a microcosm of the state, owed obedience to the male head, who was to govern those in his care. The father was traditionally responsible for ensuring the safe transition of girls from child-hood to marriage without loss of honour, and were expected to prevent adolescent males, attributed with 'a lively sensuality and weak capacities of reason', from slipping into dissolute living.[54] These texts warn men that a father who lacked authority risked allowing corruption to set in, since a mother's love was considered inferior to paternal love. Her judge-ment, her greed and her vanity all contributed to making her a most unsuitable figure for the guardianship of young people.[55] Although in the latter half of the sixteenth century the church had begun to accord women greater responsibility within the family, these moralising tales speak of a profound mistrust of the mother's power and influence over her children.[56]

These songs and broadsheets formed part of the cultural background to prostitution in early modern Italy. They were, however, part of a genre, and therefore profoundly influenced by long-standing moral and literary conventions, making it difficult to tell where tradition ended and contem-porary concerns began. It is the changes in the themes and imagery over time which show that their authors were aware of social change, and that these tales were intermittently refashioned with audience responses in mind.

[52] Ibid., lines 146–8.　　[53] Caption to *La vita del lascivo*.

[54] Albano Biondi, 'Aspetti della cultura cattolica post-Tridentina', in C. Vivanti and R. Romano, eds., *Storia d'Italia: intellettuali e potere, Annali 4* (Turin: Einaudi, 1981), 262, 272.

[55] Ibid., 225–302.

[56] Elisa Novi Chiavarria, 'Ideologia e comportamenti familiari nei predicatori italiani tra cinque e set-tecento. Tematiche e modelli', *Rivista Storica Italiana* 100:3 (1988), 679–723, 689. Renata Ago, 'Maria Spada Veralli, la buona moglie,' in Giulia Calvi, ed., *Barocco al femminile* (Rome and Bari: Laterza, 1992), 51–70, 68. Stanley Chojnacki, 'The Most Serious Duty: Motherhood, Gen-der and Patrician Culture in Renaissance Venice,' in M. Migiel and J. Schiesari, eds., *Refiguring Woman: Perspectives on Gender and the Italian Renaissance* (New York; Cornell University Press, 1991), 133–54.

This suggests that the texts and images considered here did indeed articulate early modern Italian attitudes towards prostitution, beliefs about it and perceptions of the dangers associated with it. Now, in order to understand the society in which these broadsheets and pamphlets were produced and circulated, we turn away from moralising discourses to the specific cultural, social and demographic conditions which underpinned prostitution in late sixteenth-century Rome.

CHAPTER 2

The social and cultural context

From the late fifteenth to the late seventeenth century, papal Rome was at the hub of Italian and European affairs, the central axis of international Catholic diplomacy. As a city it was dominated by the presence of the papacy, with its courtiers, functionaries and the elaborate processional life which accompanied the movements of the pontiffs and other dignitaries. It was also home to a great many cardinals, ambassadors and their entourages from the Italian principalities and great Catholic states. By 1603 there were fifty cardinals in residence in Rome, some two hundred important prelates and a great many ambassadors and diplomats.[1] The *Curia* was the papal administration. It relied on the presence of hundreds of well-educated men who could run administrative affairs and act as diplomats and secretaries. A position in the papal court opened the way to higher offices and benefices, providing a family with money, dignity and social status. Consequently Rome was the focus of the career hopes of a great many families from all over Europe.[2] Each cardinal and ambassador had his own court which provided employment for scores if not hundreds of people, mostly men, ranging from secretaries, courtiers and pages, to servants, stablemen and coachmen.[3] Large numbers of young men also came to the city in order to study or to join the scores of monasteries and religious institutions.[4] In the

---

[1] Delumeau, *Vie économique et sociale*, 37–8.

[2] There were 2,232 venal offices by 1521. John D'Amico stresses the very competitive nature of the *Curia* in *Renaissance Humanism in Papal Rome: Humanists and Churchmen on the Eve of the Reformation* (Baltimore: The Johns Hopkins University Press, 1983), 27. Also on the *Curia* see Peter Partner, *All the Pope's Men: the Papal Civil Service in the Renaissance* (New York: Oxford University Press, 1990). Renata Ago, *Carriere e clientele nella Roma barocca* (Rome and Bari: Laterza, 1990).

[3] In a 1656 census the Spanish ambassador's household numbered more than a hundred dependants. ASR, Camerale II, Sanità, busta 4/5, c106r–109r.

[4] The former constituted about 3.5 per cent of the total population. C. Schiavoni and E. Sonnino, 'Aspects généraux de l'évolution démographique à Rome, 1598–1824', *Annales de Démographie Historique* (1982), 91–109, 95. On the clergy see Eugenio Sonnino, 'In the Male City: the Status Animarum of Rome in the Seventeenth Century', in Antoinette Fauve-Chamoux and Solvi Sogner, eds., *Socio-economic Consequences of Sex-Ratios in Historical Perspective, 1500–1900*. Proceedings of the Eleventh

early seventeenth century there were between 4,000 and 6,000 courtiers and students in the city, whilst the clergy amounted to about 5,000 men. As Schiavoni and Sonnino have reminded us, they were 'celibate but not necessarily chaste'.[5]

Alongside 'Holy Rome' and 'Papal Rome' there was also a lay population of nobles, gentlemen and commoners over whom the popes ruled and with whom they had to co-exist. At the head of the lay social hierarchy were the noble families descended either from medieval feudal barons, or from the families of sixteenth- and seventeenth-century popes.[6] Below them came those families headed by 'gentlemen' who had been in Rome for more than a century, as well as those who had arrived more recently and who dealt in trade and finance, for Rome was also a centre of financial affairs.[7] Finally, there were the 'commoners', a mixed population of merchants, professional men, artisans, shopkeepers, servants and labourers.

Although Delumeau lamented the failure of the papacy to install any manufacturing industries in the city, recent scholarship has stressed that Rome was crowded with hundreds of artisans producing goods for the consumption of the rich.[8] Vast quantities of marble, jewels, paintings and textiles passed through the Roman customs offices, on their way to the thousands of shops, workshops and market stalls of the city, providing employment right across the social spectrum.[9] From the second half of the sixteenth century onwards, large tracts of the city became huge building sites as successive popes ordered the construction of churches, aqueducts and housing as part of the *Renovatio Roma*, the project to rebuild Rome in a manner befitting its importance.[10] Fifty-three new churches alone were

International Economic History Congress, Milan, 1994, vol. B5 (Milan: Università Bocconi, 1994), 21.

5   Schiavoni and Sonnino, 'L'évolution démographique à Rome', 95.
6   There were about seventeen such families. Laurie Nussdorfer, *Civic Politics in the Rome of Urban VIII* (Princeton and Oxford: Princeton University Press, 1992), 99.
7   Ibid. On the Roman nobility see Elisabetta Mori, 'Cittadinanza e nobiltà a Roma tra cinque e seicento', in *Roma Moderna e Contemporanea* 4:2 (1996), 379–403, 381. And Anna Esposito, '"Li nobili huomini di Roma": strategie familiari tra città, curia e municipio', in S. Gensini, ed., *Roma capitale, 1447–1527* (Rome: Ministero per i Beni Culturali e Ambientali, 1994), 373–88.
8   Delumeau, *Vie économique et sociale*, 365. Renata Ago finds that about 21 per cent of the population was involved in this kind of profession. Ago, *Economia barocca*, 3–7.
9   See Arnold Esch, 'Roman Customs Registers, 1470–80: Items of Interest to Historians of Art and Material Culture', *Journal of the Warburg and Courtauld Institutes* 58 (1995), 72–87.
10 Helge Gamrath, *Roma sancta renovata: studi sull'urbanistica di Roma nel XVI secolo* (Rome: L'Erma, 1987), 28. Sigfried Giedion, 'Sixtus V and the Planning of Baroque Rome', *Architectural Review* (1952), 217–26, 220. Gérard Labrot, *L'image de Rome: une arme pour la Contre-Réforme, 1534–1677* (Seyssel: Champ Vallon, 1987), 280–1. James S. Ackerman, 'The Planning of Renaissance Rome, 1450–1580,' in P. A. Ramsey (ed.), *Rome in the Renaissance: the City and the Myth* (Binghamton, N.Y.: Medieval and Early Renaissance Texts and Studies, 1982), 3–19.

built, mostly after 1550. At the same time cardinals, ambassadors and the great families sought to maintain their social position by building new palaces which reflected their role in the new Rome. All this exerted a powerful 'pull' on labour from the surrounding areas, bringing thousands of immigrant masons, labourers and specialised artisans and artists to the city. It is not surprising to find that by the early seventeenth century, when we have the first comprehensive records, Rome was a city populated extensively by immigrants or, as they were called, *forestieri*.[11] As the Venetian ambassador Girolamo Soranzo put it in a report sent to the Venetian Senate in 1563, Rome was:

A great throng of all the nations of the world, and of people of every state, degree and condition that you can think of. This is because everyone hopes that he will be able to realise his ambitions here . . . the gentleman of medium fortune, who finds himself with many sons, decides which one is most likely to succeed, and sends him to Rome in the hope that this route will bring him money and honour.[12]

Although there was female migration to the city, Rome was not so attractive to women. As a result, data from 1600 onwards (the first year for which reasonably accurate data are available) show that there was an extremely skewed population balance, with huge numbers of single men in the city at any given time. There were years when there were as many as 150, even 178, men to 100 women.[13] In addition, vast numbers of itinerants such as beggars and pilgrims flocked to the city annually; 139,000 pilgrims received hospitality for the jubilee year of 1574–5 alone.[14] It was thus very much a 'male city', and, as the commentator Alessandro Petronio observed: 'Next there are the women, few of whom are without a husband, and many are married, and often they are pregnant.'[15]

Despite the hubbub of activity, the majority of people in Rome lived in poverty and were always vulnerable to the next famine or wave of infectious disease. The closing years of the sixteenth century brought starvation and public discontent. An *avviso* from March 1592 describes how 'Given the

---

[11] Delumeau, *Vie économique et sociale*, 135–220.
[12] Relazione di Roma di Girolamo Soranzo letta il 14 giugno 1563, in Eugenio Alberi, *Le Relazioni degli Ambasciatori Veneti al Senato*, Vol. X, Serie 2, Tomo IV (Florence: Tipografia all'insegna di Elio, 1839–57), 84.
[13] Sonnino, 'In the Male City', 21. See also Antonio Santini, 'Le strutture socio-demografiche della popolazione urbana', in *La demografia storica delle città italiane: relazioni e comunicazioni presentate al convegno tenuto ad Assisi* (Bologna: Clueb, 1982), 125–47.
[14] Of these, 109,000 were male, staying at Trinità dei Pellegrini, whilst 30,000 female pilgrims stayed in various confraternities. Delumeau, *Vie économique et sociale*, 171.
[15] M. Alessandro Petronio da Città Castellana, *Del viver delli romani et di conservar la sanità* (Rome, 1592), 196.

continuous famine of the last several years . . . there has been no bread in Rome for the last three days, except of a little made with maize, and the people are raging around at the ovens.'[16] There was a constant threat of malaria, fever and plague, which struck with particular ferocity in 1656–7, as well as outbreaks of typhus in and around the city. The seventeenth century saw general economic decline across the peninsula. By the middle of the century thousands of immigrants were flooding into Rome from the south in search of food as conditions worsened even furthur.[17] A contemporary observer described how in 1649, when the price of bread had soared, one could hear the poor crying that they were dying of hunger, people were collapsing in the streets, 'and on the streets you saw nothing but biers and the dead and the communion being carried to the sick'.[18] This was the backdrop to the lives of the women whose stories are told here, women who had turned to or been forced into prostitution in order to survive the deprivations and hardships of early modern life.

TOLERATING PROSTITUTION IN THE HOLY CITY

Prostitution had long been an integral component of daily life in Rome, encouraged by the population imbalance as well as its atypical social composition. (This is not to assume that all, or even most, men would turn exclusively to women for the satisfaction of sexual desires; although in theory severely persecuted, sodomy was very common between males in some areas of Italy.[19]) It was also a city in which there were many men who would never marry, particularly amongst the well-to-do. Primogeniture had been widely adopted by the mid-sixteenth century, meaning that many families found a wife for only one of their sons, rather than see their estate divided and eventually diminished through inheritance partition.[20] For young men destined for a career in the *Curia*, many of whom were required to take religious orders, marriage was out of the question. Even

---

[16] BAV, Cod. Urb. Lat. 1061, c160, 20 March 1593.

[17] Eugenio Sonnino, 'Le anime dei romani: fonti religiose e demografia storica', in Luigi Fiorani and Adriano Prosperi, eds., *Storia d'Italia, Annali 16, Roma la Città del Papa* (Turin: Einaudi, 2000), 329–66.

[18] Cited in ibid, 358. From Giacinto Gigli, *Diario romano (1608–1670) a cura di G. Ricciotti* (Rome: Tumminelli, 1958), 333.

[19] Michael Rocke, *Forbidden Friendships: Homosexuality and Male Culture in Renaissance Florence* (Oxford: Oxford University Press, 1998).

[20] Renata Ago, 'Young Nobles in the Age of Absolutism: Paternal Authority and Freedom of Choice in Seventeenth Century Italy', in Giovanni Levi and Jean Claude Schmitt, eds., *A History of Young People in the West*, trans. Camille Naish (London: The Belknap Press of Harvard University Press, 1997), 283–324, 284.

men who were destined to marry, whether they were sons of the nobility, merchants or artisans, usually had to wait until their late twenties to do so.[21] Thus, the majority of men in the city under the age of about twenty-eight were without a legitimate way of satisfying their carnal appetites.[22]

Such a society, dominated by the presence of young, unmarried, immigrant males, must have generated its own particular set of social dynamics and sexual tensions. Although sexual intercourse was ideally only performed within the sanctity of matrimony, in this social and demographic context it is hardly surprising that there was explicit toleration of prostitution in Rome, as elsewhere in Italy during the period, on the grounds that it provided an outlet for male 'lusts'. But we cannot explain prostitution purely in terms of biological essentialism. The cultural and social factors underlying the use of prostitutes on such a large scale are of equal importance in explaining the phenomenon. The authorities of some early modern cities actively promoted prostitution as an alternative both to homosexual sodomy and to illicit sex with 'honest' women. The government of early fifteenth-century Florence, for example, established the office of 'Decorum', with the explicit aim of attracting foreign prostitutes into the city in the hope of turning 'young men away from homosexuality'.[23]

The rationale underpinning the acceptance of prostitution was based on the Galenic understanding of the body. This saw illness as the result of the disturbance of the balance of fluids within the body. The build up of both male and female 'seed' over prolonged periods (or its excessive discharge) represented one way in which an imbalance could be caused. Regular but not excessive sexual intercourse was believed necessary for the sake of one's health, particularly for men, according to their age.[24] Alessandro Petronio, a late sixteenth-century writer on health, specified that between the ages

---

[21] In late fifteenth-century Tuscany the average age of marriage for men was thirty, whilst about 10–20 per cent of people in Europe never married. See Maryanne Kowaleski, 'The Demographic Perspective', in Judith Bennett and Amy Froide, eds., *Singlewomen in the European Past, 1250–1800* (Philadelphia: University of Pennsylvania Press, 1999), 43–5. Stanley Chojnacki calculates that of 952 men whose patrician birth was documented in fifteenth-century Venice 43.3 per cent never married. 'Subaltern Patriarchs: Patrician Bachelors', in Chojnacki, *Women and Men in Renaissance Venice* (Baltimore: The Johns Hopkins University Press, 2000), 244–56, 249.

[22] For a sophisticated discussion of the problem of patrician bachelorhood and patriarchy see Chojnacki, 'Subaltern Patriarchs: Patrician Bachelors'.

[23] By using foreign prostitutes, or at least women from outside the city, the city's own reputation was less tarnished. Richard Trexler, *Public Life in Renaissance Florence* (New York: Cornell University Press, 1991), 380.

[24] Joan Cadden, 'Western Medicine and Natural Philosophy', in Verne L. Bullough and James A. Brundage, eds., *Handbook of Medieval Sexuality* (New York and London: Garland, 1996), 51–80. And Cadden, 'Medieval Scientific and Medical Views of Sexuality: Questions of Propriety', *Medievalia et Humanistica* (new series), 14 (1986), 157–71, 157, 162.

of twenty-one and thirty-five men could 'use coitus very liberally', from thirty-five to forty-nine rather less so, and thereafter even less, until the age of sixty-three after which they should abstain totally.[25]

Interestingly, despite widespread beliefs that women were inherently lusty and little able to exercise self-control over their voracious sexual appetites, it was not widely assumed that women became prostitutes because of their need for sex. Tracts on medicine lead us rather towards the conclusion that women were less in need of intercourse than men. This is because women, unlike men, had alternative uses for their excess bodily fluids. Menstruation, the creation of nutrients for the foetus and lactation were all ways in which fluids were converted in the female body, making their expulsion through intercourse a less compelling matter. Certainly this might explain why there are so few arguments linking lust and recruitment into prostitution. Legal commentators generally blamed poverty, Thomas Aquinas believed women were attracted to it by their innate greed, others laid the blame on astrology; only Hortensius attributed prostitution to women's exceptional lustiness.[26] However, once a woman had become a harlot it was believed that her body was subject to physiological changes which made her lustier and hotter, as it were turning her into a 'true' whore, 'because they are made hot from the motion that the man makes during coitus', and his hot sperm 'warms' her entire body, strengthening her.[27] These beliefs are evident in the moralising broadsheets which show women initially being seduced by men with music, dancing, fine words and gifts. It is only once they have lost their virginity that they become sexually insatiable.

Men had no alternative methods for expelling excess 'matter' apart from bloodletting and through masturbation, which was not encouraged. Certainly, it was hoped that virtuous men would learn to control their appetites, but it was recognised that this required great self-discipline, particularly in younger men. These deeply rooted beliefs go some way towards explaining why, despite the best efforts of church and city authorities across early modern Europe, mores and sexual behaviours seem to have remained impervious to church teachings, well beyond the sixteenth century.[28] As James

[25] Petronio, *Del viver delli romani*, 340–1.
[26] James Brundage, *Law, Sex and Christian Society in Medieval Europe* (Chicago: University of Chicago Press, 1987), 464.
[27] Cadden, 'Western Medicine and Natural Philosophy', 62. See also Thomas Laqueur on beliefs that the heat in prostitutes generated sterility. *Making Sex: Body and Gender from the Greeks to Freud* (Cambridge, Mass.: Harvard University Press, 1990), 101–3.
[28] See, for example, Michael Rocke's study of male sodomy in fourteenth- and fifteenth-century Florence, *Forbidden Friendships*, and Ruggiero, *The Boundaries of Eros*, esp. 146–68.

Brundage observes, there was a 'huge disparity' between sexual norm and conduct in late medieval Europe, and canon laws on sexual matters 'were so widely disregarded that ordinary people could and frequently did treat these high-flown theories as having scant relationship to daily life'.[29] In this context, the situation in Rome was not an anomaly. Prostitution was seen as preferable to the two main alternatives: violating honourable women (virgins or wives), or keeping a concubine.[30] Concubinage had previously been considered a less dishonourable and less severe sin than prostitution, but after Trent the position was reversed. Concubinage was not only assimilated to prostitution, but was seen as a more serious form of immorality, because it undermined the institution of marriage.[31]

TAXES AND TRIBUTES

Prostitution was not just the necessary evil portrayed by city regulations. It was also a convenient source of revenue. Although some medieval canonists believed that the church should not take tithes or accept alms from prostitutes because the money was earned through sin, the papacy and the secular authorities had no such scruples.[32] In fifteenth- and sixteenth-century Rome prostitutes were taxed, like other professional groups in the city. Under Sixtus IV (1471–89) they paid a weekly tax of a gold *giulio* to the Holy See (*Camera Apostolica*) which apparently brought in 20,000 ducats a year,[33] and this continued throughout most of the sixteenth century.[34] The tax acted as a kind of licence, payment of which protected courtesans from further judicial harassment, and from extortion by the prison guardians.[35] This corresponded to practice in Bologna and Florence in the same period: hence the surprise when Porzia the Jewish courtesan was arrested. Courtesans also paid death duties, known as the 'spoglio', worth one-fifth, and later one-third, of their estate, which financed the home for repentant prostitutes known as the Convertite. Finally, courtesans were required to pay

[29] James Brundage, 'Prostitution in the Medieval Canon Law', *Signs* 1 (1976), 825–45.
[30] In 1563 the council declared concubinage between unmarried people illegal. See Emlyn Eisenach, *Husbands, Wives and Concubines* (Kirksville, Mo.: Truman State University Press, 2004), 137.
[31] Concubinage was more 'dangerous' than prostitution, because of its similarity to marriage, without the sacraments. For a lengthy discussion of this position see Ferrante, 'Il valore del corpo', 217.
[32] Others suggested that it was possible to take tithes from prostitutes but the church 'could not accept her payment until she had reformed'. Brundage, 'Prostitution in Medieval Canon Law', 838.
[33] Rome, Biblioteca Vallicelliana, Codice Corvisieri, busta 3, fasc. A, c9r–11r: Cortigiane.
[34] There are many references to this *tributi meretricis* in the Vatican archives. See ASV, Diversi Camera vol. 108, c47, 30 August 1537.
[35] Presumably the prison guards were paid so little that it was virtually expected that they would extort money or goods from those in their care. ASR, Bandi del Governatore, a 1529 –1733, c71, 24 October 1560.

'occasional' taxes, such as the 1548 tax levied on those who lived near and used the Ponte Santa Maria, in order to re-pave it.[36] However, on at least one occasion an 'extra' *tributo* seems to have been inflicted upon the *cortigiane* in the spirit of a punishment and a desire to extract as much money as possible from them. Thus when forty-two *cortigiane* were arrested for travelling by coach in 1582, Pope Gregory XIII ordered that they 'pay the tribute until sixty-six galleys have been rebuilt . . . as they used to do',[37] apparently setting their fine at 2,500 *scudi*, a huge amount. Whether they actually paid it is not clear. Throughout the sixteenth century prostitution represented a certain and consistent source of revenue both for the Holy See and for the municipal authorities, financing the costs of their own or their colleagues' 'rehabilitation' in the Convertite, and paying for the upkeep of the streets they used in their professional lives.

The fact that prostitutes contributed to the running of the city did not mean that their presence was regarded with equanimity, and various institutions were founded with the intention of offering women an alternative. The Compagnia del Divino Amore started to raise funds to help prostitutes in the early sixteenth century, leading to the establishment by papal bull in 1525 of the Monastery of Santa Maria Magdalena for repentant prostitutes (the afore-mentioned Convertite).[38] At the time Leo X had cited a passage from Luke which stated that 'there is more joy in heaven over one sinner who repents than ninety-nine righteous', which remained the premise of Catholic toleration of prostitution.[39] From the 1530s Ignatius Loyola, leader of the Jesuits, campaigned to reduce the numbers of prostitutes in the city. He and his followers proselytised in the streets, rallying the support of men and women of the nobility in an attempt to gather together 'fallen women' and find them alternative ways of life.[40] With their financial aid he founded a house for repentant prostitutes in 1542, the Casa Santa Marta. This was so successful that another building was purchased in 1559, and in 1563 a house for the 'ill-married', or *malmaritate*, was founded, named Casa Pia. The Jesuits also put pressure on Pope Paul III to support an institution

---

[36] This was calculated as a tenth of their yearly rent. ASR, Camerale I, Fabbriche, busta 1514, Tassa fatta alle cortigiane.

[37] BAV, Codice Urbinate Latine, vol. 1050, c252v–253r, 18 July 1582.

[38] For the most comprehensive study of Jesuit institutions in Rome for women, particularly prostitutes, see Lance Gabriel Lazar, *Working in the Vineyard of the Lord: Jesuit Confraternities in Early Modern Italy* (Toronto: University of Toronto Press, 2005), 40. See also Charles Chauvin, 'La Maison Sainte-Marthe: Ignace et les prostituées de Rome,' *Christus* 149 (1991), 117–26.

[39] Lazar, *In the Vineyard*, 40.

[40] For the work of Loyola and the Jesuits generally see Pietro Tacchi-Venturi, *Storia della Compagnia di Gesù in Italia: narrata col sussidio di fonti inedite* (Rome: La Civiltà Cattolica, 1950), 161–72. John O'Malley, *The First Jesuits* (Cambridge, Mass.: Harvard University Press, 1993).

(Santa Caterina della Rosa) in which to house young virgins, particularly the daughters of prostitutes, who it was feared might fall into a life of sin.[41] This was active by 1550 and by 1601 reputedly housed 160 girls.[42]

'THIRTY THOUSAND WHORES'

Rome, like Venice and Naples, was known throughout the sixteenth and seventeenth centuries for the great number of its 'whores'. Speculation on their numbers formed a kind of literary topos in descriptions of the city. Stefano Infessura's late fifteenth-century estimate of 6,800 prostitutes was exceeded by the observation in Delicado's comic novella from the 1520s that there were 'Thirty thousand whores and nine thousand procuresses' living in the city.[43] Neither of the earliest 'censuses' of the city, parish surveys, corroborates these impressions. The first, from 1517–18, identifies 193 women as prostitutes living throughout the city. The second, carried out just before the sack of Rome, in 1527, identified a mere 26 women as prostitutes, out of a total population of about 60,000, of which 2,015 households were headed by women.[44] Discussion about the discrepancies between contemporary estimations and the census data have largely focused on the problems of collection and interpretation. Yet rather than take the numbers at face value, the large numbers of prostitutes reported in the later accounts were probably intentionally wild exaggerations, intended to criticise female morality in general, and using prostitution as a vehicle for a thinly veiled attack on the hypocrisy of the Roman court. Contemporaries may also have been expressing a genuine *perception* that there were a great many more prostitutes in the city than before. This may have been triggered by changing practices of prostitution and new anxieties about prostitution itself, rather than any real increase in actual numbers. The arrival of the

---

[41] For a detailed study of this institution see Alessandra Camerano, 'Assistenza richiesta ed assistenza imposta: il Conservatorio di S. Caterina della Rosa di Roma', *Quaderni Storici* 82 (1993), 227–60.

[42] Ibid., 228–9. And Lazar, *In the Vineyard*, 89–90.

[43] Cited in Joannis Burchardi, *Diarium sive Rerum Urbanarum Commentarii, 1483–1506*, in the Italian edition, *Diario del Burchardo*, April 1498, vol. II (orig. 1498), ed. L. Thuasne, 3 vols. (Paris: Ernest Leroux, 1884), II, 442–3. Delicado, *La Lozana Andalusa*, 276.

[44] The merits and problems of these two early censuses have already been much discussed by Renaissance scholars. For detailed analysis one should turn to M. Armellini, 'Un censimento della città di Roma sotto il pontificato di Leone X', *Gli Studi in Italia* (1882), 69–84, 161–92, 321–55, 481–93. Domenico Gnoli, 'Censimento di Roma sotto Clemente VII', *ARSRSP* 17: 2–4 (1894), 375–520. Egmont Lee, 'Foreigners in Quattrocento Rome', *Renaissance and Reformation* (new series) 7: 2 (1983), 135–46. And Lee, 'Notaries, Immigrants, and Computers: the Roman *Rione* Ponte, 1450–1480', in Paolo Brezzi and Egmont Lee, eds., *Sources of Social History: Private Acts of the Late Middle Ages*, Papers in Mediaeval Studies 5 (Toronto: Pontifical Institute of Mediaeval Studies, 1984), 239–49.

'French disease', syphilis, was a cause of great public concern, and it was soon apparent that prostitutes were particularly likely to catch it. Preoccupations about prostitutes may well have been linked to anxiety about the disease. Equally dramatic, however, had been the change in practices of prostitution at the end of the fifteenth century. Over a period of about twenty years a new kind of prostitute appeared in the city, the so-called *cortigiana onesta*, or 'honest courtesan'. Initially they were linked specifically to the papal court and to the elite world of the Roman humanists, though this soon changed. Neither tied to a single man, as was a concubine, nor linked to the more controlled environment of baths and brothels, courtesans were free to roam the city with their lovers and admirers, with little control exercised over their behaviour.[45] The social visibility and wealth of the successful courtesan was apparently shocking, with many commentators, particularly foreign visitors, expressing astonishment that they were so well dressed that they could not be distinguished from noble women:

In some places of Italy, specially where the churchmen do reign, you shall find of that sort of women (courtesans) in rich apparel, in furniture of households, in service, in horse and hackney and in all things that appertain to a delicate lady, so well furnished that to see one of them unknowingly she should seem rather the quality of a princess than of a common woman.[46]

This was the background to the fierce debate which took place in the summer of 1566, when Pius V put forward his proposals for the reduction and control of prostitution in the city.

---

[45] According to Brundage, canon lawyers apparently had an ambivalent attitude towards concubinage for the laity, which was not prohibited by the church until 1563. *Sex, Law and Marriage in the Middle Ages*, 10.

[46] William Thomas, *A History of Italy* (1549), edited by G. B. Parks (Ithaca: Cornell University Press, 1963), 16.

CHAPTER 3

Debating prostitution

GOVERNING THE CITY

Late sixteenth-century Rome was a violent and lawless place.[1] Bandits roamed the surrounding countryside, plaguing travellers and those bringing merchandise into the city, while within the city walls there was a huge floating population of pilgrims, migrant day-labourers and beggars.[2] Despite legal prohibitions men carried knives and swords as a matter of course, and seem to have used them with alarming frequency, giving rise to violent brawls in the streets and taverns. Amidst the general disorder and throng of this city of some hundred thousand souls were the thousand or more women who worked as prostitutes.

This was the city which the post-Tridentine popes inherited as their immediate spiritual and temporal domain. Pius IV (1559–65), Pius V (1566–72) and their successors, particularly Sixtus V (1585–90) and Clement VIII (1592–1605), responded to the perceived crisis in the social and moral order of Rome by seeking to refashion the city and improve the morals of its population. Social disciplining and physical rebuilding of the city would provide evidence to the rest of Christendom of the renewal of the church, 'an outward and visible sign of her moral reform',[3] and act as a testimony to its sanctity, magnificence and charity. The physical fabric of the city was to reflect these moral changes, as roads, piazzas, churches and palaces were

---

[1] On violence and banditry see Irene Polverini Fosi, *La società violenta. Il banditismo nello stato pontificio nella seconda metà del cinquecento* (Rome: Edizioni dell'Ateneo, 1985). On public order see Peter Blastenbrei, 'I Romani tra violenza e giustizia nel tardo cinquecento', *Roma Moderna e Contemporanea* 5:1 (1997), 67–79. And Blastenbrei, 'La quadratura del cerchio. Il Bargello di Roma nella crisi sociale tardocinquecentesca', *Dimensioni e Problemi della Ricerca Storica* 1 (1994), 5–37.

[2] Luciano Palermo, 'Espansione demografica e sviluppo economico a Roma nel Rinascimento', *Studi Romani* 44:1–2 (1996), 21–47. This demographic expansion was a general feature of the second half of the sixteenth century across Europe. Also Athos Bellettini, *La popolazione italiana* (Turin: Einaudi, 1987), 23–4.

[3] Frederick McGinness, 'The Rhetoric of Praise and the New Rome of the Counter-Reformation', in P. A. Ramsey, ed., *Rome in the Renaissance: the City and the Myth* (Binghamton, N.Y.: Medieval and Renaissance Texts and Studies, 1982), 355–70, 361.

built or improved, fashioning Rome into a new Jerusalem.[4] This process was even more urgent in view of the approaching Jubilee years of 1575 and 1600, when huge numbers of the faithful, whose opinions and experience of the city would later carry far and wide, were expected to descend upon the city.

In order to implement these reforms the pontiff had a range of powers at his disposal. As Bishop of Rome he had numerous ways of seeking to improve moral discipline and understanding of the faith in the city. Amongst the many more general reforms, those which touched specifically on prostitution were the instruction to parish priests to undertake a yearly survey of their parishioners, noting those, such as prostitutes and concubines, who were morally unfit to receive communion.[5] Prostitutes were also ordered to attend weekly sermons at the church of San Rocco, in the most run-down part of town by the port, where they were exhorted to leave their sinful way of life.[6]

The Pope was also temporal ruler of the city of Rome, with a great deal of power over its day-to-day running. His appointees were responsible for improving roads, defending and provisioning the city, setting up charitable institutions to alleviate poverty, and mendicancy.[7] In practice the papacy did not exercise complete power over the city, having traditionally shared power with other elite groups with which there were conflicting interests and overlapping jurisdictions. Ultimately the popes would centralise and rationalise the tribunals and courts which governed the city, concentrating power in the hands of fewer bodies.[8] But by the mid-sixteenth century this process was only partially underway, and the body which represented the greatest obstacle to the papacy's authority was the *Popolo Romano* (the Roman People). A lay civic body it was established in the middle ages and its elected representatives ran the Capitoline administration and governed municipal affairs. About 1,256 men (10–12 per cent of adult laymen in 1569) were designated as *cittadini*, or 'citizens', which gave them the right

---

[4] Gamrath, *Roma sancta renovata*, 28. Giedion, 'Sixtus V and the Planning of Baroque Rome', 220. Labrot, *L'image de Rome*, 57, 280–1.

[5] These are known as the *Libri di Stati delle Anime* and were compiled from the late sixteenth century. They are housed in the Archivio del Vicariato di Roma.

[6] Avviso di Roma, 2 November 1566, in Bertolotti, *Repressioni straordinarie*, 10.

[7] A. D. Wright, *The Early Modern Papacy: From the Council of Trent to the French Revolution* (Harlow: Longman, 2000), 34–6.

[8] The encroachment of papal sovereignty on the civic institutions is debated in Paolo Prodi, *Il sovrano pontefice* (Bologna: Il Mulino, 1982), 108. And Emmanuel Rodocanachi, *Les institutions communales de Rome sous la papauté* (Paris: Alphonse Picard, 1901), 282. However their view has been challenged by Michele di Sivo in 'Il tribunale criminale capitolino nei secoli XVI–XVII: note da un lavoro in corso', *Roma Moderna e Contemporanea* 3:1 (1995), 201–15.

to vote in its public council.[9] Like the Pontiff, the *Popolo Romano* oversaw much of the practical running of the city: cleaning and repairing roads and bridges, maintaining the city walls, adjudicating in trade disputes, running the markets and ensuring the price and quality of bread.[10] They also had the power to draft the city statutes but these had no legal force without the Pontiff's approval. Likewise, in practice the Pope could not enact legislation regarding the city without the agreement of the *Popolo Romano*, since they could refuse to enforce his rulings, as happened in 1566, when the papacy attempted to limit prostitution in the city.

The financial interdependence of these two bodies was a further complication. In his temporal capacity as Prince of Rome and ruler over the Papal States the Pontiff had innumerable financial burdens and an ever pressing need for revenue, much of which was raised by the *Popolo Romano*, from customs duties.[11] Nor was the relationship between the papacy and *Popolo Romano* easy. By the late sixteenth century the kind of men holding office and entitled to vote on the latter's councils comprised four main groups: members of the old baronial houses such as the Orsini, Colonna and Savella; those ennobled by virtue of their descent from papal families, such as the Aldobrandini and Borghese; the nobility created from the merchant and banking families; and 'gentlemen', members of the liberal professions and merchants who met the criteria for citizenship.[12] As a result the Capitoline administration was composed of a broad lay social elite which had a range of interests to protect in the city and represented a considerable counterweight, socially if not always politically, to the clerical hierarchy of the *Curia*. Nussdorfer has pointed out that it also had a long and vital tradition of irreverence towards the papacy and a 'life and logic' of its own, masked by its political subordination to the Pope.[13]

By the 1560s the *Popolo Romano* was 'on the defensive'. The papacy had added new laws and officials to the city administration which threatened the *Popolo*'s powers. Papal proposals such as requests for raising additional income could therefore expect to meet with considerable hostility from delegates. The two principal forums for discussion were the *consiglio publico*,

---

[9] For a discussion of methods of election, and comparison with other Italian states, see Nussdorfer, *Civic Politics*, 66–8.

[10] Ibid., 118–67.

[11] On the complexity of their financial relationship see ibid., 66. For Spain's contribution to papal finances and its political influence see Thomas J. Dandelet, 'Politics and the State System after the Habsburg–Valois Wars', in John A. Marino, ed., *Early Modern Italy, 1550–1796* (Oxford: Oxford University Press, 2002), 11–23.

[12] The criteria were based on property, income and five years' residence in the city. Nussdorfer, *Civic Politics*, 66–8.

[13] Ibid., 64.

which could be attended by all *cittadini*, and the *consiglio secreto*, which was attended only by elected officials. These were 'the only vehicles of public, or at least semi-public, political negotiation that existed in Baroque Rome, the means by which to establish the consent or rally the resistance of the upper classes to controversial requests'.[14] As we will see, this arena for debate was particularly valuable in view of the power struggle which was in course between the papacy and the Capitoline administration. This struggle was made particularly clear when Pius V attempted to expel and re-settle the city's prostitutes in 1566, as part of the wider battle for the reform of morals in the city.[15]

PIUS V VERSUS THE ROMAN PEOPLE, 1566

Elected as Pope in January 1566, Pius V's reign was characterised by his zeal to reform the Catholic world and fight against heresy. On the broader European front he sent troops against the French Protestants in the latter half of the 1560s and he formed the Holy League, an alliance of Spanish, French and papal troops, which defeated the Turks at the Battle of Lepanto in 1571.[16] Closer to home, alongside his reforms of the clergy, he took up his predecessor Paul IV's efforts to tackle the problems of public order and immorality in the Holy City, starting with a comprehensive statute (*bando*) issued against a range of activities, such as sodomy, blasphemy, public disorder and the carrying of arms.[17] By early summer he had turned his attention more specifically to the problem of prostitution. As this was a question of civic order, traditionally under the jurisdiction of the *Popolo Romano*, on 20 May 1566 the *Popolo Romano* was informed that he wished them 'to use every means to find a place for prostitutes and dishonest women, because he absolutely didn't want them mixing and living amongst honest women'.[18] Nothing happened and several weeks later the Pope's agent repeated the request, stressing its urgency and making the additional

---

[14] Ibid., 76–82, 82.
[15] Rodocanachi cites the 'rebellion' over the question of the *meretrici* as his example of the Capitoline's resistance to 'the massive attacks' made on its powers. Rodocanachi, *Les institutions communales de Rome*, 282.
[16] Maurilio Guasco and Angelo Torre, eds., *Pio V nella società e nella politica del suo tempo* (Bologna: Il Mulino, 2005).
[17] ASR, *Bandi*, vol. 3, 16 January 1566, and ASR, *Bandi*, 3 April 1566. ASV, Arm. IV, vol. 7, c2, 4: vol. 47, c6.
[18] Archivio Capitolino (AC), Credenza I, vol. XXIII, Decreti di Consigli Magistrati (DCM), Cittadini Romani, c7r–28r. 20 May 1566, c7v. The minutes indicate that Honofrio Camiano, probably the Pope's fiscal procurator, conveyed the Pope's wishes. For a discussion of his role see Nussdorfer, *Civic Politics*, 85.

request that prostitutes be ordered to 'wear a sign so that everyone will recognise them'. The prostitutes would therefore have been treated much like the Jews, who had been confined to the ghetto by Pope Paul IV on 14 July 1555. The men had been ordered to wear a yellow hat and the women a veil of the same colour.[19] However, the Pope's apparently simple request was not at all straightforward to implement and months of intense discussion and debate were to follow. These would reveal profound divisions between the papacy and the *Popolo* and within the ranks of the *Popolo* itself, over the problem of what to do with the city's prostitutes.

When the *Popolo* was first notified of the Pope's intentions it decided that the issue would have to be debated further at a meeting of the *consiglio secreto* on 30 May 1566. The topic must have been controversial, since it had to be reconsidered at two further meetings in June, despite which the *Popolo* was no nearer to reaching an agreement.[20] Finally it was decided that a delegation comprising 'the gentlemen Conservators, the Prior and other gentlemen go to meet his Holiness and explain the difficulties, inconveniences, disorders and scandals which had arisen'. Presumably they hoped that a discussion with the Pope would break the deadlock.[21] In the meantime the Pope's patience had worn thin. Angered by the delay of the *Popolo Romano* he took matters into his own hands in the one district of the city over which he did have full powers: the area immediately surrounding the Vatican known as the Borgo, which was traditionally an area in which a great many courtesans had lived.[22] On 28 June he ordered that all the prostitutes be expelled from there, and as the governor of the Borgo was answerable only to him, the order was executed the same evening.[23] This was followed on 22 July by an order from the Pope's Vicar General that 'twenty-four of the most famous courtesans' were either to repent and 'convert' (i.e., become nuns of the Convertite), marry or leave Rome within six days, and the Papal States within twelve days. 'All the others' were instructed to go

---

[19] AC, Cred. I, vol. XXIII, DCM, Cittadini Romani, 18 June 1566, c13v. *Dizionario di erudizione storico-ecclesiastico*, Cav. Gaetano Moroni Romano, vol. XXI (Venice: Tipografia Emiliana, 1843), 16–18.

[20] Rumours were already circulating about these laws in May. Biblioteca Apostolica Vaticana (BAV), Codici Urbinati Latini (Urb. Lat.) 1040, c231v, Avviso di Roma, 25 May 1566. Many of them are printed in Ludwig F. von Pastor, *Storia dei papi dalla fine del medio evo. Compilata col sussidio del'archivio segreto pontificio e di molti altri archivi, vol. VI*, trans. and ed. Mons. Prof. Angelo Mercati (Rome: Desclée, 1958), 599. The subsequent meetings were called on 18 June and 29 June 1566. AC, Cred. I, vol. XXIII, c9v, DCM, Cittadini Romani, 30 May.

[21] AC, Cred. I, vol. XXIII, c15v, DCM, Cittadini Romani, 30 May 1566.

[22] The governor of the Curia di Borgo was usually a relative of the Pope. Augusto Pompeo, 'Procedure usuali', 115.

[23] BAV, Urb. Lat., vol. 1040, c248, Avviso di Roma, 29 June 1566.

to live in Trastevere. The writer of the *avviso* who reported this added that
the Pope had said 'he didn't want this city to be a copy of Babylon, when
it should be the head and an example to the others'.[24]

This order opened a new chapter in the negotiations. Trastevere was
a crowded, run-down area of the city, downstream from the Vatican and
across the river from the principal banking and market areas around Campo
dei Fiori and Piazza Navona. As it was home to numerous important monasteries and churches, the proposal to send the prostitutes there caused uproar
amongst its inhabitants who were not keen to welcome an influx of such
women. On 27 July, four hundred residents gathered with their *capori-
one* (head of the locality) and went to beg Cardinal Morone, who lived
in the area, for his protection and support against the Pope. Meanwhile
the *Popolo Romano* had finally been galvanised into action and at last it
presented the Pope with an alternative, but far less radical proposal. This
was that courtesans should not be allowed to live on principal streets, near
the churches and monasteries and the homes of gentlewomen, 'but should
be allowed to live in the less public streets of Rome'.[25] The Pope's answer
to this was that some courtesans might live along Strada Giulia, a fashionable street on the opposite bank of the Tiber to Trastevere, as long as 'the
rest' lived in Trastevere.[26] At a meeting held on 30 July the *Popolo* found
that this was still too radical a change for them and they resolved to send
a second delegation, this one consisting of forty council members, for an
audience with the Pope.[27] This infuriated Pius V. According to one contemporary observer he considered it to be 'an act of sedition', and he retorted
by berating his opponents for their infamy and preference for vice over
virtue:[28]

'All this morning you have been ringing your nasty little bell (*campanozzo*) calling
your members to congregate, to what end? To conserve the infamy which we, for
your sakes, your honour and your common satisfaction are trying to get rid of. Nor
is it right that the most beautiful streets in Holy Rome are lived in by prostitutes,
where the blood of all the holy martyrs has been spilled, where there are so many
relics, so many devotions, the Holy Seat and much religion. This city which should
be the mirror of the whole world and weeded of vice and sins to confuse the infidels

---

[24] Camillo Luzzara from Rome to the Duke of Mantova, 22 July 1566, in Bertolotti, *Repressioni straordinarie*, 8. Also Fabio Mutinelli, *Storia arcana e aneddotica d'Italia raccontata dei Veneti Ambasciatori,
vol. I* (Venice: 1865), 50–3.

[25] BAV, Urb. Lat., vol. 1040, c264, Avviso di Roma, 27 July 1566.

[26] AC, Cred. I, vol. XXIII, c24r, DCM, Cittadini Romani, 30 July 1566.

[27] This delegation included a *conservatore*, prior, a captain and Chancellor and several nobles. Ibid.

[28] Cited in Mutinelli, *Storia arcana*, 3 August 1566, 53.

and heretics. But you don't know what is good for you.' And he got up and went away.[29]

Despite the Pope's outburst, the minutes of a meeting held on 3 August show that the *Popolo Romano* was still not happy with the situation. The citizens were asked to decide whether or not to present 'a lengthy petition to the Pope which had been composed by an affectionate citizen, Geronimo de Picchij'. The hope was that the written word would persuade Pius V, where 'verbal persuasion, and supplication' had failed.[30] So it was that on 10 August the *avvisi* reported that 'The Conservatori of Rome, in the name of the People, have presented a letter with much information about the *meretrici*, and their expulsion, with many reasons attached for the conservation of the honour of the city, married women and virgins.'[31]

The letter appears to have achieved its purpose, for on 24 August the Vicar of Rome announced that the prostitutes would not be banished, after all, and could live in the area of Campo Marzio. However, since the *Popolo* wanted them to stay in the city, henceforth it would have to take responsibility for them itself, since 'building a brothel and looking after them is not a task suited to the Prince'.[32] It seemed as if the *Popolo* had finally won its battle. The prostitutes were to be neither exiled nor banished to Trastevere, but rather they were to be accommodated in the new quarter of Campo Marzio, some near the river, some off the main streets.

Campo Marzio was a recently developed area of the city. At the northern end was the great Porta del Popolo and its piazza, which was the principal entry point for voyagers coming into Rome from the north along the Via Cassia. This made it something of a transit area for large numbers of travellers, and there were ten taverns, hotels and hostelries – *osterie* – in the area.[33] The Via Lata (Via del Corso) ran south from here down to Piazza San Marco, dividing the quarter in two. On the western side was the port of Ripetta and the area known as the Ortaccio, or Otto Cantoni. It was low-lying and damp, often subject to flooding, and it had been identified as a breeding ground for disease in the earlier part of the century. On the eastern side was the increasingly fashionable Piazza Trinità dei Monti and main streets where the palaces of several cardinals and ambassadors were located. With their retinues of courtiers and 'cavaliers', they were assiduous clients of the city's prostitutes.

---

[29] BAV, Urb. Lat., vol. 1040, c264, Avviso di Roma, 3 August 1566.
[30] AC, Cred. I, vol. XXIII, c25v, DCM, Cittadini Romani, 3 August 1566.
[31] BAV, Urb. Lat., vol. 1040, c27, 10 August 1566.   [32] Ibid., c27v.
[33] Mario Romani, *Pellegrini e viaggiatori nell'economia di Roma dal XIV al XVII secolo* (Milan: Vita e Pensiero, 1948), 70.

There were several advantages to housing prostitutes in Campo Marzio, from the point of view of both prostitutes and their clients. It was located along a main thoroughfare and it had a very mixed population including many travellers and visitors, which meant that men going to visit prostitutes would not be particularly obvious. It was also at the centre of the city's 'night-life', with its many *osterie*. Unlike Trastevere, there was little danger that an area like Campo Marzio could become a 'ghetto'.

Yet if the *Popolo* thought the Pope was going to stop interfering in matters regarding prostitution, they were wrong. Over the following months and years the papacy continued to issue edicts concerning prostitutes. Not even a month had gone by before the Vicar General issued an order which made nonsense of the lengthy and subtle negotiations which had just been concluded, ordering all the courtesans to leave the city within fifteen days.[34] Then in November prostitutes were warned not to leave the designated 'places of prostitution', the *luoghi*, on the pain of whippings. Those who were 'worth more than 200 *scudi*' were ordered to 'convert' or marry, whilst all the others were once again instructed to attend mass in one of the churches where there was preaching nearly every day.[35] In May 1567 there was a decree that prostitutes should either convert or flee the city, and two months later 'sixty of the best courtesans still here' were told to leave Rome.[36] Some of the prostitutes who ignored these edicts, or resisted them, were dealt with severely and there are many *avvisi* reporting the whippings dealt out to them. One from March 1567 recounts how a prostitute named Nina da Prato, having gone to church to hear the sermon, berated the preacher, telling him to 'get on with preaching the word of the lord and stop interfering in our business'. And when the priest tried to close the church at the end of the sermon she called out, 'We spend the whole year in the *bordello* (brothel), can't we even stay an hour in church?' Another woman, Isabella Venetiana, was accused of running a brothel from her home, which was outside the *luoghi*. For this the two women were first imprisoned in the Torre di Nona. Then they were taken, bound together, with their faces covered and with a placard stating their crimes around their necks, through the streets to the Piazza d'Ortaccio. They were followed by a crowd estimated at three thousand people, who then watched them receive twenty-five lashes each, 'on their naked buttocks'.[37]

[34] Avviso di Roma, 7 September 1566. Cited by Bertolotti, *Repressioni straordinarie*, 10.

[35] BAV, Urb. Lat., vol. 1040, c314v–315r, 2 November 1566. On the order to attend churches and 'those who are worth more than 200 *scudi*' see Bertolotti, *Repressioni straordinarie*, Avviso di Roma Alla Corte di Mantova, 2 November 1566, 10.

[36] BAV, Urb. Lat., vol. 1040, c395v, 29 May 1567.

[37] BAV, Urb. Lat. vol. 1040, c370v, 15 March 1567.

Apart from occasional exemplary punishments of the kind meted out to Isabella and Nina, which were intended as deterrents as much as punishments, it must have proved difficult to enforce the many ordinances which appeared throughout the following years. This would explain why a more definitive kind of segregation was proposed in 1567, taking the form of a wall which was to be built around the *luoghi*, so as to enclose the prostitutes in a kind of ghetto 'like the Jews'.[38] The first steps towards this were taken in early October 1569 when according to one *avviso*, 'two principal streets were taken away from the prostitutes, and they have been packed into very narrow alleyways . . . and they are being given the place called Otto Cantoni'. Soon afterwards work started on erecting the walls around the area known as the 'Ortaccio' – the nettle bed – which suggests that it had a long-standing reputation as an unpleasant area.[39] By January 1570 all *meretrici* were instructed to move to the Ortaccio, and to near the Trinità.[40] Evidently, however, walls were not sufficient to keep the prostitutes in and their clients out. Less than a month later it was decided that doors with locks would have to be made for the Ortaccio and guardians would be put on duty in order to control the movements of 'these poor courtesans'.[41] The final act in this increasingly desperate attempt to control the prostitutes came later in February when the Pope ordered the closure of the doors to the Ortaccio for the whole of Lent so as to prevent carnal commerce completely during this holy period. Bizarrely, in order to prevent the prostitutes from starving as a result of their loss of commerce, the city then had to provide 'the poor prostitutes so much a day for them to live off out of the public purse'.[42]

The attempt to create a 'ghetto' for the prostitutes appears to have been very short lived. Even though the Ortaccio long remained one of the principal living areas for the poorest prostitutes, its doors, walls and keys are never mentioned again, whilst repeated edicts during the 1570s and 1580s suggest that periodically prostitutes had to be rounded up and sent back there to live.[43] Less than thirty years later in February 1592, the 1560s were evidently already considered as a golden age of discipline. When Clement VII announced that the prostitutes would be obliged to wear a long yellow

[38] BAV, Urb. Lat., vol. 1040, c421v, 19 July 1567.
[39] BAV, Urb. Lat., vol. 1041, c158v, 5 October 1569, and, c180, 17 October 1569.
[40] Avviso di Roma, 10 January 1570, in Bertolotti, *Repressioni straordinarie*, 14.
[41] BAV, Urb. Lat., vol. 1041, part 1, c231v, 4 February 1570.
[42] BAV, Urb. Lat., vol. 1041, part 1, c224v–225r, 18 February 1570.
[43] BAV, Urb. Lat., vol. 1043, c303v, 12 September 1573; vol. 1045, c601, 20 October 1576; vol. 1050, c24r, 27 January 1582; vol. 1060, c70, 8 February 1592.

sleeve and were to be confined once again to the Ortaccio and the Trinità, he specified that this was 'as they had been under Pius V'.[44]

REACTIONS AND RESISTANCE

It has been argued that the frequent repetition of ordinances in the early modern period indicates not a lack of success in implementing them so much as the need repeatedly to remind the populace of the new behavioural norms and outlawed practices.[45] This argument is not particularly convincing in the case of Counter-Reformation Rome. Prostitutes could hardly have been unaware of the new laws issued. They were first read in public, and on average about one hundred copies of each *bando* were printed and then affixed in a number of public places, including Campo dei Fiori, outside the major churches, outside the taverns and at the entrances to the city.[46] In the summer of 1566 news of the proposed changes to their status quo had evidently travelled very quickly, since the *avvisi* noted that prostitutes were 'appalled and bewildered' and in their terror, large numbers of them fled the city, particularly the better off.[47] Another reported that 'Over 300 of the principal prostitutes of Rome have already left, and continue to leave because of the warnings, and many have married, withdrawn and converted, and the wretched women can't find anyone who will buy their things . . . since they seem to be a bad purchase'.[48]

Interestingly, the tone of the *avvisi* and diplomatic letters were consistently sympathetic towards those courtesans who had fled and the misfortunes which befell them in consequence. In his dispatches to the Venetian Senate the Venetian ambassador described how:

In the flight of the courtesans from the city a great many unpleasant things have happened to them, because some have been killed on the roads, others drowned in the Tiber by people moved by selfishness and greed for the money they were carrying with them, and we are still hearing about the woundings and other disorders which have been going on.[49]

---

[44] BAV, Urb. Lat., vol. 1060, c80–81, 15 February 1592.

[45] Karl Härter, 'Disciplinamento sociale e ordinanze di polizia nella prima età moderna', in Paolo Prodi, ed., *Disciplina dell'anima, disciplina del corpo, disciplina della società tra medioevo ed età moderna* (Bologna: Il Mulino, 1994), 635–58, 644.

[46] A. Cirinei, 'Bandi e giustizia criminale a Roma nel cinque e seicento', *Roma Moderna e Contemporanea* 5:1 (1997), 81–95, 83–5.

[47] Camillo Luzzara to Duke of Mantua, 17 August 1566, cited in Bertolotti, *Repressioni straordinarie*, 9.

[48] BAV, Urb. Lat., vol. 1040, c270, 10 August 1566.

[49] 17 August 1566. Cited by A. Bertolotti, *Repressioni Straordinarie*, 54.

However, after the initial alarm many women drifted back to the city as the situation eased. Sources also indicate that as the years passed prostitutes learned to resist legislative changes both actively and passively: either by simply ignoring the laws, finding ways to get around them, or by complaining about them. On one occasion in particular the city's prostitutes put up a spirited defence of their livelihood and living spaces by protesting against proposals to force them to live in the Ortaccio and around Piazza Padella. Rather as in 1566, they found support for their cause in unexpected quarters. This time it was not the lay elite but members of the clerical elite who came to their defence. Pope Clement VIII found his plans opposed by a number of his own cardinals, most notably by his Vicar General, the man in charge of executing the orders. The rebellion was sparked off in February 1592 when Clement VIII issued his edict which instructed the *meretrici* to move back into the Ortaccio, particularly those in the Borgo.[50] A few days later the *avvisi* reported that four cardinals, Paleotti, Salviati, Rusticucci and Dezza, had opposed Clement, on the grounds that:

This undertaking was too difficult . . . and dangerous, as has been witnessed on the other occasions it has been tried, and Rusticucci particularly told his Holiness that there were over 1,300 women of this condition in the city, and that the edict could be moderated, so as to prevent them from living near the churches, the homes of honourable women and certain principal streets.[51]

Cardinal Dezza also pointed out that since his palace was located at the top of the Piazza d'Ortaccio it would be surrounded by prostitutes if the plan went through, meaning that he would have to sell it and leave. However, apparently unmoved by the opposition, the Pope went ahead with his proposal a few weeks later. The cardinals stepped in once more, this time arguing that it was 'an extremely complex issue to tackle and of little importance, and it would cause great disorder because the whole city would be turned upside down'.[52] Since Cardinal Rusticucci was the Vicar General, and the prostitutes were under his jurisdiction, he must have failed to implement his orders. As a result, to his dismay, Clement stripped him of his powers over the courtesans, and jurisdiction was handed over to the Governor of Rome, who acted immediately:[53] 180 courtesans, most

---

[50] BAV, Urb. Lat., vol. 1060, c70, 8 February 1592.
[51] The text shows a '13' surmounted by an 'M' over a line. This may have been intended to mean 1,300 or 13,000. The former number is very close to the number of prostitutes in the city according to surviving parish records. The latter is a wild exaggeration. BAV, Urb. Lat., vol. 1060, c88, 19 February 1592 and c94r, 22 February 1592.
[52] BAV, Urb. Lat., vol. 1061, c94r, 22 February 1592.
[53] BAV, Urb. Lat., vol. 1061, c94r, 26 February 1592.

of whom were Spanish, left the city and headed towards Naples. Most of them were robbed and killed (presumably by the bandits who roamed the Roman Campagna and were a constant scourge to travellers).[54] Of those who remained in the city, rather than meekly complying with the eviction order, many went to complain to the Governor, 'lamenting that they could not find anywhere to live and that there was chaos, which hadn't been provided for, which could have been foreseen from the start'.[55] As a result the Pope and his Governor bowed to pressure, issuing a much-amended version of the edict. This granted the courtesans more living space, specifying that if there was not enough accommodation in the Ortaccio they could live on the nearby streets, provided they stayed away from churches and monasteries.[56] Amnesties were also promised for all prostitutes who agreed to live honestly in future. Despite this, in early March a great many *meretrici* were still evicted, 'with infinite imprecations and laments especially because of the costs involved'.[57] The women were outraged by the expense and a great many of them, 'poor and miserable', presented appeals to the courts to force their landlords to repay them rents which had already been paid in advance.[58] As a result of their outcries yet another version of the ordinance was issued, acknowledging that the authorities had not been successful in their attempts to segregate the prostitutes, that insufficient space had been allocated to them and that some prostitutes had therefore been granted licences enabling them to live outside the *luoghi*.[59]

In the new version the boundaries of the *luoghi* were greatly enlarged. As long as prostitutes did not live near churches, monasteries and the houses of the nobility, they could live virtually throughout Campo Marzio, except for four main streets in the area of the Trinità. *I luoghi* included all the district from Piazza Padella and the Ortaccio to Trinità dei Monti, and from the Arco di Portogallo up to Piazza del Popolo. A map showing the newly extended zone was then hung in the offices of the notaries of the relevant tribunal.[60] The courtesans were given ten days to move into the new streets, but in order to avoid the complaints and litigation which had ensued earlier that month, this eviction was to be overseen by Cardinal Rusticucci who had been reinstated and he now went about his duties with zeal. His officials were to make notes on the type of accommodation each woman lived in, and of the rent paid, so as to be able to assign a new

---

[54] Again the text notes '18' surmounted by a line, which I read as 180, not 1, 800. Ibid.
[55] BAV, Urb. Lat., vol. 1060, 26 February 1592.   [56] Ibid.
[57] BAV, Urb. Lat., vol. 1060, c112, March 4 1592.   [58] Ibid.
[59] ASV, Miscellanea, Arm. IV–V, vol. 66, c217, 26 March 1592.
[60] BAV, Urb. Lat., vol. 1060, c159v, 28 March 1592.

house to each woman: 'to each one according to her condition and wishes'. Those women who failed to comply with the legislation were to leave Rome and the Papal States, or be whipped and have their wealth confiscated.[61] (See Map 1.)

A DEFENCE OF THE PROSTITUTES

At first glance the disagreement between the papacy and *Popolo Romano* can be read as a simple clash between rival authorities. On the one hand, the *Popolo Romano* was trying to preserve its communal rights, obstinate because it was affronted at having its power usurped. On the other, the papacy was attempting to assert its authority over those who had traditionally held local power. Upon closer examination, however, it becomes clear that even if for the papacy it was merely a question of a power struggle, for the *Popolo Romano* the terms of the debate were actually quite subtle, revealing complex attitudes towards prostitution.[62]

Ostensibly the papacy's position on the presence of prostitutes in Rome was very straightforward, hinging on an understanding of them as a corrupting, contaminating presence in the Holy City. They were an offence to the memory of the martyrs, to those who had taken religious vows, and their presence detracted from the city's claims to be 'head' of and example to all Christendom. Yet, reading the texts of the statutes and *avvisi* with care, we realise that in practice the papacy was willing to tolerate the presence of some prostitutes more than others, provided that those who remained in the city were segregated across the river in Trastevere. This area was evidently chosen because it was a relatively out-of-the-way part of the city, rather left behind by the new building projects on the more fashionable side of the river, and joined to the busy commercial area of Ponte by a bridge. (We can hypothesise that the authorities might have hoped to control access to the area *via* the bridge.) What is significant is that the chief targets of the Pope's ordinances were not the miserable, poor and unsightly prostitutes whom he intended to keep out of sight in Trastevere, but the wealthy, the famous and the 'best' of the courtesans. In July 1566 the *avvisi* reported that 'twenty-four of the most famous courtesans have been banished from Rome and the Papal States, if they don't marry or convert'.[63] Another commentator wrote, 'many must leave, that is, the most scandalous, and the others

---

[61] Ibid.

[62] My understanding of the papacy's position is, however, limited to what can be gleaned from the *avvisi* and the texts of the statutes.

[63] Camillo Luzzara to Duke of Mantua, 22 July 1566, in Bertolotti, *Repressioni straordinarie*, 8.

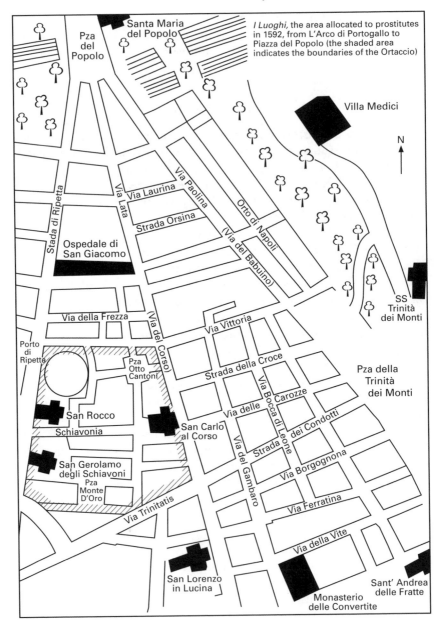

Map 1   *I luoghi*, the area allocated to prostitutes in 1592

can go to Trastevere'. '*Scandalose*' in this context meant the most obvious, showy and extravagant courtesans.[64] In November 1566 it was reported that 'they want to issue a *bando* against those courtesans worth more than 200 *scudi*, who must marry or go with God'.[65] The following summer we read of a warning 'issued against about sixty of the best courtesans, of those who remained from last year, that within six days they must leave Rome'.[66] The wealthy courtesans were clearly being targeted, which suggests that it was not so much the moral failings of prostitutes which were troubling the papacy as their very evident 'wages of sin'. One concern presumably was that the sight of such wealthy prostitutes in the city would induce critics to draw unfavourable conclusions about the sexual morality of the city's richest men. Furthermore, it may have been feared that the visible presence of such well-off prostitutes might undermine the church's efforts to warn women away from prostitution.

One might well have expected the good citizens of Rome to have been as opposed to the presence of prostitutes as the Pope was, given that it was their womenfolk who were most in danger of 'corruption', and the reputation of their city which was ultimately at stake. However, although these issues clearly worried the *Popolo*, if we look back at the accounts of the events of 1566, it is evident that attitudes amongst them were by no means uniform, which must explain how difficult it was for them to respond to the Pope's requests. As the secretary of the council meetings noted on one occasion, the topic had raised many 'difficulties, inconveniences and disorders' amongst the members of the council.[67] Two letters in particular give us insight into the issues which concerned the *Popolo Romano*. One of them is the letter (or a copy of it) composed by Girolamo Picchij which was handed to the Pope in August 1566 to explain the *Popolo*'s viewpoint on the questions surrounding the toleration and segregation of prostitutes. *Lettera scritta da incerto a Papa Pio Quinto*.[68] The other anonymously authored letter, *Lettera sulla tolleranza delle meretrici in Roma*, appears to be a critical appraisal of Picchij's letter, or of an

---

[64] BAV, Urb. Lat., vol. 1040, c260v–261r.   [65] BAV, Urb. Lat., vol. 1040, 2 November 1566, c314.

[66] Bertolotti, *Repressioni straordinarie*, 11, 19 July 1567.

[67] AC, Cred. I, vol. XXIII, c15v, DCM, Cittadini Romani, 18 June 1566.

[68] ASR, Fondo Santa Croce, Filza 188. Lettera scritta da incerto a Papa Pio Quinto acciò che gli ebrei e le meretrici non si scacciano da Roma con le ragioni allegati per il medemo effetto dai Romani. The document might well be a seventeenth-century copy of the original. It was amongst the papers of the Santa Croce family, two of whom were made *conservatori* in the summer of 1566. Many thanks to Mirabelle Madignier for pointing it out to me.

earlier draft of it, and was presumably composed by another of the council members.[69]

Like the papacy, the *Popolo Romano* was concerned about its international reputation and the question of public order in the city. As the anonymous writer of the *Lettera sulla tolleranza* pointed out, 'since Rome is the Head of Christianity, Rome should be ordered so as to set a good example, especially now that the heretics have their eyes and tongues upon the Catholics'. But for the *Popolo* this did not translate into their expulsion; indeed there was vehement opposition to this threat. Picchij's letter to the Pope outlined all the reasons why this was both detrimental and unnecessary, starting with an appeal to tradition. Prostitutes, they pointed out, had been tolerated under ecclesiastical law since the time of Solomon, on the grounds that it protected the honesty of wives and virgins from 'men's incontinence'. They then alluded to the extent of the problem facing Rome, with the large numbers of foreign men and of courtiers in the city. In such a city, they argued, the presence of prostitutes acted as a guarantee of honesty amongst its womenfolk.[70] They also warned that if prostitutes were no longer tolerated legally, the problem would become more intractable since women would simply use the pretence of honest work as a cover for dishonesty:

Marrying, working as servants in the courts, washing clothes and renting rooms . . . in fact only changing the title of their profession . . . which would mean that it would be impossible to take them away from their sin . . . indeed, there will be a greater number, when they believe that they can sin secretly.[71]

These, however, were fairly familiar arguments in favour of toleration. Perhaps they had to pay lip-service to these well-worn principles before launching into a rather more unusual defence of prostitution on economic grounds. Point by point the letter then lists the ways in which the city's

---

[69] Although anonymous and undated it was undoubtedly written as a contribution to this ongoing debate, probably by another member of the *Popolo Romano*, since it opens by stating that, 'The reasons and defences which your honours adduce in favour of tolerating the *meretrici* throughout Rome are of little import, if you cannot find other, better reasons.' It then suggests that they think over the points which he has drafted in order to prepare themselves for a tough dispute with the Pope and his advisers, and the text makes clear reference to the points raised in the second and third parts of the letter written by Girolamo Picchij. BAV, Cod. Vat. Lat., vol. 9729, Tributo di Miscellanee di Roma, sacre, politiche, erudite, istoriche, in prosa ed in verso offerto da Francesco Cancellieri a sua ecellenza Milord Francis Henry Egerton nel mese di Aprile dell'anno MDCCCVIII, c104r–107r, Lettera sulla tolleranza delle meretrici in Roma.

[70] Lettera a Papa Pio Quinto, c5v. See as a comparison Coryat's notes on the reasons for the presence of prostitutes in Venice in the first decade of the seventeenth century in Thomas Coryat, *Crudities*, *vol. I* (orig. 1611) (Glasgow: James MacLehose and Sons, 1905), 402–3.

[71] Lettera a Papa Pio Quinto, c5v.

economy would suffer if prostitutes, particularly the wealthier ones, were banished, suggesting that prostitutes were perceived as occupying a crucial position at the heart of the city's financial and economic networks.

It will damage those who have already paid their rents, some for long periods, and they would not be able to recover them. It will also damage the contacts which so many of those women have with merchants, bankers, brokers, and also there are some who are rich and have investments and partnerships. But it will also damage their creditors, because they will not be able to pay them back; it will damage landlords whose houses will remain un-let and will be forced to repay money which they had already spent; it will damage the customs and excise, and as a result, the Camera [Apostolica], because the *meretrici* have good taste, and they buy many precious goods, and goods from abroad.

The case was also put for the immediate economic needs and rights of the courtesans themselves. It was observed that they would have no time to sell their belongings, nor to arrange for them to be sent on to them, nor to decide how to dispose of them; that they would be exposed to grave danger on the roads when they left the city if they took their possessions with them (as indeed, happened), since they would be easy prey for thieves.[72] The Venetian ambassador in Rome echoed these economic concerns in his report to Venice on the dispute between papacy and *Popolo*. He noted that people feared that if all the prostitutes were sent away, they would be followed by such a great number of people that altogether about twenty-five thousand people would leave the city (about one-quarter of the population). He added that the customs officers estimated the potential loss in import duties at about 20,000 ducats a year, which would have implied that the Apostolic Camera stood to lose a sizeable portion of its revenue.

Because if they are sent away it would be too great a thing, and it has been affirmed that between them and the others who would follow them, twenty-five thousand people would leave; and those who run the customs in Rome have made it clear that if they have to renounce the duty payments, they will insist on being paid 20,000 ducats a year in reparations.[73]

The *Popolo* may have been overstating its case for the sake of strengthening its arguments, but if so, this was presumably because the expulsion of the wealthy courtesans would have impinged directly on the individuals involved, both financially and in other ways. Without a doubt many of

---

[72] Material possessions acted as a surety since most women would not use banks and investments, so jewellery, clothing, fine materials and pictures were effectively their savings. Lettera a Papa Pio Quinto, c6r–7v.

[73] 3 August 1566, Mutinelli, *Storia arcana*, 53.

them could be counted amongst the clientele of the better-off courtesans. The men who sat on the assemblies and councils of the *Popolo Romano* would have included representatives of a whole range of commercial and mercantile interests, for it was above all men like themselves who rented the courtesans their accommodation, who imported and sold them the materials for their dresses, and who arranged their loans and investments.[74] As the Venetian ambassador sagely remarked: 'This problem is troubling the Roman People greatly, as much as any other, for many reasons, but principally because of the profit they make from them.'[75] According to Larivaille, economic leverage was applied on an even more dramatic scale by bankers and merchants in 1585 when Sixtus V also sought to expel the city's courtesans, with one bank declaring itself bankrupt to the sum of 170,000 *scudi*.[76]

The *Popolo's* letter did not just cite practical and economic reasons for permitting prostitution, but was prefaced by a long theological exposition in which it argued that it was only by keeping prostitutes in the city that the Pope would be able to construct a truly Holy City.[77] Their arguments were built around the fundamental principles of reformed Catholicism, echoing the emphasis placed by conservative reformers (the *zelanti*) on the importance of acts of charity and the belief in free will. During the Council of Trent, Catholic doctrine had emphasised these principles as a reaction against the Lutheran emphasis on original sin and its insistence that man remained a sinner despite baptism or good works.[78] Tridentine theology countered this with a belief in free will, stressing that each person was responsible for his or her own destiny, celebrating the value of repentance and the importance of the 'active' Christian life. In this way believers who performed good works could demonstrate their faith, earning 'the grace of God by which an unjust person becomes just'.[79] It was in this theological

---

[74] Thomas Coryat similarly observed that the *courtezans* were tolerated in Venice because of the revenue they generated for the Venetian state. Coryat, *Crudities*, 403.

[75] Mutinelli, *Storia arcana*, 53.

[76] Larivaille, *La vita quotidiana delle cortigiane*, 198–9. Unfortunately, however, he does not cite any sources for his comments.

[77] One of the main points raised by the anonymous critic of the letter that was originally to be presented to the Pope was that the *Romano Popolo* would have to find some more convincing arguments if they wanted to pursuade the Pope and his ministers to agree to their proposals. Since he does not allude to any of the theological reasons presented in the Lettera a Papa Pio, it is possible that he was commenting on an earlier version, and that the theological section was therefore an afterthought.

[78] The Council of Trent had three periods of session: December 1545 to January 1548; May 1551 to April 1552; January 1562 to December 1563.

[79] I have referred here to Delumeau for my interpretation of the theological points. Jean Delumeau, *Catholicism between Luther and Voltaire*, trans. Jeremy Moiser, intro. John Bossy (London: Burns and Coates, 1977), 9–15. Also useful is John Jeffries Martin, 'Religion, Renewal and Reform in the Sixteenth Century', in John A. Marino, ed., *Early Modern Italy, 1550–1796* (Oxford: Oxford University Press, 2002), 30–45.

context that the *Popolo Romano* pointed out to Pius V that God himself, rather than 'extirpating all vices' from the world, had chosen to confer 'the gift of free will' on man.[80] They argued that since God himself 'tolerates the presence of Jews, adulterers and prostitutes' in the world, it followed that he, the Pope, should do likewise, and like God should be guided by tolerance and grace when drawing up legislation.[81] They even went on to argue that 'If the wicked women, like the Jews and all the other people . . . were to leave the city, your holiness would have no one to convert to goodness and no one to punish.'[82]

It was a clever argument. By tolerating prostitutes (like the Jews) in the city, these sinners would be provided with the opportunity to convert, 'through delight rather than through violence, which is not lasting'. This, it was implied, would ultimately bring far greater glory to Catholicism than if they were merely expelled.[83] Indeed, in this 'economy' of wickedness and salvation, the more wicked a person was, the greater her redemption if she converted, and the greater the glory for the Catholic church. Furthermore, by allowing the 'wicked' to live in the city, ordinary Romans would be able to proselytise and perform acts of charity to them, thereby giving them a chance to redeem themselves and demonstrate the power of their faith.

Thus the letter by the *Popolo Romano* framed the whole problem of the presence of prostitutes in the city as a kind of 'doctrinal challenge' for Catholicism: as a litmus test of the tolerance of the ruler and as a demonstration of belief in the doctrine of free will and divine mercy. The *Popolo Romano* drew on frequently used imagery of Rome as a theatre, a stage upon which the eyes of all the world were turned, whether seeking to follow its example, or seeking to find fault. In this particular 'play', the prostitutes are envisaged as 'actresses', who, aided by pious citizens and clergy, were to play out a drama of sin, repentance, conversion and forgiveness before the eyes of the Protestant and Catholic world, thus demonstrating the efficacy of Catholicism.

SEGREGATION OR INTEGRATION?

Whilst the *Lettera a Papa Pio Quinto* gives us an idea of the final arguments presented to the Pope, the *Lettera sulla tolleranza*, read in conjunction with it, give us insight into what seems to have been the most contentious issue raised, which was whether or not the prostitutes should be segregated from honest people, and if so where. The arguments for segregation were put

---

[80] Lettera a Papa Pio Quinto, c1.   [81] Ibid., c3r.   [82] Ibid., c4r.   [83] Ibid., c3v.

quite forcefully in the *Lettera sulla tolleranza*; reading between the lines, we learn more about the arguments of those who opposed it.

As for the release of carnal appetites, it is true that in well-run cities they do tolerate public women, and for this reason perhaps we should tolerate them in Rome, but this doesn't mean that they should be mixed up with the honest. Men's incontinence will be provided for well enough if they are allowed refuge somewhere in the city. Those who say they want to keep the *meretrici* near and closer to hand are not solving the problem of male incontinence but are simply encouraging vice.[84]

The anonymous writer perhaps spoke for a great many Romans when he argued that the dishonest women posed a considerable danger to honest women, in terms of setting them a bad example and possibly corrupting their virtue. He also pointed out that it was quite unfair that honest folk should have to go to such great lengths to avoid seeing prostitutes, to the extent that they could barely set foot outside their houses, adding, 'Whilst in Germany, Switzerland and amongst the other Lutherans *meretrici* are confined to woods and wild places, in Rome they can be seen mixing with Gentlemen, living in and contaminating the most beautiful streets of Rome'.[85] By taking the part of the ordinary Romans whose day-to-day lives were affected by the presence of prostitutes, he was also evidently setting himself against those who were seeking to protect the interests of 'outsiders' who used prostitutes when they came to the city. These virtual promoters of Roman 'sex tourism' were against segregation on the grounds that it would make life more difficult for foreign men who wished to seek out prostitutes.[86] It might be dangerous for them to go to a red-light district or damage their honour to be seen in such a place, thus putting them off seeing courtesans all together. Our writer dismissed these concerns with contempt:

You speak of the difficulties and even the dangers facing foreign gentlemen who might wish to visit 'public spaces', but these are nothing compared with those faced by our own citizens who usually have to mix with the wicked. And these foreigners or whoever else these incontinents are, either esteem their honour or they do not. Those who do esteem their honour have ways of bringing prostitutes to wherever they wish. Those who don't esteem it can go to see them openly, as grooms and *sbirri* do now.

He clearly favoured the idea of creating a 'public space' for prostitution also on the grounds that since prostitutes were associated with public disorder

---

[84] Lettera sulla tolleranza, c104r–v.   [85] Ibid., c104v.
[86] It is enough to read Thomas Coryat on Venice to appreciate the extent to which men from outside Italy hoped to visit their courtesans whilst on their travels.

and disreputable people, it would be far better if there were only 'three or four places in the city' where such disorder was likely to occur, since that would also make it easier for the police to control.[87]

Those who were against segregation turned these arguments upside down. They claimed that by creating a single space for prostitution a greater number of 'scandalous' people would be attracted to those streets, exacerbating problems of disorder and turning Trastevere into a kind of dangerous ghetto, particularly since it was 'sequestered' on the other side of the river.[88] The commerce on the Tiber would be under threat from the presence of 'low life'; the boatmen would be upset, and the poor people living there would be damaged by the influx of prostitutes, because it would raise the rents in the area.[89] The *Popolo* was also concerned with the way this would degrade the whole neighbourhood, affecting members of 'ancient families' and those who went there in the course of their daily business. If it became a red-light district, wrote Picchij, 'which gentlewoman would go to visit her daughter in one of the many monasteries of noble and honourable nuns over there, even if she were on the point of death?'[90]

The creation of a red-light district would not only have affected the honour of foreign men, of course, although they were a convenient scapegoat. At the heart of this debate lay the question of how to maintain the hierarchical structure of the profession and the distinctions between different classes of prostitute. As things stood, honourable courtesans could live in honourable streets, which honourable men needn't fear being seen in. But by forcing all prostitutes into one area, regardless of their 'status' or the status of their clients, it would be extremely difficult for gentlemen to carry on visiting their courtesans without tarnishing their own reputation.[91] Understandably these issues were not addressed explicitly in the letter to the Pope, although the *Popolo*'s defence of the wealthy prostitutes was implicitly a defence of this hierarchical system of prostitution. But in the *Lettera sulla tolleranza* the author goes into the kind of details which reveal some of the differences of opinion amongst the gentlemen of the Capitoline administration. It also clarifies further the ways in which the distinctions between prostitutes and honest courtesans were understood to operate.

The more famous, the richest and the least dishonest will effectively be left to get on with their lives more than the whores, but then these [the more famous] will

[87] Lettera sulla tolleranza, c105r.   [88] Lettera a Papa Pio Quinto, c8r.
[89] Ibid.   [90] Ibid., c7v.
[91] Men commonly had courtesans brought to their rooms, perhaps to avoid this kind of scandal.

earn respect for themselves more than the others, and they will make themselves appreciated by living honourably, by being better paid, and with the other qualities which signal the differences between them, just as they are recognised and more honoured in Valencia, where there are different grades of prostitute, according to their quality. And wherever they live people will make more allowances for them than of scoundrels and they will not be visited in the public places but will at the very least be called out by nobles and by the rich, and they can be content with this.[92]

PROSTITUTES AND THE COMMUNITY

Who finally 'won' the battle over prostitution? *Roma Sancta*, written by Gregory Martin and published in 1581, claimed that the policies of successive papacies on prostitution had been extremely successful. As an English Catholic who had fled to Rome and spent several years there teaching at the English seminary, Martin intended the book as a guide to the holy sites and charitable institutions of Rome. He aimed not only to educate and inform those fellow Catholics who were confined to England, but to contribute to the religious debate by providing a defence of the faith through praise of the new *Roma Sancta Renovata* of the Counter-Reformation.[93] Hence there were several passages on the prostitutes and courtesans, including a description of their living conditions, intended to show how the papacy had triumphed over immorality.

The notorious harlottes were banished not only out of the city, but out of the territorie of the Romane Diocese . . . and yet some remayned still, but pent up into one place of the citie in corners and bylanes and small outhouses in the basest streetes . . . Marke then . . . the miserable condition of them that continew in their lewdness, sufficient . . . to weary them and to drive them from it.[94]

But how much of this was accurate and how much was wishful thinking? Judging from the legislative changes, neither party was the outright winner. On the one hand the papacy was forced to back down from its most severe proposals for reform; on the other hand, the move to Campo Marzio meant that the *Popolo Romano* had to accept a certain degree of 'zoning', which facilitated policing. Also, the numerous discipline ordinances issued over the following years must have brought about some changes to the status quo of prostitutes. Ultimately the solution agreed upon represented a compromise between the two points of view.

[92] Lettera sulla Tolleranza, c106r–v.
[93] Editor's preface, Gregory Martin, *Roma sancta* (1581), ed. George Bruner Parks (Rome: Edizioni di Storia e Letteratura, 1969), 14–25.
[94] Martin, *Roma sancta*, 148, 145.

Concrete evidence of where prostitutes actually lived forty years after the first debates sheds light on the success of this policy. The sources are the parish records, known as the *Stati delle Anime*.[95] These were registers kept on a yearly basis, usually around Easter, in which the priest indicated the number of people living in each household in the parish and their relationship – if any – to their co-habitees, their name, age and profession. The priest then added an indication of whether each person was old enough or morally fit to take communion and whether or not it had been taken that year. Known prostitutes were recorded with some care, since they were unfit to take communion. Women whose reputations were in doubt had the word 'suspected' (*sospetta*) added to their names, and those with a serious reputation were marked as *cortegiana famosa* or *cortegiana scandalosa*.[96]

The *Stati delle Anime* show that by 1600 most of the *meretrici* did indeed live in that area of the city which had been designated by the 1592 laws and was broadly referred to as the *luoghi*, 'the spaces'. Campo Marzio fell under the tutelage of three parishes: the parish of San Lorenzo in Lucina, which was one of the most densely populated areas of the city;[97] the parish of Sant'Andrea alle Fratte, which encompassed the more fashionable streets; and the parish of Santa Maria del Popolo. This included the new hospital for incurables, much new housing for workers near the Piazza del Popolo, and the vineyards and shacks just outside the walls, where about half the parish's population lived. Overall, the records for the Parish of Santa Maria del Popolo show that in 1610 about 10 per cent of the households in that parish that year included a courtesan.[98] However, they were not evenly spread through the parish. Some streets had a far higher density of prostitutes than others. In 1607 in the parish of San Lorenzo in Lucina there were prostitutes living in nineteen streets, and four of these streets had more than twenty. Similarly in Schiavonia, one of the poorest streets in the Ortaccio, there were

---

[95] The priest and his assistant handed out a printed slip which had to be filled in and returned. For a detailed analysis of the source see Rosa Traina, 'Caratteristiche di registrazione dello stato delle anime a Roma', in Carla Sbrana, Rosa Traina and Eugenio Sonnino, eds., *Gli stati delle anime a Roma dalle origini al secolo XVII* (Rome: La Goliardica, 1977), 345–75. Also Schiavoni and Sonnino. 'Aspects généraux de l'évolution démographique'. Eugenio Sonnino, 'Intorno alla "Sapienza". Popolazione e famiglie, collegiali e studenti a Roma nel seicento', in *Roma e lo studium urbis: spazio urbano e cultura dal quattro al seicento*, Atti del Convegno, Roma 7–10 June 1989 (Rome: Ministero per i Beni Culturali e Ambientali, 1992), 341–68.

[96] In general the words *meretrice*, *cortegiana* and various abbreviations were adopted, such as 'M', 'cort', or a large 'C'. Sbrana et al., *Gli stati delle anime a Roma*, 361–4.

[97] It had 5,076 inhabitants in 1599.

[98] There were 486 households, and a total population of 3,091. Amongst these there were sixty courtesans, living in forty-seven households. Archivio del Vicariato (AVIC), *Stati delle Anime* (SA), Santa Maria del Popolo, 1610.

Table 1 *Showing the streets favoured by prostitutes
and courtesans in the parish of S. Lorenzo in
Lucina, 1607 (see also Map 1)*

Street	Number of prostitutes
Strada Ferratina	3
Via Borgognona	4
Via Condotti	7
Alla Serena	8
Via della Croce	9
Via Vittoria	9
Vicolo del Grillo	10
Bocca di Leone	12
Nr. Palazzo Strozzi	15
Vicolo Vittoria	16
Vicolo del Gambaro	18
Via Paulina	29
Otto Cantoni	36
Schiavonia	40
Vicolo San Germano	44

a total of 233 people, of whom about 40 (18 per cent) were prostitutes, and in
the nearby Vicolo del Grillo nearly 50 per cent of households were headed
by prostitutes.[99] The high concentration of prostitutes in this area presumably resulted in part from their having been relocated there, in part from the
low rents, and also reflected the area's proximity to the port. Peopled with
sailors and passing travellers this was an ideal area for casual prostitution.[100]
The wealthier courtesans lived in the more elegant streets which were officially out of bounds, such as Via Lata, Via Ferratina and Piazza Trinità.
(See Table 1.)

With the exception of Schiavonia and one or two other alleys, very few
of these streets were exclusively occupied by dishonest women, as Gregory
Martin's description would have had us believe. Prostitutes tended to live
with just a few other 'dishonest women', alongside their honest neighbours.
Apart from a few streets which seem to have been dominated by professional

---

[99] Thirty-two of sixty-six households.
[100] The church of San Rocco and the hospital had been built there in order to offer assistance to the
poor and sick in the area, and the confraternity of San Rocco was supported largely by artisanal
groups such as the Vignaroli, Barcaroli, Legnaioli, Sonatori. See Luigi Salerno and Gianfranco
Spagnesi, *La chiesa di San Rocco all'Augusteo* (Rome: Desclée e C. Editori, 1962), 1–8.

groups, such as boatmen (Vicolo del Oca), cow-herds (Vicolo de Fenili), or in which there was a high concentration of beggars (such as the Borghetto), most streets seem to have had a very mixed population: artisans, widows, coachmen, vine-dressers, tavern keepers, cooks, musicians, artists and their families all rubbed shoulders with one another.[101]

Whilst official documents suggest intolerance towards prostitutes, in practice attitudes were more nuanced. Elizabeth Cohen has pointed to the 'uneasy but complex integration of prostitutes into the social fabric of the city', which can be traced both to their long-standing presence in Rome and to their social role, 'in the defence of collective public order'.[102] Despite the extent of immigration to the city and the high levels of residential mobility amongst the poor, the evidence suggests that in Rome prostitutes were widely tolerated, provided they observed the community ethos and maintained the 'appearance' of honesty. This is illustrated by a number of similar letters which were sent to the Governatore by residents writing to protest about the presence of prostitutes in their streets.[103] One of these, written in 1624, was signed by ten gentlemen, who pointedly noted down how many unmarried daughters they had living at home. They complained about the 'scandalous behaviour' of a number of prostitutes who had moved into their street.

Living extremely impure lives and publicising their dishonesty by day in the streets, touching men's shameful parts and doing other extremely dishonest acts in front of married women and virgins with great scandal. We neighbours, being unable to be at home for the (. . . ?) of our families, especially at night because of the great tumult and noise which is going on in the area, and as a result of which there are arguments and stones are thrown at their windows, with the risk that an onlooker or passer-by will be killed.[104]

They asked the Governor to have these women evicted, to which end they supplied a list of names. This was divided into two parts. The first part contained the names of the women whose scandalous behaviour had

[101] AVIC, *Stati delle Anime*, San Lorenzo in Lucina, 1607, c10r–41r.
[102] Cohen, 'Seen and Known', 394. Rossiaud, 'Prostitution, jeunesse', 307–8, 324. Trexler says they functioned to 'underpin the community ethic'. 'La prostitution florentine', 984. Roper discusses the contradictions and ambiguities of what she calls the 'symbolic marginality' and 'symbolic centrality' of prostitutes. 'Discipline and Respectability', 19.
[103] There are four such letters, all pleas addressed directly to the Governor of Rome asking him to intervene in order to settle disputes. The letters are written by men who refer to themselves as *honorati, curiali principali* (three), *Artegiani buoni e da bene* (three), *gentilhuomini* (two). ASR, Tribunale Criminale del Governatore (Henceforth TCG), Atti di Cancelleria, Busta 105, Fasc. 158, Cortegiane, 2, c38, 12 September 1601; and c34.
[104] Ibid., c34.

outraged them, and whom they wished to have evicted immediately. The other list held the names of those courtesans whom they did not object to, provided they remained well behaved.[105] This distinction draws our attention to the fact that even in an extreme case like this, it was not the physical presence per se of courtesans in a street of honourable gentlefolk which was under attack, but the 'dishonest' and shameless behaviour of a few. This view coincides closely with the sentiments expressed in the *Lettera sulla tolleranza*, where it is argued – perhaps in response to Picchij's comment about 'secret' prostitutes – that it does not matter if women prostitute themselves secretly, provided they behave respectably. If they began to behave scandalously, then they should be transferred elsewhere.

As for the difficulties about dividing prostitutes from the honest, I don't see this as being such a great problem as you do. Because for prostitutes I mean those who make a public profession and who are manifestly before the eyes of all, and these are very well known and so vituperous that they cannot, nor should they be tolerated in the community of others. And you can see that these even live in the most beautiful and busy streets of Rome. Those who are dishonest . . . in their homes, and others not knowing about it, or pretending not to, or tolerating them, or whether it is brothers or fathers or husbands, do not have to consider themselves amongst these prostitutes, even if they are not really living honestly. As long as no disorder or scandals follow, like those caused by the women mentioned above. And if there should be trouble, and if they should gradually become infamous, they can be sent to the assigned spaces with the others. Which would encourage them to improve themselves.[106]

Consideration also needs to be made of the way in which prostitutes might have established networks for themselves within their communities, through their friendships with clients. These may have been far stronger and more 'formalised' than we suppose, judging from a witness statement given in 1619. Domenico Marsigli from Rome described how, on the evening of 22 February, he had been called upon for assistance by Donna Vittoria, mother of a courtesan named Maddalena. He knew the family because his brother 'had dealings with Maddalena'. Maddalena's house had been threatened earlier in the evening by one of her former clients. She had gone to her parents, who lived nearby, asking for help emptying the house of all her possessions so they shouldn't be damaged in the expected attack. Donna Vittoria had called on various neighbours to help them carry Maddalena's belongings out, and they were doing this by the light of a lamp when Domenico passed by. 'I said to her, "sister-in-law, are you moving house

---

[105] Ibid., c39.   [106] Lettera sulla Tolleranza, c105v.

because you have debts?" And she replied, "Oh, brother-in-law, come here a moment, I would like you to help me.""[107]

The casual way in which Domenico reports this conversation suggests there was nothing unusual about the bond of 'extra-marital kinship' which had evidently been established between himself and his brother's prostitute and her family. Like official kinship bonds, this appears to have implicitly created solidarity between the two families, and conferred responsibilities upon the new 'kin'. Prostitutes would certainly have benefited from a system which strengthened their standing in the neighbourhood and provided a network of people upon whom they could depend.

Given the symbolic significance of prostitutes in the Counter-Reformation, Catholic rhetoric encouraged the belief that prostitutes had largely been banished from Rome. Likewise promulgation of legislation has frequently been read as being synonymous with its implementation.[108] A closer look at the sequence of events and at the debates which took place suggests that reform was driven by aims which were more nuanced than is usually assumed, and that the outcomes were less dramatic. Pope Pius V did not succeed in banishing wealthy courtesans, nor did he marginalise the poorer prostitutes; even the compromise solution took the city authorities some forty years of repeated ordinances, enforced moves, re-setting of boundaries and police harassment to enforce. Reasons for Pius's lack of success embrace cultural, economic and social factors, highlighting just how far removed lay concerns about prostitution were from those of the religious elite.

There was a fundamental gap between the papacy's concerns about the immorality of prostitutes, and lay perceptions that the sexual promiscuity of prostitutes in itself was not a key issue. Although as a group they could be seen as a corrupting influence in the city, vituperation was reserved for the 'whores who hang around the streets with such licence and dishonesty'.[109] Those prostitutes who observed a decorum of appearances and manners were not just tolerated but accepted in their communities, embedded there by virtue of neighbourliness, friendship and even local 'kinship' solidarities. There were also powerful economic reasons for allowing the wealthier prostitutes to remain in the city, which were rehearsed in the *Popolo*'s letter to the Pope. Its comments may have been calculated simply to play on popular beliefs about the wealth of courtesans, or they may have been a

---

[107] ASR, TCG, Processi (sec. XVII), vol. 154, c128r–v, 22 February 1619.
[108] Elizabeth Cohen also finds a significant gap between the ideals and practices regarding the presence of prostitutes in the city in 'Seen and Known'.
[109] Lettera sulla Tolleranza, c104v.

reflection of the real economic concerns of the city's lay elite. The fact that they emphasised the revenues which elite prostitution generated suggests that there was more than a grain of truth in their arguments. The *Popolo's* letters also draw attention to the social structures of prostitution, under-lining how important it was to maintain the hierarchy of prostitution, by upholding the distinctions between different kinds of prostitutes. Forcing all prostitutes to live in the same area or streets would have eroded these social distinctions which marked out elite prostitutes and signalled the sta-tus of their clientele, just as swiftly as banishing the wealthy courtesans from the city would have done. In so doing, it would have swept away the principles which had underpinned practices of prostitution in Rome for more than half a century.

CHAPTER 4

Policing prostitution

The campaign to bring order to the streets of Rome continued well into the seventeenth century, with some 458 statues (*bandi*) on criminality and the administration of justice issued between 1590 and 1623. The majority were concerned with repressing the violence and disorder which reigned on the streets, by targeting vagabonds, banditry and the carrying of weapons.[1] Yet although prostitutes were the subject of numerous statutes, there was no further attempt to expel them, nor was prostitution itself criminalised. Instead the focus was on restricting prostitutes' freedom of movement around the city, on reducing the occasions of violence and disorder associated with them, and on preventing prostitutes from wearing disguises and from riding in coaches and carriages.

The forecourts and piazzas beside churches were important social spaces where people traditionally gathered, especially on Sundays, feast days and in Lent. They were also seen as 'amatory' spaces: places to observe potential suitors and brides.[2] Courtesans and their admirers had long since adopted these places for purposes of 'courtship' and display, as in Aretino's description of a famous courtesan arriving at the church of Sant'Agostino, which was particularly popular amongst courtesans during the early Cinquecento.

I saw everyone bow down to her, and many left the Mass so as to drift around near her. So they are not witches, and if they are, they adorn the churches and palaces and people run to feast their eyes on them. Do you believe, you dunce, that at the churches of Sant'Agostino, La Pace and San Salvatore the festivals would be so well attended if those women you are speaking of did not go?[3]

By the mid-sixteenth century the church increasingly perceived this promiscuity of sacred and 'amorous' space as intolerable. For example, men

[1] Cirinei, 'Bandi e giustizia criminale', 87.
[2] Adrian Randolph, 'Regarding Women in Sacred Space', in Johnson and Matthews Grieco, *Picturing Women*, 17–41, esp. 34–8.
[3] Aretino, *Il piacevol ragionamento de l'Aretino*, 51.

were prohibited from going to the church of San Sebastiano on Sundays in May with 'women and courtesans and to play games outside the doors';[4] prostitutes were ordered not to occupy the benches in the 'best' places in church nor sit near *donne oneste*;[5] they were forbidden to 'stay longer than necessary' at stations of the cross, to procure clients in the vicinity of the church and to participate in the Corpus Domini procession which took place in the Borgo.[6]

Hostelries and taverns were favoured by prostitutes and clients, which in the eyes of the city authorities posed grave problems to public discipline. Drink and women encouraged a wide variety of sins, and immorality in *osterie* gave a poor impression of the city to the many foreign travellers and pilgrims who frequented them.[7] The authorities were also concerned that the *osterie* might be used as brothels and in particular that tavern-keepers would use the presence of dishonest women to lure in more clients. As a result prostitutes were forbidden to enter *osterie*, and the hosteller from having women 'of any sort, age, or condition, whether their wives, daughters, sisters, aunts, nieces, in-laws or whatever kind or relation' from living there.[8] The *birri* could and did check by examining the book in which the host was obliged to write the names of those staying the night.[9]

In order to prevent general disorderliness after dark, the *luoghi* were placed under a curfew and prostitutes were forbidden to move about after the Ave Maria had sounded.[10] The penalty was a hundred *scudi*, a whipping and perpetual exile from the Papal States. To reduce the occurrence of violent brawls, the penalty for carrying weapons in the company of prostitutes was a fine, 'the rope' for men (a form of torture which involved being hung by the arms) and a public whipping for the prostitute.[11] Parties were forbidden, and rowdy, vulgar behaviour was also criminalised.

We command that from henceforth nobody, especially no courtesan or dishonest woman of whatsoever condition may dare go about the city in groups walking abreast, whether on foot or on horseback making a hullaballoo, causing an uproar, fighting and shouting or saying slanderous or indecent words.[12]

---

[4] ASR, Bandi del Governatore, Bandi 1, 1529–1733, c17, 2 May 1556.

[5] ASR, Atti di Cancelleria, vol. 1, Bando Generale, 13v, 18 February 1556.

[6] ASR, Bandi del Governatore, vol. 410, 6 March 1557. ASR, Bandi 1, 1529–1733, c75, 8 June 1563.

[7] ASV, Miscellanea, Armadio IV–V, vol. 52, c1, 2 October 1566.

[8] ASV, Miscellanea, Armadio IV–V, vol. 52, c5, 9 November 1592.

[9] Fornili, *Delinquenti e carcerati a Roma alla metà del '600*, 54.

[10] ASV, Miscellanea, Armadio IV–V, vol. 66, c212, 6 January 1586.

[11] ASV, Miscellanea, Armadio IV–V, vol. 66, c212, May 12 1586.

[12] ASV, Miscellanea, Armadio IV–V, vol. 66, c210, 24 September 1564.

Whilst the intentions behind most of the laws show a desire to improve public order, others were concerned with enforcing distinctions of social hierarchy. Riding in a carriage was a valuable and sought-after status-marker and a steady stream of edicts were issued between 1558 and 1674 which prohibited courtesans from doing so. These prohibitions appear to have been routinely flouted. As a result a 1592 edict specified that the entrances to the streets in which courtesans lived would be narrowed by the placing of columns at both ends, so as to prevent carriages from entering their streets at all – rather like twenty-first-century attempts to deter cars from pedestrian areas. A 1624 ordinance expressed exasperation at the way in which courtesans rode about in carriages, relying on the belief that their clients' status and access to power networks would enable them to evade punishment.

Notwithstanding the rigorous edicts which prohibit *meretrici* and other dishonest women from travelling by coach, they nevertheless have the *brazen cheek* to disobey them . . . Hence on express orders of Pope Urban VII, no *meretrice, cortigiana* or dishonest woman may dare to go by carriage by day or night, in the city or two miles outside it, alone, or in company, *however privileged the company, for any pretext or reason, however pre-eminent the title or dignity of the people they are with.*[13] (My italics.)

Disciplining prostitutes and courtesans was one matter, but trying to control the activities of their elite clients was another, since it was they who allowed the women to borrow or ride in their coaches, and instructed their coachmen to drive them. Coachmen could be punished with 'three pulls of the rope' if they drove a courtesan anywhere;[14] the men who owned the carriages were threatened with the confiscation of their carriages and heavy fines. However, it was easy enough to threaten elite men, but hard to punish them. The disparity in status and power between the *birri* and men of the elite made it extremely difficult for the police to arrest and bring them to trial, except under exceptional circumstances, and the next best thing was to target their courtesans.

THE *BIRRI*, 1594–1606

Issuing laws was one thing: enforcing them quite another. Law enforcement depended largely on the efficacy and honesty of the city's courts and police-men, known as *birri*, whose role it was to maintain public order, enforce

---

[13] ASV, Armadio IV–V, vol. 60, c218, 18 October 1624 (italics added).
[14] BAV, Cod. Urb. Lat., vol. 1040, c245v, 22 June 1566.

edicts and perform underground surveillance. The Governor of Rome had by far the largest police force, commanded by corporals and a Captain, the Bargello, who took orders directly from the Governor himself.[15] In the late sixteenth century the Bargello del Governatore had eighty men stationed around the city, who went out on three daily patrols in groups.[16] They were aided by a special nucleus of police concerned with morals, named the Polizia del Buon Costume, directed by the Cardinal Vicar. The police (*birri* or *sbirri*) were authorised to proceed *ex abrupto*, which meant that they could arrest anyone and take them off for preliminary questioning. Prisoners were generally interrogated by the court the very next morning.[17]

The *Relazioni dei Birri* are volumes which were compiled daily by the corporals who were supposed to make a record of the name and profession of anyone arrested that night, including details of where they had been arrested, why, and the events or verbal exchanges which had taken place. They would also note where they had been imprisoned. We can safely assume that the number of arrests of prostitutes and clients recorded in the *Relazioni dei Birri* moderately under-represents arrests, and vastly under-estimates transgressions occurring in the city. Loss of records, arrests by other courts and bribery are just some of the reasons. There were also practical difficulties. The capacity of the *birri* to act was limited by their numerical weakness, by the fact that they were regarded with much hostility by the whole society,[18] and by the extensive areas of the city which were out of bounds. The palaces of cardinals, ambassadors and nobles, like religious buildings, enjoyed 'immunity' from the city laws.[19] Finally

---

[15] He also paid them. Blastenbrei, 'La quadratura del cerchio', 15–16.

[16] However, a hundred years later there would be three hundred. Giulio Pisano, 'I birri a Roma nel '600 ed un progetto di riforma del loro ordinamento sotto il pontificato d'Innocenzo XI', *Roma* 10 (1932), 543–56.

[17] This is clear from the dates of the *Costituti*, in which most people state that they had been arrested a few hours earlier or at most the previous day or night.

[18] Steven Hughes points out that the *birri* were recruited from the criminal classes as it was one of the least honourable and most despised of jobs. In the late seventeenth century it was claimed that they took bribes from prostitutes in exchange for protection. See 'Fear and Loathing in Bologna and Rome: the Papal Police in Perspective', *Journal of Social History* 21:1 (1987), 97–116. And Pisano, 'I birri a Roma nel '600', 546–7.

[19] Fornili, *Delinquenti e carcerati*, 57. The most important noble families with a presence in Rome were the Altieri, Massimi, Boccapaduli, Cenci, Muti, Santacroce, Maffei, Pamphili, Orsini, Colonna, Farnese, Aldobrandini, Farnese, Medici, Este and Savoia. Laurie Nussdorfer, 'Il popolo romano e i papi: la vita politica della capitale religiosa', in Luigi Fiorani and Adriano Prosperi, eds., *Storia d'Italia, annali 16, Roma, la città del papa* (Turin: Einaudi, 2000), 241–62, 247.

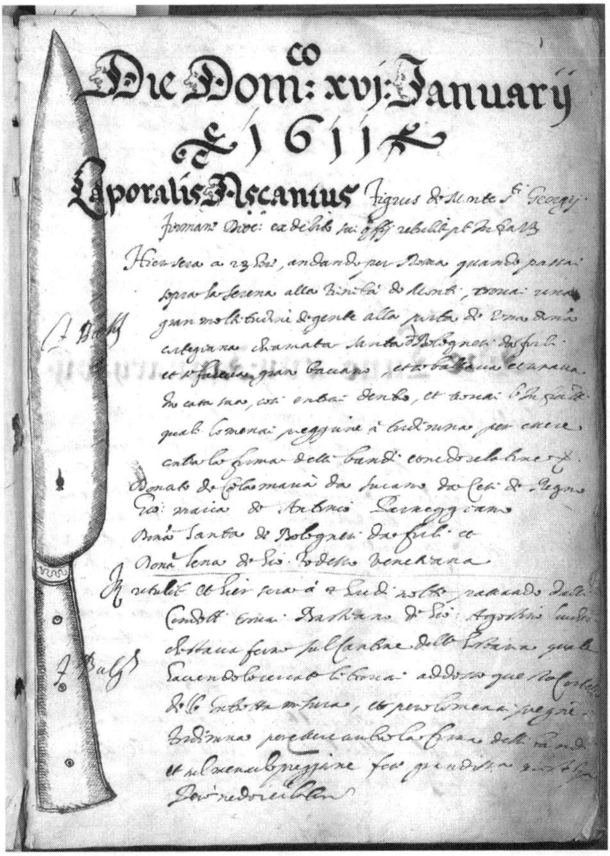

Fig. 6 An example of a page from the police reports. First page of the *Relazioni dei Birri*, vol. 104. Translation of first entry. Sunday 16 January 1611. Corporal Ascanio Figro (or Tigro) of Monte San Gregorio in the diocesis of Fermo: In the course of duty [I relate the following]. Yesterday evening at 23 hours, [an hour before sundown], I was going about Rome when I passed above la Serena at the Trinità dei Monti, I found a great multitude of people at the door of a woman, a courtesan called Santa Bolognesi from Forlì and they were making a terrible racket, and there was dancing and music playing in her house, so I went inside, and I found those named below whom I led to prison at Tor di Nona because they were contravening the regulations in the manner I have described. Donato de Colamaria da Lucano da Cesi di Regno. Gio Maria di Antonio Parmeggiano, Dona Santa di Bolognesei da Forlì and Dona Lena di Gio Todesco Venetiana.

we must question the commitment of the Bargello and his men to the enforcement of the law and the keeping of such records in the first place. It was easier to roam the streets looking for parties to interrupt than to track down adulterers or even to check on who was sleeping in the hundreds of *osterie* in the city.[20] Therefore this study of police records and depositions can only very loosely indicate the actual effectiveness of policing at the start of the seventeenth century. They can be read, however, as a testimony of policing policies and the inclinations of the police with regard to different illegal activities. They also give us insight into practices of prostitution in the city and the nature of the sociability which revolved around the city's prostitutes and courtesans.

This chapter is based on the *Relazioni dei Birri* for the period between 1594 and 1606. It represents records pertaining to 369 prostitutes and courtesans arrested by the Governor's *birri* during this period, picked up on their nightly rounds.[21] They did not record all arrests of prostitutes made in the city. Still, for the chief law-enforcement agency in the city, this is not a great many arrests, averaging out at about thirty-one per year, or 3 per cent of prostitutes, given that their numbers oscillated at around 1000–1,200 in this period. Even in the years when there was the greatest will to discipline prostitution, around the years of the Jubilee for example, the numbers arrested (sixty-five in 1600 and eighty-eight in 1601) represent about one-tenth of the city total. From numbers alone we can surmise that policing cannot have constituted a very effective deterrent to breaking the law (see Table 2).

Since most of the women were guilty of more than one infringement of the law on any given occasion, it is only possible broadly to categorise the causes of arrest.[22] A majority were arrested inside their homes (42 per cent), whether for holding parties or for being in their homes with an armed man, or involved in a fight; 33 per cent were arrested outside in the streets, while a further 5 per cent were arrested in connection with an act of violence committed against their house, in the form of stones being thrown at their windows or the door being battered (see Table 3). These 369 women were arrested in 170 different places scattered throughout Campo Marzio, with a very few arrests taking place elsewhere in places such as Trastevere. This suggests that the *luoghi* had indeed very much become the principal space of sociability linked to courtesans and was also subject to the most frequent police patrols. Courtesans were most likely to be arrested in or near Trinità dei Monti (twenty-eight cases), which was the most fashionable area in Campo Marzio. Twenty-six were arrested in or near an *osteria*, ten of which were located in this part of the city, and all other localities are reported far

---

[20] Ibid., 242.   [21] I do not count women merely suspected of being prostitutes.

[22] A prostitute might have been out in the streets by night with an armed man, disguised as a man and making a great deal of noise, each of which constituted an offence. For statistical purposes I have taken a decision as to which seemed to be the 'major' offence, but this is often open to interpretation.

Table 2 *Numbers of courtesans
arrested as recorded in the
Relazioni dei Birri, 1594–1606*

Year	Number
1594	24
1595	28
1596	19
1597	26
1598	28
1599	22
1600	65
1601	88
1602	2
1603	16
1604	9
1605	4
1606	1

less;[23] for example, twelve in the Leoncino, and seven each in Otto Cantoni, Schiavonia and the Serena.

POLICING THE STREETS

Although the following analysis is centred on the activities of courtesans and their *amici* it is important not to let this distort our perceptions of the overall situation in the streets. Far fewer prostitutes were arrested than were men, and the *Relazioni dei Birri* are above all a record of the nocturnal activities of gangs of armed men who wandered around the *luoghi* by night, frequently getting into fights. Let us consider a 'typical' night in May 1601. Having arrested four soldiers at about 6 p.m. the *birri* found themselves below Trinità dei Monti, where 'Every night a great uproar came from groups of soldiers armed with swords and daggers outside the *Osteria* of the Serena.'[24] Accordingly they arrested nine men, before carrying on their rounds. At about 12 p.m. in the same place, they found seventeen armed men all of whom were arrested. Another eight were taken at the Osteria del Moro under Trinità dei Monti. 'Carrying on towards the Babuino' they arrested two more men and at Borghetto delli Pidocchi they noticed a large

---

[23] Romani, *Pellegrini e viaggiatori*, 70.
[24] ASR, TCG, Relazioni dei Birri, RB, vol. 101, c67v, 16 May 1601.

Table 3 *Principal causes of arrest recorded
in the* Relazioni dei Birri, *1594–1606*

64	With a man
45	At a party
35	With an armed man
29	Violent behaviour
20	Outside permitted areas
19	Out walking (*a spasso*)
17	In a carriage
22	Argument between women
15	Argument between man and woman
14	Theft
13	Dressed as a man
12	Adultery
11	Making a racket
11	Going about by night
5	In an osteria/inn
2	Wearing a shirt with no front
1	Disobeying a court order
1	Escaped from monastery
1	Leading young men to her home
1	Running a brothel
1	In bed with a man
1	Swearing
1	Damaging words
1	Sheltering bandits
1	Murder
1	Gambling
1	Man disobeying court order
1	Kept by a man
1	Insulted the court
1	Contumacy
1	Had meat on the table
1	Men fighting over her

number of people, among whom were some *donne meretrici*, one of whom
was arrested. Five more men were finally arrested in a house at the Babuino.

'I STOPPED THEM AND ASKED THEM WHAT THEY WERE DOING AT THAT HOUR IN THOSE DANGEROUS STREETS'[25]

The *birri* automatically suspected the motives of women who were found
out and about in the streets by night and quite often arrested them. Perhaps

[25] ASR, TCG, Processi, sec. XVII, vol. 20, c1248r–9r, 4 July 1602, Hieronimus Baroncellis Urbis.

they had good reason to, or perhaps they believed the stereotype according to which honest women would not risk going out alone. This certainly was the line they took when interrogating Bernardo the barber, whose wife Dianora had been caught virtually *in flagrante delicto*: naked in the top-storey room of a gentleman's house.[26] Asked by the court what she had been doing there, Bernardo denied all knowledge of his wife's whereabouts that night, asserting that she had gone off alone that evening. The court was disbelieving: 'How can you think that she came alone, considering that she is so beautiful and looks so glamorous, especially at that time of night?'[27] But Bernardo asserted that she was 'a spirited woman (*una donna ardita*) and would think nothing of going off at midnight through Rome',[28] adding that she often went to see relatives, especially when they had had an argument! Dianora herself also made little of her escapade, refuting the suggestion that it was particularly dangerous or unusual for a woman to be out alone: 'I am used to going out at night. I have been to my mother's house and my uncle's, who live near by.'[29]

Under the circumstances, this construction of Dianora as an independent and wilful woman was presumably an attempt made by the couple to conceal Bernardo's complicity in the affair. Yet similar defiance is implicit in a great many of the replies made by women who were picked up by the *birri*, including those given by women merely suspected of being prostitutes. We are, it seems, witnessing a conflict between divergent expectations of behaviour. Moralists may have presumed that any woman who was out after sundown was implicitly a prostitute. But considering the large numbers of women who were heads of households, who had families to maintain and money to earn, there was no reason automatically to suspect that single women out and about in the evening were prostitutes. They might indeed have been doing the washing or delivering laundry to a client, as they claimed.

Nonetheless, sometimes such suspicions were well founded. One evening the corporal of the *birri* went along to the Arco di Parma, having heard that there was a woman who ran a bawdy house in those parts. He hid and waited to see what happened. Sure enough at about ten or eleven o'clock 'whilst I was in the street I saw the afore-mentioned woman and she was leading a young woman with her and they entered the house, so I took them both'.[30] On another occasion Portia Rastrelli Romana, 'who is a famous

---

[26] Ibid.   [27] Ibid., c1256r, Sisigmondo Attavanti Florentino, 4 July 1602.

[28] Ibid., c1254r, Bernardinus q. JoMatthei Romanus, 4 July 1602.

[29] Ibid., c1267r, Dionora Uxor Bernardini Barbiero, 4 July 1602.

[30] ASR, TCG, RB, vol. 101, c127r, Santa Fiorentina, 10 October 1601.

prostitute', was found at night near La Pace, accompanied by her servant and Mesi, wife of Camillo Fiorentino. 'And since Mesi lives at Quattro Fontane, and Portia was leading her towards the Borgo, perhaps it was in order to be screwed by someone.'[31]

Whatever their real destination or motives, on the whole prostitutes and courtesans did not go out alone. Of sixty-two arrests which occurred in the streets between 1594 and 1606, only fifteen of the women were alone when arrested and the remaining forty-seven were in couples or groups of varying sizes. The majority (twenty-seven) were with one other person, eleven were in groups of three, and nine women were arrested in groups of four or more. Quite often they were accompanied by a servant. Cinzia was arrested on the way to see her compatriot, a gentleman from Siena. She was accompanied by Primavera, her servant, her friend Rosa and Rosa's male friend.[32] Likewise Laura Ventimiglia, arrested one night in November 1602: 'I was arrested yesterday evening, at around 11 p.m. near Montecitorio with Giulia my servant, and we were both going to Signor Mario Piccolomini's house, since I was going there to speak to him, since he is my friend and has carnal relations with me.[33]

Portia Rastrelli and her servant were on their way to a vineyard at Porta Salaria, when they were arrested one evening in June 1593, presumably intending to meet friends for the evening.[34] Courtesans may have taken their servants along for company, for 'safety', to signal their status and for help with the preparations for their sexual encounter. Dianora, the beautiful barber's wife, had been accompanied to her client's home by her man-servant. He described having undressed her and having 'pulled off her stockings' before returning home.[35]

Usually the women out in the streets were in the company of men, in numbers ranging from one to twenty-five! If they were with a single man he often hung back, trailing behind the woman at some distance, pretending they were not together.[36] Often the woman was accompanied by a man who was not her client, but an escort. On at least one occasion when the Governor's Bargello, Captain Valerio, wanted to have sex with one of his prostitutes, he sent along one of his *birri* to collect her rather than go to

---

[31] ASR, TCG, RB, vol. 101, c117v, 12 September 1601.
[32] ASR, TCG, Costituti, vol. 509, c177v–178r, Rosa Vannocci and Cinzia Gabrielli Senese, 1 January 1602.
[33] ASR, TCG, Costituti, vol. 521, c58v, Laura Ventimiglia Panormita, 13 November 1602.
[34] ASR, TCG, Costituti, vol. 442, c177v, Donna Portia Rastrelli, 28 June 1593.
[35] ASR, TCG, Processi, sec. XVII, vol. 20, c1262–1263, 4 July 1602.
[36] ASR, TCG, RB, vol. 101, c76v, 15 June 1601.

her house himself.[37] Diana Biondi Ferrarese was arrested just as she was leaving home with Pompeo, a musician who had been sent to get her out of bed, in order to take her over to the German Guardsmen.[38] The fact that a musician should have come to collect her was probably quite natural, since so many social occasions seem to have required the presence of both courtesans and musicians: these two groups must have known one another well.

On other occasions courtesans were accompanied by their *amici*, often not going anywhere at all, but merely strolling about the streets, singing and chatting. Indeed, the city was teeming with bands of young men drifting around with one or two prostitutes in tow.[39] The case of the Cavaliere Gironimo was exceptional: he took Vincenza Serena da Vicenza for a stroll (*per andare a spasso*), along with twenty-five gentlemen.[40] *Andare a spasso* is a term which appears repeatedly in these records. In a sense it resembles the modern Italian *passeggiata*, but its meaning was not necessarily limited to indicating that a person was out walking in the streets, in a purely physical sense. Although dependent on the context, it was also a term used by the wealthy to convey that they did not have to work for a living and therefore could spend their time ostentatiously enjoying their leisure. Ago cites a man who, when asked what his profession was, replied, 'My profession is to go out strolling, and I have no other profession.'[41] So when we read in the records that a group of men and a courtesan '*andavano a spasso*' we should consider the possibility that this casual wandering around the streets by night had its own particular social significance, which was not lost on the rest of the community.

One of the methods employed by courtesans attempting to escape detection was disguise. The *bandi* mention numerous ingenious disguises they were forbidden to adopt, ranging from wearing masks to dressing as nuns, men and lay-religious women.[42] Relatively few arrests were made on this count, however, and then only for dressing as men. This may have been because the disguise was successful. Julia Rossi Ferrarese recounted her arrest one night in September 1602. 'Yesterday evening at 10.30 p.m. in Via del Babuino behind the vegetable garden of Naples they took me

---

[37] ASR, TCG, Processi, sec. XVII, vol. 34, c92r, Donna Hieronima Lena figlia Giuseppe, 13 October 1602.

[38] ASR, TCG, RB, vol. 101, c130v, Diana Biondi Ferrarese, 16 October 1601.

[39] ASR, TCG, RB, vol. 99, c123v, Magdalena Romana and Ludovica d'Ancona, 27 November 1597.

[40] ASR, TCG, RB, vol. 102, c20r, Vincenza Serena da Vicenza, 16 April 1603.

[41] Renata Ago points this out in *Economia barocca*, 94–5.

[42] ASV, Miscellanea, Armadio IV–V, Vol. 66, c219. Editto delle meretrici e donne disoneste e loro fautori e ricettatori, 27 November 1624.

because I was wrapped in a *ferraiolo* [a man's short cloak] and I had a hat.'[43] Another woman claimed: 'We were not dressed as women, but we were each wearing a *ferraiolo* . . . because I was cold in my *zimarra* [a cloak-like over-garment].'[44] Yet another insisted that she had been dressed as a woman (meaning presumably that she had a dress on), but had a man's hat and *ferraiolo* on as well.[45]

IN THE CARDINAL'S PALACE

Although it was not considered advisable for courtiers, prostitutes were often entertained in the great palaces and villas of the city.[46] By 1600 there were some sixty-seven of the former and twenty of the latter in and around the city.[47] These vast buildings were usually built on three floors around a central courtyard and towered above the narrow city streets, dominating the piazzas with their austere façades. Sometimes hundreds of people lived in the warren of rooms and apartments, where, bustling with the coming and going of visitors and of the '*familiari*' (those who belonged to the household, in whatever capacity), a few courtesans could easily be slipped in unnoticed. The *palazzi* and even the streets beside them were out of bounds to the police and immune to the dictates of the city authorities, acting as a forceful reminder that the power of the Governatore and his men was strictly limited when it came to disciplining the men of the nobility.[48]

One evening Aquilina *cortigiana* was arrested on her way to the palace of Cardinal S. Giorgio, and she was quite open about the fact that she was expected by a *gentiluomo*, with whom she would dine and then sleep, as she had often done before. Her companion Flaminia was allegedly coming along just for the dinner.[49] Clelia and Betta were arrested near S. Andrea delle Fratte with two young men, one of whom was a seventeen-year-old courtier armed but with a licence for his sword. One of the youths, Alberto, claimed that the women had called on him, asking him to escort them through the streets to Cardinal Alessandrino's palace. 'She begged me to go, as she wanted to go to dinner in Cardinal Alessandrino's palace and

---

43 ASR, TCG, Costituti vol. 520, c74v, Julia di Rossi Ferrarese, 26 September 1602.
44 ASR, TCG, Costituti vol. 520, c126v, Madalena Perugina, 3 October 1602.
45 ASR, TCG, Costituti vol. 520, c17v, Martia Pollastrella de Cavignano, 3 September 1602.
46 See John Woodhouse, 'La Cortegiania di Niccolo Strozzi', *Studi Secenteschi* 23 (1982), 141–93, 184.
47 Delumeau, *Vie économique et sociale*, 277–8.
48 See Woodhouse, '*La Cortegiania*', 184.
49 ASR, TCG, Costituti, vol. 448, c124r, Aquilina filia Clementis da Todi, 13 December 1605.

told me that they were going to give her the key to a room.'[50] A nobleman or a highly placed ecclesiastic would not have been seen walking about the streets with a courtesan, and Alberto may have been sent to escort Betta and Clelia to the palace. Women who had assignations with gentlemen and dignitaries behind the palace walls may often have stayed there for some days, affording themselves cover from the law, as occurred when Giulia from Lubriano was accompanied some thirty kilometres to Narni in order to have sex with the Governor of the city. Once in Narni she was lodged with one of his employees and then escorted into the palace when called for. She stayed there for several days at a time before being taken back out to await the next 'summons'.[51]

'I HAD BEEN TO MASS'

With increasing frequency after about 1610 prostitutes and courtesans picked up by the *birri* asserted that they had been out in the streets because they were coming from or going to Mass. Truthful or not, this certainly shows an awareness that going to church was regarded as the one laudable reason a woman could offer for going outside the house alone. However, courtesans preferred to attend Mass suspiciously early in the morning, which presumably explains the court's interest in their movements. Maddalena Fiorentina, asked to recall her movements on a specific day, described how 'That morning I was coming from the church of the Trinità, where I had gone to early Mass, as I usually do, because I always go there at 4 a.m.'[52] Dianora Lupi Romana wasn't quite such an early riser. She was arrested near the Madonna dei Monti and said she had been to Araceli for Mass with her mother at about 5 or 6 a.m.[53] Another woman, Domenica, defended her choice of timing defiantly.

I was arrested this morning at 6 a.m. more or less in the Strada della Croce, since I wanted to go to Mass in S. Carlo del Corso where I usually go to Mass every morning . . . it was 6 a.m., and I can see that it is no longer night time then, because it is morning.[54]

[50] ASR, TCG, Costituti, vol. 508, c198r–199r, Clelia Michaelis Guelfi Romana, Alberto Ferrarese and Betta Francesco de Castiglione Florentina, 7 January 1602.

[51] ASR, TCG, Processi, sec. XVII, vol. 63, c17v–23r, Giulia Uxor Horatio Petri di Lubriano, 9 March 1607.

[52] TCG, Processi, sec. XVII vol. 46, 764v–769r, Maddalena Santini Fiorentina, 23 May 1605. She says at six hours, which, if the sun set at around 10 p.m. would have been 4 a.m.

[53] ASR, TCG, Costituti, vol. 715, c31, Dianora Lupi Romana, 25 November 1623.

[54] ASR, TCG, Costituti, vol. 715, c32, Domenca Mognicini, 25 November 1623.

Julia Vimentis claimed that she was returning from the Madonna dei Monti where she went to Mass every Thursday, 'and I was going by night because I don't like going by day'.[55] Even without their preference for attending church at irregular hours, it is easy to dismiss their claims not only as false, but as an attempt to portray themselves as 'honest' courtesans in the hope that they would be treated differently by the court. However, we ought not to be excessively sceptical for it is interesting that they do not mention either of the churches which they were obliged to attend (San Rocco or San Ambrogio), or their parish churches. They favoured churches and chapels scattered about the city, a fact echoed in their wills. Many courtesans left pious legacies to far-flung churches and religious houses, suggesting that they were familiar with and had a particular affinity for these establishments.[56]

GARDENS, VINEYARDS, THEATRES AND OTHER AMUSEMENTS

Parties and picnics were often held in the gardens and vineyards around the city. Some were elegant *conviti* attended by ambassadors, noblemen and, inevitably, elite courtesans.[57] Carpets were put down on the rough ground, banquets laid on and music was provided for dancing. In 1566 Cardinal Alessandrino had to be forbidden from leaving the palace because he 'went too often to the vineyards and . . . this life appeared too licentious'.[58] Forty years later the famous courtesan Domenica Calvi was arrested after a great banquet held by the Marchese Peretti, in the garden of the Medici at which several cardinals were present.[59] In 1624 a coachman described how he had delivered Angela Tropetti to a party in a vineyard, and later collected her.[60] These were not necessarily exclusive events, however, as we learn from a report made in late October 1600, when the *birri* were informed 'That there was a party for craftsmen in a vineyard near San Giovanni, and that

[55] ASR, TCG, Costituti, vol. 715, c155r, Julia Vimentis Romana, 1 February 1624.
[56] From my examination of fifty wills drawn up by courtesans, 66 per cent of them left pious bequests in their will, and 40 per cent left a second pious legacy, whilst 14 per cent named a church or religious foundation as their heir.
[57] Riccardo Bassani and Fiora Bellini, *Caravaggio assassino: la carriera di un 'valenthuomo' fazioso nella Roma della Controriforma* (Rome: Donzelli, 1994), 127–8. Although questions have been raised about the accuracy of the scholarship in this book, it conveys an extraordinary sense of place and atmosphere.
[58] BAV, Cod. Urb. Lat., vol. 1040, c245v, 22 June 1566.
[59] ASR, RB, Vol. 6, Menica di Francesco di Siena, 9 August 1601.
[60] ASR, TCG, Costituti, vol. 716, c203–4, Michael Joannis Teutonius Cocchiere, 3 May 1624.

although most of them were married, they were with whores and having eaten together they were making an uproar in the vineyards'.[61]

Plays were also a popular destination for men and courtesans seeking entertainment. According to an *avviso* dated 23 January 1593 the 'theatre' season in Rome had just opened 'in public' in a place called Il Carbone in Strada Giulia.[62] The entrance cost was a minimum of one *giulio*, a price which had been determined in order to 'prevent rowdiness', and a large part of the proceeds were to go to the upkeep of pious buildings. Despite this, a few days later an *avviso* reported that 'To the great displeasure of the whole court plays have been prohibited by the Pope and it is believed that next we won't have masques, nor the diversion of races, but only certain tragedies and spiritual representations which will be put on by the fathers of the *Chiesa Nuova*.'[63] This disruption to what was evidently one of the high-spots of the Roman social calendar, and the attempt to substitute comedies with moralising dramas acted out by the enthusiastic priests, did not pass uncontested. Plays were defended as 'pastimes traditionally used by the Roman people for their enjoyment and consolation' and accordingly some 'illustrious gentlemen' went to complain to the Pope to ask that the ban on public comedies be lifted.[64] The Pope relented, giving permission for comedies, but only in the houses of certain noble families.[65] Shortly afterwards the gentlemen Conservatori of Rome were also permitted to hold a great party in the Campidoglio, with a play and various games at which 'a great many Romans and gentlewomen were present'.[66]

A few chance arrests show that courtesans mingled with the rest of Roman high society behind the walls of these palaces. One evening as the police corporal and his men made their rounds they came across a carriage in which a number of gentlemen and four '*donne cortigiane*' were travelling. They were 'returning from a play which had been put on in the house of the Marquis of Pallavicino at San Giovanni dei Fiorentini'.[67] The corporal duly arrested them, and carried on his way through the streets to Via del Corso. When he reached the church of Sant'Ambrogio he came across another coach, also carrying three courtesans, Giacoma Rena and her daughters Giulia and Margarita, accompanied by two gentlemen. As he noted, 'they

---

[61] ASR, TCG, RB, vol. 100, c268r–v, 29 October 1600.
[62] BAV, Cod. Urb. Lat., vol. 1061, c46, 23 January 1593.
[63] BAV, Cod. Urb. Lat., vol. 1061, c53, 27 January 1593.
[64] BAV, Cod. Urb. Lat., vol. 1061, c58, 30 January 1593.
[65] Ibid.   [66] BAV, Col. Urb. Lat., vol. 1061, c97, 17 February 1593.
[67] ASR, TCG, RB, vol. 101, c27r, 12 February 1601.

too were coming back from the same play'.[68] Lower-status Romans and their prostitutes attended plays in less glamorous surroundings, as was discovered one evening in May 1603 when the corporal heard that a play was being staged in a barn near 'la Consolazione'. 'Having gone along with my company, I found that they were performing the play, so I arrested all the actors, whose names are below, and also some women who are assumed to be of ill repute.'[69]

'WE HEARD THAT THERE WAS A CARRIAGE FULL OF WHORES'[70]

Carriages were an increasingly important status symbol in late sixteenth- and seventeenth-century Rome. When Montaigne visited Rome in the 1580s he commented that respectable people travelled only by carriage, never by horse, which was suitable only for the more humble, or for young men.[71] Nobles vied to acquire as many ornate carriages as they could afford and then show them off by having them driven through the streets, emblazoned with the family arms, by coachmen in their livery. The ambassador of France, for example, drew up to a papal audience with 131 carriages in the mid-seventeenth century.[72] By 1594 there were 883 carriages in the city, approximately one per thousand inhabitants, and travelling in one could be a highly public act.[73] When Angela Adami Troppetti from Rome was arrested, far from being driven to a discreet assignation, she was on a family outing in her client's coach: 'I was out for a drive (*a spasso*) with my mother, one of my sisters, the servant and two of my brothers.' The drive had evidently been a long one, since they lived at Santa Maria in Via and had been to Santa Croce in Gerusalemme before returning to see a procession in Piazza del Popolo, where they were arrested. Her client's coach enabled Angela to participate in this fashionable pursuit, driving around ostentatiously *a spasso* – out 'doing nothing' in a coach[74] – and it also signalled the quality of her clientele, and hence her own place in the social

---

[68] Ibid. This is probably the same Margarita Rena mentioned in chapter 7 in a case from 1613.

[69] ASR, TCG, RB, vol. 102, c34r, Silvia de Santi da Celasso, 4 May 1603.

[70] ASR, TCG, RB, vol. 100, c273r–v, 29 August 1600.

[71] Michel de Montaigne, *The Diary of Montaigne's Journey to Italy in 1580 and 1581*, ed. and trans. by E. J. Trechmann (London: Hogarth Press, London, 1929), 156.

[72] Ignazio Ciampi, 'Un periodo di cultura in Roma nel secolo XVII', *ARSRSP* 1:13 (1877), 257–389, 393–458.

[73] Wolfgang Lotz, 'Gli 883 cocchi della Roma del 1594', *ARSRSP* 23 (1973), (1877), 247–66, 248.

[74] ASR, TCG, Costituti, vol. 716, c204v–206v, 3 May 1624. The coachman calls her 'a small whore'. Ibid., c203–4, Michael Joannis Teutonius.

hierarchy. Men may also have loaned their coaches to their courtesans for the purposes of displaying them, but it was a practical way for a member of the elite to have a courtesan brought to his apartments: it would have been unthinkable for her to traipse through the streets in her finery, exposing her to the risks of being attacked, robbed or simply picked up by the police.

The preference for carriages had been combated through ordinances since the 1560s, and in 1588 the punishment established was a fine and the loss of the jewels and clothing being worn by the woman at the time of her arrest.[75] However, police records do not give the impression that this transgression was pursued with great zeal. As a result courtesans and their clients took a very relaxed attitude towards the prohibition. One night two men 'and two whores' were travelling by coach and on passing by the corporal of the *birri*, they simply greeted him amicably and carried on their way, passing right in front of the prison of Tor di Nona. The *birro* evidently took umbrage at their lack of respect, followed them and stopped the coach at the prison, upon which he arrested the men and one of the women, although the other prostitute managed to escape.[76] In the ten years studied, only fifteen courtesans were noted as having been arrested on this count, all during the Jubilee of 1600–1 when policing was stepped up. Yet this can have borne no relation to the number of women out riding illegally in carriages. A single courtesan, Angela Adami Tropetti, estimated that she had been out in her Spanish client's carriage about 'twelve or thirteen times' in the one or two months since she had met him, and several times in that of another of her clients.[77]

Stopping a carriage belonging to a nobleman to inspect its passengers presented innumerable difficulties to the *birri*.[78] The noblemen not only refused to bow down to the authority of the Governor and his policemen, but considered it extremely humiliating to have to do so, considering it their prerogative to behave as they wished. This presumably explains why the *birri* did it so rarely. Two accounts from the 1630s illustrate the kinds of problems they faced. The first took place in the summer of 1635 when 'the Governor heard that *cortegiane* were being taken about the city at night with extraordinary licence'. Going to see for himself he found that the police

---

[75] ASR, Armadio IV, tomo 60, c212, 16 October 1588.
[76] ASR, TCG, RB, vol. 104, c162, Camilla Grassi da Modena, 16 July 1611.
[77] ASR, TCG, Costituti, vol. 716, c204v–206v, 3 May 1624.
[78] Successive papacies struggled to subdue the Roman barons, who opposed the authority of the Governor and his *birri* at every opportunity. See Polverini Fosi, *La società violenta* and Blastenbrei, 'La quadratura del cerchio'.

were doing nothing, so he warned the corporal responsible that 'if he didn't catch some women that evening he would be stripped of his office'. That night three courtesans were imprisoned, whipped and exiled 'to terrorise the others'. Fired with enthusiasm for his new task the following night the corporal found the Count Giulio della Massa with a woman. He arrested her and, despite the fact that the Governor was in bed, took her directly to him. This time the corporal had overstepped his brief. The Governor ordered her immediate release but it was too late. The count had been seriously offended, the Governor was warned of his ire, and a long letter of apology was duly sent and published in the *avvisi*. It was still not enough, and finally the Governor had to go and apologise in person.[79]

Two years later, during the *Carnevale* of 1637, the Governor was once again exasperated by courtesans: particularly their routine flouting of the laws forbidding them to ride in carriages and from wearing disguises.[80] On 18 February the *birri* therefore stopped a hired carriage in which Checca Buffona, *cortigiana scandalosa*, was travelling dressed as a man. She was accompanied by Scipione Gonzaga, ambassador to the Holy Roman Empire. Checca was arrested and imprisoned, at which Gonzaga complained to the Bargello. Annoyed at this interference, the Bargello told his superior, the Governor of Rome, who in turn spoke with the 'Cardinal Padrone', Francesco Barberini.[81] Gonzaga asked for Checca's release, on the grounds that she had been unfairly singled out for arrest. The Governor replied that an example had to be made, and Checca had broken the law on two counts: she had been riding in a carriage, *and* was dressed as a man. The ambassador retorted that it would damage 'his reputation and his office', at which the Governor pointed out that the arrest had been made very carefully: 'Because the woman was not travelling in his name, nor was she in his carriage, nor had they been able to tell that it was driven by his men, so his Excellency was in no way offended.'[82] When the Pope confirmed that Checca should be whipped as a punishment, the ambassador sought help from the Cardinal of Savoy, protector of the Holy Roman Empire at court. He then sent letters to Vienna, raising the stakes considerably. A

---

[79] BAV, Codice Corsini, 34.E.10. c1ov, *Racconto delle cose più considerabili che sono occorse nel governo di Roma in tempo di mons. Giov. Battista Spada*, 18 January 1635.

[80] The following account has been summarised partly from the version reported in BAV, Codice Barberiniani Latini (Barb. Lat.), 4975, c49v–52, and also from a discussion of this incident in an article by Ermete Rossi, 'Un curioso incidente diplomatico tra Vienna e Roma', *ARSRSP* 60 (1937), 243–55.

[81] This would be a young nephew or grandson of the Pope, elevated to the position of chief cardinal, vice-chancellor and secretary of state.

[82] Ibid.

spokesman for Emperor Ferdinand III described his shock at 'the damage done to the reputation of the gentlemen of our ambassador', warning that he hoped that this incident would not bring about a more definitive rupture. The dispute dragged on for some time. The ambassador was not given the satisfaction he hoped for, but despite his complaints to Vienna, little more happened. Checca was then released from prison, exiled and given fourteen days to leave the city for good. However, if she did leave, she was soon back. The next year she appeared on the streets similarly masked, but this time accompanied by the Spanish ambassador.

According to sources used, we receive very different impressions about the relative success or failure of the city's police to discipline prostitution and all those aspects of city life which pertained to it. On the one hand, the *avvisi* convey the savage punishments meted out to the men and women who were caught transgressing the new laws: prostitutes publicly whipped and humiliated; a man with his nose cut off and eyes gouged out for prostituting his wife.[83] These exemplary measures, one imagines, must have instilled terror in the hearts of many. Yet other sources, such as the *Relazioni dei Birri* or the descriptions given in court-room depositions, suggest that notwithstanding the occasional ferocity of the authorities, prostitutes and their clients continued about their daily business, frequently breaking the law, with nonchalance. The *luoghi* appear to have been teeming with life by day and by night: prostitutes drank in taverns, sat on their doorsteps drying their hair and enticing customers; courtesans perambulated about the city in forbidden coaches, calmly going to visit a religious procession, out for a drive with the family or on their way to join other revellers in the vineyards. Rather than privilege either of these views, it seems best to assume their co-existence. Men and women knew of the possible consequences of transgressing the ordinances, but given the randomness of punishments, hoped that nothing would come of it. Some also presumably calculated their chances not only of arrest, but of offering a bribe, or simply of paying their way out of prison, since as we will see in chapter 7, there was always the chance of being granted bail.

The task facing the Governor of Rome and his eighty-odd *birri* was immense. On the one hand, there was the quest to discipline prostitution and impose greater public order on the city, with laws directed largely at the lower-status prostitutes and their clients. But huge numbers of men, many armed, drifted continuously into the city. They were pushed by famine, or

---

[83] BAV, Barb. Lat., 4592, c64, 26 March 1592.

the search for work, or were washed up in the aftermath of the numerous wars and battles which lacerated Europe throughout the late sixteenth and seventeenth centuries. They inevitably socialised with one another in the company of prostitutes, and violence frequently broke out. It would take more than a few score policemen to control so many men and women, and more than a few decades to eradicate such well-entrenched practices.

Meanwhile, men of the elite were able systematically to protect their courtesans from the legislation aimed at eroding their privileges, by means of licences, exemptions and immunities, over and above the fact of their crude social dominance. Like their early sixteenth-century predecessors, courtesans in post-Tridentine Rome were frequented by cardinals, by intellectuals, the nobility and the gentry. They attended the theatre, they had one or more servants, they often lived outside the areas controlled by the police and they travelled ostentatiously about the city in borrowed carriages. Indeed, far from dying out, the kind of sociability once associated purely with the *honest courtesan* and men of the elite appears to have infiltrated the social practices of men lower down the social spectrum. In Baroque Rome it was not just high-ranking nobles and cardinals who gathered round courtesans for music and dancing, but the young men sent to Rome as courtiers and students and even artisans. For more thorough reforms of prostitution to succeed, a complete change in social attitudes was necessary, which would take away the status associated with courtesans, making it no longer respectable and acceptable for elite men to frequent prostitutes publicly. Although the negative connotations associated with more intensive policing would contribute towards this, ultimately this was a task for priests, preachers and moralising pamphlets.

CHAPTER 5

A profile of Roman prostitutes

One of the reforms brought about by the Council of Trent was the require-ment that parish priests keep records of the moral state of their parishioners. This was achieved by the keeping of registers, known as the *Stati delle Anime*. They were compiled annually at Easter by the priest and his assistants who undertook a door-to-door survey of households, noting the names, ages, professions and moral 'status' of all those living in the parish. This was par-ticularly intended to pick out those who were prostitutes, concubines and any others who should not take or had not taken communion. According to these records, the number of prostitutes living in Rome in the first half of the seventeenth century oscillated between 604 and 1,200: in 1600 this meant that for every hundred adult women there were 2.5 prostitutes. This is undoubtedly an underestimation of the actual numbers of women who prostituted themselves, and not only because of the inevitable loss of some of the parish registers.[1] Despite the apparent care taken on the part of the priests to note the presence of prostitutes, and although this was a 'face-to-face' society, working people moved frequently. The city's population varied enormously from year to year, decimated by floods, famine and disease, or augmented by the arrival of pilgrims and those fleeing from poverty and famine elsewhere: between 1599 and 1600 (Holy Year), it increased by as much as 19,000, to 109,000, and by 1604 it had dropped to 99,000, before rising again.[2] More importantly, many women did not view occasional acts of prostitution as providing their main source of income. It was just one of a panoply of expedients taken in order to feed themselves and their chil-dren on an occasional or part-time basis. Such women may not have been

---

[1] Many parishes never kept continuous and complete registers, especially prior to 1650, while others have been lost. See Eugenio Sonnino, 'Gli Stati delle Anime a Roma nella prima metà del secolo XVII: entità e qualità delle registrazioni', in Sbrana et al., *Gli Stati delle Anime a Roma*, 19–39, 22, 25. Schiavoni and Sonnino, 'Aspects généraux de l'évolution démographique à Rome'.
[2] Schiavoni and Sonnino, 'Aspects généraux de l'évolution démographique à Rome', 98.

considered by their neighbours as prostitutes, or have been noted in the parish records as such.

IDENTIFYING PROSTITUTES: COMPLICATING THE CATEGORIES

The very fact that women known to live from prostitution were specifically identified in the parish records is a reminder of the importance attached to the distinction between two opposing forms of womanhood – the honest and the dishonest – in early modern society. The rhetorical and institutional classification of women into one of these two groups was certainly aimed at by contemporary authorities. One of the key terms used in definitions of the prostitute during this period was that she was a 'public' woman. Such was the stress on the essentially 'public' nature of prostitution that the definition of which women were to be called *meretrici* often lay with the community: a prostitute was a woman considered to be so by a certain number of witnesses, or by public reputation – *voce pubblica*.[3] As Ferrante has pointed out, in medieval canon law prostitution was qualified principally by the multiplicity of partners and not by its venality.[4]

To be a 'public' prostitute, however, in the sense of working openly rather than illicitly, was not always seen in a negative light. As has recently been shown, in mid-seventeenth-century Rome two forms of prostitute were legally recognised. Firstly there were those who were publicly recognised as practising the profession, termed the *meretrices honestae*, or 'honest prostitutes'.[5] These women were allowed to reside and own property in the city, were able to dispose of their goods and make a valid will, provided they paid the annual tribute to the Corte Savella and left a fifth of their estate to the monastery of the Convertite. The 'dishonest' prostitutes were the part-timers, those who prostituted themselves secretly or occasionally. These women could be chased from their homes if neighbours complained, had no rights over their property and would have their entire patrimony requisitioned by the Monastery of the Convertite on their death.[6] This intolerance and persecution of the 'secret' prostitute reflects a powerful

---

[3] In Bologna in the sixteenth century five witnesses were called on, although later this was reduced to three. Canosa and Colonnello, *Storia della prostituzione*, 76. Camerano cites a Roman jurist named Gualtieri, who states the same general principle. 'Donne oneste o meretrici?', 643.

[4] Ferrante, 'Il valore del corpo', 213.

[5] Camerano, 'Donne oneste o meretrici?', 638. The legal position of prostitutes is clarified in Scanaroli, *De visitatione carceratorum*.

[6] Camerano, 'Donne oneste o meretrici?', 637–8.

social anxiety: a need to distinguish clearly between types of women, and so to identify and hence regulate what women were doing.

In daily life the borders between these two states of womanhood do not seem to have been as clearly demarcated as didactic, moralising and institutional literature would suggest. On the one hand, a great many women appear to have preferred to operate as clandestine prostitutes, despite the legal and economic sanctions this might bring.[7] On the other hand, neither honesty nor dishonesty was an irreversible state, and there were legitimate routes through which dishonest women could make the transition back to honesty, through monachisation or marriage.[8] Also, although didactic and legislative sources give us a clear idea of the ways in which patriarchal society sought to define and identify women's bodies, they give us limited insight into whether such clear-cut divisions were accepted in practice. Camerano has found evidence of the difficult decisions facing the many women who had prostituted themselves long ago, or on an occasional basis, when they came to drawing up their wills. She suggests that they were clearly unsure whether to describe themselves as prostitutes, and enjoy the freedom to dispose of their goods as they wished, or whether to reject this identity, thereby risking confiscation of everything they had on their deaths. As a result in their wills many denied, modified or explained their interpretation of the title of *meretrice*.[9] Here I shall use court-room testimonies to explore how women interpreted concepts of honesty and dishonesty in the context of their daily lives, and the extent to which these taxonomies of sin, dishonesty and shame were accepted or rejected by women who prostituted themselves.

Julia Silvestri Caponarij from Velletri was a married woman whose husband was a cowherd. She was arrested one night in September 1605, three hours after the curfew, in the home of a Spanish gentleman, a doctor in canon law and gentleman to a cardinal. The next day in court, questioned as to what she had been doing at the time of her arrest, she initially tried to present her activities as entirely honourable. She had merely gone there, she said, to pick up the washing, 'as I live honestly. I do his washing and

---

[7] See Camerano's thorough discussion of the ways in which women approached this problem when it came to making a will: ibid., 642–6.

[8] One of the principal ways was by entering one of the convents specifically set up for former prostitutes, the Convertite. See Sherrill Cohen's *The Evolution of Women's Asylums since 1500: From Refuges for Ex-Prostitutes to Shelters for Battered Women* (New York: Oxford University Press, 1992), 50–1. Marriage was another way out of prostitution. In Rome male prisoners were offered an amnesty if they promised to marry a prostitute, whilst the Pope sometimes promised amnesties to married prostitutes if they returned to their husbands.

[9] Camerano, 'Donne oneste o meretrici?', 638–9.

I do his cooking and he pays me one *scudo* a month, five *giulii* from him and five from a certain Pietro who I believe is Spanish who eats there but sleeps elsewhere'.[10] Asked, as all those who appeared before the court were, how she earned her living, she then asserted, 'I sew, I spin, I wash: I do what other women do.'[11] Clearly not convinced by her protestations the court pressed her further about why she had gone to the Spaniard's house and she soon admitted what the court evidently already suspected. 'I will tell the truth. Yesterday evening I had gone to that Spaniard's room to sleep with him, and then the *birri* came, and I had already slept with him previously.'[12]

The fact that Julia tried to cover up her activities is hardly surprising. As a married woman, adulteress and an 'occasional' prostitute, her case would have been pursued with some zeal by the police. Yet one supposes that she wouldn't even have tried to argue that she was collecting his washing unless she had had her washing basket there as an 'alibi'. Probably Julia did make an 'honest living' from some women's work, but supplemented her income with commercial sex. Her story illuminates the pitiful sums of money involved in honest women's work, one *scudo* a month for doing one gentleman's washing, though presumably she could have washed for several others. It also reveals the ease with which working women came into contact with men, as they not only went to men's homes to pick up and return laundry, but also habitually spent time on the premises, engaged in domestic tasks such as cleaning and cooking.

Many other women made no secret of their sexual activities when interrogated, simply linking them to their other 'legitimate' ones without acknowledging the ostensible 'clash' in values. Margarita Angeli di Santis was a widow. When asked what she did for a living she replied: 'I spin, sew, and occasionally get laid . . . and I am pregnant too.'[13] Isabella Gaudena explained, 'I get laid sometimes because my husband can't support me.'[14] Santa Mancina told the court that she had 'a husband in Chieti but I haven't heard from him for twelve years and it is because of that that I sometimes get laid'.[15] The English term 'get laid' seems the best translation of an expression commonly used in these sources: '*faccio qualche scappata*'. It conveys the notion of something swift and also of a minor transgression, in the sense of an escapade or prank. The context makes it clear that there was financial remuneration involved. However, their choice of this term

---

[10] ASR, TGG, Costituti, vol. 555, c71r–76v: 71v, 9 September 1605.
[11] Ibid., c72r.   [12] Ibid., c73r.   [13] ASR, TCG, Costituti, vol. 550, c94r, 20 May 1605.
[14] ASR, TCG, Costituti, vol. 448, c200r, 22 February 1605.
[15] ASR, TCG, Costituti, vol. 523, c49v, 25 November 1602.

was surely not entirely casual, since it seems to be used to downplay the significance of their sexual commerce, defusing the moralistic connotations of prostitution by placing it in the context of their other, perfectly honest occupations.

Studies of normative sources dealing with prostitution lead us to the assumption that the distinction between honesty and dishonesty was so clear cut that any woman who had sex for money in this period would automatically have seen herself as a prostitute, or understood her activities as 'prostitution'. Yet the criminal records suggest otherwise. These women, in court, implicitly or explicitly rejected the identity of the prostitute/ courtesan on the grounds that they had sex just occasionally, had one or very few partners, or that it was not their main source of income. Although the Counter-Reformation was in full swing, such attitudes can probably be explained with reference to lingering medieval conceptions of marriage, concubinage and prostitution; for the medieval church the defining characteristic of prostitution was not the venality of the relationship, but promiscuity. Accordingly, women who lived as concubines had traditionally been less severely judged than were prostitutes.[16] This attitude presumably lingered on in the tolerance accorded the 'honest courtesan' who took few clients (discreetly), as opposed to the public *meretrici* who took clients indiscriminately. It is certainly referred to in some testimonies.

Dianora Lupi Romana, a widow, was arrested with her mother after the curfew one evening in November 1623. She had been arrested by the police on the grounds that as a courtesan she was not allowed to move about the city after the curfew. Although Dianora made no attempt to hide the fact that she engaged in the occasional *scappata* with gentlemen, she claimed ignorance of the laws regarding courtesans, arguing that 'I do not consider myself to be a public courtesan but I just have occasional sex with a few gentlemen.'[17] Isabella Speranza Hispana was a cobbler's widow who made her living as a shoemaker in Campo Marzio. She also appeared to find no contradiction in her situation, asserting that she was an honest woman who worked and lived off her labour, but sometimes had a *scappata*. 'I don't have a husband, although I had one but he died six months ago, and I am an honest woman and work and live from my labour, and sometimes I get laid.'[18] Nor can we dismiss this distinction between the occasional *scappata* and full-time prostitution as merely one

---

[16] Ferrante, 'Il valore del corpo', 213.   [17] ASR, TCG, Costituti vol. 715, c31, 25 November 1623.
[18] ASR, TCG, Costituti, vol. 518, c187r, 11 August 1602.

which had suddenly been created in self-defence by women who were trying to maintain their dignity in court. The frequency with which the term *scappata* was used indicates that it was common currency amongst women. Indeed, the fact that it was regularly cited in court suggests that lawyers and judges also recognised this distinction between 'occasional' and 'professional' prostitutes, or at least that plaintiffs expected it to be taken into consideration. When Vincentia Sinna Romana was arrested for travelling in a carriage in September 1602 she argued that, although she was a courtesan, she was 'not the kind who takes one man one day, and another the next'. Indeed, she claimed exemption from the law on the grounds that 'I am not one of those who is forbidden to ride in a carriage, because I am in the employ of just one man only.'[19] She was explicitly differentiating herself from those women who took many clients, implying that she considered herself to be a cut above them. This was the same kind of distinction between prostitutes referred to in the *Lettera sulla tolleranza*, discussed in chapter 3.[20] This relaxed attitude towards discreet prostitutes, and the sense that there was a shared understanding about these distinctions, appears to contrast with the mid-seventeenth-century juridical view of 'secret' versus 'public' prostitutes, according to which the former were to be condemned. Whether this signals that attitudes had changed significantly by the later seventeenth century, or whether it is merely a demonstration of the extent to which juridical and normative concerns could be contradicted by common opinion or practice, would require further research.

The fact that women and men embraced relatively tolerant and subtle understandings of precisely what constituted 'professional' prostitution does not mean that they were ignorant of normative discourse or the attitudes of the authorities in such matters. Two women took a defiant stance before the court. Rather than making light of their recourse to occasional prostitution, they justified it in terms of their economic hardship, arguing that they had a choice between sin and starvation. Domitilla from Civita Castellana was interrogated in October 1602 because she had transgressed a court order not to have carnal relations with a certain Giobattista. She justified herself by saying that when the ban had been issued she had been married, and working as a laundry woman. Her husband had since died and she had been left with two small children to maintain, so she had no alternative but to prostitute herself. 'And having nothing to live on I was forced to turn to a wicked life and become a whore.'[21] Indeed, she went on

---

[19] ASR, TCG, Costituti, vol. 519, c113r, 3 December 1602.
[20] BAV, Cod. Vat. Lat., vol. 9729, Lettera sulla tolleranza delle meretrici in Roma.
[21] ASR, TCG, Costituti, vol. 520, c134r, 7 October 1602.

implicitly to challenge the court to condemn her for her choice, pointing out that, 'I am not obliged to obey the law since if I do I will die of hunger, and if I do not do this I cannot live.'[22] Magdalena Jacobi was arrested later that month in bed with a man named Paolo. She evidently suffered from what we would describe as a mental disorder and as a result had been abandoned by her husband some four years earlier. She made an impassioned outburst before the judge, challenging him to find fault with her actions. 'He left me when I was possessed by the spirits . . . I don't know if he is dead or alive, but I am possessed, and what do you expect me to live off if no one will take me into their homes because I am possessed? I have been possessed for seven years.'[23]

Another identity adopted in court by many women which flew in the face of Counter-Reformation sexual morality hinged on women's assertion that they were 'free women' and therefore there was nothing intrinsically wrong with their sexual activities. The term '*Donna Libera*' appears in the court records in the late sixteenth century, becoming increasingly common in the early seventeenth century, and was used to indicate the status of being single and unmarried. It was therefore not a term used exclusively by women who prostituted themselves. It was, however, a way in which 'unmarried women often expressed the idea of being able to dispose freely of their body, unlike married women'.[24] Thus Chiara Jacobi, arrested by night in 1628 and asked 'what her condition was and how she lived', replied: 'I, Sir, am a free woman, and sometimes I work and sometimes I am a *courtesan* according to what comes my way, and I live as best I can.'[25] This expression does seem to have connoted something over and above the mere fact of being unmarried and therefore judicially free of ties, for it was also used in a context in which the woman's unmarried status had already been established and was therefore not in question. When Magdalena de Chieti was called to testify, she first declared that she did not have a husband, and then added that she was a 'free woman', which would surely have been unnecessary if the phrase were merely another expression for celibacy. 'I don't have a husband but I am a poor courtesan and a free woman.'[26] *Donna Libera* was therefore being used by women to emphasise that *since* they were unmarried they were indeed 'free' to do as they chose, and that included the freedom to prostitute themselves. This is particularly evident in the deposition by Julia Vimentis: 'I am a widow, and have been for seven months since my husband died . . . now I am pregnant, and I don't know by whom, because I am two

[22] Ibid.   [23] ASR, TCG, Costituti, vol. 523, c54v, 28 October 1602.
[24] Ferrante, 'Il valore del corpo', 219.   [25] ASR, TCG, Costituti, vol. 721, c51, 13 January 1628.
[26] ASR, TCG, Costituti, vol. 716, 7 September 1624.

months pregnant and I have *amici* and I am a woman who is free with my own life and I do whatever I want to do.'[27]

This is not to suggest that all women rejected the terms or labels generally applied to women who prostitute themselves. When eighty-four women were asked in court to describe themselves and how they lived, half chose to describe themselves as a *cortigiana*, and perhaps not surprisingly, only twelve women chose to call themselves by the more derogatory terms of *puttana, meretrice, donna di malavita* or *donna di partito* (roughly translated into English as 'whore', 'prostitute', 'fallen woman' and 'on the game'). This does not mean that they were necessarily high-class prostitutes. The terms *puttana* and *meretrice* were essentially 'labelling judgements', conveying dishonour, misery and indiscriminate promiscuity. The term *cortigiana* had an 'evocative' power suggesting glamour and beauty, and was clearly a preferable identity.[28] Indeed, its use and meaning had shifted noticeably since the early sixteenth century, a process which had been noted by a contemporary commentator who complained that, 'Every starving whore I see from Piazza Padella calls herself a courtesan.'[29] He may not have been exaggerating wildly. In 1548 when a tax was levied on prostitutes who lived near the bridge Ponte Santa Maria to pay for its rebuilding, the four hundred women whose names were listed were described collectively as *cortigiane* and not as *meretrici*. This suggests that increasing numbers of prostitutes were appropriating the title *cortigiana* in order to be or acquire that which the term conveyed, and/or that Roman society had accepted this less derogatory appellative as a general term for prostitutes.

The process by which the term 'courtesan' gradually spread into common usage obviously resulted in a devaluation of the word. Documents show us that even by the 1560s it could no longer unambiguously signal distinction and differentiation as it had done fifty years earlier. Yet the actual distinctions between the women per se had remained, and therefore had to be conveyed through rather more elaborate means. By the 1570s legislators and commentators discriminated between different kinds of courtesan and prostitute according to 'the other qualities which distinguish them from the others'.[30] They were variously distinguished by how much they earned, and by their social visibility as 'principal courtesans' or 'the best courtesans' or

---

[27] ASR, TCG, Costituti, vol. 715, c155r, 1 February 1624.
[28] On stigma and labelling see Pierre Bourdieu, *Distinction: a Social Critique of the Judgement of Taste*, trans. Richard Nice (London and New York: Routledge and Kegan Paul, 1984) (first published as *La distinction: critique sociale du jugement* (Paris: Les Editions de Minuit, 1979), 475, 479.
[29] *Vocabolario degli accademici della Crusca*, 5th edn (Florence: Succ. Le Monnier (1905)), 116 under 'Cortigiana'.
[30] Lettera sulla tolleranza, c106r–v.

'the most famous, the richest, and the least dishonest'.[31] The 'better sort' of courtesans were also distinguished by the way in which they were treated by other people in the community. 'They earn themselves respect more than the others, and they win appreciation for themselves by living honourably', and crucially, 'they make sure they are better paid'.[32] As all these attempts to locate and differentiate between courtesans shows, the courtesan's place on the social hierarchy was a matter not purely of money, but of her behaviour, manners and '*habitus*'.[33] Having selected a 'label' these women also had a choice of verbs available to them. Some used the verb 'to be': 'I am a courtesan', 'I am a prostitute.' Others used expressions like 'I follow the life of a courtesan' or 'I live as a whore' or 'I work as a whore.'[34] We might also agree with Margherita Pelaja's argument that these different linguistic forms suggest that, in the first case, they are somehow implying that they 'are what they do', while in the second, they were distancing themselves as a person from the life they led.[35]

This leads us on to the question of whether women who prostituted themselves and accepted this definition of their activities had an awareness of themselves as having a 'collective' identity with other women engaged in similar sex-work, and as being in some way different from other women. When Antonia Segnoverde Palermitana appeared before the criminal court in October 1602 she was asked how she had lived since coming to Rome. To this she replied, 'I have done what *the other women* do.'[36] When asked for clarification Antonia explained that she had been 'kept' by a man and in turn had kept house for him and had been his lover, until recently when she had moved out into her own apartment and prostituted herself to other men.[37] Evidently when she declared that she did what 'the other women do', she was referring to women who prostituted themselves. Later, in her account of a meeting which had taken place between her former lover and two of her new clients, she uses the expression again. Her jilted ex-lover had challenged her clients by asking what they were doing with her. One of the men replied, 'We are merchants at Ripa . . . and we have come here to do that which one does in the house of *the other women*.'[38] Another courtesan

[31] As in the 1566 statute directed at those courtesans 'worth' more than two hundred *scudi*. BAV, Urb. Lat., vol. 1040, c314v–315r, 2 November 1566. And Lettera sulla tolleranza, c106r.

[32] Lettera sulla tolleranza, c106r.

[33] As used by Bourdieu in *Distinction*.

[34] 'Tengo vita da corteggiana', 'vivo da puttana', 'faccio la puttana'.

[35] Margherita Pelaja, 'Relazioni personali e vincoli di gruppo. Il lavoro delle donne nella Roma dell'ottocento', *Memoria* 30:3 (1990), 45–54.

[36] ASR, TCG, Processi, sec. XVII, vol. 23, c42v–49v: c42v, 8 October 1602 (italics added).

[37] Ibid., c43v.   [38] Ibid., c111v–113v: c112r, 16 October 1602.

also used the expression in her testimony, explaining the phrase for us by saying: 'I do what the others do, I am a courtesan.'[39]

Some women further clarified this sense of collective identity by locating themselves in terms of the places of prostitution (*i luoghi* or *il bordello*), as if the existence of a special living area in the city had become a constitutive part of the prostitute's identity. Some defined themselves in terms of their promiscuous sexuality. For example, when Antonia Menici Piedmontese was asked who the father of her child was, she replied: 'I . . . don't know who the father is because *we others* who live in the *luoghi*, sometimes we have sex with one and sometimes with another.'[40] Maddalena Santini Fiorentina stated, 'You know how things are for *us other women*, one leaves today, another comes tomorrow.'[41] Livia de Blanchus said simply, 'I am a courtesan and I live in *i luoghi* and I am a poor woman.'[42] Domitilla di Civitacastellana explained that after her husband's death she had gone to live '*in bordello*'.[43] Giulia Crista said that she initially had worked as a servant but had ended up '*in bordello*'.[44] In both cases this term seemed to speak for itself.

Women therefore employed a variety of expressions in order to confirm, qualify or deny the normative or legal identities which were applied to them by *birri*, lawyers, churchmen and by their clients. We have also seen how in many cases the identities which they claimed for themselves bear little relation to what we know and understand of early modern concepts of womanhood. Many women implicitly rejected the idea that occasional acts of commercial sexuality marked them out as being prostitutes, or that this could undermine their claim to 'living honestly'. Others might accept the stigmatised identity of prostitute but distance themselves from the moral questions attached to their behaviour, asserting that it was simply a question of economics. Others expressed a sense of their 'otherness', in terms both of their activities and of where they lived. Yet one of the most powerful things to emerge from their testimonies is just how fine the line was between honesty and dishonesty, and that women saw little to distinguish between the two, especially those who had been living an 'honest' life until economic or marital crises had precipitated them into prostitution. Indeed, most of these testimonies remind us above all of the broken relationships which

---

[39] ASR, Sforza Cesarini (SFZ), II, S1, Giu. Ovale, V498, cnn., 2 September 1605.
[40] ASR, TCG, Costituti, vol. 523, c85r, 21 December 1602.
[41] ASR, TCG, Processi, sec. XVII, vol. 46, c718r–719v: c718r, 6 May 1605.
[42] ASR, TCG, Costituti, vol. 523, c63v, 2 December 1602.
[43] ASR, TCG, Costituti, vol. 520, c124r, 7 October 1602.
[44] ASR, TCG, Costituti, vol. 450, c15r, 21 October 1594.

led women from 'honesty' into prostitution. Prostitution offered them the hope of earning their living, as other forms of work evidently did not. In some cases it appears as though having to be self-supporting was considered to be virtually synonymous with prostitution.

PLACES OF ORIGIN

Numerous studies have observed that prostitutes were often outsiders to the communities in which they worked. This was also true for Rome, suggesting that many of them were likely to be economically vulnerable and lacking the kind of support networks which were so vital to survival in early modern cities. An analysis can be made of the origins of prostitutes from their place-name surnames. Of 1,577 prostitutes living in Rome between 1590 and 1630 (whether recorded in parish records, criminal archives or notarial records), 25 per cent failed to state a place-name surname.[45] It has been persuasively argued that such people would have been considered to be functionally Roman, perhaps from the near hinterland.[46] To these can be added the 12 per cent who were described as Roman, making a total of 37 per cent of prostitutes who were actually or functionally Roman. The remaining 63 per cent were then evidently first- or second-generation migrants, largely from the Papal States (29 per cent) or from other, mostly northern states in the Italian peninsula (27 per cent); 7 per cent were from abroad. (For a detailed breakdown of their origins see Table A1 and Map 2 in the appendix.)

From place-name surnames alone we cannot tell whether these women had migrated to Rome or had been born in Rome to immigrant parents. However, the fact that they used a place-name surname suggests a strong tie with this place, whether it was their or their parent's place of origin, perhaps because of other people's perceptions of them. Places of origin would have been signalled aurally and visually by people's accents, dialects and clothing, as well as through their social networks, which were often with people from their home town or country. It is also important to note that, in contrast to assumptions that prostitutes necessarily had a weak sense of identity, 54 per cent of the women in the early seventeenth-century sample and

---

[45] The registers used are those covering Campo Marzio, Santa Maria del Popolo, San Lorenzo in Lucina and Sant'Andrea delle Fratte, and two of those on its fringes: Santa Maria in Via and Santissimi Dodici Apostoli. The years consulted range from 1600 to 1621. See Appendix 2 for the list of parishes and registers consulted.

[46] Lee interprets the absence of a place name as indicating that a person considered themselves, or was considered by others, to be Roman 'in a loose and functional sense', and thus felt no need to add anything to their name. Lee, 'Foreigners in Quattrocento Rome', 140.

81 per cent of those in a 1656 sample gave three names, suggesting a very strong sense of family and geographical identity. In approximately 9 per cent of cases prostitutes gave two different places of origin in their names, presumably those of both their father and mother (for example, Giovanna Ferrante Romano Napolitana), and in eighty-three cases, the woman's second and third names were those of her mother rather than of her father, such as Amabilia Lucrezia Antognetti Romana.

By the last decades of the sixteenth century travelling to Rome was a well-organised affair, with three main routes into the city, two from the north and one from the south.[47] People could travel along these in organised groups either under the protection of the '*Procaccio*', or by renting horses and travelling '*a vettura*'.[48] The former was a kind of armed guide who accompanied and guarded 'caravans' of mules and horses carrying merchandise, the post and travellers with their baggage.[49] The latter was cheaper and slower and could travel along routes other than the 'post routes'. By 1600 there were weekly departures of the *Procaccio* between Rome and the major Italian cities, such as Venice, Florence and Naples, with more frequent trips to Bologna, and Delumeau estimates that the journeys took less than a week.[50] For those who could afford it the hazards of lonely travel were reduced, although one would nonetheless still have been exposed to the dangers of attacks from bandits. According to a contemporary observer the *Procaccio* also helped travellers deal with the fears and difficulties they encountered on their journey, especially by helping with language problems, and making sure they were well treated.[51] At least one courtesan profited from the *Procaccio*'s connections on her arrival. This was Antonia Segnoverde Palermitana, who arrived from Naples in about 1597. She had travelled with her sister-in-law and her son and took lodgings on her arrival with a woman at the Porta di Napoli, presumably where the Via Latina from Naples entered the city walls.[52] Within a short time she was frequently seen at the *Procaccio*'s house, perhaps prostituting herself to him, or using him to make contacts in the city. Not long afterwards the Bargello of Rome, Captain Valerio, chief of the Governor's police force, called upon

---

[47] The main route from the north was via Bologna, Scarperia, Florence, Siena and Viterbo. Romani, *Pellegrini e viaggiatori*, 1–4.

[48] Armando Serra, 'Viaggiatori e servizi di posta o a vettura nel bacino tiberino preferroviario', in Enzo Mattesini, ed., *Vie di pellegrinaggio medievale attraverso l'alta valle del Tevere* (Città di Castello: Petruzzi Editore, 1998), 152–91, 152.

[49] Delumeau, *Vie économique et sociale*, 40–65.   [50] Ibid.

[51] O. Codogno, *Compendio delle poste* (Milan: Cuavanni Battista Bidelli, 1623), 98–102, cited in John Day, 'Strade e vie di comunicazione', in *Storia d'Italia*, vol. V, *I Documenti*, (I), eds., Ruggiero Romano and Corrado Vivanti (Turin: Einaudi, 1973), 89–116, 89.

[52] ASR, TCG, Processi, XVII sec., vol. 23, c42v–46v: c42v–43r, 8 October 1602.

her and asked her to work for him as a servant. Soon afterwards she became his concubine.[53]

Many other women evidently had contacts in the city prior to their arrival – friends, relatives or villagers with whom they could stay. Dianora Hieronima Pisana had travelled down from near Pisa with her *amico* and after a night in lodgings, they had gone to stay with her aunt who ran a lodging house down by the busy port at Ripa Grande. Her aunt turned them out when she realised that instead of marrying Cesare, as she had claimed, Dianora was intent on living 'dishonestly'. She then moved on to stay with an old acquaintance, from a previous spell in Rome, a man in whose house she was arrested.[54]

THE PROSTITUTE'S HOUSEHOLD

The average Roman prostitute was not only likely to be an 'incomer' in some sense, but she was probably also quite young – in line with findings from other studies.[55] This said, prostitution in Rome was also characterised by a remarkable number of comparatively 'older' women still registered as *cortigiane* or *meretrici*. A sample of 254 prostitutes from the first two decades of the seventeenth century shows that 66 per cent were under the age of thirty.[56] A similar sized sample from 1656 shows that 30 per cent were younger than twenty, 47 per cent were between twenty-one and thirty and 21 per cent thirty-one or over.[57] Their youth, and the fact that many prostitutes were relatively recent arrivals in the city, points to their extreme economic vulnerability: a picture reinforced by an analysis of their living arrangements. In early modern Europe the family or kin group was the core provider of financial and economic stability and of access to trade, professional and patronage networks. It was relatively unusual for people to live on their own: only 17 per cent of Romans did in the mid-seventeenth century, and the vast majority of Roman households (76 per cent) were composed of people related to one another. Of these, about 25 per cent of households contained unrelated co-habitees.[58] An analysis of the households of 941 prostitutes between 1600 and 1621 shows that almost the

[53] Ibid., 124v–133r: c130v, Valerio Armenzano, 18 October 1602.
[54] ASR, TCG, Costituti, vol. 464, c21v–22r, 19 October 1596.
[55] See the discussion in the Introduction.
[56] Bearing in mind the inaccuracies of people's memories. The majority of ages, for example, cluster around 'easy' numbers, like twenty, twenty-five, thirty and so on.
[57] Data drawn from the 1656 census. ASR, Camerale II, Sanità, Busta 4 \ 5, Contagio di Roma. Descrittione del rione di Campo Martio, fatta il mese di luglio 1656.
[58] Sonnino, 'Intorno alla "Sapienza"', 342–67, table 5.

reverse was true: 45 per cent of them lived on their own, 55 per cent lived in households containing unrelated co-habitees, and only 30 per cent of the total lived in households containing a relative.

These differences are hardly surprising. For those from Rome the relative absence of family members, particularly parents, from their households can be seen either as a cause or as a result of their recruitment to prostitution. Those who were migrants would have had few or no relatives to rely on. The picture is complicated slightly, however, if we divide the households of prostitutes into two groups: women who appear more than once in the parish registers over a number of years, and those for whom there is only a single record. We find that 47 per cent of the prostitutes with multiple records lived with family members, as opposed to only 25 per cent of the women with single records. This seems to suggest that prostitutes for whom there are multiple records were more stable residents in the area because they had family ties to root them there. It also raises the question of whether prolonged residence in the area indicated professional continuity and stability, and hence, relative success. A profession like prostitution was heavily dependent on networking, social ties and local reputation, all things which it took time and stability to build, so this may have been the case. This may even explain why 16 per cent of the 'multiple-record' courtesans had servants living with them, whilst only 9 per cent of the single-record courtesans had them, implying that the multiple-record women were better off.

Living with relatives may have had benefits, in terms of economic security and possibly emotional or financial support, but it brought additional financial burdens. If we examine the 30 per cent of prostitutes who lived in family groups, we find that 52 per cent of them had their children living with them, 39 per cent were living with their mothers, and 21 per cent with a sibling or other relatives (the odd nephew, niece or uncle.)[59] Assuming that their children and their mothers were dependants, or at least partially dependent, then in the majority of cases the prostitute was the principal, if not sole, breadwinner. The exceptions are the cases in which the mother and sisters are indicated as also being courtesans, which occurs in 17 per cent of these family groups.

Overall, only 13 per cent of the total had children living with them, and some of these were not their own but children whom they were wet-nursing for the Ospedale Santo Spirito, for a fee (despite hospital regulations prohibiting prostitutes from acting as wet-nurses). This figure seems

---

[59] These categories are not mutually exclusive.

remarkably low given the nature of their profession. It leads us to the assumption that prostitutes had some knowledge of contraceptive practices, how to miscarry or abort, knowledge which certainly circulated in early modern societies,[60] as reflected also by Sixtus V's 1588 prohibition of such practices. For those who did give birth, babies could be abandoned. A late seventeenth-century commentator wrote that until the mid-seventeenth century the abandoned children in the hospital of Santo Spirito were very largely the children of prostitutes.[61] In addition the Ospedale di San Rocco, known colloquially as the Ospedale delle Donne, provided a place where women could give birth in anonymity and have the child taken away from them for care. Situated as it was in the heart of the poorest part of the Ortaccio, it was probably well used by prostitutes. Furthermore, an unknown percentage of female children were taken away by the authorities of Santa Caterina dei Funari, an institution authorised forcibly to remove the daughters of prostitutes, between the ages of about ten and twelve, to prevent them from falling into prostitution.[62] In theory this institution could accomodate a maximum of a hundred people, including the nuns who ran it, and in 1659 there were thirty-six *zitelle* (unmarried girls) living there.[63] Of the children living at home whose ages are noted, 86 per cent were younger than twelve and 66 per cent of them were boys.[64] Fewer than 1 per cent of all the courtesans in this study had daughters at home of a 'corruptible' age. This was considered to be between the ages of nine and twelve; after this girls were no longer seen as innocent and in need of protection – it perhaps coincided with the average age of the onset of menstruation. In view of contemporary anxieties that prostitutes would corrupt their daughters and force them into prostitution, we must either assume that the legislation

---

[60] Angus McLaren, *A History of Contraception: From Antiquity to the Present Day* (Oxford: Basil Black-well, 1990), 161. Also John M. Riddle, 'Oral Contraceptives and Early Term Abortifacients during Classical Antiquity and the Middle Ages', *Past and Present* 132 (1991), 3–32. The four principal methods of contraception were the avoidance of coitus, which clearly did not apply in the case of prostitutes, prolonged breastfeeding, coitus interruptus and abortion. Marina d'Amelia, 'La presenza delle madri nell'Italia medievale e moderna', in Marina d'Amelia, ed., *Storia delle donne in Italia: storia della maternità* (Rome and Bari: Laterza, 1997), 3–52, 15. Raul Merzario finds that men in a small mountain village practised coitus interruptus which had been learned from prostitutes in the big cities such as Rome. *Anastasia, ovvero la malizia degli uomini* (Rome and Bari: Laterza, 1992).

[61] The citation is taken from Claudio Schiavoni, 'Gli infanti esposti del Santo Spirito in Saxia di Roma tra '500 e '800: numero, ricevimento, allevamento e destino', in *Enfance abandonneé et société en Europe, XIVe–XXe siècle*. Collection de l'École Française de Rome (Rome: École Française de Rome, 1991), 1017–64, 1026–7.

[62] See Camerano, 'Assistenza richiesta e assistenza imposta'.

[63] For the first figure see ibid., 233. On the number for 1659 see ASV, Armadio VII, no 36, Sacre Congregazioni, Visitationis Apostolica pro Monialibus, c498 (new numbering).

[64] We know the ages for 112 of them.

was extremely successful, and that the monastery of Santa Caterina was managing to remove the daughters of prostitutes, or that the prostitutes themselves sent their daughters away before they could be taken away from them. As to the 55 per cent of courtesans who lived in households with unrelated co-habitees (perhaps alongside kin), the co-habitees tended to be women. In 18 per cent of cases they were other courtesans, in 11 per cent of households they were servants: boys aged between about twelve and sixteen, women over twenty, or sometimes just 'girls' under the age of ten.

WOMEN'S WORK IN ROME

Roman prostitutes were mostly young, many were migrants, some had mothers or children to keep, and they were also, crucially, women without men. They were 'singlewomen' (unmarried, never married or widowed), and as such they were potentially extremely vulnerable, economically, socially and physically.[65] Recent research suggests that by the middle of the seventeenth century the numbers of 'singlewomen' in the Italian population accounted for between 15 per cent and 25 per cent of all adult women.[66] In Rome specifically we know that in 1645 about 22 per cent of households were headed by women whom we must presume were functionally singlewomen (that is, about five thousand women).[67] As historians have frequently pointed out, women without men were often amongst the poorest members of society, unable to access the higher wages paid to men, yet often still with dependants to keep.[68] Certainly economic hardship is the chief reason cited by women in court as the explanation for turning to prostitution. Given the paucity of economic opportunities for women in early modern Italy, it is easy to see why.

The economic situation in Italy by the end of the sixteenth century was catastrophic. The Italian states were showing signs of overpopulation, whilst

[65] The term 'singlewomen' is coined in Judith Bennett and Amy Froide, eds., *Singlewomen in the European Past, 1250–1800* (Philadelphia: University of Pennsylvania Press, 1999).

[66] Kowaleski, 'Singlewomen in Medieval and Early Modern Europe', 50–1. Although compared with data for fifteenth-century Tuscany this seems to be a very high proportion of singlewomen, it is comparatively low relative to the situation in northern Europe where as many as 40 per cent of women might be single.

[67] Sonnino, 'Intorno alla "Sapienza"', 353–4.

[68] Perhaps the scholar to have engaged most comprehensively in discussions of female poverty seen in the context of women's life-cycle and employment opportunities is Olwen Hufton. See her 'Women without Men: Widows and Spinsters in Britain and France in the Eighteenth Century', *Journal of Family History* 9:4 (1984), 355–76. Hufton, *The Poor of Eighteenth Century France, 1750–1789* (Oxford: Clarendon Press, 1974). And more recently, Hufton, *The Prospect Before Her: a History of Women in Western Europe*, vol. I, *1500–1800* (London: HarperCollins, 1995).

there was a general decline in agricultural output after 1580 and a series of extremely poor harvests in the 1590s which caused widespread famine.[69] This resulted in a dramatic increase in rural poverty and unemployment and a move towards towns and cities where commerce and productivity also began to falter after about 1620.[70] By 1650 the Italian population had decreased by 1.8 million.[71] Economic decline led men to desert smaller towns and villages in favour of the great cities in their quest for employment, resulting in extremely unbalanced populations in early modern Italy. Of 105 towns and cities between the sixteenth century and the nineteenth, 85 per cent showed huge surpluses of females.[72] In the sixteenth and early seventeenth century only the greatest cities on the Italian peninsula – Venice, Milan, Turin, Naples and Rome – could hope for a surplus of men, and in these cases the sex-ratio was reversed.[73] In practical terms there would have been a 'surplus' of between twenty and thirty thousand men in Rome in the early seventeenth century.[74]

Women throughout Italy had traditionally been part of the workforce, working both inside and outside the home, in agriculture and particularly in the textile industry.[75] With the decline of the last, the skewed sex-ratios led to intense competition for jobs in female occupations. In towns and villages across the peninsula the chances of earning a dowry or finding a marriage partner were greatly reduced, making migration to Rome or another of the great cities the obvious remedy to both problems. However, once in the Holy City there was little if any organised work available for women, and they had to improvise in order to make a living. Those looking for honest employment could expect to find work in the traditional

---

[69] Bellettini, 'La popolazione italiana', 509.

[70] Ruggiero Romano, 'La storia economica dal secolo XVI al settecento. I mecchanismi', in Romano and Vivanti, *Storia d'Italia, dalla caduta dell'impero romano*, 1841–904. And Bellettini, 'La popolazione italiana', 513–16. Carlo Marco Belfanti, 'Rural Manufactures and Rural Proto-industries in the "Italy of the Cities" from the Sixteenth through the Eighteenth Century', *Continuity and Change* 8:2, (1993), 253–80.

[71] Sonnino, 'Le anime dei romani', 356.

[72] Antonio Santini takes 97 women per 104 men to represent a 'normal sex-ratio' in 'Le strutture socio-demografiche della popolazione urbana', 131. See also Solvi Sogner, 'Introduction', in *Socio-economic Consequences of Sex-ratios in Historical Perspective, 1500–1900, Proceedings of the Eleventh International Economic History Congress, Milan, Sept. 1994* (Milan: Università Bocconi, 1994), 9–16, 10–11. See also Van de Pol, 'The Lure of the Big City: Female Migration to Amsterdam', in Els Kloek, Nicole Teeuwen, and Marijke Huisman, eds., *Women of the Golden Age: an International Debate on Women in the Seventeenth Century: Holland, England and Italy* (Hilversum: Uitgeverij Verloren, 1994), 73–83.

[73] Even Venice towards the end of the century had more women than men, in 1581, 1586 and 1593. Santini, 'Le strutture socio-demografiche', 74.

[74] Sonnino, 'In the Male City', 21.

[75] M. T. Bettarini and Roberto Ciapetti, 'L'arte della seta a Firenze: un censimento del 1663', *Ricerche Storiche* 12:1 (1982), 35–49, 38.

female occupations generated by the courts and large households: taking in washing and sewing, cooking and cleaning, starching lace collars, and some work as servants, although serving was largely a male preserve in this period.[76] There was also money to be earned from taking care of the sick, accompanying people to mass, teaching school, and renting out beds and linen.[77] Some women carried on a deceased husband's workshop and an indeterminate number of young women may also have worked as 'apprentices' for artisans, often informally, but without being able to become *maestre* (masters). They would have ended up turning their hand to whatever came their way and would have earned very little from it.[78] A fourteen-year-old girl would have earned only her bed and board for ten years, with a payment of twenty *scudi* at the end of this period.[79] This was not even enough to match the average poor-woman's dowry handed out by the charitable institutions.[80] As for the earnings to be had from 'regular' honest work, we noted earlier a woman who claimed she earned one *scudo* a month doing one man's washing. Isabella di Abruzzo earned the same as a servant, with her bed and board. When she worked as a wet-nurse she earned two *scudi* a month in 1603.[81]

In recognition of the economic vulnerability of women, Catholic Italy went to great lengths to try and relieve female poverty, partly with the intention of removing women from those situations which drove them to prostitution. Apart from more traditional confraternal charity, the 'new philanthropy' of the Counter-Reformation had led to the foundation of institutions to help the kind of women excluded from other help, such as fallen women, orphans, widows and abandoned wives.[82] However, despite

---

[76] Angiolina Arru, *Il servo: storia di una carriera nel settecento* (Bologna: Il Mulino, 1995), 31.

[77] Renata Ago, 'Di cosa si può fare commercio: mercato e norme sociali nella Roma barocca', *Quaderni Storici* 91:1 (1996), 113–33, 121–2. Also for later centuries: Marina D'Amelia, 'Scatole cinesi: vedove e donne sole in una società d'ancien régime', *Memoria* 18:3 (1986), 58–79, 77.

[78] Angela Groppi, 'Lavoro e proprietà delle donne in età moderna', in Angela Groppi, ed., *Storia delle donne in Italia: Il lavoro delle donne* (Bari: Editori Laterza, 1996), 131.

[79] Renata Ago explains that the *maestro* was only interested in 'employing' such girls if he knew he didn't have to pay them and could count on their help for many years. *Economia barocca*, 183.

[80] Santa Caterina dei Funari gave a dowry of fifty *scudi* and a white dress. Maria Elena Vasaio, 'Il tessuto della virtù: le zitelle di S. Eufemia e di S Caterina dei Funari nella controriforma', *Memoria* 11–12: 2–3 (1984), 53–64, 57. Those girls who were found a post as servant were given two hundred *scudi* after two years' service. Alessandra Camerano, 'Assistenza richiesta', 246.

[81] ASR, TCG, Testimoni per la Difesa, vol. 190, c73r–81v:73v–74r, 17 March 1603.

[82] Eighty-four confraternities had been founded in the sixteenth century and there were several well-established long-stay hospitals for the sick. There is a vast body of literature on the subject. I cite just a few. Camerano, 'Assistenza richiesta'. Chauvin, 'La Maison Sainte-Marthe'. Tacchi-Venturi, *Storia della Compagnia di Gesù in Italia*. Cohen, *The Evolution of Women's Asylums*. Marina D'Amelia, 'La conquista di una dote. Regole del gioco e scambi femminili alla Confraternita dell'Annunziata (secc. XVII–XVIII)', in G. Pomata, L. Ferrante and M. Palazzi, eds., *Ragnatele di rapporti. Patronage e reti*

the impressive array of institutions, their actual ability to relieve poverty significantly has recently been questioned.[83] In terms of providing young women with an alternative to prostitution, they were probably more a palliative than a solution.[84] On the whole they were small, under-endowed institutions, not able to attract large donations, especially several decades after their foundation. In general there was a low turnover in all these institutions, with girls staying for seven to ten years, resulting in comparatively little space for newcomers at any given time. There were in addition a wide range of entry restrictions or requirements in operation which made them significantly less accessible to the average poor girl than one might initially suppose. As an example the convent of Santa Marta had been founded in 1543 initially as a 'half-way' house for prostitutes who were seeking an alternative life, but who were not prepared to take vows. By 1573, however, it had become exclusively a convent for virgins who were able to pay a monthly fee.[85] The Casa Pia, founded in the early 1560s took those prostitutes who could no longer be housed in Santa Marta. It was also intended specifically to act as a half-way house for unhappily married women, the '*malmaritate*', and to tide them over periods of difficulty by helping them find work, or giving them shelter until they could be reconciled with their husbands.[86] In 1599 it cost five *scudi* per month bed and board and by 1604 it cost six *scudi*.[87] By this time it had already changed its aims: a meeting in May 1599 had agreed to take in only unmarried girls for education.[88] As Lazar points out, these institutions were in a sense victims of their own success. Within several decades new accommodation had to be found as they

---

di relazione nella storia delle donne (Turin: Rosenberg and Sellier, 1988), 305–43. Anna Esposito, 'Ad dotandum puellas virgines, pauperes et honestas: Social Needs and Confraternal Charities in Rome in the Fifteenth and Sixteenth Centuries', *Renaissance and Reformation* 30:2 (1994), 5–19. Angela Groppi, *I conservatori della virtù, donne recluse nella Roma dei Papi* (Rome and Bari: Laterza, 1994). Brian Pullan, 'Support and Redeem: Charity and Poor Relief in Italian Cities from the Fourteenth to the Seventeenth Century', *Continuity and Change* 3:2 (1988), 177–208.

[83] Sandra Cavallo points out that the amount of historical literature devoted to this topic is also out of all proportion to their 'actual function in relieving poverty'. 'Donne, famiglie e istituzioni nella Roma del sette–ottocento', *Quaderni Storici* 92 (1996), 429–39.

[84] In 1601 there were seven institutions which officially took in children between the ages of six and twelve, caring for a total of 1,890 orphans of both sexes, which represented about 10 per cent of the children in the city. Eugenio Sonnino, 'Between the Home and the Hospice: the Plight and Fate of Girl Orphans in Seventeenth and Eighteenth Century Rome', in Richard Wall and John Henderson, eds., *Poor Women and Children in the European Past* (London and New York: Routledge, 1994), 94–116, 100.

[85] Chauvin, 'La Maison Sainte-Marthe'.

[86] Pamela Askew, *Caravaggio's Death of the Virgin* (Oxford: Princeton University Press, 1990), 84–107. O'Malley, *The First Jesuits*, 182.

[87] There is record of a payment of five *scudi* received for a month's stay and food, paid in advance, in ASR, Trenta Notaii Capitolini, vol. 42, Ottavio Scaravetius, 11 December 1599, c686r.

[88] Askew, *Caravaggio's Death of the Virgin*, 90–1.

expanded to allow for the separation of professed nuns from the reformed prostitutes, and they ultimately gave up helping the latter, for whom the options had narrowed by the 1630s to a newly founded Convertite.[89] Similarly, by 1678–1700 only 1 per cent of the girls in Sant' Eufemia were orphans, in an institution initially created specifically for female orphans.[90] Santa Caterina dei Funari, as we saw, had a total capacity of about a hundred women. By 1656 many of them had already been there for perhaps ten years, and the low turnover caused concern to contemporaries who suggested that all those over the age of thirty-five be sent away.[91] It was also quite costly to place a daughter there, because, although it continued to take in daughters of courtesans in the early part of the century, it only took in those whose mothers could afford to pay the sum of five *scudi* per month for their keep. It also started to admit older women in need who could afford to pay this sum, thus reducing the number of places for the poor daughters of courtesans.[92] Bearing in mind that the monthly wage of a servant girl was only one *scudo* such institutions were clearly out of reach of most young women. Similarly the various forms of 'outside' relief such as dowry payments were restricted to a very particular kind of girl. The Confraternity of Santissima Annunziata gave dowries only to girls 'of good fame' who had never been 'to shop alone in the Piazzas or into hostelries', or had never been to public washing areas, hoed, cut wood or picked chicory.[93] This was obviously specifically aimed at excluding the daughters of the working poor, and those who had migrated from the countryside. The confraternity also required the opinion of a trusted referee about the girl's honour and reputation, something which was also dependent on having lived for some time in the city, and on having good social ties. While entry to the Convertite al Corso had initially been free, at a later stage entry was also dependent on paying a dowry. As Sandra Cavallo's study of charitable institutions in Turin makes clear, such places were progressively aimed at helping the daughters of local '*poveri vergognosi*' (the shamefaced poor, or distressed gentlefolk), thereby protecting the status quo by assisting daughters of the gentry who had fallen on hard times. This process was well underway in late sixteenth-century Rome.[94] Finally, we should also question the extent to which young women actually wished to enter

---

[89] Lazar, *In the Vineyard of the Lord*, 66–9.   [90] D'Amelia, 'La conquista di una dote', 316.

[91] ASV, Armadio VII, no. 36. Sacre Congregazioni: Visitazionis Apostolicis pro Monialibus, c230 and c355 (498 new numbering).

[92] Camerano, 'Assistenza richiesta', 227–8.   [93] D'Amelia, 'La conquista di una dote', 312–13.

[94] Sandra Cavallo argues that charitable provision was restricted to women of a certain social station. *Charity and Power in Early Modern Italy: Benefactors and their Motives in Turin, 1541–1789* (Cambridge: Cambridge University Press, 1995), 113. Sherrill Cohen terms them 'A haven for the daughters of the

these institutions, or the extent to which their parents wished it for them. Sant' Eufemia has been described as 'the most miserable place in Rome', whilst not only did courtesan mothers resist handing their daughters over to Santa Caterina dei Funari, but frequently the 'alternative' path through life mapped out for them by the institution was rejected by the girls themselves, who found that they preferred their independence to enclosure, and often to marriage.[95]

To contextualise prostitution so firmly within the Roman economy and a debate on women's work is a contentious step. It implies that prostitution can be viewed and understood as a neutral form of work and the prostitute as a 'sex-worker', thus ignoring or negating views of prostitution as being principally about stigma, sexuality, male power and the victimisation and exploitation of women.[96] Ruth Mazo Karras addresses this issue at great length in her work on prostitution in medieval England. She argues persuasively that we cannot view prostitution in strictly economic terms because it was viewed socially not as principally a commercial activity, but as a sexual behaviour or identity; that 'a woman was a prostitute because she was a lustful woman, not because of a specific behaviour of accepting money for sex'.[97] Furthermore she argues that prostitution cannot be viewed merely as 'labour' since society viewed the work as degrading and its practitioners as degraded.[98] She challenges concepts of the prostitute's freedom and 'agency' as a 'worker', arguing that women entering prostitution were constrained by a lack of alternatives and gendered power relationships, so that entry into the 'profession' was ultimately a form of economic coercion. In particular, she states that their identity as 'common women', publicly and indiscriminately available to men, was a defining feature of prostitution within that society, which meant that prostitutes were brought very

---

propertied class'. *The Evolution of Women's Asylums*, 68–9. A report by a mid-seventeenth-century apostolic visitor explains that Santa Marta was full of nuns, some of whom were noble, who had large incomes. ASV, Armadio VII, no. 36. Sacre Congregazioni: Visitazionis Apostolicis pro Monialibus, c355 (498 new numbering).

[95] D'Amelia, 'Scatole cinesi', 71. Santa Caterina offered care until such an age as the girl could be married with a dowry of fifty *scudi*, or the chance to go into service for six years and a subsequent dowry of one hundred *scudi*. Camerano, 'Assistenza richiesta', 231, 245.

[96] This debate is discussed in depth in Noah D. Zatz, 'Sex Work/Sex Act: Law, Labor, and Desire in Constructions of Prostitution', *Signs* 22:2 (1997), 227–308.

[97] Ruth Mazo Karras, 'Prostitution and the Question of Sexual Identity in Medieval Europe', *Journal of Women's History* 11:2 (1999), 159–77, 162. This article stimulated a certain amount of debate which is printed in the same journal. See Theo van der Meer, 'Medieval Prostitution and the Case of a (Mistaken?) Sexual Identity', 178–91. And Carla Freccero, 'Acts, Identities and Sexuality's (Pre)-Modern Regimes', 186–91. And Ruth Mazo Karras's response, 193–7. She also discusses these issues at length in her book *Common Women*.

[98] Mazo Karras, *Common Women*, 8–9.

much under male control, unable to work independently, forced to work in brothels, not allowed particular lovers and so on. Evidence from early modern Rome does not entirely support this interpretation of prostitution, reminding us that although it is often termed 'the oldest profession', the nature of prostitution differs according to the social and economic context in which it operates. It is particularly affected by the presence or lack of 'specific regimes of criminalization and denigration that serve to marginalize and oppress sex-workers'.[99]

Karras's interpretation of prostitution as inevitably stigmatised both reflects Christian morality and derives from a radical feminist interpretation of sexual essentialism. According to Zatz, this view identifies sexual acts with the body and the self, assuming a specific relationship 'between sexual acts and identity', with the result that 'commercial sex is assumed to be "inherently degrading" to women'.[100] Although this was precisely the view which the Catholic church was seeking to impose in early modern Europe, the evidence from the court records suggests that neither prostitutes nor their clients had accepted this interpretation of commercial sexuality. Furthermore, whilst the church stigmatised prostitutes, there were other, competing or parallel discourses which greatly complicated the discursive world around prostitution, even within theology and canon law. James Brundage has shown that the carnal and venal aspects of prostitution were inseparable in the work of those jurists who had progressively fashioned the official views of the church which were enshrined in canon law. It was understood, for example, that financial need was 'a root cause of prostitution', although canon lawyers 'did not consider poverty or economic necessity as mitigating circumstances', and in theory a woman should starve rather than prostitute herself.[101] Moreover, although the church condemned the act of fornication outside marriage, especially multiple fornication, it was not a crime to take money (or goods) in exchange for sex, and such monies were regarded as a woman's legal property and her earnings could therefore be defended before a court.[102] The logic behind this has been explored by Ferrante and it is particularly helpful for our understanding of how practices of prostitution were constructed in early modern Italy generally.

[99] Zatz, 'Sex Work/Sex Act', 289.   [100] Ibid., 289–90.

[101] Brundage, 'Prostitution in the Medieval Canon Law', 836.

[102] 'What she did in return for her fee might be wrong, but the taking of money for it was no crime . . . Once she had taken the fee, it became her property outright and her rights to it were legally valid.' Ibid., 836–7. Also particularly Lucia Ferrante, 'La sessualità come risorsa: Donne davanti al foro archivescovile di Bologna (sec. XVII)', *Mélanges de l'École Française de Rome* 99 (1987), 989–1016. And Ferrante 'Pro mercede carnali.'

Ferrante explains that the prostitute's right to payment was explained by sixteenth-century jurists and theologians in terms of 'gifts' and 'counter-gifts' or exchanges. This paradigm stressed the idea of the 'liberty' of the contracting parties. According to this logic, the prostitute made a gift of her body, and in return received a 'gift' from a man. Furthermore, since the exchange was deemed unequal (since the women had to labour and expose themselves to dangers, while the men experienced pleasure), the 'gift' became a 'natural obligation' which the man was legally bound to honour, and which women had the right to demand in court.[103] Importantly, according to this formulation, the relationship between the two parties was structured in terms of friendship and mutuality: the prostitute 'giving pleasure', the man 'giving' her 'gifts' which would please her in return, and both parties relying to a certain extent on concepts of trust. This is particularly important for our understanding of the way in which prostitutes, clients and those around them understood their relationships in early modern Italy. We will see later how these concepts of friendship, of gifts as well as payments, of promises kept and of broken trust appear over and over again in the accounts of relationships between prostitute and client in criminal records.

All women were living under the constraints of patriarchy, and we cannot account for why some women prostituted themselves and others did not without recourse to a concept of choice, or 'agency'. Whilst the economic odds were stacked against women in general, and there is evidence of forced recruitment – which will be discussed in a later chapter – there were nonetheless some women who turned to prostitution when others did not. It is therefore valid to speak of a 'choice', and in the following chapters I explore what it was these women – and those around them – believed they would gain by making this choice. Finally, an important difference between prostitution in early modern England and in Italy lay in the 'commonality' or otherwise of prostitutes, and the extent to which they were controlled by men. English prostitutes were very much 'common women', in the sense that they were available to all men and lived under strict patriarchal control. Even though the term 'public woman' was a key element in defining and identifying Italian prostitutes, this did not mean that prostitutes were officially or practically available to all. One of the most defining features of the profession in Rome, at least, was the tendency towards 'particular' relationships between prostitute and client, and the prostitute's right (though clearly not always observed) to pick and choose her clientele.

---

[103] This is based on Ferrante, 'Pro mercede carnali', 43–4.

As to the extent of their subjection to men, apart from the daily encounters with clients, Roman prostitutes were comparatively free to go about their business. Certainly, the laws on prostitution restricted them in certain ways and these were occasionally enforced by the police, who had the opportunity to extort money from them in exchange for protection. Yet, they were not confined to a brothel, nor were they placed under the control of specific men. They had the liberty to enter into official financial agreements – sales, purchases, investments – and to draw up a will. Finally, and crucially, they could and frequently did turn to the court for help in defending their honour and economic interests; and, as we will see later, they could also be successful.

The economic outlook for poor women in Rome was bleak, especially for young migrant women. By 1600 those institutions which had been set up specifically to prevent girls from falling into the kind of poverty which led to prostitution had either changed their function, or were inadequate as a means of preventing or alleviating prostitution on a significant scale. If a girl had migrated recently from outside Rome, if she was over the age of twelve (the age after which girls were no longer considered innocent), if she was poor in the sense that she had to run errands, go to the marketplace alone or do the washing alone, then there was no question of her receiving formal charitable assistance. Widows and abandoned or ill-treated wives unable to afford the three or five *scudi* per month were similarly excluded from assistance, except for very short-term relief. If we couple this with the low wages paid to women, and the frequency and ease with which poor young women came into daily contact with much wealthier men about the city, particularly if they offered domestic services, it is easy to understand how many women became involved in prostitution. Precisely why women came to prostitute themselves, the kinds of circumstances which led to their being recruited into the profession, and the roles played by relatives – whose job it should have been to protect them – are the subjects of the following chapter.

CHAPTER 6

Becoming a prostitute

Luigi Mocingo, Venetian ambassador to Rome for several years and a well-placed commentator on the internal dynamics of the Roman elite, noted in his dispatches to the Venetian Senate in 1560 that prostitution played an important role in the family economy of many Romans. He stressed that it was not only the poor who turned to this expedient:

Nearly all the natural inhabitants of the city are unemployed, so that they nearly always live in poverty. That is the reason why the majority of women sell their honour so easily, and also that of their daughters. This also happens because of the great rewards which they hope for from papal nephews and from the many rich and powerful clerics and laymen who come to Rome . . . People who hope to acquire a dowry for their daughters and people who aspire to better things. And I assert that such corruption has spread so widely that in many very respectable families such things go on, although discreetly, with the consent of fathers, mothers and brothers.[1]

How widespread such practices were, whether amongst the elite or the poorer classes, is difficult to elucidate, and criminal records are unlikely to reveal the dark secrets of the upper classes. But the Catholic church certainly harboured grave doubts about the safety and suitability of the family unit as a place to raise children, issuing an enormous amount of advice literature and prescriptive texts about the roles and responsibilities of parents.[2] In particular it was concerned that mothers, fathers, brothers and husbands, whose duty it was to protect women, would instead act as their procurers. A 1586 edict specified the death penalty for this crime, and for those who induced women to commit adultery.[3] To a certain degree the criminal

---

[1] Eugenio Alberi, *Le Relazioni degli Ambasciatori Veneti al Senato*, vol. X, serie II Tomo IV (Florence: Società Editrice Fiorentina, 1857), 35–36, although it is important to bear in mind his possible bias against the city.
[2] Adriano Prosperi, 'Intellettuali e chiesa all'inizio dell'età moderna', *Storia d'Italia: annali 4, intellettuali e potere* (Turin: Einaudi, 1981), 161–252, 246.
[3] I am citing the 1632 re-issue of this edict, 'Editto renovatorio della costituzione della santa memoria di Sisto V per preservare la publica honestà', ASV, Armadio IV–V, vol. 60, c224, 1632.

records reflect these concerns. There are many trials of husbands, fathers and mothers accused of prostituting their womenfolk, and in the course of routine questioning, much evidence emerges about mothers who lived with their prostitute daughters. However, this view of the family as a hot-bed of corruption should not blind us to the many other testimonies which omit any mention of women's 'initiation' into prostitution. These dwell not on a specific moment of 'corruption' but on the economic circumstances and geographical peregrinations which had led them to Rome and to 'live a dishonest life'.

Some women had already been working as prostitutes prior to their arrival in Rome, and, as we saw in the discussion of migration above, some had contacts already in place in the city. Ursolina Faustina originated from a small village near Orvieto. At some point she had moved to Orvieto where, around the turn of the century, she lived and worked as a courtesan. She had a high-class clientele composed of four gentlemen friends, who enjoyed conversation and musical evenings in her rooms. In 1602 the murder of a man known to them all led to their arrest and interrogation. The outcome of the trial is not known, but perhaps it was this which prompted her to move away, since three years later she was living in Rome in the parish of Santa Maria del Popolo, still working as a courtesan.[4] It would be interesting to know whether any of the men had come too.

Twenty-year-old Prudentia Silvestri Infantis de Florentino, also interrogated in 1602, told the court that she had already been living a 'wicked life' for a year prior to her arrest. She had come to Rome only a month earlier, looking for work as a servant, but since she had not yet managed to find an employer she was still living 'dishonestly'.[5] Her claim that she was trying to find honest work could, of course, have been true. But given that she was living with her 27-year-old sister, Laureta, also a courtesan, who had arrived in Rome two years previously, it seems equally likely that she had come to join her sister in the city and benefit from her contacts in the world of prostitution. Diana Filippi Lauri di Formio had originally left her home town because she had become a prostitute. Whether she was chased away or had moved in search of a better clientele she didn't specify. She had gone initially to Foligno where

---

[4] For Orvieto, see Archivio di Stato, Sezione Orvieto, Archivio del Governatore, Processi, vol. 121a: 1600–1602: cnn. Ursolina Faustina Rosatini di Monte Testis, 17 January 1601. For Rome, Archivio del Vicariato (AVIC), Santa Maria del Popolo (SMP), Stati delle Anime (SA), c15v, 18 March 1605; c18r, 23 February 1606. She lived in Via Paulina.
[5] ASR, TCG, Costituti, vol. 511, c109r–110r, 11 February 1602.

she had lived for six years, before coming on to Rome where she had been resident for two years.[6]

Other women described themselves as economic migrants, claiming that they had turned to prostitution only after trying their hand at honest work. Giulia Crista, examined in 1594, had been brought to Rome from Segno eight or nine years earlier by her mother, who couldn't afford to keep her in their village. She had come to find work as a servant and had initially worked for a Sicilian baroness, then for other gentlewomen, until about three years before her arrest she had ended up living *in bordello*.[7] A similar story was told by Dianora, interrogated in 1624. She had come to Rome in about 1615 and for six years she had found work as either a wet-nurse or servant. It was just in the two years prior to her arrest that she had been 'living independently, having sex with whoever wanted her'.[8]

MOTHERS AND DAUGHTERS

The concerns voiced in contemporary literature and legal discourse about maternal influences in prostitution would seem to be corroborated by the finding that just over 11 per cent of Roman prostitutes lived with their mothers, the majority of whom were aged between about forty and sixty, and many of whom were widowed.[9] Given the geographical mobility of prostitutes, its links with family breakdown and earlier ages at death, this is quite a high proportion. Furthermore, as we will see later in this chapter, in many court records evidence emerges which suggests that mothers often played some kind of role in their daughter's professional life. There is also evidence that some girls were destined for prostitution at a very early age, instructed in what can be called the 'arts' of the courtesan by their mothers, female relatives or other women who had care of them. Although the idea that courtesans had knowledge to pass on to younger members of the profession was the subject of savage literary satire in the period, it is not unreasonable to assume that there were things to be taught to those women seeking entry into the profession at higher levels.[10] There were the skills of the body, not only how to seduce and pleasure clients, but care of the body and the appearance. In 1603 the courts interrogated Delia, an orphan

[6] ASR, TCG, Costituti, vol. 550, c20v, 15 January 1605.
[7] ASR, TCG, Costituti, vol. 450, c15r, 21 October 1594.
[8] ASR, TCG, Costituti, vol. 715, c68, 3 January 1624.
[9] Of the 1,056 courtesans in the parish records, 122 are indicated as living with mothers.
[10] As in Aretino's *oeuvre*, in *Il Ragionamento del Zoppino* and to a lesser extent in Delicado's *La lozana andalusa*. They stress that the only arts to be learned are seducing, fleecing and stealing from gullible men.

who had been placed by her uncle with a 'gentlewoman', Sueca, when she was aged about fourteen. Sueca, whom she also referred to as her aunt, was known to have been a courtesan, indeed, in her prime 'she had dealings with cardinals', but now she was old.[11] She nonetheless continued to use her professional know-how, as Delia revealed when she boasted to another woman that Sueca 'knew the remedies which allow a woman to pass as a virgin three or four times'. She explained that 'she took a thread of crimson silk and sewed it into the skin, so that when a woman had intercourse with a man she bled'.[12] This was obviously a useful skill – one worth passing on – in a profession in which a high premium was placed on virginity. As much as one hundred *scudi* could be asked from a man hoping to deflower a young woman.[13] Methods of birth control and knowledge of abortifacients would likewise have been necessary, whilst the ability to prepare cosmetics, amatory potions and perform spells would have come in handy. Research has shown that prostitutes were commonly versed in love magic which presumably also acted as an extra, often lucrative income.[14] Equally it was useful for courtesans to be literate and well versed in music and singing, all of which would ideally be learned at an early age, given that entry to the profession was in the mid-late teens. Camerano describes the case of a thirteen-year-old girl named Caterina who was forcibly removed from her mother's care in 1607 and placed in the Monastery of Santa Caterina dei Funari, from which her mother tried unsuccessfully to free her. She was 'beautiful and skilled as a singer and in playing the harpsichord', and had also been taught to read and write.[15] Since her mother was reputed to live an 'extremely dishonest life' and had tried so hard to prevent her daughter from being 'saved' by the monastery, it is reasonable to suspect that she had intended her daughter to work as a courtesan and had therefore invested in her education.

The fact that only 1 per cent of prostitutes had unmarried daughters living with them, but that 11 per cent of older prostitutes lived with their mothers, suggests that at an early age daughters were sent to live with other women, possibly as servants or 'apprentices', but that contact could

---

[11] ASR, TCG, Testimonii per la Difesa (hereafter TD), vol. 190, c14v, Duns Abertus Brecatius Lucrentis, 17 March 1603.

[12] Ibid., c78r, Isabella Uxor Camilli Tenantis de Abruzzo, 17 March 1603.

[13] Camerano, 'Assistenza richiesta', 233.

[14] See examples from Fantini, 'La circolazione clandestina'. Guido Ruggiero, *Binding Passions* and 'Re-Reading the Renaissance', 10–30. I found evidence of a woman who must have made a good deal of money from love magic. ASR, TCG, Processi, vol. 114, sec. XVII, c254–7, 3–7 August 1613. The woman was Maddalena Tessitrice.

[15] Camerano, 'Assistenza richiesta', 250–3.

be resumed in later years.[16] In 1607, at the age of only eight, a girl named Maddalena Grilli moved in to a household in the fashionable Via Ferratina, headed by the successful courtesan Fillide Melandrone di Siena.[17] She was initially described in the parish records as her niece. Five years later, at the age of thirteen, she was still living in Fillide's household, which had moved to the foot of Trinità dei Monti, though now described as a *'zitella'*, or unmarried girl. It is only through Fillide's will, drawn up in 1614, that we learn the real nature of the relationship between the older and younger woman, since Fillide left Maddalena the handsome sum of a hundred *scudi*, describing her as her *'alumna'*, in other words, her pupil.[18] In order to prevent such relationships it became illegal after 1624 for courtesans to take anyone under the age of twenty into their houses as servants. There would have been ways of getting around this: one involved the apprenticeship of much older women. The parish records often describe women living with courtesans as 'servant-courtesans', who were probably getting themselves established in the profession and working as a servant in exchange for lodgings. Another example which suggests that some kind of 'training' was involved emerges from the parish records. The courtesan Amabilia Antongetti Romana lived with her mother, also a courtesan, in the high-class area of Via Paulina. When in 1605 Faustina da Perugia joined the household, she was described in the parish records as Amabilia's 'companion'. Only two years later she appears in the parish records living on her own, in a neighbouring apartment, registered as a 'courtesan'.[19] It seems likely that she had been brought from Perugia through family networks (since Amabilia's mother was from Perugia), so as to be instructed in the 'arts' of the profession, and introduced to a clientele network under Amabilia's guidance.

Some of the mothers were actively involved in their daughters' professional activities, rather like business managers. Angela Adami Tropetti recounted how she had first met Sig. Gerolamo, a Spanish gentleman, because she had seen him from the house on several occasions. (Many literary accounts stress that prostitutes frequently attracted their clientele by standing at the window, so she was probably doing just this.) She claimed that he had first approached her when her mother was out, but that she had initially declined to receive him because her mother had forbidden

[16] Ibid., 244.
[17] For Maddalena in Fillide's household see AVIC, SMP, SA, 1603, c106,107r–v; SMP, SA, 1604, c128r; SMP, SA, 1605, c17r; SLL, SA, 1607, c13r; SAF, SA, 1611, c30r; SAF, SA, 1612, civ.
[18] ASR, TNC, U19, vol. 95, c380r, 9 October 1614.
[19] For Faustina da Perugia see AVIC, SMP, SA, 1605, c15v; SMP, SA, 1607, c12r.

it. She had eventually persuaded her mother 'to look favourably on him', presumably thanks to the payment and terms which were agreed.[20] We should not imagine, however, that Angela was a virgin, whose first clients had to be negotiated by her mother. The parish records show that five years earlier she had been living away from home, and was already working as a courtesan.

Camilla di Faenza was a 'poor woman', both of whose daughters were courtesans.[21] She lived with the younger of the two, Menica, behind the monastery of San Silvestro. When one of Menica's clients, a stable-hand named Pietro, was murdered, Menica, her mother, and others associated with Pietro were interrogated. Their testimonies show the extent to which Camilla's life revolved around that of her daughter and men who visited the house. Camilla knew the names of several clients, how long they had been coming to the house and when they had last visited:

> I couldn't say exactly how long it is since Pietro started having carnal commerce with my daughter, but it wasn't very long ago. He sometimes came by night, in the early evening . . . and he stayed a very short time with Menica, passing some nights when there was nobody else, and then he went away. A gentleman called Sig. Antonio, who has had dealings with my daughter hasn't been to her for about forty days, since *Carnevale*.[22]

On one occasion Camilla was in the house when Pietro passed by. Seeing Camilla at the window he asked after Menica, was told that Menica was ill in bed, but he was nonetheless allowed up to see her. Pietro's servant confirmed Camilla's involvement in Menica's daily life, identifying Menica by saying that she was 'big and she has a mother'.[23] He went on to describe an occasion when he had been sent to take some gifts to Menica: he had handed them over to her mother, not to Menica. At night Camilla seems to have acted as door-keeper for Menica, as she had another evening when Pietro had come by with a friend and asked if he could go up and see her. Camilla told him that he couldn't go in because Menica 'was accompanied by a French gentleman'.[24] It appears then that Camilla lived openly off her daughter's earnings and played a useful role in her daily life as an intermediary, door-keeper and cook. She was also fully aware of the kinds of clientele her daughter received and the subtle deceptions in which she was involved, and in court participated in her daughter's attempt to portray herself as a high-class courtesan.

[20] ASR, TCG, Costituti, vol. 716, c204v–206v, 3 May 1624.
[21] ASR, TCG, Processi, vol. 46, sec. XVII, c709–769, 6 May 1605.
[22] Ibid., c714r–c718r; c714v.   [23] Ibid., c722r, Petrus Joannus Marie Lutis, 9 May 1605.
[24] Ibid., c738r, Menica Pauli di Remedis, 11 May 1605.

Santa and Angela, both unmarried, also lived with their courtesan daughters.[25] From the similarities and differences in their accounts before the court, we are given two slightly different 'models' of the kind of relationship a mother might claim to have with a daughter who was working as a courtesan. Santa's account of how her daughter lost her virginity (and implicitly, then became a prostitute) reminds us of the worries about the 'careless' mother portrayed in the moralising images. She told the court that her daughter Virginia 'lost her virginity during the Holy Week of the Holy Year' (the Jubilee year of 1600). She herself was out, having gone to do the washing, when her daughter was raped by a stranger who 'didn't give her anything'. After that, Santa was closely involved with Virginia's working life. They insisted that they preferred her not to receive clients at home so Santa would accompany Virginia when she went out to see her gentlemen. Virginia gave her earnings to her mother who then paid the rent with them.[26] The fact that Santa always accompanied Virginia when she went out was of some relevance to the court, with Santa maintaining that it was better if she went along, rather than paying someone else to go. This may have been a reference to the dangers on the streets, or may have been a matter of professional form, a way of reassuring the clients that Virginia was being 'chaperoned' and thus protected from the attentions of other men; it is an example of the 'aping' of higher-class mores which was part of the professional persona of courtesans who wished to consort with gentlemen.

Angela was apparently less involved in her daughter Lucrezia's 'negotiations'. She maintained that when Lucrezia went out to clients she paid a woman called Giulia a small fee to accompany her, rather than go along herself. This was to hide the fact that Angela benefited from the commerce, for as Lucrezia explained: 'My mother knows that I have sexual commerce, but she does not get involved and she told me that she does not want to be considered as my procuress.'[27] So although both mothers openly lived off their daughters' earnings, there appears to have been some ambiguity about what was permissible and the fine line dividing them from *ruffiane*. Evidently Lucrezia and Angela thought that chaperoning a courtesan daughter about the city might compromise her reputation, even though Virginia and Santa did not seem overly concerned about it.

---

[25] ASR, TCG, Costituti, vol. 508, c18v–25r, Verginia Thome di Dominicis, Angela Thome . . . Romana, Santa Nicole da Fabriano, Lucretia Vangeli Romana, Natalins Riccins de Acqua Sparta, 29 October 1601.
[26] Ibid., 20r.   [27] Ibid., c22v.

Although mothers living with prostitute-daughters could be intimately involved in their 'professional' lives, these are just snapshots of a particular moment in their careers. They were not necessarily long-term solutions, nor purely to the mother's advantage. Evidence from parish records shows that rather than being permanent units, courtesan–mother households could serve as a temporary anchorage, and that they probably benefited the daughter as much as the mother. The Antognetti women, a mother and two daughters, were all courtesans who lived together or near to one another in the parish of Santa Maria del Popolo throughout the first decade of the seventeenth century. In 1600 the two girls were in their late teens or early twenties and their mother, Lucrezia, was aged forty-five. She was probably no longer making a living from prostitution but dependent on her daughters, especially since she still had a young son with her at home.[28] In 1601 and 1602 Amabilia, the elder daughter, was living with her baby son and her mother in Via Paulina, while Maddalena, the younger sister, was living on the other side of the river in the Borgo. However, in 1604 Maddalena took an apartment in the Via del Corso, which was nearer, and then moved in with her mother and sister in 1606. She stayed for at least two years, before finally moving out again, leaving Amabilia with her mother and their younger brother in 1610. We see much the same pattern with the Nerone Senese family. Angela and Isabetta Nerone Senese were aged twenty-six and eighteen and both worked as courtesans. In 1602 they were living together in Via Margutta, to be joined in 1604 by their mother Ginevra Biondi, described as 'a widow' and 'courtesan', and by their twelve-year-old brother.[29] This domestic arrangement was not to last long, since in 1605 Angela married and left home, followed by her mother Ginevra, who found herself a husband in 1606, when the household broke up.

This case suggests that mothers and daughters turned to each other for help when times were hard, or when it was convenient. Living independently was presumably a sign of success, particularly if the apartment was paid for by a wealthy client. But they might fall ill, perhaps they stopped working in the later stages of pregnancy, or perhaps they lived with a

[28] Lucrezia is still indicated as a *cortigiana* in 1605, when she was fifty. AVIC, SMP, SA, c15v, 1605. For Amabilia Lucrezia Antognetti Romana, AVIC, SMP, SA, c18v, 1601; SMP, SA, c55r–v–56, 1602; SMP, SA, c106v–107r–v, 1603; SMP, SA, c15r, 1605; SMP, SA, c15v, 1606; SMP, SA, c12r, 1607; SMP, SA, c37r, 1610. There is a biography of Maddalena in Bassani and Bellini, *Caravaggio assassino*, although questions have been raised about the accuracy of their sources.

[29] For Angela Nerone Senese, AVIC, SMP, SA, c40v, 1604; SMP, SA, c40v, 1604; SMP, SA, c106v, 1603; SMP, SA, c55r–v, 1602; SMP, Matrimoni, c70r, 12 May 1606. For Ginevra Biondi, her mother, AVIC, SMP, SA, c40v, 1604; SMP, Matrimoni, c74v, 17 January 1606.

relative when there was a small child to be cared for. Above all the fact of living together was not necessarily the indication of something sinister. It could equally point to strong affective bonds between mothers, daughters and siblings. Other sources corroborate this. Camerano observes that despite being shut away in the Monastery of Santa Caterina della Rosa for between ten and seventeen years, in an effort to remove them from a corrupting environment, many young women managed to maintain contact with their prostitute mothers, often returning to live with them when they were finally released.[30] My analysis of fifty wills drawn up by prostitutes in the years around the close of the sixteenth century reveals that nearly 20 per cent of the women included their mothers in their wills. Seven left them their entire estate, and two left them a legacy, suggesting both continued contact with them and ongoing concern for their economic well-being.[31]

HUSBANDS AND WIVES

Husbands who forced their wives into prostitution are much harder to track down, since this only comes to light when a legal action has been filed. This must have been a risky thing for a woman to do, since the tenor of the edicts issued in the 1570s and 1580s suggests that suspicion was automatically directed at the wife, assumed to have married so as to have a cover of respectability for her dishonest inclinations.[32] A woman who brought a case against her husband must have felt confident not only that she could win the case, but that her reputation would not suffer as a result, that he would not seek revenge later, and that she would have something to live off afterwards.

Caterina Saffiari had been married for about fifteen months to Pietro Paolo, a copyist, when she complained that he wasn't keeping her 'as befitted a wife' and asked him what 'his game was'. He replied that he hadn't enough to keep her, and that 'I should find myself three or four male friends and that my earnings he would have put aside, keeping some for himself and some for me.'[33] He apparently added, 'you will help yourself and me . . . because I don't want to work at my writing all the time', before beating her.[34] Yet Pietro Paolo wasn't desperately poor, compared with many. He

[30] Camerano, 'Assistenza richiesta', 244.   [31] This study of wills is as yet unpublished.
[32] See, for example, *avvisi* dated 14 July 1570 and 5 December 1568, from Rome to Mantua cited by Bertolotti, *Repressioni straordinarie*, 11, 14. And BAV, Urb. Lat., vol. 1060, 26 February 1592. And ASV, Armadio IV–V, vol. 60, c224, 1632.
[33] ASR, TCG, Processi, sec. XVII, vol. 174, c584r–586v, 5 September 1621.
[34] Ibid., c584v, Sebastianus Q Francisi Tozzi.

earned 15 *scudi* a month from his work, and her dowry was worth 135 *scudi* in cash as well as linens and clothing. As Caterina's father pointed out, he had married her to him 'knowing he was a copyist, and believing that he was intending to earn money . . . it would have been enough to keep his family . . . but he didn't want to stick at it and went to the dogs'.[35] Paolo's defence in court was simply that he couldn't afford to keep her. In reality it was probably more a problem of aspirations and expectations: he wanted to live a more comfortable life, since according to two witnesses he had explained that if she did prostitute herself they would 'be able to go out and about and live happily'.[36]

Not unlike Pietro Paolo, Gaspare Tronasarello had married his wealthy wife Livia and shortly afterwards 'put her out to earn'.[37] Educated in the monasteries of Sant' Anna and Santo Spirito, Livia was married to Gaspare in 1603 with a dowry of two thousand *scudi*, plus her *trousseau*, at a wedding in which a cardinal had acted as a witness. She is not the kind of woman we normally associate with the world of prostitution. However, Gaspare had a great number of debts, presumably accumulated in his attempt to maintain appearances and live as a gentleman.

My husband led me to do ill with other men, and to know Mr Loreto Campello carnally in his house three times . . . and he also wanted me to do ill with others, asking the tailor Antonio Critio, to bring people to me for this purpose, and he didn't want me to waste time because he wanted to pay his debts.[38]

When her mother learned of this she had Livia examined by the Vicario, initiated judicial proceedings against her son-in-law and had Livia placed in Casa Pia. According to one of his friends, Gaspare had actually wedded Livia so as to pay his debts, saying: 'Idiot, why don't you do as I have, take a wife. I took a pretty one and that way I will never be short of money.'[39] Once married, he had cast around among his acquaintances looking for people who would pay him to 'make free' with her. 'More than once he sought me out, as he did Gio Giacomo here, asking us whether we could find him some gentlemen . . . and take them to him so he could give them a free rein with his wife who was fresh merchandise, and he didn't want to waste any time, so he could earn something.'[40]

[35] Ibid., c585v, 15 September 1621.   [36] Ibid., c858r–v, Jo Baptista Laurentis de Nizza.

[37] ASR, TCG, Processi, sec. XVII, vol. 36, 1–89v, 2 June 1604. On the order of the Vicar General she was placed in Casa Pia for the duration of the trial.

[38] Ibid., c17r, 2 June 1604.

[39] This man had initially been Gaspare's accomplice and had defended him in earlier testimonies. Ibid., c79r–v, 79r Alexander di Aricia Romano, 14 August 1604.

[40] Ibid., c70v, Antonio Critio, 7 July 1604.

The expression 'to put the wife out to earn' is a term used several times, equating the woman's body implicitly with a market value.[41] Certainly, Gaspare seems to have had high expectations about what she could earn for him. Michelletto, a former friend of Gaspare's, asserted that Gaspare had asked whether he would help find men he could 'take' her to, 'so that he could earn a few hundred *scudi*'.[42] Her body could also be exchanged for services. Livia described being prostituted to Loreto Campello, a notary in the Camera Apostolica, in exchange for a stay of a court order for bankruptcy which he obtained for Gaspare.[43]

Although debt and bankruptcy were extremely common in seventeenth-century Rome, they were viewed very seriously. Ago explains that those who were bankrupt had to 'flee or hide, possibly somewhere out of reach of the civil courts', and risked permanent damage to their reputation.[44] In view of this it is interesting that Gaspare was far more concerned about the social dishonour resulting from his indebtedness than the dishonour of prostituting his wife, selling all his household goods and then going into hiding in St Peter's palace, taking Livia with him.[45] Indeed, his former friend testified that 'He confessed that he cared nothing about his honour because he wanted to get out of debt with his wife's body because otherwise he would not be able to [get out of debt]'.[46]

Given the suspicion with which married women's claims to being victims were treated, Livia was expected to explain why she had not resisted her husband's demands. Her account of events was that of the model Counter-Reformation wife: ingenuous, obedient and loving. 'I loved my huband a great deal, because I was so young and had been in a monastery and when I was married to him he was my first love, as I had never loved a man, nor thought of loving one.'[47] That explained why she had willingly accompanied him into hiding when he was declared bankrupt: 'Because I loved him so much I said I would go with him.' When they had gone into hiding and she was first left alone by her husband with Loreto Campello, he asked her 'to please him', to which she replied, erroneously as it turned out, that her husband had not married her for that. Her account of his physical advances and her refusal echo countless other tales of rape and a woman's attempt to protect herself. 'And so he took me by the hand, squeezed it and he wanted to kiss me and touch me, but I drew away from him and went over to

[41] Ibid., c4r–v, Jo Jacobus Michelozzi, 2 June 1604.   [42] Ibid., c5v.
[43] Ibid., c16f–26v.   [44] Ago, *Economia barocca*, 148.
[45] ASR, TCG, Processi, sec. XVII, vol. 36, 4v–5r, Jo Jacobo Michelozzi, 4 June 1604.
[46] Ibid., c7v–8r.   [47] Ibid., c17r.

where my husband was.'[48] Gaspare at first told her not to let Loreto have his way, until finally he told her that Loreto had obtained a stay of debt for him and that in return she should let him touch her. To impress this upon her he threatened her with a knife, claiming that her mother had given her in marriage to him and it was his right to do as he wished with her, saying 'he was the master and he wanted me to do as he saw fit'.[49] He went away, leaving her with Loreto, who locked the door behind him and raped her.

Gaspare was not the only man to assert his claim to total authority over his wife's body, both through his words and using the threat of violence. Caterina and Livia, above, were both fortunate in that they had a parent who intervened on their behalf, taking them back in, or seeking institutional care for them. Giulia, whose story unfolds next, had no such luck. She was apparently trapped between her parents and her husband, all of whom, it seems, were equally keen to exploit her.

GIULIA FROM CASTEL LUBRIANO

Castel Lubriano is a tiny village perched high above wooded valleys and sharp ridges, on a rocky outcrop, some 80 km north of Rome near Orvieto. Enclosed within medieval walls and dominated by a tall tower, it was an isolated, tightly knit, though not harmonious, community. In 1607 the villagers allied themselves with Horatio Petri against a deeply unpopular couple, Tarquinio and Artemetia, who were accused of prostituting their daughter, Giulia, Horatio's young wife.[50] Tarquinio, Giulia's stepfather, was a man of thirty-one, from Lucca in Tuscany, and considered to be a 'foreigner'.[51] He turned his hand to almost any kind of work – butchering, running the village hostelry (*ostaria*), selling bread and groceries, and also working the land. Between them they were worth about 150 *scudi*.[52] Artemetia, aged forty-five, had a reputation as a procuress (*ruffiana*), having been whipped for this crime in Orvieto some six years earlier.[53] An argumentative woman, she was disliked intensely and she herself listed thirteen villagers

[48] Ibid., c18r.   [49] Ibid., 19r.

[50] ASR, TCG, Processi, sec. XVII, vol. 63, c1–101r; c57r, 24 March 1607.

[51] Artemetia uxor Tarquinio, 47v–48v, 20 March 1607. Tarquinio claimed that the accusations had been levelled against them because he was a 'foreigner', c44r, 18 March 1607.

[52] Ibid., Artemetia, 49v, 23 March 1607.

[53] One of the villagers saw her being whipped in Orvieto. Ibid., c15, 5 March. We find that trial in Archivio di Stato, Sezione Orvieto, Archivio del Governatore: Cancelleria Criminale B.121A 1600–1602: Processum Diversorum, 1600. 8 January 1601 and 13 January 1601, Alrinic Gentilis de Castro Lubriano.

with whom she had an ongoing quarrel. Blind in one eye as a result of an attack by a man who had accused her of procuring for his daughter, she herself put it thus: 'I believe that everyone in this village hates me.' Giulia was aged about sixteen at the time and according to her husband was 'so beautiful and young that you worry about her honour and mine'. Sadly, from the trial proceedings it would appear that her honour had long since been irrevocably compromised.[54]

Giulia had first been prostituted in the city of Orvieto at about the time of her marriage, when she was only thirteen. The circumstances surrounding this event are somewhat blurred. Artemetia was in prison in Orvieto, and, perhaps even straight after the marriage, Horatio took Giulia to dine in the Governor's palace with Ludovico, *Auditore del Governatore*. Horatio then left and Giulia 'stayed to sleep with Lodovico, remaining in the palace for about three days'.[55] It was probably not a coincidence that Artemetia was freed a few days later, since given his position Ludovico probably had some influence over the gaols. This was not a 'one-off' event, however, and according to the villagers over the next few years Giulia was taken here and there as a prostitute. For example, it was claimed that Artemetia had taken Giulia:

Many times to Castigione della Teverina (a nearby village) . . . and let whoever wanted to have sex with her, and in particular by the Castel keeper there, and she also led her to Orvieto for the same reason, and wherever suited her, and this is public knowledge and well known and I've heard it said in diverse places, and occasions, by diverse people.[56]

Another villager claimed he had seen Giulia in Rome where Artemetia had taken her, and where she had apparently been prostituted to 'some monks', and generally offered on the market.[57] Most importantly, however, she continued to see Ludovico, whom she referred to as her 'old man'. Very early one morning during Lent of 1607, Giulia was accompanied out of the village by one of Ludovico's servants, probably her father and perhaps Horatio (according to which story one believes). She was taken to the city of Narni, a formidable walled city about 50 km away, where Ludovico was now *Auditore*. It would have been a long walk. A mule track would have wound down through the woods, joining the busy Via Flaminia which ran along the Tiber valley towards Rome, before turning up once more into

---

[54] ASR, TCG, Processi, sec. XVII, vol. 63, c1r–2v, Horatio Petri, 5 March 1607.
[55] Ibid., c22–23v, 20 March. Artemetia later describes him as 'auditore del procuratore del Governatore', c26.
[56] Ibid., 24v–25r, Vianci di Castro Lubriano, 14 March 1607.
[57] Ibid., c10r, Marchangeli della Verduccia, 7 March 1607.

the hills. Giulia was lodged the first evening with the servant and his wife. Next day, one hour after sunset a messenger came and she was taken to the Governor's palace where she dined at Ludovico's table and then went to bed with him. That first night he did not have sexual relations with her: 'Because he is a white-haired old man, and he just caressed me a little, and kissed me, as one does, and he didn't have relations with me all the time I was there, and I slept with him more than five or six times, but he had carnal relations with me only on one night.'[58] She stayed in Narni for about fifteen days, spending two or three days at a time in the Governor's palace. Then his servant Giulio would come to collect her 'early in the morning' and take her back to his house, where she waited until he called for her once more. Finally she sent a message to her stepfather asking him to come and collect her, and she was taken back home.

It was not long after her return that Horatio filed his *querela*, or complaint, to the court. The trial lasted for nearly a month. Artemetia, Tarquinio and Giulia were imprisoned in the nearby village of Bagnorea (now Bagnoregio) in the custody of the Vicar. Tarquinio was placed in secure cells, Artemetia in a room with the policemen, but Giulia was taken away by the Vicar's chancellor who wanted her to sleep with him. Horatio was suddenly 'moved to compassion for his wife, mother and father-in-law, and went to revoke his denunciation'.[59] At this point he too was arrested, although he subsequently escaped. But despite the revocation of Horatio's complaint, the Vicar refused to release Artemetia and Tarquinio, torturing Artemetia and then releasing Giulia, though not without first putting her in the stocks and having her publicly humiliated. It was this which was to prove to be Giulia's downfall, for it evidently dishonoured Horatio more than anything which had happened before, and 'because of this shame, he stabbed his wife with a dagger in front of the church door'. Still the Vicar refused to release Artemetia, 'her poor mother', to care for her, and she lay wounded for two days before she died. Somehow, perhaps thanks to the coral necklace and two gold rings which Giulia had sent to Artemetia in prison to help her buy their release, her parents then escaped from prison and made their way to Rome. They then presented themselves before the court, protesting their own innocence and demanding that justice be done, in view of the 'extreme cruelty of the court in Bagnorea'.[60]

[58] Ibid., c18v, 9 March 1607.   [59] Ibid., c96, 26 May.
[60] Ibid., c98, 26 May. Hence the trial records are in two parts. The original trial documents from Bagnorea and then the summaries of what had happened subsequently and the petition for justice.

In the course of the interrogations which took place in Bagnorea, the questions focused on the character and reputation of each person, trying to establish who had really 'governed' Giulia's actions. From the conflicting accounts we can see how each family member justified their actions or inaction in terms of a logic based on power, obligation, privilege and responsibility. Furthermore, each person's character bore a remarkably close relationship to those portrayed in contemporary public narratives of prostitution of the kind discussed in chapter 1. In their characterisation of Giulia, the villagers' comments alternated between portraying her as a victim and as an arrogant, greedy hussy. This echoes the moralising narratives in which the prostitute is portrayed as a girl who is initially the victim of parental neglect, but who subsequently becomes an ambitious, greedy whore. One aspect of the villagers' depositions hinged on the power her parents had over her: 'And so he led Giulia to Narni and put her in the power of the Auditore.'[61] 'It was she who induced her daughter Giulia to a dishonest life.'[62] 'She had her screwed by the Castle keeper of Castiglione della Teverina.'[63] Yet they then went on to describe Giulia as being a '*donna de cattiva vita*' (a shameless hussy), whose immoral behaviour was compounded by a strong and wilful character. She had tried to 'get rid of' her husband, 'in order to have her way with other women's husbands'.[64] She was arrogant and unconcerned about other people's perceptions of her behaviour and comments about her. She was imputed on one occasion to have said: 'I couldn't care less what the other women of Lubriano do.'[65] On another occasion she had apparently boasted of her relationship with the old *Auditore*, throwing a handful of *scudi* on to the table of the *osteria*, saying: 'Here is the money my old man has given me.' And when asked whether she was pregnant she replied, 'I wish to God he had impregnated me. That would have been my luck, and me and my old man would have held it dear to us.'[66] A recurrent image in their depositions is of her appearing in the village wearing new clothes and jewels, openly flaunting her ill-gotten wealth. These newly acquired objects took on great importance in the eyes of the witnesses, whose lists of her possessions grew longer and longer, betraying a kind of fascination bordering on envy: 'Giulia was carrying pieces of some kind of light woollen cloth to make herself a dress, and also two rings, shoes,

---

[61] Ibid., Angelica Proculi Meci da Lubriano, c4r, 7 March 1607.
[62] Ibid., c13v–14r, Emilius Romanus Potestà, 7 March 1607.
[63] Ibid., c24r, Felix Alexandri di Lubriano, 14 March 1607.
[64] Ibid., c3v, Bernardina Ascanij, 7 March 1607.
[65] Ibid., c 5v, Persia uxor, Thome Jacobi, 7 March 1607.
[66] Ibid., 12v, Biellus Jacobi, 7 March 1607.

mules, bonnets, money and many other things which the *Auditore* had given her.'[67]

In contrast, Giulia's account of events was remarkably neutral. She recalled having passively gone along with whatever she had to do: 'He sent for me so that I would go and stay with him'; 'He had his way with me'; and 'He sent me to Giulio's house.' Although Giulia cast Horatio as the chief protagonist in this commerce (and not her parents), there was no protestation of her innocence, no stylised account of rape, and she was certainly not interested in saving her honour. Her narrative was a disjointed 'chronicle' of events with no sense of cause and effect, with no reason or explanation given for anything which happened. So when she described how she had been obliged to have 'carnal relations' with an elderly stranger, as a girl of thirteen, there was no mention of her honour or shame, and no mention of resistance. Her only expression of displeasure was that she had no idea what was going on that first time that she was taken to him.

My husband Horatio took me . . . that evening we went together and my husband left me to sleep with Sig. Ludovico and he slept in another room . . . that night [Ludovico] had carnal relations with me twice but I didn't want to because he had said nothing to me and I didn't know him, nor did I know what he did, as I had never seen him.[68]

Although Giulia described herself as having been a victim, there were two occasions when, obliquely and perhaps unintentionally, she offered an explanation for not having offered any resistance to this commerce. On one of these occasions she described how she, Horatio and her father had set off from the village for Narni. Horatio had been giving her advice on what she should expect to take away from this encounter in material terms. He had told her to 'skin that old man, get what you can out of him; after all, he is old'.[69] To this she had replied indignantly that she could look after her own interests: 'And I told him . . . I was going to do myself some good, since my husband Horatio didn't. I have never had anything from him, but for a pair of shoes.'[70] Thus she moved away from a narrative of exploitation, asserting her own agency, and placing her actions in an interpretative framework in which a husband had responsibilities towards his wife which, if not upheld, gave her licence for transgression. He had failed her as a provider, so she was justified in using other means to obtain what she wanted; and what she wanted was money and material goods. She also recalled a 'Monday during

[67] Ibid., Ursolina uxor Petri Antonij, c6r, 7 March 1607. Angelica Proculi, c3–4v, 7 March 1607.
[68] Ibid., c21v, 9 March 1607.   [69] Ibid., c58r, 24 March 1607.   [70] Ibid.

Carnevale' when Horatio had come to Narni and she had seen him talking to Ludovico and taking money from him, but he had not spoken to her. This was because she had been going off to a party to 'dance with other women at a Castle called Schifanoia', which lay a few kilometres outside the city walls.[71] That brief phrase suggests that there was another, more positive aspect of the commerce in which she was entangled. For the poor daughter of despised parents, in Narni as the *Auditore*'s beautiful young prostitute, she found not just money and clothes, but parties, and perhaps friends: entertainments of a kind which were probably unknown to her in her home village.

Artemetia was portrayed by all (except her daughter) as a strong and wilful woman, reputedly the key figure in these events. She was accused of dominating the men around her, of accompanying Giulia to assignations, of openly offering her daughter's body to men and, in a key moment in the construction of her character, of having actually held Giulia down so that she could be deflowered. 'It is said publicly that when Artemetia had Giulia deflowered by a man from [?], I can't remember his name, she herself held her so that she would lie still and be quiet.'[72] The fascination with the mother–daughter relationship, especially in the graphic details of her deflowering, reminds us of the stress placed on this bond in early sixteenth-century literature, particularly in the pornographic literature by Aretino. Unsurprisingly, the salacious descriptions of her sexual behaviour were given by men, rather than by women.

Artemetia's account of her own actions presented a total contrast to this picture. 'I work hard, like other poor women . . . [and] I have always lived honourably.'[73] She had been a responsible and caring mother, saving a dowry of forty *scudi* with which to marry her child.[74] She had been let down by her son-in-law, who had failed to maintain Giulia, so that in the end she was forced to return home: 'She came back home again, because he gave her neither bread, nor wine, and if he had looked after her, she wouldn't have come home.'[75] 'Good mother' that she was, she had received her daughter back with open arms, fearing that otherwise she might 'go astray'.[76] She claimed that it was Horatio who had first prostituted Giulia in Orvieto, and that she, on learning what was going on, had advised Giulia that she should beg rather than prostitute herself.[77] The only person who kept silent about Artemetia was Giulia, who hardly ever referred to her mother, and did not accuse her of anything. However, the

---

[71] Ibid., c20r. [72] Ibid., c13v–14r, 7 March 1607. [73] Ibid., c25r, 14 March 1607.
[74] Ibid., c27r. [75] Ibid., c25v. [76] Ibid., c25v. [77] Ibid., c27r.

fact that when her mother was imprisoned in Bagnorea she took her jewels to the prison guards suggests her filial loyalty and concern for her ill-famed mother.

Although husbands and fathers were mentioned in the legislation against procuring, as we saw in chapter 1, they barely featured in most prostitution narratives. Those male kin who are portrayed are never guilty of actively corrupting women, but are depicted as ignorant, naive and powerless to overcome the feminine wiles of wife and daughter. Both these narrative identities emerge in the depositions by and about Horatio and Tarquinio. Despite the fact that Tarquinio seems to have played a specific and active role in prostituting Giulia, relatively little was said about him by the villagers. There were no salacious details, few accusations other than that by Horatio, and his character fails to acquire substance in the course of the interrogations in the way that Artemetia's does. Tarquinio also sought to make himself 'invisible', denying any involvement in anything to do with Giulia. He had not been present at her wedding because Artemetia had arranged it, and he was away harvesting and looking after the sheep. The evening he was accused of having accompanied her to Narni he was 'out working, chopping wood'.[78] His story was initially backed up by Artemetia and Giulia who both tried to protect him. They claimed that he had nothing to do with this commerce, as if they were colluding to keep his role in the shadows.[79] It was Artemetia who emerged as the 'central' guilty figure in the narratives, as if she were the repository of all female vices in the village, even though she had not had any visible involvement in Giulia's departure for Narni.

Given that Horatio was Giulia's husband, she should by rights have been 'in his power': obedient to him, ruled by him, and his financial responsibility. However, the accusations and counter-accusations which were traded by Horatio and his parents-in-law focused on the fact that Horatio had not worked, had not been able to provide for Giulia as a husband should, and that she had therefore returned to live with her parents, who provided her with food and shelter. Horatio's inadequacy as provider also implicitly offered an explanation as to why he would have wanted to prostitute Giulia, since 'in order to keep himself he led my daughter to Ludovico in order to earn something'.[80] Their account of Horatio, whose village

---

[78] Ibid., c31v, 18 March 1607 and c39r, 20 March 1607.

[79] Drawn in the margin is a picture of a finger pointing at the words where Artemetia admitted that Tarquinio had accompanied Giulia to Narni. Ibid., c46–7, 23 March 1607.

[80] Ibid., c52r.

nickname was inauspiciously *volpino* (little fox), was of an 'inadequate' husband, capricious, unbalanced and unable to maintain her. Artemetia described him thus: 'My son-in-law is cunning and mad, and on several occasions he has gone about naked, swearing and taking the name of Christ and the saints in vain like a dog.'[81] Horatio likewise saw himself as naive, powerless and utterly deceived by his parents-in-law. 'How do you expect me to know what my wife had gone to do in Orvieto, in the company of my mother-in-law and her stepfather? They told me she was going as a wet-nurse.'[82] Since she had given birth that winter and now kept a child in Lubriano, there had been occasion to go to the city. But the glaring weakness in Horatio's argument was that he failed to explain convincingly how it was that she had been working as a prostitute for the past three years without his realising, especially when it seems that the rest of the village knew perfectly well what was going on.[83]

The debate at the heart of this trial revolved around issues of responsibility, power and, ultimately, recompense. We are privy, through the archives, to this battle for control over Giulia, who was essentially a financial 'resource', as Ferrante would describe it, even though she was figured by her family as a financial burden for whom somebody had to provide. The subtext of each party's accusations was that the person who took responsibility for her and provided for her had a right to a 'return' on their investment. Artemetia implied that Horatio had lost his marital 'rights' over her, and that by continuing to maintain her, they had kept their 'parental' rights. As Artemetia said, 'I kept her, she was in my care,' while Tarquinio said that 'Although Giulia is kept in my house at my expense, she also works hard . . . to pay her own way.'[84] Yet Horatio as husband also claimed this right to benefit from his wife's body, as illustrated when Giulia described how a letter had arrived from Ludovico asking that she be sent to Narni to see him. She claimed that Artemetia, Horatio and Tarquinio were all there together, discussing whether or not to send her. Horatio then told her to go, telling her parents that if they had hoped to remain Giulia's 'masters' they should never have married her off in the first place: 'Go there, go! I am the master. And you should never have found her a husband if you wanted to be her masters!'[85]

[81] Ibid., 19v, 9 March 1607. Also Artemetia, c25r–v, 23 March 1607.
[82] Ibid., c11r, 5 March 1607 and 60r, 24 March 1607.
[83] Ibid., c24v–25r, Attilius Ciani de Lubriano, 14 March 1607.
[84] Ibid., 44r, Artemetia, 24 March, 1607 and 31v–32r, Tarquinio, 18 March 1607.
[85] Ibid., 57r, Giulia, 24 March 1607.

'BELIEVE ME, SIR, THAT MY FATHER WAS NEVER THERE'

Hieronima Lena, daughter of Giuseppe the cobbler, was about fifteen when she was first prostituted to Captain Valerio, the governor's Bargello, mentioned in chapter 5. He had dealings with many prostitutes in the city and was under investigation for murder in connection with rivalry over women. Hieronima had first come to Valerio's attention when he rode past her house whilst on his nightly rounds and he had seen her at the window. They had subsequently met more formally at a christening at which she was godmother and Captain Valerio godfather, something her father seems to have arranged. Soon afterwards Valerio came to her house by night. Leaving his men outside he knocked, entered and told her that he wanted sex with her, to which she refused to agree. He left some money and went away, only to return a few nights later, leaving a 'great many of his men' outside the door, threatening to take both mother and daughter to prison if he could not have his way. Finally he got what he wanted, and she became one of his prostitutes. Over the following year he often sent his men for her or came to her house for sex.[86]

Although Hieronima and her mother presented this sequence of events as a rape – as it may well have been from Hieronima's perspective – evidence given by both parties tends to substantiate Valerio's claim that his commerce with Hieronima had been set up by her parents. Questions by the court centre on the figure of the father, Giuseppe. Where was he during all this, they asked, and why did he do nothing to protect her honour? Both mother and daughter were adamant that Giuseppe had not been present on any of the occasions when the Captain came: 'When the Captain came there by night my father was never there. Believe me, sir, that my father was never there when the Captain came to my house to know me carnally as he knew me. It was always . . . when my father was out.'[87] Yet whilst they repeatedly denied his presence in the house, they did not deny that he knew exactly what was going on. It emerged from their accounts that her father's absence was not coincidental but planned. The Captain had given him *il gioco del girello*, a gambling game, from which he earned thirty or forty *scudi*. There was an agreement that in return for the game he would be out of the house whenever the Captain came.[88] Her mother was even more

---

[86] This is a summary of events drawn from testimonies by Hieronima and her mother. ASR, TCG, Processi (XVII sec.), vol. 23, 7 October 1602, c1–340.
[87] Ibid., c90v, Donna Hieronima Lena filia Giuseppe Calzettaro, 13 October 1602.
[88] Ibid., c90v, 13 October 1602.

forthcoming. Yes, her husband had known everything, but no, he hadn't been in the house: 'This man must have given him the game so that he would stay away, and the captain used to come home at one or two hours after sundown, and my husband hadn't come home because he was out at the game.'[89]

All this suggests that Hieronima's parents were not merely passive victims of the Captain's power, but on the contrary had struck some kind of a bargain with him. Perhaps they hadn't sought out the situation in the first place, but since it had arisen there was a desire to exploit it for what it was worth. Another element which points towards the mother's/parents' complicity in the commerce emerges from some inconsistencies in the testimony. The mother claimed that she had tried to protect her daughter's honour, but Hieronima recalled an occasion on which Giacomo Francese, a well-known ruffian, had come to their house: 'He said to my mother, in my presence, that he had found me a gentleman, who would have given me bracelets, necklaces and dresses and kept me, and that we would leave that house so as not to be near Captain Valerio.'[90] According to Valerio, the mother tried to play him off against Giacomo, claiming: 'I have found a gentleman who wants to keep my daughter, feed her and do her some good.'[91]

Much of the evidence from Rome confirms the traditional stereotypes which we noted in the moralising literature about the involvement of mothers in prostitution. Mothers or other female relatives led their daughters into the trade, lived with their prostitute daughters, managed their daughter's business and pocketed their earnings. The popularity of this as a literary topos and warning was therefore perhaps linked to its contemporary relevance. Harder to explain is the absence of men from the narratives, given that husbands and fathers were also clearly complicit in this commerce. One reason for their 'invisibility' probably lies with the approach taken by the Jesuits towards the family. In the instructions written for Jesuit missionaries on how to deal with the kinds of problems which might arise between married couples, it states clearly that even if a man is known to be at fault, priests should be careful 'not to offend the husband by exposing his behaviour publicly because greater damage arises from encouraging women to indulge their vengeful instincts'.[92] If applied also to moralising

---

[89] Ibid., c98r, Sofonisba Uxor Giuseppe Calzettaro, 13 October 1602.
[90] Ibid., c93r–v, 13 October.   [91] Ibid.   [92] Cited by Selwyn, *A paradise*, 173.

literature, as it probably was, this would have resulted in the avoidance of any plots or images which attributed blame to men, for fear that this would undermine the authority and status of men and husbands. This presumably represented a greater social evil than did the spectre of men prostituting their wives and daughters!

This said, there is an uncanny resemblance between the 'invisible' male relatives in moralising discourse and the actual men who, although prostituting their wives and daughters, made themselves 'invisible' at strategic moments in the commerce, and whose acts were likewise shrouded in secrecy by those around them. Giulia of Castel Lubriano, Livia wife of Gaspare Tronsarello and Hieronima the cobbler's daughter: in all three cases the father or husband, having forced his wife or daughter into prostitution, made the symbolic gesture of absenting himself from the premises during sexual commerce. On the one hand, this may have been connected to the legal implications of his acts and an attempt to evade severe punishment. Perhaps a man's physical presence at the act of prostitution was constituted as proof of his responsibility, or as a stain on his honour, in a way in which mere knowledge of it did not. Also, punishments could be severe, though how often they were meted out is open to speculation. Certainly this concern to absolve the father from responsibility, even sometimes by other witnesses, stands out sharply from discussions of the mother, whose presence at times of carnal commerce seems to have been unproblematic and readily admitted to. At the level of court-room accounts, it is almost as though, in the absence of a cultural narrative about the 'wicked' father, there was nothing for the popular imagination to draw or elaborate upon. There was, on the contrary, an unending stock of popular imagery about the wicked mother which may have conditioned witnesses' perceptions of events as well as providing them with ready interpretations of women's actions.

More importantly, these cases raise questions about our understandings of the construction of male honour. It has widely been assumed that in early modern Europe (particularly in Mediterranean societies), men were automatically dishonoured if their womenfolk were 'unchaste'. Yet there is other evidence to suggest that the way in which these men prioritised financial concerns over the chastity of women was not exceptional. Mocigno's comments about Rome generally, as well as studies on Florence and London, have revealed similar trends, as husbands and fathers organised or consented to this commerce of their wives. Men from the lower classes sought purely financial gain, whilst amongst the upper classes such relationships were condoned in the quest for social privilege, jobs and preferment.[93] This suggests that there was a delicate balance between the dishonour brought about by female unchastity and the honour to be accrued from economic solvency and increased social status.

There also seems to have been a sharp distinction, as far as male honour was concerned, between those acts of unchastity which were 'governed' by a husband or father, and those which were initiated by a woman herself, such as a love affair or secret prostitution. My explanation of this is that in the latter case it was not the sexual act per se which dishonoured the man, but what it said about the failure of his authority and his inability to 'govern' his wife or daughter. In the former case there was no such dishonour because the woman, and her body, were still totally under his control. He had decided to initiate this commerce, had agreed a price, selected the person with whom she had sex, and crucially taken all or most of the earnings. It was an agreement between men. This might explain why Horatio, Giulia's husband, who merely denounced Giulia for prostituting herself, murdered her for being publicly humiliated in the stocks, a shameful punishment over which he had had no control.

These cases also draw our attention to the economic issues which lay at the heart of marriage and families. What is common to these 'dysfunctional' families is the expectation that every member should contribute to the family budget – whatever that might involve. It was not just that men expected women to turn to prostitution if necessary, but that if a husband did not provide for a woman she might believe herself justified in prostituting herself. All those involved in these cases also shared the perception that prostitution was a viable way to make a considerable amount of money: whether to make life easier and 'live *allegramente*' or to allow a husband to stop working, or to pay off his debts. In the following chapter we will explore the extent to which beliefs in the earning potential of prostitution were grounded in daily life, looking at how much woman earned from prostitution and the ways in which they organised their professional lives so as to maximise their economic security.

---

[93] For Florence, see Cohen, *The Evolution of Women's Asylums*, 56. For more extensive discussion, see Dabhoiwala, 'The Pattern of Sexual Immorality', 89–90.

CHAPTER 7

The business of prostitution

NEGOTIATING WITH CLIENTS

One evening in October 1601, the governor's *birri* entered an apartment where two young prostitutes, Verginia and Lucrezia, lived with their mothers. Earlier that evening an innkeeper had supplied some wine and Natalitio, a well-off goldsmith, had dropped in to 'speak in private' with Lucrezia. The couple were found together in a separate room and everyone was arrested. This may have been because the *birri* suspected the mothers of acting as procuresses, or because Natalitio had illegally been wearing a weapon in the *luoghi*. When interrogated the next day about how they earned their living, the kind of women they were, and what was going on, both younger women stated they were unmarried and admitted to living dishonestly and having casual sex. Angela, Lucrezia's mother, acknowledged the purpose of Natalitio's visit: 'I believe he had come because he wanted to *negotiate* with her, but I don't know whether he did.' In her testimony Lucrezia used the same terms: 'when I go out of the house to *negotiate* myself a women called Giulia who lives in the Borgo comes with me, to whom I pay a *scudo*'.[1]

Just as the term *scappata* was commonly employed by prostitutes to convey the sexual dimension of their profession, so the verb 'negotiare' was used to spell out the commercial nature of the transaction. Although the simplest translation into English is 'to sell myself', this does not convey the full range of meanings in Italian. It implies that they bargained, they traded, they entered into a contract with these men with their bodies or, as they expressed it, with 'themselves'. The verb also draws attention to the initial moment of an encounter between courtesan and client, when the man learned what the woman considered herself to be worth, the woman what he was prepared to offer her. Accounts of these 'negotiations' give

---

[1] ASR, TCG, Costituti, vol. 508, c 18v–22v, Verginia and Santa Nicole da Fabriano, Lucrezia Vangeli Romana and Angela Romana, 29 October 1601.

the impression that, in principle at least, prostitutes were in charge of the transaction. They set their price, refused or accepted an offer and then had to try and ensure that the client paid them. When Diana Filippi from Formio was asked about her relationship with a certain Francesco, she replied that it had begun four or five months earlier, 'as it usually does, when he asked me if I wanted to do him a service and I replied that I would if he paid me'.[2] Evidently, clients often simply paid what was asked of them, as Lucrezia Bastiani from France described: 'I have been paid by him and he sometimes gave me two *scudi*, at other times one, depending on what I asked for.'[3]

Many court cases reveal the women's vulnerability and the fragility of these agreements. Those prostitutes who accepted casual clients seem to have been paid after the event, which evidently put them in a precarious situation, placing the onus of trust on the client. They could set a price, but it might not be paid in full, and unknown clients might turn out to be dishonest or violent. In September 1597 a fight broke out between Magdalena Tarafini Napolitana and her client.

A youth had come to my house and had had 'to do with me' and only wanted to give me a *grosso*, and I wanted a *giulio* and I didn't want him to leave without giving me a *giulio*, and since I did not want him to go out he put his hands around my throat to strangle me.[4]

Luckily for Magdalena the police happened to be in the vicinity and hearing the dispute, interrupted the fight. Another Magdalena from Naples recounted how Flavio had come to sleep with her and paid her two *scudi*, 'which I put down my chest'. He then evidently repented of having paid her so much and took the money back, which led to a fight.[5] Another courtesan, Martuccia, denounced her client Menico to the *birri* for paying her with a false coin which seems to have annoyed her greatly: 'Even more so, since I have heard that he spends freely on the whores from the Ortaccio.'[6]

It seems as though prostitutes could not easily ask for pre-payment, perhaps because it was construed as a sign of mistrust and a slur on the client's honour. This is evident from a mid-sixteenth-century case concerning a Frenchman who had already acquired a reputation amongst other women

---

[2] ASR, TCG, Costituti, vol. 550, c20v, 15 January 1605.
[3] ASR, TCG, Costituti, vol. 518, c116v, 13 July 1602.
[4] ASR, TCG, Relazioni dei Birri (RB), vol. 99, c105r, 24 September 1597.
[5] ASR, TCG, RB, vol. 100, c240r, 26 August 1600.
[6] ASR, TCG, RB, vol. 101, c158r, 28 December 1601.

for not paying. When he approached Flaminia Milanese and asked to 'nego-tiate' with her, she replied that 'I wouldn't give of myself unless he paid me first.'[7] This caused great offence and the Frenchman claimed that his honour had been slurred by her lack of trust in him and he threatened to disfigure her.

Prostitutes not only stood to lose income in such cases, but they were in danger of losing their own reputations by associating with the kind of dishonourable men who did not pay. Having sex and not paying for it had powerful symbolic connotations in the community and was used by men as a kind of ritual humiliation, a way of shaming a woman and undoubtedly, a way of asserting themselves over her.[8] Maddalena Santini from Florence explained to the court that her shutters had been broken the previous evening by two young courtiers who were part of the French ambassador's retinue. She had incurred their anger by chastising them for having attacked a friend of hers. In retaliation they had threatened her:

They themselves were boasting about it and they told me that they wanted to do to me what they had done to another young woman in the Ortaccio, both having screwed her hard without paying her . . . and the following evening they had gone to break her *gelosie* with stones.[9]

Although these accounts remind us of the day-to-day violence and ver-bal abuse present in their lives, and of how vulnerable prostitutes could be, the women were not entirely alone. They lived and worked in extremely densely populated buildings in closely knit neighbourhoods. Given that windows were covered at best with waxed cloth or shutters, the sounds of disputes and fights rapidly drifted into the public arena. Even if people didn't always get on, they knew one another well and there were often peo-ple ready to come to a woman's aid and prevent disputes from escalating too far. When there was trouble, prostitutes, like anyone else, had recourse to the courts of law. They could and did take men to court for abusive behaviour and non-payment. Whilst there are no data for Rome, research on Bologna has shown that between 1600 and 1630 at least 300 prostitutes

---

[7] ASR, TCG, Costituti, vol. 55, c81v, 15 June 1557.

[8] Elizabeth Cohen explores physical and verbal attacks on Roman prostitutes in 'Honour and Gender'. On the unclear boundaries between 'rape' and consensual intercourse see my 'Fragments from the "Life Histories" of Jewellery Belonging to Prostitutes in Early Modern Rome', *Renaissance Quarterly* 19:5 (2005), 647–57.

[9] ASR, TCG, Processi, sec. XVII, vol. 46, c719r, 6 May 1605, Maddalena Santini Fiorentina. The *gelosie* were semi-transparent blinds made of oilpaper or cloth, soaked in turpentine and fixed on frames. Raffaella Sarti, *Europe at Home: Family and Material Culture, 1500–1800* (New Haven and London: Yale University Press, 2002), 93.

(of about 300–600 prostitutes in the city) denounced their clients for non-payment.[10]

A STABLE CLIENTELE: THE *AMICO FERMO*

One of the most important ways in which prostitutes protected themselves from financial instability and the problems of an ever changing clientele was by cultivating long-term clients. These were known in Rome as the *amico fermo* or 'firm friend'; they were important figures in the day-to-day lives of prostitutes.[11] An *amico fermo* was not just a long-term client but one who paid for her rent and sometimes her keep, representing economic security, as illustrated in Maddalena Santini's interrogation in 1605. Asked by the court whether or not she had an *amico fermo*, she replied that ever since her friend Agosto had 'abandoned' her, seven months previously, she had not. She was then asked whether any of her clients were grooms. She made a show of being greatly affronted by this suggestion. She wept and begged the court to believe her when she said that 'although I don't have an *amico fermo*, I would rather eat my hands and starve than associate with men like grooms'.[12] She and her interrogators therefore directly linked the loss of her *amico fermo* to economic vulnerability, and acknowledged the potential dishonour associated with taking lower-status clients.

As with more casual relationships, the details of the contract between a courtesan and an *amico fermo* had to be arranged first. Angela Adami Tropetti's mother agreed that Angela would see the Spanish gentleman Signor Gerolamo twice a week for a monthly payment of ten *scudi*. Angela gave a description of how the arrangement worked in practice.

On one occasion when he dropped by during the day he asked if I wanted to go to his house. I said yes and that evening he sent his carriage for me and I went to his house [which was in Via Condotti], where I spent the night sleeping with him, and I returned home the following evening at seven p.m. and the same coachman took me back home.[13]

As well as being taken to and from his home by carriage, which would have served partly to protect her from being seen by the *birri* (since prostitutes were placed under an evening curfew), Angela and her mother had the use of his carriage as a general means of conveyance. This was perhaps part of

---

[10] Ferrante, 'Pro mercede carnali', 48.

[11] See Elizabeth S. Cohen for a detailed discussion of prostitutes and their clients in 'Camilla la Magra, prostituta romana', in Ottavia Niccoli, ed., *Rinascimento al Femminile* (Bari: Economica Laterza, 1998), 163–96, 183.

[12] ASR, TCG, Processi, sec. XVII, vol. 46, c718v, 6 May 1605.

[13] ASR, TCG, Costituti, vol. 716, c204v–206v, 3 May 1624.

the contract, a valuable asset which we must also consider as a kind of 'payment'. Carriages were an important status symbol at this time and part of the city's sociability involved being seen riding in them around the streets: courtesans were no exception. Since they were forbidden to own and ride in them, they tried to circumvent this prohibition by riding in their clients' carriages. In this way they were not only participating in the general social 'parade', but signalling the quality of their clientele.

In Rome, although the *amico fermo* had some specific 'visiting rights', there is no evidence that men expected a woman to refrain entirely from taking other clients, as if they were concubines or mistresses, as has been found elsewhere.[14] They supplemented their income either with another *amico fermo* or with visits from occasional clients. Menica Fiorentina told the court, 'I have as an *amico fermo* a gentleman called Sig. Antonio from Modena and another, the Sig. Angelo in the Giubbonari, and I have no other firm friends.'[15]

Whether or not a client was actually described as an *amico fermo* in depositions, women often referred to *un amico* who was responsible for paying their rent, food or clothing. Verginia's mother, Santa, explained to the court that a particular gentleman friend 'dresses her and gives her money'.[16] Another woman described how her client, a mule-driver, paid her rent, gave her money and 'always gave her something for the baby'.[17] Hieronimo, a courtier, stated that he had paid his courtesan a total of twelve or thirteen *scudi* over three months, and had also paid for her food and rent.[18] Diana Filippi from Formio denied that she had an *amico fermo*, but admitted that her friend Francesco di Como none the less provided her with economic stability: he had been seeing her for four or five months and paid her rent for her.[19]

Another expression used to describe a secure long-term relationship between a client and courtesan was '*tener a sua posta*' or '*tenerla a tutte sue spese*'. This meant that he kept her and paid all her expenses – rent, firewood, food, wine, clothing, linen and tableware.[20] A witness in one trial expressed the opinion that the courtesan herself should not be obliged

---

[14] In Bologna there was an assumption that a woman would be available exclusively for a man if he kept her, and that other relationships she may have had were kept secret. Ferrante, 'Pro mercede carnali', 51.

[15] ASR, TCG, Processi, sec. XVII, vol. 46, c721r, 7 May 1607.

[16] ASR, TCG, Costituti, vol. 508, c21r–v, Santa Nicole da Fabriano, 29 October 1601.

[17] ASR, TCG, Costituti, vol. 50, c213v, Jacobella Savoiana.

[18] ASR, TCG, Costituti, vol. 509, c91r–92r, Joanna Antonio Milanese and Hieronimo Alegretti Cesis, 14 December 1601.

[19] ASR, TCG, Costituti, vol. 550, c20v–23r, 15 January 1605.

[20] Ago, 'Di cosa si può fare commercio', 123. She quotes this which comes from ASR, Tribunale del Auditor Camera; Uff. 1 Liber Testium, b69, c4v, Marcu Scipione de Angelis, 4 March 1613.

to sustain heavy expenses in order to keep up the appearances necessary for her trade. It was her client who stood to gain by being seen with a well-dressed courtesan with richly decorated apartments, and therefore it was fitting that he should be the one to pay for her finery. 'I believe that it is not right that a poor woman should pay the rent and pay for her clothing out of her own money, so that another [her client] can cut a fine figure.'[21]

Crucially, as a late sixteenth-century court summary makes clear, these objects were a prostitute's earnings and savings. It was to be expected that she would not only keep them, but subsequently dispose of them as she needed.

When one wants to keep such a woman *a sua posta* . . . it is necessary for him to dress her, shoe her and pay her expenses and give her all that she needs . . . and once a man has bought any things or furniture for a similar woman, or any woman with whom he has had carnal friendship several times, those things have been earned by that woman, and she can do whatever she likes with those things as her own. And when she breaks with that friend who has bought her those things, that man cannot have, or hope to have any expectations of those goods.[22]

Eisenach makes clear that this term '*tener a sua posta*' was particularly associated with elite concubinage in sixteenth-century Verona, and that it signalled the presence of an extremely common 'institution' with its own customs and vocabulary.[23] In Rome, where concubinage is rarely mentioned, it was in common usage in the world of prostitution.

PAYMENTS AND GIFTS

The scarcity of coinage in Rome meant that commercial transactions often relied upon the giving of objects and foodstuffs, making it very difficult to assess the average earnings of prostitutes in the city.[24] The lowest-status 'public' prostitutes who were struggling to survive could not pick and choose. They were routinely paid in food and drink; if they were lucky, they received an additional sum in coins. Diana Filippi from Formio said of her clientele: 'Whoever wants to, comes to me, and as long as they pay me, I serve them.'[25] Faustina Angeli from Orvieto, who lived in Schiavonia, the most miserable street of Campo Marzio, described herself in the following

[21] Ibid.
[22] Archivio di Stato di Roma, Archivio Sforza Cesarini, II parte, seria SXII, vol. I, filza AZ, cnn, filza 3 (interna), 26 May 1594–5.
[23] Eisenach, *Husbands, Wives and Concubines*, 139. She translates it as 'to keep at his demand', 147.
[24] As Renata Ago points out, this was an economy in which everything could be bartered, sold and traded in the marketplace. *Economia barocca*, xiv–xvii.
[25] ASR, TCG, Costituti, vol. 550, c20v, 15 January 1605.

manner: 'I am friends with everyone who wants to have sex with me and especially those who pay me with money.'[26] Diamante from Ancona asked the son of a mule-driver to pay eight *giulii* a time. As she had sex with him about six times over a period of twelve days, this should have brought her payment to about forty-eight *giulii* (nearly five *scudi*). In fact he only gave her about three *scudi* – hence her grievance against him. In her testimony she was also quite specific about the time of day at which she had seen him, which suggests that this bore some relationship to the 'extent' of the services offered him. 'He didn't stay the whole night . . . [he usually left?] in the morning before daybreak, although twice he went to bed.'[27] So although Diamante was just a 'poor' prostitute, in two sexual encounters she was none the less able to earn the amount that a washerwoman, seamstress or a servant to a gentlewoman earned in a month.

Sometimes it was hard for clients to disentangle the various elements which had constituted their payments for sex, what with cash payments, paying for the women's food and perhaps settling the odd bill. As Hieronimo Capitani from Salerno explained to the court in 1621:

I came to Rome eight days or so ago with merchants from Turin . . . and about five days ago a certain black Spaniard I knew introduced me to the aforementioned Anna *cortigiana*, his countrywoman with whom I slept two nights, and between food and that which I gave her, I spent about sixteen ducats, and calculating four ducats I gave to a Jew for her.[28]

Portia Rastrelli Romana is an example of a prostitute who numbered courtiers and merchants amongst her clients. Interrogated in February 1596 about her relationship with Aurelio, a young courtier, she told the court that he had visited her twice. Like Diamante, she was very precise in her description of when he had come and how long he had stayed. On the first occasion he 'slept the night with me, and in the morning he left, having given me three *scudi*'.[29] On another occasion he came by day, had lunch with her in the company of friends, and afterwards had sex with her 'and left me two *scudi*'.[30] So staying the night was a more costly business.

Earning between one and two *scudi* per sexual encounter Portia was better off financially than a woman reliant on 'honest' work, earning far more than a skilled artisan could in a month with just two sexual encounters. This explains why she could afford the servant mentioned in depositions made in both 1593 and 1595.[31] But this was not unusual. Angela, a courtesan from

[26] ASR, TCG, Costituti, vol. 515, c216v, 15 July 1602.
[27] ASR, TCG, Costituti, vol. 721, c8v, 2 January 1624.
[28] ASR, TCG, Processi, sec. XVII, vol. 174, c676r, 18 October 1621.
[29] ASR, TCG, Costituti, vol. 457, c40v, 20 February 1596.   [30] Ibid.   [31] Ibid.

Narni, was propositioned in the street when she was out walking with her family, and was offered two *scudi* for her services.[32] Captian Valerio, the Bargello of Rome, left at least two or three *scudi* each time he had sex with young women, whether or not they had consented. At a conservative estimate, Delia Angeli Romana, a young orphan forced into prostitution with him, had probably earned forty-five *scudi* in the eight months after she met him, averaging five *scudi* per month.[33] Hieronima Lena, the cobbler's daughter also prostituted to him, had probably earned her family between fifty-five and seventy *scudi* in seven or eight months.[34] Between twenty and thirty of these *scudi* she had been given as cash, but the remaining money had been earned by her father with the gambling game[35] which Valerio had given him as part of the agreement.

Given the economic circumstances and demographics of the city it stands to reason that the majority of men frequenting prostitutes would have been much better off than the women – though not always. Joannus Clementis, a tailor, was arrested in October 1627. He declared that he owned nothing and that 'there is no way in which I could keep a woman, although it is true that I give her something because I work with the Pope's tailor, and I earn myself three or four *giulii* a day which is what I live off'.[36] On the other hand, the wealth divide could be enormous. Natalitio Riccio di Acquasparta, the goldsmith whose arrest was described at the start of this chapter, was a 28-year-old widower. He declared that his possessions were worth '2,500 *scudi*, plus his wife's dowry of 1,500 *scudi*'.[37] Hieronimo Alegretti Cesi was arrested in bed with a courtesan in a house near the Trinità dei Monti. She was to all appearances a very low-status prostitute. Aged 'twenty-two or twenty-three' she had been in prison 'about fifteen or sixteen times' and was worth only 'ten *scudi*'. Yet thirty-year-old Hieronimo, a courtier working for Monsignore Ferratini, had 'goods worth about a thousand *scudi*'.[38] Given the kind of spare cash these young courtiers and professionals must have had, it is hardly surprising that they were expected to maintain their courtesan and provide furniture and

---

[32] ASR, TCG, RB, vol. 98, cnn, 29 August 1596.

[33] Based on accounts of how often she saw him and how much he paid. ASR, TCG, Processi, sec. XVII, vol. 23, 175v, 5 December 1602.

[34] She said that he paid her about two or three *scudi* a time, and that he had visited her perhaps eight or nine times since *Carnevale*. ASR, TCG, Processi, sec. XVII, vol. 23, c85v–95r, Donna Hieronima Lena filia Giuseppe, 13 October 1602, and c97–98r, Sofonisba filia Gironimo, Uxor Giuseppe Calzettaro.

[35] The *gioco del girello* as mentioned in chapter 6.

[36] ASR, TCG, Costituti, vol. 733, c5, 21 October 1627.

[37] ASR, TCG, Costituti, vol. 508, c24r, 29 October 1601.

[38] ASR, TCG, Costituti, vol. 508, c90v, 14 December 1601.

clothing if they formed a firm friendship. Even when they didn't, the two or three *scudi* they paid for the odd night with a prostitute can hardly have seemed lavish to them, although it was clearly of great value to the woman.

Gift giving was central to the practice of prostitution in seventeenth-century Rome, echoing the way in which canon law had theorised relationships between prostitute and client in terms of giving and receiving of gifts. It was not just that it was common for clients to pay their prostitutes with objects in lieu of coinage, but some of the objects given seem to have had a different 'status' from money, in the eyes of both parties. On the one hand, they played a role in 'courtship' rituals, as men attempted to win the favours of prostitutes they liked. On the other, they also seem to have symbolised the presence of a more intimate or long-term bond between the two parties. The 'courtship' rituals enacted between courtesans and clients were very public: Montaigne describes how 'the reward for having slept the night [with a courtesan] for a crown or for four, is to be able to pay court to her the next day in public'.[39] Accordingly, gift giving was quite a high-profile activity. Details of the gift were recollected not only by the recipient but also by the person who delivered it, and by others who had either noted the gift or had been told about it. The importance of gifts in the economy of prostitution is underlined by the interest shown by the criminal court in who had given what to whom, in its attempts better to understand the nature of certain relationships.

In 1605 the Governor's Tribunal probed into the gifts which the murdered stable-hand Pietro had given a young courtesan, Menica Pauli Romana, in the course of their friendship. Horatio, Pietro's friend and a servant in the Marchese Peretti's household, recounted having taken the white bread and wine with which stable-hands were paid directly to Menica on behalf of Pietro.[40] On another occasion Horatio saw Pietro give her a black dress embroidered in silk. Another friend of Pietro's had also acted as intermediary in this affair, and had taken her a range of foodstuffs including 'lemons, fish-roes, apples, and afterwards I took her nearly every day wine, or chickens, quails, salad, lemons, apples and other things to eat'.[41] Many of these items were presumably considered delicacies and must have represented a considerable daily expenditure for a humble groom. It suggests that he was very keen to win Menica's favour. But she was anxious to downplay her intimacy with Pietro, therefore dismissing his

---

[39] Montaigne, *Journey to Italy*, 155.
[40] ASR, TCG, Processi, sec. XVII, vol. 46, c722v–723r, Horatio Marcantonio di Amelio, 9 May 1605.
[41] Ibid., c722r–v, Petrus Joannus Maria Lutis, 9 May 1605.

gifts by enumerating the items in such a way as to make them sound mean, pointedly describing them as having been of poor quality. 'He sent me a chicken, a little bit of steak and some little birds which were not at all good, and also four seville oranges, two lemons and two loaves of white bread.'[42] He had also given her two pairs of flesh-coloured silk stockings, but the fact that Menica had confided this to a friend suggests that she had not really disdained these gifts. Indeed, the friend added that she herself had seen Menica wearing the stockings.

PAYING THE RENT

Needless to say a prostitute's earnings had to be offset against the expenses of daily life and the overheads specific to the profession. One of the first considerations was finding enough money to pay the rent for somewhere to live, or at the very least, for the use of a bed with clients. Commercial sex could and did take place outside, particularly in vineyards, and several accounts mention women going to their clients' rooms; but having a place from which they could operate professionally seems to have been preferable. At the poorest and most casual end of the profession clients would perhaps have expected little more than a straw mattress laid on the floor in a room borrowed or rented for the occasion. For others there was plenty of cheap and probably run-down accommodation in the alleys of the Ortaccio, the most down-at-heel part of the *luoghi*. Here the houses would have been two or even three storeys high, built in terraces which enclosed a central courtyard. Narrow dark alleyways ran between the blocks, where pigs, cows and goats would still have roamed freely.[43] Down at the waterfront was the church of San Rocco, which gave on to the wide esplanade and harbour of Ripa Grande where boats were anchored.

Records of the rents paid by twenty-six prostitutes living nearby the church of San Rocco, between the years 1598 and 1603, give us an idea of the rental market at the poorer end of the professional hierarchy.[44] The rents paid mostly fell into a narrow bracket of between just over half a *scudo* per month and one *scudo* per month, roughly a servant woman's monthly wage. Analysing the regularity and manner of payments we can surmise that there were considerable fluctuations in their income. In one year a

---

[42] Ibid., c733r, 11 May 1605. [43] Based on Delumeau, *Vie économique et sociale*, 225–7.
[44] Archivio di Santa Maria in Acquirio (ASMA) (kept in the Biblioteca Corsini, Rome). The original marking was Sez. H Eredità e Carteggi del XVI–XVII secoli, Eredità Sebastiano Caccini, Libro Mastro 1598–1603. The archive was being reorganised when I consulted it, so the markings may have changed.

woman named Francesca, who stayed in one of the apartments for nearly four years, made four monthly payments of less than one *scudo*, four of one *scudo*, and then a lump payment of four and a half *scudi*.[45]

Courtesans at the other end of the professional hierarchy tended to live near the Via Lata (now Via del Corso), or clustered around the fashionable streets near Piazza della Trinità dei Monte. The piazza lay at the foot of the Pincian hill and the church of the Trinità which looked down on it was a favourite with courtesans, judging from their wills. However, rents were considerably more expensive than in the Ortaccio. Aloisia Napoletana paid twenty-five *scudi* per annum for a room in Via del Corso,[46] Isabella Sances living nearby paid thirty-six *scudi* per annum in quarterly payments,[47] and Anna Albritio Hispana paid seventy *scudi* for rooms in Via Paulina by the Collegio dei Greci.[48] Domenica Calvi from Siena, one of the most famous courtesans of the time, lived nearby. She paid just five *scudi* more and her contract included a clause demanding that she behave with decorum, a sure signal that she was living in an area in which the residents did not want the social tone of the neighbourhood to drop.[49]

BUYING CLOTHES

Finances permitting, prostitutes and courtesans in Rome could dress more or less as they wished – provided they did not attempt to disguise themselves as religious women or as men.[50] Given the nature of their profession we can assume that it was viewed as an important expense to be budgeted for. None the less we should be wary of assuming that prostitutes were any different to honest women or men in the importance that they attached to clothes. In early modern Europe clothes spoke volumes about the wearer, signalling one's profession, social distinctions and political allegiances.[51] The corollary was that people were acutely sensitive to what they and others wore, noting

---

[45] ASMA, Libro Mastro 1598–1603, C41.

[46] ASR, Trenta Notaii Capitolini (TNC) Ufficio (U) 19, vol. 67, c986r–v, Diana Mangona, 26 August 1605.

[47] ASR, TNC, U19, vol. 63, c474r–v, 5 July 1604.

[48] ASR, TNC, U19, vol. 74, c292r–v, 16 October 1607.

[49] ASR, TNC, U19, vol. 56, c881, 3 April 1602.

[50] For a fuller discussion of these issues see my 'The Clothing of Courtesans in Seventeenth Century Rome', in Catherine Richardson, ed., *Clothing Culture, 1350–1650* (Aldershot: Ashgate, 2004), 95–108. For laws regarding these prohibitions see ASV, Miscellanea, Armadio IV–V, vol. 60, c215; vol. 80, c180, c218, 18 October 1624, c62–105, 17 February 1618, c216, 219, 27 November 1624. And ASR, Bandi, vol. 13.

[51] There is a growing body of work on early modern clothing, its meanings, functions and symbolism as well as analyses of inventories. Catherine Richardson, ed., *Clothing Culture: 1350–1650* (Aldershot: Ashgate, 2004). A. R. Jones and Peter Stallybrass, *Renaissance Clothing and the Materials of Memory*

the gradations in colour, types of weave and the quality of textiles. This is reflected in the descriptions of clothing given in the court records.[52] One witness was able to describe the men who had attacked a courtesan under the cover of darkness, since he recognised the sound of the fabric they were wearing. 'There were about ten or eleven of them and they were well dressed, because as they walked you could hear the sound of silk.'[53] In the descriptions of the jewellery worn by a part-time courtesan named Orsola we see minute attention to detail in the testimonies by two neighbours: 'She was wearing five or six gold rings on her fingers, two gold chains around her neck and a pair of pendants in her ears with three pearls on each pendant . . . One of the necklaces was tiny, tiny and the pendants had black strands . . . .'[54]

Prostitutes acquired their clothing from many sources: some clothes were gifts, some were home-made (numerous prostitutes owned scissors and lengths of material), and cheap clothing could be had from market stalls, pedlars and from friends. The best-documented transactions, however, were those which took place between courtesans and *regattieri*, the city's second-hand clothes dealers. These men, predominantly Jews, not only bought and sold clothes and furniture, but also unpicked old garments and refashioned them into 'new' ones.[55] Since the payments for garments were often made in instalments, a contract was drawn up before a notary which described the garment and recorded the remainder of the payment owed by the purchaser.[56] For example, on 1 September 1595 Isabella Marabacci summoned Moses Melucci to her home. She wished to buy a dress made of *panno*,

(Cambridge: Cambridge University Press, 2000). Carole Collier Frick, *Dressing Renaissance Florence: Families, Fortunes and Fine Clothing* (Baltimore and London: The Johns Hopkins University Press, 2002), 301–20, 316. Maria Giuseppina Muzzarelli, *Guardaroba medievale: vesti e società dal XII al XVI secolo* (Bologna: Il Mulino, 1999). On prostitutes in particular see James A. Brundage, 'Sumptuary Laws and Prostitution in Late Medieval Italy', *Journal of Medieval History* 13 (1987), 343–55. Diane Owen Hughes, 'Le mode femminili e il loro controllo,' in Georges Duby, Michelle Perrot and Christiane Klapisch-Zuber, eds., *Storia delle donne in occidente. Il medioevo* (Rome and Bari: Laterza, 1998), 166–93.

[52] On these 'hierarchies' of clothing in Rome, Renata Ago, 'Gerarchia delle merci e meccanismi dello scambio a Roma nel primo seicento', *Quaderni Storici* 96 (1997), 663–83.

[53] ASR, TCG, Processi, sec. XVII, vol. 36, Vincenzio Jobaptista Alexandro Romano, c224r–v, 3 July 1604.

[54] ASR, Processi, sec. XVII, vol. 146, c9v–11r, Elizabetta Antonij Romana, 25 August 1618 and c13r, Antoniius Casini Milanese.

[55] For recent work on the market in second-hand clothing in Venice see Patricia Allerston, 'Clothing and Early Modern Venetian Society', *Continuity and Change* 15:3 (2000), 367–90. For Rome see Carlo Travaglini, 'Rigattieri e società romana nel settecento', *Quaderni Storici* 80:2 (1992), 415–47. And my 'Prostitution and the Circulation of Second-Hand Goods in Seventeenth Century Rome'.

[56] So the values recorded are not usually those of the full price, but of the remainder owing.

a cheap woollen cloth, decorated with green and orange trims and bows. There were two witnesses present and having made a down payment she still owed Moses about four and a half *scudi*. She agreed to pay fifteen *giulii* 'by Wednesday evening', another five *giulii* within a week, and the rest in two lots, until the total sum was paid.[57] Orinthia Focari di Siena purchased a decorated cloak in November 1604, but still owed fifteen and a half *scudi* which she pledged to pay within three months. Giuseppe Sirona the *regattiere* must have trusted her. No mention was made in the contract of his keeping the garment until she had paid, nor did he lay out specific dates for the interim payments. This was perhaps because Orinthia was well known both to him and to the notary Tranquillo Pizzuti, since she availed herself of Pizzuti's services at least fifteen times between 1604 and 1607, buying clothes, jewellery, furniture and drawing up her will.[58]

Documents recording the purchase of fifty dresses and over-gowns in the years on either side of 1600 show that courtesans tended to buy brightly coloured clothes, particularly in turquoise, yellow and *paonazzo* – a deep purplish blue. These were mostly made up in moderately priced woollen fabrics, as favoured by the average Roman at the time, trimmed with braids and ribbons. These added a hint of luxury if they were of fur or gold or silver thread.[59] These brilliant colours were the same as those worn by brides and newly married women in this period, as bright colours were considered to signal sexual availability, fertility and beauty.[60] Despite widely voiced anxieties about the ostentatious dress of courtesans in contemporary literature only ten of the fifty garments could have been described as luxurious. They were made of cloth of gold, cloth of silver, ormuz silk, satin and velvet, or were coloured with one of the most expensive dyes (crimson), or had cost twenty-five *scudi* or more.[61]

The most expensive and visible garments in courtesans' wardrobes were their dresses and the *zimarra*. The latter was a capacious cloak-like outer

---

[57] ASR, TNC, U19, vol. 36, c1, Isabella Marabacci, 1 September 1595.

[58] ASR, TNC, U19, vol. 64, c539r, Orinthia Focari Senese, November 4 1604.

[59] *Perpignano*, a French weave, *roverso* was like baize, which was widely worn by merchants, master artisans and middle-class foreigners and *saia* was a lightweight wool or silk with a diagonal weave. *Panno* was a cheap wool weave. Renata Ago discusses the quality, types and sales of textiles in Rome in 'Gerarchia delle merci'.

[60] Diane Owen Hughes shows that regulations in Florence in 1638 restricted the wearing of colour to the first six years of matrimony – when the wife was presumably at her most fertile. In Siena colour could be worn only for the first year of marriage. 'Le mode femminili', 183. In her analysis of Roman inventories Renata Ago finds that brides wore turquoise, yellow, pink, red and green. 'Il linguaggio del corpo', in Carlo Marco Belfanti and Fabio Giusberti, eds., *Storia d' Italia, annali 19: La moda* (Turin: Einaudi, 2003), 117–48.

[61] One in cloth of silver, two in satin, one in *ormesino* and two in velvet.

garment or over-dress, which may possibly have been linked particularly with prostitutes, given that in Florence prostitutes were given the name '*zimarrine*'. Prices varied greatly. At the top end of the profession Domenica Calvi bought two dresses in January 1601 for twenty-five *scudi* apiece. One was of silver cloth with a gold trim, the other of orange and purple *drappo* (probably a woollen cloth), with some gold and eleven ounces of silver decoration. Of the prices paid for the remaining twenty-six dresses, the most expensive 20 per cent were worth between twelve and twenty *scudi*, 32 per cent were worth between six and ten *scudi*, and the cheapest 18 per cent were worth between four and five *scudi*.[62]

Very few prostitutes owned more than two or three dresses and *zimarre*. Hieronima Paglia, who owned eight dresses and six *zimarre* in 1656, seems to have been the exception rather than the rule.[63] The rest of a courtesan's wardrobe consisted of smaller items which, worn even with a single dress, could vary its appearance to some extent: shirts, aprons, bonnets, pairs of sleeves and shawls. Other essentials were cloths for binding breasts and pairs of mules.[64] It has been suggested elsewhere that nearly all courtesans owned one or two black dresses, so they could pass as widows, and a pair of trousers so as to be disguised as men after curfew. Several of the inventories studied here do contain black dresses, but only one mentions trousers.[65]

MISCELLANEOUS EXPENSES

The cost of food is rarely mentioned. One prostitute, arrested whilst she was eating dinner, had 'sent someone to buy a *giulio* of mutton and for three *fogliette* of wine'.[66] Occasional mention is made of services which must have incurred extra expense. There was the need to pay intermediaries of various kinds. There were the boys who brought food over from the *osteria*, people who took messages, go-betweens and those who accompanied courtesans

---

[62] In fact, this is the minimum cost because in some documents the amount of money owed was *pro residuo pretis*, which suggests that an initial payment had already been paid for the dress.

[63] For a comparison with honest women's wardrobes see Ago, 'Il linguaggio del corpo', 114. For Hieronima Paglia Tiburtina, ASR, TNC, U19, vol. 258, c621r–624v and 643r–644r, 9 December 1655.

[64] For textiles and clothing I have used the glossary in Collier Frick, *Dressing Renaissance Florence*, 301–20.

[65] Camerano, 'Donne oneste o meretrici?', 62. For trousers see Hieronima Paglia, U19, vol. 258, c621r–624v and 643r–644r, 9 December 1655 and Caterina Chiavari, U19, vol. 257, c234r, 28 July 1655.

[66] ASR, TCG, Costituti, vol. 448, c58v, Magdalena uxor Luca Muratore, 20 December 1604.

to their clients' homes – which could cost one *scudo*.[67] However, the sinister figure of the procuress who took a chunk of a prostitute's earnings is not as visible in the court records as we might have anticipated. Courtesans sometimes referred to a woman or friend who had found them a client, but mention is never made of whether or how much they paid them.

Another expense was the cost of getting out of prison, though this expense was often shouldered by clients.[68] In 1601 Santa Nicole da Fabriano told the court that on one occasion she and her daughter had been arrested and that seven *scudi* had been paid for their release. However, this money had been paid not by her but by a gentleman in the service of Cardinal Visconti, presumably a client.[69] In the same year Magdalena, a married woman who had been imprisoned for carnal commerce with a soldier named Pietro, explained that she had been in prison for about two months at Corte Savella and managed to 'get away': 'Because I paid I can't rememer how much, because I paid for the whip – although they should have paid me, because I was pregnant . . . I learned afterwards that the money for my freedom was paid by Pietro who was arrested with me.'[70]

There were also expenses like medicines, doctors' bills and servants' wages which courtesans' wills reveal were sometimes paid for out of their estates.

SAVINGS

Women go into this profession in order to live and save something for their old age . . . and not for a change of air.[71]

The witness who made this statement in court was merely reaffirming a perception present in much contemporary literature: that prostitution could be a way out of poverty and a way of saving for the future. How much prostitutes saved or, to use a contemporary phrase, how much they were worth, is the subject of the remainder of this chapter. It will explore a range of sources which allow us to see different aspects of their finances. By piecing them together we obtain a general impression of the economic hierarchy within the profession.

---

[67] ASR, TCG, Costituti, vol. 508, c21r, Santa Nicole da Fabriano and c22v, Lucretia Vangeli Romana, 29 October 1601.

[68] Pisano, 'I birri a Roma nel '600'.

[69] ASR, TCG, Costituti, vol. 508, c21r, Santa Nicole da Fabriano, 29 October 1601.

[70] ASR, TCG, Costituti, vol. 448, c58v, Magdalena Luca Muratori, 20 December 1604.

[71] Cited in Ago, 'Di cosa si può fare commercio', 123.

Table 4 *Proportions of courtesans
leaving cash bequests (based on
fifty wills), 1594–1609*

Bequest (*scudi*)	Percentage
No cash bequest	38
1–6	22
10–30	18
31–50	14
51–90	8

Source: ASR, TNC, U19, vols. 33–79.

Women examined in court were routinely asked what they were 'worth', which referred to their savings, movable and immovable possessions. Of fifteen prostitutes interrogated between 18 October 1601 and 31 March 1602, nine (that is, almost two-thirds of them) seem to have been living hand-to-mouth, two had savings of ten *scudi*, and four declared savings of between forty and a hundred *scudi*.[72] We might have expected this source to privilege prostitutes from the lower spectrum of the profession, since the better-off were less likely to appear in court.[73] Despite this, nearly one-third of the respondents had substantial savings, if we consider that between half and one *scudo* could buy a month's rent in cheap accommodation.

When drawing up a will it was standard to leave at least one pious legacy, if nothing else.[74] Many women left several, in addition to bequests to family and friends. From this it is reasonable to assume that the 38 per cent of prostitutes who made no specific monetary bequests whatsoever had nothing to bequeath and were virtually destitute: 22 per cent left small sums, less than ten *scudi*. Of the remaining 40 per cent the wealthiest 8 per cent had saved between fifty and ninety *scudi*, a tidy sum which would have covered rental payments in the Ortaccio for more than five years.

Another source which casts a different light on the financial arrangements of prostitutes is the records of bails granted by the Governor's Tribunal. Bail was obviously only granted to prostitutes from the upper echelons of the profession. Such women may have been suspected of involvement in

---

[72] These are from ASR, TCG, Costituti, vols. 508 and 511, 1601 and 1602.

[73] They would have been able to offer a bribe to the *sbirri*, could have obtained a licence or might have had access to the protection of their well-off clients.

[74] As Camerano points out, 'Donne oneste o meretrici?', 638–9, they still had to draw up such a will even if they had not prostituted themselves for some time.

Table 5 *Bails granted to twelve courtesans in 1601*

Bail (*scudi*)	Number of women
25	5
50	3
100	3
200	1

Source: ASR, TCG, Fideiussioni vols. 44–6 (1601–3).

a crime and awaiting trial, or may merely have been called as witnesses. What they all had in common was the money and the connections to escape the overcrowded and demeaning conditions in prison by promising to pay a large bail. Of twelve women granted bail in the first few months of 1601 all had at least twenty-five *scudi* available, and the majority could raise between fifty and two hundred *scudi*. These documents also reveal the close links of trust and interdependence they had established with men of the elite. Most of them needed to have this promise underwritten by a man who agreed to stand as surety for them. It seems most likely that these would have been friends or clients, people who themselves stood to lose if the courtesan they associated with was imprisoned. For example, on 13 April 1601 Isabella Veneta and Ursula de Fuschis di Cesena promised to pay twenty-five *scudi* as a penalty if they failed to appear in court and Alessandro Gentili Romano promised to represent them and make sure that they would appear. A further two gentlemen pledged to pay the penalty if they failed to do so.[75] Settimia Luchetti Romana was placed under house arrest rather than be sent to jail on the condition that she paid two hundred *scudi* if she left the house.[76] However, she was bound over to stay not at her home, but at that of a nobleman, the Illustrissimo Signor Carlo Galli. He lived in the already fashionable Via Condotti 'near the fountain', whilst D. Alessandro Caglio from Rimini stood surety for the two hundred *scudi*. It is hard to imagine a nobleman offering shelter in this way to a courtesan unless she was his own *amica* or that of his friend Alessandro.

One difficulty facing the more successful courtesans was how to keep their money safe. Although much was invested in furniture, clothing and

75 ASR, TCG, Fideiussioni, vol. 44, c94r, 13 April 1601.
76 ASR, TCG, Fideiussioni, vol. 44, c26r, 7 January 1601.

jewels, other forms of investment were also used. Women at the top end of the profession could invest their money in several ways. The most common form of investment was a kind of savings bond called a *società d'ufficio*, a high-risk investment which successful courtesans frequently entered into with men of the nobility.[77] In 1607 Amabilia Antognetti Romana invested fifty *scudi* in a *società d'ufficio*, along with a nobleman, Ascanio Plumuon from Rome.[78] Quite a different kind of 'investment' is revealed by a notarial contract drawn up in the same year which shows that a courtesan called Anna de Arbritio from Spain had lent a total of two hundred and fifty *scudi* to a young nobleman, the Illustrissimo Fabius filio Stephani Latini from Rome. The first loan was an interest-free *mutuo*, for a hundred *scudi*, followed by a second loan of a hundred and fifty *scudi* which he undertook to repay within four months.[79] This loan would not have given Anna any financial return, but tying this young man to her financially may ultimately have served as an 'investment' in her clientele. What is particularly interesting is that he chose to borrow from a courtesan and not another man of his own social class.[80]

Another form of savings lay in property. In 1605 Diana Mangona, *cortigiana*, who lived in Via Sirena, rented out 'a ground-floor room' in her house in Via del Corso to an apothecary for twenty-five *scudi* per annum.[81] Flora Timodei de Marincola also had a house and a piece of land 'with oaks and walnut trees' located in the Marche, 'her home' which had been her dowry, and in her will she left them to her legitimate son.[82] When Santa Bastiani de Camerino was arrested one night in 1604 and asked what she was worth, she stated that she had a small house and vineyard in Camerino.[83] These few examples remind us of the narrow divide between honesty and dishonesty: many prostitutes would once have been 'honest' married women who could never have foreseen that one day they would be living a *vita dishonesta* in Rome.

Research from Venice suggests that during the early sixteenth century there was concern at the numbers of prostitutes who had been drawn into

[77] Camerano, 'Donne oneste o meretrici?', 652–3.

[78] ASR, TNC, U19, vol. 73, c77r–v, 28 May 1607.

[79] We do not know from this document that Anna was a *cortigiana*, but she appears in the parish records. AVIC, SMP, SA, 1610. The loan is recorded in ASR, TNC, U19, vol. 73, c413, 11 June 1607. And in 1607 she rented an apartment in Via Paulina for seventy *scudi*. ASR, TNC, U19, vol. 74, c292r–v, 16 October 1607.

[80] For more detail on *mutui*, see Camerano, 'Donne oneste o meretrici?', 650–3.

[81] ASR, TNC, U19, vol. 67, c986r–v, 26 August 1605.

[82] ASR, TNC, U19, vol. 64, c647r–v, 15 November 1604.

[83] ASR, TCG, Costituti, vol. 548, c44r, Santa Bastiani da Camerino, 17 December 1604.

debt by hiring clothes and furnishings at exorbitant rates.[84] Indebtedness was such a common condition in Rome that about 10 per cent of the population were in prison for debt at any one time.[85] Likewise twelve of the fifty prostitutes whose wills I have studied had outstanding debts. Some women owed money for food and care from servants during their illness.[86] Three owed rent,[87] three owed money to an *aromatario* (perfumier),[88] and four had loans outstanding on clothes and shoes which they had bought.[89] Five of them owed less than fifty *baiocchi*, three women had debts of between four and ten *scudi*, two owed between thirty and forty *scudi*, but these last two left movables of comparable or greater value than the debt.

POVERTY, WEALTH AND THE 1656 CENSUS

Poverty was endemic in early modern Europe and depending on how it has been defined, estimates of the number of poor in early modern Italy range from 75 per cent to 98 per cent of the population.[90] However, definitions vary. Brian Pullan has characterised poverty in terms of deprivation, insecurity and vulnerability, dividing the general population into three groups. First there were the indigent poor living permanently on charity or as vagabonds, who made up about 4–8 per cent of the population. Second were those who were occasional recipients of charity in times of crisis, comprising 20 per cent of the population. Finally there were those

---

[84] Patricia Allerston, 'Reconstructing the Second-Hand Clothes Trade in Sixteenth- and Seventeenth-Century Venice', *Costume* 33 (1999), 46–56. And 'Clothing and Early Modern Venetian Society'.

[85] Nearly 6,000 people in 1583–4. Blastenbrei, 'La quadratura del cerchio', 10–11. The population was about 50,000–60,000 and 25,609 loans were made. And in 1589, approximately half the population of the city had relied upon the Monte di Pietà, a charitable institution which provided loans and pawned goods for the poor. Mario Tosi, *Il Sacro Monte di Pietà di Roma e le sue amministrazioni (1539–1874)* (Rome: Cassa di Risparmio di Roma, Libreria dello Stato, 1937), 81.

[86] ASR, TNC, U19, vol. 36, c2r–v, 1 September 1595, Aurelia Mattei Barbarrossa and Lucretia Joannis Sori Fiorentina mentioned above.

[87] ASR, TNC, U19, vol. 45, c399r–v, Plautilla Antini Nepi, 4 November 1598. U19, vol. 74, c230r–v, 231r–v, Felice Intaglini Montepulciano. U19, vol. 70, c431r–v, Eugenia Marini de Rubeis, Orvieto, 22 June 1606.

[88] ASR, TNC, U19, vol. 67, c941r–v, Diana Pandolfini Quorli, 22 August 1605. U19, vol. 68, c993r–v, Floralisa de Octavius Macerata. U19, vol. 74, c230r–v, 231r–v, Felice Intaglini Montepulciano, 7 October 1607.

[89] ASR, TNC, U19, vol. 64, c483r–v, Lucretia Sori Fiorentina, 27 October 1604. U19, vol. 64, c765r–v, Hieronima Simonis di Castro, 28 November 1604. U19, vol. 68, c993r–v, Floralisa de Octavious Macerata, 20 December 1605. U19, vol. 70, c431r–v, 22 June 1606, Eugenia Marini di Orvieto.

[90] For example, Carlo Cipolla suggests 75–80 per cent in 'Economic Fluctuations: the Poor and Public Policy, Italy 16th and 17th Centuries', in Thomas Riis, ed., *Aspects of Poverty in Early Modern Europe* (Florence: EUI, 1981), 65–77. Brian Pullan suggests 98 per cent, in 'Poveri, mendicanti e vagabondi (secoli XIV–XVII)', in C. Vivanti and R. Romano, eds., *Storia d'Italia. Dal feudalismo al capitalismo. Annali I* (Turin: Einaudi, 1978), 981–1048, 988.

whose livelihoods were insecure, becoming threatened when times were hard, comprising 50–70 per cent of the population.[91]

Such classifications are useful in recognising the potential vulnerability of most people's economic condition. Yet they simultaneously sweep away the rather subtler distinctions and differences in economic rank which people used as reference points in their day-to-day lives. Recognising this, other historians have added more subjective facets of poverty to this core 'economic' definition. They stress the importance of social context, and argue that once a subsistence level has been attained, poverty is 'relative and culturally determined.'[92] For example, Ago's 'economic anthropology' of Baroque Rome finds that a great many people categorised themselves as poor. They ranged from those who had no income, work or possessions, to those in possession of all three.[93] On the other hand, very few described themselves as rich, usually considering that other people were rich but never themselves.[94] Overall she notes that, 'It is their social position, not their income, which orients perceptions and definitions of the economic condition.'[95]

Where did prostitutes and courtesans figure in these classifications of wealth and how did they estimate their own wealth? Fortunately there is a census from 1656 of the *rione* (district) of Campo Marzio, which allows us to contextualise the wealth of prostitutes within the broader community and gives us data on the (perceived) wealth of a large number of prostitutes.[96] The census was drawn up in response to the news that the plague was approaching Rome. It was intended to identify the poor and the miserably poor, those groups who would be most critically in need of alms if the city ground to a halt, and to discover who and how many people were already ill.[97] The taking of the census was entrusted in each *rione* to a prelate, two gentlemen, two doctors and a surgeon. The prelate was supposed to

[91] Pallan, 'Poveri, mendicanti e vagabondi', 989.

[92] Michel Mollat, 'The Poor in the Middle Ages: the Experience of a Research Project', in Thomas Riis, ed., *Aspects of Poverty in Early Modern Europe* (Florence: EUI, 1981), 29–37. And Wim Blockmans, 'Circumscribing the Concept of Poverty', in Riis, *Aspects of Poverty*, 39–45.

[93] See chapter 3, 'Un'antropologia economica', in Ago, *Economia barocca*, 81–109. She takes the replies given by fifty-five men when asked whether they were rich or poor and how they lived.

[94] Ibid., 87.   [95] Ibid., 89.

[96] ASR, Camerale II, Sanità, Busta 4/5, Contagio di Roma. Descrittione del rione di Campo Martio, fatta il mese di luglio 1656 (cnn, except introduction). This census is also discussed in Didier Bodart, 'La descrizione del rione di Campo Marzio di Roma: artistes à Rome durant la peste de 1656', *Bulletin de l'Institut Historique Belge de Rome* 38 (1967), 475–531.

[97] 'Lo scopo di individuare le famiglie già "povere e miserabili".' Eugenio Sonnino and Rosa Traina, 'La peste del 1656–57 a Roma. Organizzazione sanitaria e mortalità', in *Demografia Storica delle Città Italiane: Relazioni e comunicazioni presentate al convegno tenuto ad Assisi, 1980* (Bologna: Clueb, 1982), 433–52.

go personally to visit each house, and the head of household was asked to estimate his or her own wealth, which was perhaps confirmed from a glance around the premises.[98] Two artisans, nominated as 'heads of the streets', assisted, and perhaps offered local knowledge about families.

Campo Marzio was the largest and most populous *rione* of Rome, housing 3,599 families and a total of 15,543 people, about 12 per cent of the total population of the city.[99] The census calculates the wealth of 3,511 households (of the 3,599) in this *rione*, and the author explains the criteria adopted when classifying people's wealth.[100] The population is divided into four categories. The poorest of the poor were the *miserabili*; they were the needy poor who depended on charity and alms and constituted 2.8 per cent of the population.[101] Next came *i poveri*, the working poor. These were people whose labour would not be needed in a general crisis, or who lacked sufficient goods to sell to tide them over hard times. They were servants, labourers, artisans and small shopkeepers: 66 per cent of the population fell into this category. Thirdly there were the *commodi*, the comfortably off, a category for which no definition or professional group was offered, presumably because it was self-explanatory. A range of professions were represented here: an architect, a barber, a collar-maker, a painter, a priest, a grain measurer, a musician, a notary, a carpenter and a boatman. It was indeed not the professional 'tag' which counted as much as whether people had a 'comfortable lifestyle', an entirely subjective measure based on the person's status and expectations.[102] Included under this heading were 28 per cent of the population. Last, and certainly least in terms of numbers, were the *ricchi*, who accounted for 2 per cent of the total, amongst whom were numbered the cardinals, princes, prelates, ambassadors and *cavalieri*.

A similar census was carried out in other *rioni* of the city, allowing a comparison with the districts of Ponte and Trastevere, which shows that Campo Marzio was a comparatively well-to-do area. For example, in the *rione* of Ponte 44 per cent of the population were described as *miserabili*, the needy poor.[103] Trastevere was even poorer, which might explain why Pius V had originally desired to send the *cortigiane* there: 94 per cent of its

98   Bodart, 'La descrizione del rione di Campo Marzio', 476.
99   In 1656, prior to the plague, the total population was 120,595. Sonnino, 'Intorno alla "Sapienza"', 344.
100 ASR, Camerale II, Sanità, Busta 4/5, Contagio di Roma, Introduction.
101 And this is discounting those living in the city's *ospedali*. In that year there were 782 'poveri d'ospedale' in the city as a whole.
102 See Ago's lengthy discussion of this issue in *Economia barocca*, chapter 3.
103 Sonnino and Traina, 'La peste del 1656–57 a Roma', 438.

Table 6 *The wealth of the general population of Campo Marzio, as calculated from 3,511 households of 3,599 from the 1656 census*

Wealth	Number of households	Percentage
Ricchi	79	2
Commodi	1,002	29
Poveri	2,330	66
Miserabili	100	3
Total	3,511	100

households were designated as needing to receive alms. Indeed, during the 1656 plague the area was fenced in overnight, and alms were distributed daily to the entire population.[104]

The *Stati delle Anime* show that 21 per cent of the city's prostitutes lived in Campo Marzio – some 240 courtesans out of a city total of 1,138.[105] We can therefore compare their estimated wealth with that of the rest of the population. These 240 courtesans were living in 203 households: 27 of the households contained two or three courtesans and 14 consisted of sisters, mothers and daughters who were all courtesans. Of these households, 195 had a wealth category assigned to them: 43 per cent were considered to be comfortably off, 57 per cent were considered to be poor. None were classified as *miserabili*, and none as *ricchi*.

Used as we are to considering prostitutes as amongst the poorest and most economically disadvantaged sections of the population these are somewhat surprising data: not only because such a large percentage of this group of courtesans was classed as comfortably off, but because this was a larger percentage than is found amongst the general population, only 28 per cent of whom were considered to be *commodi*. There are inevitably some problems with the data. Given that only one-fifth of the city's known prostitutes were living there, it is possible that by the mid-seventeenth century the *rione* of Campo Marzio was the area where only the richest courtesans lived. The remaining four-fifths, living elsewhere in the city (such

[104] BAV, Chigi, E III, 62, f.784.
[105] This total comes from the summaries of the population given for 1656 in the *Stati delle Anime* in Archivio di Stato di Firenze, Carte Strozziane (Parti), *Summarium Animarum Romae Existentium Anno*, c139.

Table 7 *The wealth of households headed by*
prostitutes/courtesans in the 1656 census

Wealth	Number of households	Percentage
Ricchi	0	
Commodi	83	43
Poveri	112	57
Miserabili	0	
Total	195	100

as Trastevere), may have been poor.[106] This is, however, unlikely, given the district's long association with prostitution. Furthermore, the courtesan households in the *rione* were distributed across thirty-one streets, some of which were more 'fashionable', others, such as Schiavonia, the Ortaccio and the Port of Ripetta, which were still poor areas. Another difficulty is that, from a survey of heads of households, it is impossible to estimate the numbers of destitute vagabonds who prostituted themselves in a city in which poverty was endemic. Nor can we estimate the numbers of those other women who formed part of the hidden face of prostitution: prostituting themselves part time and trying to cover their traces. Finally it could be argued that courtesans may have lied about their wealth so as to give a better account of their professional success. However, since they were subject to an inheritance tax, they would have had more reason to hide their financial situation than boast of it in an official context.

Comparing and contrasting the data from these different sources it is possible to draw some conclusions about the wealth of prostitutes in early modern Rome. Of the 60 per cent who were poor, I suggest that about 40 per cent were very poor, by which I mean living hand to mouth. This proportion corresponds to those who left nothing in their wills (38 per cent) and to the nine women interrogated by the courts who replied that they were 'worth nothing'. I estimate that the remaining 20 per cent of the poor had some savings put by. These were the 20 per cent of women who left less than ten *scudi* in pious bequests, and the two women who estimated their savings at ten *scudi*. The remaining 40 per cent were the 'comfortably-off' courtesans. At the bottom of this category would have been those who could afford to pay four *scudi* for a new dress and two

---

[106] I do not know how many prostitutes lived in Trastevere, where the general population was so poor.

scudi a month in rent. At the top were those like Orinthia Focari who spent sixty-five *scudi* for two pearl necklaces and a pair of pearl earrings, or Domenica Calvi whose furnishings and savings could well have exceeded a thousand *scudi* – given that just her bedroom was worth three hundred *scudi*.[107]

The obsessive focus in early modern literature on the wealth of prostitutes, and the perception that prostitution was a quick way to make good money, was, after all, not merely an archaic trope. On the contrary, it appears as though these texts were expressing very real concerns, possibly even resentment, at the high wages to be made from sin. The way in which prostitution was organised in Rome, particularly the institution of the *amico fermo*, meant that many women had regular, long-term clients within a recognised framework. This lent stability to an otherwise precarious profession. Carnal commerce could be very lucrative, but not all the clients were courtiers who could be free with their money, or intended to play by the rules and pay up. Luck and networking skills were also needed if a woman was to meet stable and honourable clients who would not try to dodge payment or turn to random violence. But the preponderance of wealthy men in the city meant that their small change could feed and clothe a great many women and, if necessary, their families too.

The majority of early modern sources concerned with financial matters are those produced by the wealthy or by institutions. As a result we are all too familiar with the vast sums of money spent on the clothing, palaces, furnishings and dowries of the wealthy. But there was a staggering difference between the wealth of the elites and that of the popular classes.[108] By comparison it can be hard to take these accounts of earning five or ten *scudi* very seriously, or to convey what these sums may have meant to those involved, not just in terms of what they could purchase, but in terms of how women felt about themselves and their prospects. In seventeenth-century Rome ten *scudi* was the difference between wearing rags and buying a good-quality new dress; between being homeless and paying one year's rent. What is more, these meagre amounts of money meant something else, something which cannot be quantified: connected with self-respect, with escaping from desperate poverty and with not being at the bottom of the social heap. An account of a party held by a group of courtesans illustrates this very clearly.

---

[107] ASR, TNC, U19, vol. 71, c181, Orinthia Focari di Siena, 20 October 1606. ASR, TNC, U19, vol. 53, c122r–v, Domenica Calvi, 18 January 1601. See also chapter 8.
[108] Selwyn also comments on this income disparity for Naples, in *A Paradise*, 38.

The party was held in Eugenia's apartment and she had arranged for two married women (Onofria and Speranza) to come and help out. Onofria explained to the court that Eugenia had come 'asking whether I would please go to her home to [. . .] and to sweep the house since several women were coming to lunch'.[109] Both women were also present during the party, so perhaps they were also helping with food preparation or waiting at table. The 'honest'/'dishonest' division of women had clearly gone awry, when carefree young courtesans were paying honest married woman to come and clean their houses. This impression is reinforced by the pitying remarks one of the courtesans made about the married women:

We were only eight at table, but there were two other women in the house who are married women, one is called Onofria, wife of Orlando the baker, the other is Speranza, wife of Dente the policeman, and *these two married women are poor souls (poveraccie) and they came to earn something.*[110]

Much scholarship on the history of women has emphasised the importance of honesty, shame and reputation in women's lives, with chastity, institutions and marriage as the only safe harbours for women. In this context the ten *scudi* earned by a prostitute supposedly lacks meaning, since the woman who has earned it has, at the same time, lost her place in honest society. Yet in her choice of words to describe the 'honest' women who had come to do her cleaning, Jan (who was by no means a high-class courtesan) paid no lip-service to the concepts of honesty or shame which were extolled for women. Instead she emphasised only something far simpler, which was to do with crude social status, with being able to have fun and having someone else to do her dirty work for her.

Her comments are a reminder of just how important it is to consider concepts such as honesty, dishonesty, wealth and poverty from the perspectives of those at the bottom of the social heap, rather than the reverse. In the 1656 census, although the terms *commodo* and *povero* were subjective and dependent on the subject's social position, the assessments of the economic status of prostitutes in the census were made in relation to the social context: as compared with other female heads of household and with the community's expectations of what prostitutes could earn. Perhaps above all they were dependent on the prostitutes' own perceptions of their wealth. One hundred *scudi* would have been a derisory sum of money for a woman of good family, who probably needed more than a thousand *scudi*

---

[109] ASR, TCG, Processi, sec. XVII, vol. 44, c124–5r, 25 January 1605.
[110] Ibid. (italics added).

in order to live 'comfortably'.[111] Yet that same sum would have signified a very 'comfortable' life to the average young prostitute. In comparison with the poverty of the life they had left behind, and the twin spectres of homelessness and starvation which they must have hoped to avoid through prostitution, it is understandable that they should have been perceived by others, and, importantly, have perceived themselves, to be 'comfortably off'.

[111] See Ago's thorough discussion of this issue in *Economia barocca*, 80–109, 89.

CHAPTER 8

At home

> For when you come into one of their Palaces . . . you seeme to enter
> into the Paradise of Venus. For their fairest roomes are most glorious
> and glittering to behold . . . She may minister unto thee the stronger
> temptations to come to her lure, she will shew thee her chamber of
> recreation . . . But beware notwithstanding all these *illecebrae* (allure-
> ments) and *lenocinia amoris* (ornaments of love), that thou enter not
> into termes of private conversation with her.[1]

One of the central images in the visual and literary iconography of prostitution was that of the glamorously attired courtesan in her richly furnished
apartments. Her home and its contents were a symbol of all that she aspired
to and all that she stood to lose. It was also an alluring but dangerous trap
for men: a luxurious palace of delight in which men were robbed of their
reason, their health and their patrimony. This emphasis on the courtesan's
home in contemporary commentary was a reflection of the importance of
their apartments in their daily lives. By the seventeenth century courtesans had a long tradition of receiving their clients and other guests in their
rooms, whether for conversation, music, parties or dinners. They were
expected to provide comfortable, even luxurious surroundings, according
to their means, aspirations, and the status of their clientele. At the same
time these were also homes: places where the women slept, ate with their
friends and family, gave birth and raised children. This chapter explores the
status and function of the home and its contents in the day-to-day lives of
prostitutes and their clients. Particular emphasis is given to the courtesans'
apartments as a social space and to the function and meaning of domestic
objects within the context of that professional sociability.

---

[1] Coryat, *Crudities*, 403–5.

MOVING HOUSE

All the whores change house every three months so as to seem fresh like fruit.[2]

Prostitutes were a highly mobile sector of the population, as were other poor city dwellers across early modern Europe.[3] Of 941 prostitutes who appear in the parish records between 1600 and 1621, only 176 appear in subsequent years in the same parish.[4] Those for whom there are multiple records had often moved house at every appearance in the registers, although sometimes they had only moved down the street. Of the twenty-six prostitutes who rented accommodation near the church of San Rocco at the end of the sixteenth century, eleven stayed in the accommodation for just one to two months, five stayed for between three months and a year, whilst only six stayed for between one and four years.[5]

The court records reveal more about this kind of mobility. Called to give testimony in court in August 1618, a prostitute named Orsola Brunetta Veneta described her movements over the previous two years since her arrival in Rome. She had spent six months in Tor Sanguina, nine months in Sant' Andrea delle Fratte, seven months living by the Convertite and three months living in Via del Bufalo, twenty days of which were spent in a 'well-known house' owned by a certain Bartolomeo. Then she had moved to the Vicolo di Santa Caterina della Rota with another woman, leaving because they got on badly. She then stayed in another house whilst waiting for a place in Vicolo Calabraca for which she had paid a deposit.[6] Poverty, difficulties paying the rent, rapidly changing relationships, arguments, or suddenly changing circumstances (including for the better) all contributed to this kind of extreme mobility which must have inhibited a woman's chances of acquiring a stable clientele. Moving very frequently may also have seemed dishonourable, given that better-known prostitutes were commonly identified in trials by the street they lived in, or a nearby landmark. One witness described his acquaintances with prostitutes in the following manner.

---

[2] Delicado, *La lozana andalusa*, 144.

[3] For example, see James R. Farr, 'Crimine nel vicinato: ingiurie, matrimonio e onore nella Digione del XVI–XVII secolo', *Quaderni Storici* 66:3 (1987), 839–54, 842. Daniel Roche finds that nine out of ten servants in early modern Paris moved each month. *Le peuple de Paris. Essai sur la culture populaire au XVIIIe siècle* (Paris: Fayard, 1998), 96.

[4] See Appendix for registers consulted in the Archivio del Vicariato.

[5] Archivio di Santa Maria in Acquirio, Sez. H. Eredità e Carteggi del XVI–XVII secoli, Eredità Sebastiano Caccini. Libro Mastro, 1598–1603, c46–53.

[6] ASR, TCG, Processi, sec. XVII, vol. 146, c39r–40r, 12 September 1618.

A Spanish girl at the Fontana di Trevi called Donna Eugenia, with another Spanish girl who lives in that street that goes to the Madonna of Constantinople . . . whose name I forget, and a Venetian who lives at . . . called Aurora Turchetti, and one who lives at San Giacomo degli'Incurabili, called Giovanna if I remember well.[7]

A POOR ROOM

We can piece together what a poor prostitute's room or a wealthy courtesan's apartment might have been like, and the kinds of activities which went on there, from fragmentary descriptions from the court records, coupled with wills and inventories.[8] In 1600 the walls of most prostitutes' rooms would have been bare, with at most one or two cheap religious paintings on the walls. However, since it was common for men to drop by with their friends, even poor prostitutes would have tried to provide seating for guests. In 1602 Beatrice Gualtieri sold a great many household goods to a second-hand dealer for just ten *scudi*. Amongst these she had seating for ten, and a small table with a striped cloth. It was a motley assortment of furnishings, as if collected over time from different sources: five walnut chairs covered in 'used' embossed red leather, two old and broken stools, a small chair and two chairs seated with straw.[9] Costantia Stacheimburgh left some furniture in her will of 1615, amongst which were three tables, four 'used' walnut chairs and four old stools.[10] Although these were only 'lowly' prostitutes, this abundance of chairs is not unusual, given that they were living in an urban environment. Studies suggest that whilst homes in rural areas often had no chairs at all, those in cities often had seating for many people, even amongst the lower classes.[11] It also points to the particularly sociable nature of prostitution in Rome.

[7] ASR, TCG, Processi, sec. XVII, vol. 114, c2256r–v, Marcantonio Brillo Romano, 3 August 1613. See also Elizabeth Cohen's discussion of prostitutes' homes. 'Open and Shut: the Social Meanings of the Cinquecento Roman House', *Studies in the Decorative Arts*, Fall–Winter (2001–2), 61–84.

[8] Alessandra Camerano has tried to identify and distinguish prostitutes from courtesans using their inventories. There are some similarities in our findings. The differences may be explained by an evolution in availability of goods and fashions of interior furnishing, since most of her material is drawn from the earlier sixteenth century. 'Donne oneste o meretrici?', 658–63. Particularly helpful for this discussion of the quality of goods is Renata Ago's article 'Gerarchia delle merci'.

[9] ASR, TNC, U19, vol. 64, c888r–v, 17 December 1604.

[10] ASR, TNC, U19, vol. 68, c7, 12r–v, 5 September 1615.

[11] Raffaella Sarti mentions that in Paris in the period there were on average twelve pieces of furniture in each apartment for seating. *Europe at Home*, 123–4. Doctors in sixteenth- to seventeenth-century Paris had an 'incredible number of chairs accumulated in the sitting room', ranging from twenty-two to thirty-seven. Françoise Lehoux, *Le cadre de vie des médecins parisiens aux XVIe et XVII siècles* (Paris: Editions Picard, 1976), 177. However, a study of seventeenth-century Montpellier finds that very few owned chairs. Valérie Lafage. 'Le gîte, le couvert et l'habit. Aspects de la culture matérielle à Montpellier dans le premier tiers du XVII siècle', *Annales du Midi: la culture matérielle dans le midi*

Such a room would also have contained one or more chests, like Caterina Hieronima's 'pair of old smooth walnut chests',[12] for clothes, crockery, linens and valuables, all of which could be safely locked away. Chests were also the means by which a woman's possessions were transported. When a courtesan named Antonia got married she moved in with her new mother-in-law, taking three chests full of goods and a bed, which were carried through the streets on two carts.[13] Those who could afford it also had a sideboard (*buffeto*) or dresser (*credenza*) for storage and for displaying crockery. Antea Matthei di Anguillara had, unusually, two chests containing her linens which were made of *albuccio*, a softer white wood commonly found in women's inventories. This was probably of inferior quality to walnut and cheaper, hence its frequency in women's households.[14]

Courtesans needed light and heating in the winter, since much entertaining took place during the evenings. In her account of dining with the city's police chief, Captain Valerio, Sueca Saracinelli described his amazement at the misery of her apartment. He exclaimed, 'how can you stay like this, without a fire when it is so cold, you will be so miserable', sending his man out for food and coal.[15] In order to keep out the cold even quite poor women such as Beatrice Gualtieri and Caterina Hieronima had *gelosie*, waxed textile blinds for the windows which kept the draughts out. Beatrice also possessed four brass candlesticks, 'two big and two small', some women had a lantern, whilst pairs of 'fire irons with brass balls on the end' were very common. It is possible that courtesans particularly favoured apartments with fireplaces for the way they created a warm, intimate interior and a focal point for sociability, as described in an account of an evening spent in company at a courtesan's home: 'And all of the company except for Cesare gathered around the fireplace, playing and singing as you do.'[16] The police records also reveal that fireplaces were considered good hiding places. One evening in May 1595 the police broke down the door of the

de la France à l'époque moderne 115 (2003), 2–41. For Venice see Patricia Fortini Brown, *Private Lives in Renaissance Venice: Art, Architecture and the Family* (New Haven and London: Yale University Press, 2004.)

[12] ASR, TNC, U19, vol. 72, c276r–v, Caterina Hieronima di Siena, 7 February 1607. Lafage mentions that chests or dressers featured in nearly all inventories in Montpellier. 'Le gîte, le couvert', 14.

[13] ASR, TCG, Costituti, vol. 461, c205v, Francesca uxor dominici Florensis, 25 September 1596.

[14] Whether white wood was a sign of poverty or femininity is, however, not clear. Renata Ago, 'Middling Sort Domestic Interiors in Seventeenth-Century Rome', unpublished paper given at 'Domestic and Institutional Interiors in Early Modern Europe', held at the Victoria and Albert Museum, London, 19–20 November 2004.

[15] ASR, TCG, Processi, sec. XVII, vol. 23, c175v, 5 December 1602.

[16] ASR, Sezione Orvieto, Archivio del Governatore, Processi, vol. 121A: 1600–1602, cnn. Hieronimo Gualtieri, 17 January 1601.

apartment where Semidea, a courtesan from Pistoia, lived, 'and once inside with my colleagues we found a young man hidden in the chimney and Semidea was upstairs in another room'.[17] Candlesticks also had alternative uses: Pasqua *cortigiana* beat Sabbatina *cortigiana* over the head with a candlestick, accusing her of acting as a spy.[18]

What is striking overall about most of the documents is the recurrence of adjectives which denote that these objects were not new: they were usually 'old' (*vecchie, usate*) and sometimes battered and broken (*rotte*), and many of them would probably have seen a great many previous owners. Some of the stools and tables were painted, which may have hidden poor-quality wood. Yet there are also elements which hint at a faded elegance, past glory, or simply unrealised ambitions. Most of the courtesans' furniture was made of walnut, an expensive and durable wood, used particularly for elegant carved chairs.[19] Also, nearly all had at least one item (a casket or perhaps a chair) covered in *corame*, the embossed leather used by the better-off for wall hangings, which provided a hint of luxury and glamour within their limited budgets.

AN ELEGANT *SALA*

Wealthier courtesans often had more than one room, one of which was described as the *sala*. This was a reception room in which the most public forms of entertainment took place. It would have been frequented not only by actual clients, but by their friends, potentially new clients. Like their poorer colleagues, higher-status courtesans sought to cater for the presence of many guests by providing extensive seating arrangements; the difference was the quality, quantity and ability to afford matching sets of objects.[20] Orinthia Focari had sixteen matching chairs, eight big and eight small, all upholstered in printed calf-hide with a red fringe.[21] Such courtesans also had walnut chests and dressers for storage and display, just more of them and with more elaborate decoration. Caterina Chiavari, for example, had

---

[17] ASR, TCG, RB, vol. 97, c187v, 19 May 1595.

[18] ASR, TCG, Costituti, vol. 550, c93v, Sabbatina Urbivetri, 20 May 1605.

[19] Thera Wijsenbeek Olthuis, 'A Matter of Taste: Lifestyle in Holland in the Seventeenth and Eighteenth Century', in *Material Culture: Consumption, Life-Style, Standard of Living, 1500–1900*, Proceedings of the Eleventh International History Congress, Milan, 1994, vol. B4 (Milan: Università Bocconi, 1994), 48–9.

[20] Camerano finds that the bedrooms of high-class courtesans were extravagantly furnished, whilst other rooms remained comparatively bare. This distinction does not pertain to the mid-seventeenth-century inventories I have seen. 'Donne oneste o meretrici?', 659.

[21] ASR, TNC, U19, vol. 71, c487r–v, 26 October 1606.

two walnut buffets, a *credenza*, and two large walnut chests with carved lion's feet.[22]

The richer courtesans hung their walls with wall-coverings made either of *brocatello* (brocade) or more commonly, *corame*. The latter consisted of rectangles of leather which were sewn together, often dyed in quite brilliant colours, embossed with patterns in silver or gold leaf and then glazed. When new a room hung with this must have glimmered and shone, conveying a sense of great wealth and splendour, and indeed, new *corame* was very costly and fashionable.[23] Orinthia Focari Senese, who lived on the Via del Corso, had not one but two rooms decorated dramatically in this way: one room had the walls covered in new glazed black *corame* five skins high, the other room was hung with gold and silver *corame*.[24]

Such fine furnishings were necessary if a woman was entertaining gentlemen and noblemen in her apartments. They would have expected to be entertained in a place which was not only comfortable, but appropriate to their social status. Yet it was not always necessary to be able to buy all these objects in order to cut a fine figure, for anything and everything could be rented. A courtesan who wished to impress but couldn't afford to buy the necessaries, or a well-off courtesan recently arrived in the city, could give a very good impression of herself for a few *scudi* a month.[25] Angela Biraghe rented a luxurious bedroom, including the wall-hangings, chairs, a chest and canopy from a Jewish dealer for only four silver *scudi* a month.[26] One of the witnesses whom she used as her guarantor was a nobleman, probably the very man whom she hoped to receive in this splendid room.

This raises interesting questions about the relationship between the courtesan's domestic interior and her clientele, and how much influence clients had over their courtesans' choices of furnishings, if any.[27] In January 1596, the courtesan Dianora Petri Siciliana left a down-payment for a room of 295 skins of embossed and gilded leather wall-hangings, worth twenty silver *scudi*. She pledged the rest in monthly payments of two *scudi*, and her witness was a nobleman, the 'Magnifico' Christophoro Gripho, presumably her *amico*.[28] Was he just her guarantor? Was it her money, her choice, her taste and her status which these hangings would have advertised? Or were

[22] ASR, TNC, U19, vol. 257, c233r–235r, 28 July 1655.
[23] This is pointed out by Thornton, *The Italian Renaissance Interior*, 85.
[24] ASR, TNC, U19, vol. 71, c487r–v, 26 October 1606.
[25] On rentals generally see Ago, 'Gerarchia delle merci'.
[26] ASR, TNC, U19, vol. 34, c5r–6v, 4 May 1594. The *regattiere* was Gratiano Tedesco.
[27] Thornton discusses the relationship between courtesans, their clients and furnishings in *The Italian Renaissance Interior*, 354–5.
[28] ASR, TNC, U19, vol. 37, c70, 11 January, 1596.

they chosen by him, as a surrounding worthy of his rank and that of his friends when they came for the evening?

Thornton has hypothesised that courtesans were somehow 'fashion leaders' when it came to interior decoration, which is confirmed by notarial documents which show that elite men bought some of their furnishings from courtesans.[29] Semidea Jacobi Bianchi was a fifteen-year-old courtesan from Cortona who lived in Via Paulina. In 1606 she sold a very colourful 'room' for the princely sum of forty-four *scudi* and sixty-four *baiocchi*. It consisted of 183 skins of gold and silver *corame* enamelled in green and red. One of the buyers was a nobleman, the Illustrissimo Mario Cenci, captain of the militia, and the other was 'a well-known soldier'.[30] This was not an isolated case. Other documents show that courtesans bought and sold furnishings, presumably relying on their extensive client networks to act as brokers on the Roman second-hand market.[31] It was not just that they might buy goods in order to sell them on immediately, or that the odd chair or bed could be resold for ready cash when needed. A courtesan could either accumulate furnishings which could then be rented out individually, or if she had enough to furnish an entire apartment, she could rent or sub-let that apartment.[32] This would have given her a steady and more reliable income than she would have from prostitution, particularly once she was past her prime. This might explain why in September 1605 Orinthia Focari put the wherewithal to furnish three fine apartments into storage in another woman's house.[33]

THE TRAPPINGS OF THE PROFESSION

Musical instruments, writing desks and paintings often appear amongst the possessions of well-to-do courtesans. Books have also been found, though not in my sample.[34] These were all usually inexpensive objects, in terms of monetary values, but of great symbolic value as a statement of the courtesan's education and professional persona, and were kept in the *sala*. Hieronima Paglia had a '*pulpite* for writing' covered in *corame*, which was worth a mere thirty *baiocchi*, whilst Caterina Chiavari had a small walnut

---

[29] Thornton, *The Italian Renaissance Interior*, 354–5.
[30] ASR, TNC, U19, vol. 71, c382r–v, 16 October 1606. We know she was a courtesan from AVIC, SMP, SA, 1605, c17v, 18 March 1605.
[31] See my 'Prostitution and the Circulation of Second-Hand Goods'.
[32] Thanks to Patrizia Cavazzini for pointing out the possibilities of renting out furniture.
[33] ASR, TNC, vol. 68, c232r, 28 September 1605. See my 'Prostitution and the Circulation of Second-Hand Goods'.
[34] Camerano, 'Donne oneste o meretrici?', 661.

studioletto worth two and a half *scudi*.[35] In the 1650s Hieronima Paglia had a small harp, worth two *scudi*, and Flavia de Baronis had a *cembalo a coda*, worth ten *scudi*.[36] Indeed, the cost of the instrument was far less than the cost of the lessons required to master it. Just one month's music lessons, given to a Roman courtesan in 1590, cost fifteen *scudi*, which, multiplied by the number of months it would take to become reasonably proficient in an instrument or singing, suggests that a great premium was set on these skills.[37] Given the link between music and the arts of love, however, this is not surprising.[38]

Although relatively few instruments are mentioned in inventories, this vastly under-represents the amount of music taking place within the walls of courtesans' apartments. Many of the instruments played would have belonged not to the courtesans themselves but to their clients, friends or hired musicians. Music was not only the chief form of entertainment, but it must have constituted a form of conspicuous consumption. With windows hung usually with waxed cloth and shutters, neighbours and passers by would have heard music and singing drifting out from the apartments. The kind of music and instruments played, the quality of the performance and the number of musicians would all have conveyed important information about the nature of the sociability associated with a particular courtesan, as well as the social status of those who frequented her apartment.

Several scholars have noted that courtesans owned paintings, including portraits of themselves.[39] Veronica Franco, the late sixteenth-century Venetian courtesan, is reported to have presented a miniature enamelled portrait of herself to Henri III of France.[40] Fillide Melandrone di Siena, a courtesan working in early seventeenth-century Rome, had her portrait painted by Caravaggio on commission of her lover, Giulio Strozzi, who then presented it to her; in her will she provided for it to be returned to him.[41] As to their paintings more generally, Cathy Santore finds that a mid-sixteenth-century

---

[35] ASR, TNC, vol. 258, c280r–v, Hieronima Paglia, 3 November 1655, and vol. 257, c233r, Caterina Chiavari, 28 July 1655.

[36] ASR, TNC, U19, vol. 257, c607r–609v. Flavia di Baronis, 20 September 1655. Her will is TNC, Uff. 19, Testamenti, vol. 21, c686v, 19 September 1655. For musical instruments in Roman inventories more generally see Vera Vita Spagnuolo, 'Gli atti notarili dell'Archivio di Stato di Roma: saggio di spoglio sistematico: l'anno 1590,' in B. Antolini, A. Morelli and V. V. Spagnuolo, eds., *La musica a Roma attraverso le fonti d'archivio* (Lucca: Libreria Musicale Italiana, 1994), 19–65.

[37] Spagnuolo, 'Gli atti notarili'.

[38] Linda Phyllis Austern, '"Sing Againe Syren": the Female Musician and Sexual Enchantment in Elizabethan Life and Literature', *Renaissance Quarterly* 42 (1989), 420–48.

[39] Margaret F. Rosenthal, *The Honest Courtesan: Veronica Franco, Citizen and Writer in Sixteenth-Century Venice* (Chicago and London: University of Chicago Press, 1992), 106.

[40] Ibid.   [41] Helen Langdon, *Caravaggio: a Life* (London: Chatto and Windus, 1998), 145.

Venetian courtesan named Julia Lombardo owned twenty-eight paintings.[42]
She draws attention to the similarity between the subjects of her paintings
and the paintings shown hanging on the walls of the courtesan in Curzio
Castagna's series of engravings, and suggests that the schema might have
been common to Venetian courtesans. It included paintings of armed men,
of gentlemen, pictures of nude women and goddesses, as well as the more
predictable religious imagery.[43] This tradition seems to have held firm a
hundred years later in Rome.

By the mid-seventeenth century cheap paintings had become more
widely available, and all those who could afford to covered their walls
in paintings in elaborate frames of all shapes and sizes.[44] The inventories
of four 'comfortably-off' courtesans living in the mid-seventeenth century
reveal that they each had between twenty and fifty-six paintings gracing
their walls. One of these, Hieronima Paglia Tiburtina, had forty *scudi*
(one-fifth of her movable estate) invested in just over thirty paintings and
their frames.[45] Most of the women's paintings had white frames, though
many were gilded, and a handful were in black and gold. They tended to
be small and were probably of quite indifferent quality. Worth at the most
two and a half *scudi*, probably much of the cost lay in the frame. Eight of
Hieronima's towels or a single veil were of comparable value.

There is a significant difference in the genre of paintings owned by
Hieronima and other courtesans, compared with those owned by other city
women.[46] Nearly two-thirds of paintings owned by women in Rome were
of religious subjects; just a quarter of Hieronima's were.[47] These were predominantly of female religious figures, whilst the remaining three-quarters
of her paintings were secular subjects, strongly favouring portraits.[48] However, the subjects of the portraits were striking, and included a portrait of 'a
woman painting' and 'a cupid'. In the room in which she slept, alongside a
well-appointed bed and another desk, she had the remaining twenty-three
paintings, which included a Lucrezia, a Venus, a Saint Cecilia and a Judith.
It would certainly seem as though these paintings were intended to express

---

[42] Santore, 'Julia Lombardo', 54–6.

[43] These are the engravings on which the series 'La vita et miseranda fine della puttana' (Venice, 1650),
      is based, see Figure 3.6.

[44] This comparison is drawn from the data presented by Renata Ago, in 'Quadri e libri a Roma tra
      XVI e XVII secolo', *Quaderni Storici* 110:2 (2002), 380–4.

[45] ASR, TNC, U19, vol. 258, c621r–624v and 643r–644r, Hieronima Paglia Tiburtina, 9 December
      1655.

[46] For all comparisons with other women in Rome see Ago, 'Quadri e libri a Roma'.

[47] Hieronima had four Madonnas, two Maddalenas, a Saint Cecilia and a Saint Francis.

[48] Only 15 per cent of paintings in the women's inventories studied by Ago were portraits.

something either about Hieronima herself, or more generally about her profession. There were allusions to the Classics, a reminder of her musical skills in the portrait of Saint Cecilia (patron saint of music) and an allusion to artistic ability or taste in the portrait of the female artist. Finally, as we might expect, voluptuousness and the erotic are connoted through the Cupid, the Venus, and the images of Judith and Lucrezia in her bedroom.[49] These images were all in some respects images of 'strong', independent women: Saint Cecilia was martyred for her beliefs, Judith killed Holofernes and Lucrezia killed herself rather than be shamed. Rather more unusual is the portrait of a female artist, implicitly an image of independence, of a woman living by her 'art'.[50]

The interest in 'strong women' evinced in Hieronima's collection is intriguing. Research has shown that paintings of women such as Judith and Lucrezia were quite popular amongst male collectors in the city, presumably thanks to the erotic connotations.[51] Therefore, these paintings probably tell us more about her clientele than about herself. As we have already seen with the purchases of wall-hangings, there is no simple way of explaining the relationships between objects of interior decoration, the courtesans who owned them and the men who frequented their apartments. Thus we cannot assume that the objects which we find in a courtesan's household inventory necessarily reflected the taste, choice or personality of their owner. Judging from contemporary literature and imagery, the portrayal of prostitutes as strong-willed, independent women was a well-established cultural trope, one which appears to have been shared by men and women on the streets.[52] Men may therefore have expected courtesans to project an image of themselves as 'strong' women, corresponding to a set of culturally framed fantasies about sexually dominant or active women. As Bette

---

[49] Camerano also finds courtesans who owned a painting of a woman with a satyr, of a Lucrezia and a nude Venus. Camerano, 'Donne oneste o meretrici?', 662. There is a heated debate amongst art historians as to how Renaissance images of naked women in particular should be interpreted. David Frantz views erotic images 'in the context of erotica and audience response'. See *Festum Voluptatum: a Study of Renaissance Erotica* (Columbus: Ohio State University Press, 1989), Introduction and the chapter entitled 'The Loves of Men and Gods'. Another important work on the erotic in Renaissance art is Bette Talvacchia's *Taking Positions: On the Erotic in Reniassance Culture* (Princeton: Princeton University Press, 1999).

[50] Interestingly, though probably unconnected, is the fact that the artist Artemisia Gentileschi who had lived earlier in the century had overcome rape, and had also painted a Susanna, a Judith, a Lucrezia and a self-portrait of herself whilst painting.

[51] My thanks to Patrizia Cavazzini for her comments on this topic. See Patrizia Cavazzini, 'La diffusione della pittura nella Roma di primo seicento: collezionisti ordinari e mercanti', *Quaderni Storici* 2 (2004), 353–74.

[52] For a more elaborate discussion of this, related to contemporary narrative practices, see my 'Storie di prostituzione'.

Talvacchia has observed, the portrayal of women as active, self-directed participants in sexual intercourse 'would have been extremely transgressive of the norms of sexual comportment in both moral and social terms', and therefore ideally associated with prostitutes.[53]

Elizabetta (Betta) Ciocchetta was another mid-century courtesan who owned a wealth of paintings and objects of interior furnishing.[54] An inventory was drawn up when she sub-let her apartments in Via del Corso to three gentlemen in February 1656. It shows she had thought carefully about how she wanted to arrange the objects in the apartment and did not want her scheme tampered with. The rental contract stipulated that the tenant 'cannot take things from one room to put them in another', and there is a clause forbidding them from making good any losses or breakages (Sig. Elizabetta would see to that herself) and from sub-letting any part of the apartment without her agreement. The first room in the first apartment, which had a fireplace, was furnished with two walnut buffets, six chairs in the 'French style' and two in red and yellow damask with fringes, and a cembalo painted with landscapes.[55] The walls were clad in red and silver *corame* and hung with about twelve paintings, all of which had elaborate black frames decorated with 'threads and flowers of gold'. The main pictorial interest must have lain in 'the portrait of the above mentioned Sig. Betta', surrounded by visual references to the erotic and love: a Bacchanalia, a Venus and a 'profane' *putino*, painted as Eros. The bedroom was hung with a large 'Maddalena', making a very clear distinction between the two rooms. By contrast, in the second apartment one room was clearly designated just for sleeping, but the second room had a mixed function, containing a large table, three chairs and a stool as well as a gilded walnut bed. In here the paintings were more mixed, very clearly more 'masculine' in theme. There were four portraits of Frenchmen, including a French king, an armed horseman, four large paintings of battles and three portraits of women and some landscapes. The only reference to sensuality was a large painting of Susanna (and presumably the elders), a biblical scene renowned for its erotic possibilities. This was hanging over the door leading to the

---

53 See Talvacchia's discussion of Giulio Romano's *I Modi*, in *Taking Positions*, 26. Meanwhile Lynne Lawner has argued that the models for the female figures in Giulio Romano's *Modi* were courtesans – indeed, some of them are named in the accompanying sonnets by Aretino. Lynne Lawner, ed., *I Modi nell'opera di Giulio Romano, Marcantonio Raimondi, Pietro Aretino e Jean-Frédéric-Maximilien di Waldeck* (Milan: Longanesi, 1984), 27.

54 ASR, TNC, U19, vol. 259, c283r–v, 284r–v, 4 February 1656 (she appears in the 1656 census as a courtesan). She sub-lets to Giovanni Francesco Dumai and Francesco and Pietro de Cacines.

55 Peter Thornton also finds reference to 'French chairs' in a Medici inventory from 1598, but does not know what they looked like. *The Italian Renaissance Interior*, 188.

first room. Whilst the paintings in her first apartment are very much what
we 'expect' a courtesan to have, what of the paintings hung in the second
apartment? These were the kind generally associated with male collectors.
Since there is no reference to these women having been widowed, these
objects may have been a gift from a client, or purchased to create a more
'masculine' mise-en-scène, whether for previous clients or specifically for
this rental.

Many literary stereotypes portrayed courtesans as fickle, unstable and
randomly avaricious; but it must have taken years of effort for Betta to
accumulate these material goods, to the point at which she could provide
fully furnished apartments to rent out to men of the nobility. If she can be
likened to any fictional courtesan, it would be to *La lozana andalusa*, the
Spanish prostitute-turned-procuress, who saved up until she could retire to
the island of Capri. As the narrator comments: 'There are some . . . who
are so clever at saving that when they die they make a great many people
rich.'[56]

BEDS AND BEDROOMS

For all the parties, music and conversation which went on in a prostitute's
company, ultimately her rooms were a place in which to have sex. At this
point the bed, mattress and bed-linen were the most crucial objects of
furnishing. For those who could afford it, the aim was to provide comfort,
warmth and the feel of luxury. Beds were the most expensive single items of
furniture, and appear rarely in prostitute's wills.[57] Most prostitutes would
have been able to afford just a straw mattress (*pagliariccio*) thrown on
the floor in their single-roomed apartment; the more fortunate would have
had planks or boards resting on low trestles, upon which they could place
their mattresses.[58] The few who could afford a *letto completo* would have
had a walnut four-poster bed, often with gilded and carved posts. This
would be hung with curtains and a canopy above, exactly as depicted in *La
vita et miseranda fine della puttana* (see Figure 3.7).[59] Wealthier courtesans
could have afforded mattresses stuffed with thickly twisted wool, and some
women had several of different kinds which could be piled on top of one
another to make a more comfortable bed.[60]

---

[56] Delicado, *La lozana andalusa*, 91.
[57] ASR, TNC, U19, vol. 64, c544r–v, Caterina Jo Petri Ferenza, 4 November 1604.
[58] Sarti, *Europe at Home*, 120.
[59] For example, Olimpia Novarese's beds, Caterina Chiavari's bed, and Orinthia Focari's three beds.
[60] On the wool, see Frick, *Dressing Renaissance Florence*, 311. See Sarti on the use of mattresses, *Europe at Home*, 120.

Judging from Malanima's study of Tuscan furnishings, the best part of a woman's patrimony of fabrics would have been found on the bed, starting with the sheets. The inventories reveal huge differences in the quality and quantity of sheets.[61] One prostitute left a pair of tatty cut-down sheets in her will,[62] while Helena Brunelli had some 'used hemp sheets' which sound extremely uncomfortable.[63] On the other hand, in 1602 Joanna Andrei Molinari bought a pair of sheets which were 'new, triple thickness, with a lace decoration in turquoise and white', costing two *scudi* thirty *giulii*.[64] A penniless orphan, Joanna had arrived in Rome six years previously to work as a prostitute. By the time she bought these sheets she must have been in her mid-twenties, and they were a sign of her relative success.

It seems there was a chronic shortage of bed-linen in Rome, so obtaining and then managing to conserve several pairs of sheets in good condition was a small earner for women needing to supplement their income. They could be pawned, rented out and sold in times of need.[65] Some obtained as little as ten or twelve *giulii* for pawning one sheet,[66] but the procuress and weaver Magdalena Ricci from Bologna pawned some pieces of cloth and five sheets for nine *scudi*, which was a tidy sum of money.[67] When Betta Ciochetta sub-let her apartments she also undertook to provide the tenants with a four clean pairs of sheets every fifteen days.[68]

To give an idea of how a 'complete' bed was 'furnished' by a well-off courtesan we can turn to Olimpia Novarese's inventory. She owned two walnut beds, one of which was a four-poster, its columns crowned with spheres. She had eleven mattresses of varying quality, six pairs of sheets made of embroidered linen, two pillows, a red woollen blanket and one of embroidered cotton, a relatively expensive item. There were two *padiglioni*, or canopies, one for each bed. One was of a woollen cloth striped with red silk and edged with a fringe, and the other was domed, made of turquoise silk with red and white stripes.[69] *Padiglioni*, curtains and drapes kept out the draughts and created an intimate space, making the bed the focal point of the room; matching coverlets and bolsters added to the air of elegance

---

[61] Paolo Malanima, *Il lusso dei contadini: consumi e industrie nelle campagne toscane del sei e settecento* (Bologna: Il Mulino, 1990), 12, 14, 17–18.

[62] ASR, TNC, U19, vol. 73, c800r–v, Maria Taliari de Checchis, 3 August 1609.

[63] ASR, TNC, U19, vol. 79, c147r–v, 17 September 1606.

[64] ASR, TNC, U19, vol. 57, c420r, 17 June 1602.

[65] Ago, 'Di cosa si può fare commercio', 122.

[66] ASR, TNC, U19, vol. 63, c804r–v, Isabetta Graffignano, 21 August 1604. And vol. 257, c233r, Catarina Chiavari, 28 July 1655.

[67] ASR, TCG, Processi, sec. XVII, vol. 114, c221v, 28 July 1613.

[68] ASR, TNC, U19, vol. 259, c283r–v, 284r–v, 4 February 1656.

[69] ASR, TNC, U19, vol. 35, c552, 11 June 1595.

and glamour.[70] These drapes were also expensive luxuries, if made of good-quality material. In 1601 Domenica Calvi from Siena, a rising star amongst the city's courtesans, paid forty-four *scudi* for bed-hangings. They were made of turquoise spun silk from Bologna, worked over in the 'style of damask', and there were a blanket and bedspread to match.[71] Fifteen years later she had what must have been an exquisite bedroom in her apartment on Piazza Trinità dei Monti. The room was hung in Venetian brocade cloth, and there were a *padiglione*, bedspread, blanket, cushions, a small table and 'many other linens'. These she sold to a nobleman, the Illustrissimo Cassiano del Pozzo di Vercelli, collector and patron of the arts, for the princely sum of three hundred *scudi*.[72]

THE RELIGIOUS AND THE EROTIC IN THE *CAMERA*

The seventeenth-century engraving of 'The Life of the Rake' (*Vita del lascivo*) shows elegant courtesans entertaining their gentlemen friends in a beautifully furnished room. The four-poster bed nestles in the corner, whilst the dining table and cembalo are in the foreground (see Figure 4.7).[73] This suggests that even wealthy courtesans did not necessarily have two separate rooms which could be assigned the function of *camera* (bedroom) and *sala*.[74] Nor should we imagine too sharp a distinction between the *sala* and *camera*, in terms of where the 'public' were received. A courtesan would presumably have encouraged visitors and friends to see her bed if it was in a separate room, hoping to tempt them with its seductive furnishings.

When there was a *camera*, there certainly were differences in how it was furnished. In keeping with the importance of the bed and its links with sleep and death, sexuality and life, religious objects were more likely to be placed there.[75] Flavia Baronis and Caterina Chiavari both had walnut kneelers for prayer, Hieronima Paglia had a 'holy water' container of crystal, an 'archangel' and several religious paintings.[76] It is unlikely that these objects

---

[70] On beds and their hangings see Sarti, *Europe at Home*.

[71] ASR, TNC, U19, vol. 53, c122r–v, 18 January 1601.

[72] ASR, TNC, U19, vol. 96, c87r–v, 1 September 1615.

[73] *Vita del lascivo*, Civica Raccolta Achille Bertarelli, Popolari Profane, Venice, 1660s.

[74] Sarti points out that whilst specialised rooms were on the increase in the seventeenth century, their functions were only slowly disentangled from one another. Sarti, *Europe at Home*, 139.

[75] My thanks to Jenn Band who has stressed the 'liminality' of the bed, as a threshold to other states.

[76] ASR, TNC, U19, vol. 257, c607r–609v, Flavia di Baronis, 20 September 1655. Her will is TNC, Uff. 19, Testamenti, vol. 21, c686v, 19 September 1655. ASR, TNC, U19, vol. 259, c283r–284v, Elisabetta Ciocchetta, 3 February 1656. ASR, TNC, Uff. 19, vol. 258, c621–624v, Hieronima Paglia, 3 November 1655, and ASR, TNC, Uff. 19, vol. 257, c233r–234v, Caterina Chiavari, 28 July 1655.

were mere 'formalities' or part of a façade of respectability. Religion played a part in the lives of prostitutes as it did in the lives of other women, though the differences between the two groups, if they existed, have yet to be explored. They would probably have come into contact with the city's Jesuit 'missionaries', were expected to attend obligatory sermons at San Rocco and Sant' Ambrogio, and from their testamentary dispositions, seem to have worried about their souls.[77] Despite this, there was no clear separation between the sacred and profane in their rooms, for they hung paintings with clearly erotic connotations in the *camera* beside the religious paraphernalia. In her bedroom Hieronima Paglia had a painting of Lucrezia with a white frame, a large painting with a white frame of a Maddalena and a three-quarter-sized painting of a Venus with a golden frame.[78] In one of Elizabetta Ciocchetta's rooms, containing a gilded walnut bed with red and yellow damask hangings, she had some large paintings including a Saint Catherine, an anonymous saint, a 'languishing Maddalena', the three Magi, and a Madonna and child. Alongside these religious images was a large painting of 'a nude women', measuring 'seven by five'. Flavia Baronis had a kneeler and a painting of a 'nymph and satyr'.[79]

Other objects in the inventories of courtesans remind us that care of the body would have been fundamental to their professional success. Mirrors were common, and in several inventories or wills we find evidence of commodes, one of which was even made of walnut.[80] None of the inventories notes where these were placed, though Betta Ciochetta had a walnut hand-basin in the *camera* of her first apartment. There are also numerous basins and bowls, some specified 'for washing her hands', made of copper and earthenware.[81] Having washed, they also needed to dry their hands, and there are a great many pieces of material which are identified as towels, serviettes or handkerchiefs. Peregrina de Grandis (a widow turned courtesan) had seventeen towels, 'some good some bad', and forty handkerchiefs.[82] Towels were used to 'rub' the body clean, and they would also have been used during menstruation. Hands were washed at table before eating, and

---

[77] I draw this conclusion from a study of the number of those making pious legacies in their wills and from the evidence of their relationship to various city churches.

[78] ASR, TNC, U19, vol. 258, c 621–624, 9 December 1655.

[79] ASR, TNC, U19, vol. 257, c607–609, 608r, 20 September 1655.

[80] ASR, TNC, U19, vol. 68, c7, 12r-v, Costantia Stacheimburgh Flandram, 5 September 1615, and U19, vol. 79, c147r–v, Helena Brunelli, 17 September 1601.

[81] ASR, TNC, U19, vol. 74, c230r–v, Felice Aloysis, 7 October 1607. And U19, vol. 35, c552, Olimpia Novarese, 11 June 1595. And U19, vol. 63, c230r–v, Santa Joanna da Foligno, 1 June 1604.

[82] ASR, TNC, U19, vol. 259, c283r–284v, 4 February 1656. And vol. 258, c42r, Peregrina de Grandis uxor Petri Candelini, 7 October 1655.

having basins and towels in visible positions in the house may well have had connotations linked to hygiene, class and status.

EATING TOGETHER

There is ample evidence that common prostitutes and their clients ate together in the prostitutes' rooms. Court records commonly mention meals taken together, which were both prepared on the premises and brought in from a nearby *osteria*. For example, a young courtier described lunching at the home of Lucrezia, *cortigiana*: 'Yes sir, I know Lucrezia *cortigiana* because I have been to her place with Quintiliano and with Aurelio . . . and they had food brought in from the hostaria *del Gambaro*.'[83]

A courtesan named Menica Pauli gave a more detailed account of sending out for a meal one night in May 1606:

Last Thursday I was in bed because I wasn't feeling well and that evening at about eight p.m. I dined with Angelo the notary, my friend, and having dined he went away, and the dinner was brought to us by a boy working for Bernardo host at the Turchetto, called Tata . . . because he usually comes to bring us things and to take away the bowls the plates and other things.[84]

So Menica needed neither to cook nor to wash up, for even the crockery was provided by the *oste*.[85] Certainly from the majority of accounts it appears as though ordinarily food was not kept in the house, presumably because of the difficulties associated with its storage. When it came to meal times people simply sent someone for what they needed. Therefore this food had to be easy to transport: something like a piece of meat, a plate of fish or a hunk of bread and cheese. Ready cooked and prepared foodstuffs were also available from street vendors: they sold foods such as fresh ricotta, tripe, hot pastries, vermicelli, cooked pears, calves' feet and pigs' heads.[86]

Nevertheless, many prostitutes also had the wherewithal to serve food at home and some had items usually involved in food preparation. Beatrice Gualtieri had a copper cooler, a copper jug, two pans, a griddle and a grater.[87] Santa Joanna from Foligno could count twelve plates and five different knives amongst her kitchenware, although at the time she drew

[83] ASR, TCG, Costituti, vol. 457, c33v, Hieronimo de Castro Novo, 21 February 1596.

[84] ASR, TCG, Processi, sec. XVII, vol. 46, c737r–v, 11 May, 1605.

[85] ASR, TCG, Costituti, vol. 448, Magdalena uxor Luca Muratore, c58v, 20 December 1604.

[86] J. A. F. Orbaan describes some engravings of *Venditori ambulanti*, by Brambilla (late sixteenth century) in *Documenti sul Barocco in Roma* (Rome: Miscellanea della R. Società Romana di Storia Patria, 1920).

[87] ASR, TNC, U19, vol. 64, c888r–v, 17 December 1604.

up her will she was living in another woman's house, and had a daughter in the hospital of Santo Spirito.[88] Some things could also be borrowed. A neighbour described how the collar-maker and courtesan Ursola Veneta had called on her asking whether she could borrow her iron griddle because she wanted to cook some fish.[89] The inventories of wealthier courtesans also suggest that dining on quite a large scale formed part of their ordinary sociability. Caterina Chiavari had a large elm table in her *sala*, and there was a walnut table placed in the *loggia* of one of Betta Ciocchetta's two apartments. This also had a well-equipped kitchen, one of only two mentioned.[90] Both were equipped with grills, three-legged trivets for the cooking pots, and various fire-irons and tools. Flavia Baronis even had a bed in the kitchen, suggesting that a live-in cook or servant slept there.[91] As for serving the food, Felice Aloysis Intaglini had twenty-five plates and twenty-five matching terracotta bowls.[92] Olimpia Novarese had twenty flat majolica plates and matching bowls as well as thirteen earthenware plates – presumably for everyday use. She also had five covered glass *fiaschi*, for the wine, though only one crystal glass to drink from.[93]

Although these women clearly had sufficient crockery and table linen to allow groups of people to dine in their rooms, the sources are ambiguous about whether they relied mostly on fingers or on cutlery. Frequently the inventories of better-off courtesans mention the presence of silver cutlery, but there are never enough pieces to form a 'set', even for a handful of guests. Antea, for example, whose total movable goods were worth almost a hundred *scudi*, had only 'two spoons and two small forks in silver weighing about three ounces'.[94] Betta Ciocchetta agreed to supply her two tenants with only four spoons and forks a week, along with two clean tablecloths.[95] Despite Elias's theory of the spread of a more 'civilised' courtly behaviour in the sixteenth century, this suggests the lethargy with which refined table manners actually spread across Europe.[96] It also reflects the kinds of foods

---

[88] ASR, TNC, U19, vol. 63, c230r–v, 1 June 1604.

[89] ASR, TCG, Processi, sec. XVII, vol. 146, c10r–v, Elizabetha Uxor Antonij Muratore Romana, 25 August 1618.

[90] ASR, TNC, U19, vol. 257, c233r–235r, Caterina Chiavari, 28 July 1655. TNC, U19, vol. 259, c283r–v–284. Elisabetta Ciocchetta, 4 February 1656. This, however, reflects the fact that most of my sources are wills, not inventories.

[91] ASR, TNC, U19, vol. 257, c233r–235r, 28 July 1655. And vol. 257, c607–609, 608r, 20 September 1655.

[92] ASR, TNC, U19, vol. 74, c230r–v, 7 October 1607.

[93] ASR, TNC, U19, vol. 35, c552, 11 June 1595.

[94] ASR, TNC, U19, vol. 257, c308r–109v, Antea de Anguillara, 8 August 1655.

[95] ASR, TNC, U19, vol. 259, c283r–284v, 4 February 1656.

[96] Norbert Elias, *The Civilizing Process*, vol. I (Basel, 1939), ed. and trans. Edmund Jephcott (New York: Urizen Books, 1978).

and dishes which were being eaten: all cooked very simply, perhaps grilled or roasted in pots, without messy sauces. The small numbers of pieces of cutlery suggest that a silver fork or spoon was used to take food from the main dish to the individual plate, and that fingers were used otherwise. These could then be washed in finger bowls, and wiped on one of the many towels and serviettes which filled the courtesans' linen chests.[97]

'*PRATTICARE IN CASA*': SOCIABILITY IN THE COURTESAN'S HOUSEHOLD

Using approaches drawn from cultural anthropology, Tom and Elizabeth Cohen have explored the 'cultural meanings of domestic space' in early modern Rome.[98] With particular reference to women, especially prostitutes, they have emphasised that a house 'embodied' its owners' honour or shame, and like the female body could be violated and dishonoured.[99] It was therefore as important for a prostitute to control and protect this domestic space and defend its boundaries as it was to protect her body. Whilst the Cohens have emphasised the ways in which a prostitute's home and honour could be violently and dramatically attacked, I would add that in addition it could be stained and brought into disrepute gradually by the type of people who frequented it on a day-to-day basis.

The homes of courtesans were key spaces of sociability for the city's men: groups of friends dropped by for a meal, to make music or just to pass the time of day. The term used to describe this was '*pratticare in casa*', to 'frequent' a household. This did not necessarily allude to having sexual relations, but had the broader meaning of spending time, seeing friends and being a common visitor in someone's home. Far from being a question of a man's 'private' life, his practice with courtesans was a matter of his 'public' life. The courtesans he frequented, as well as the other men who frequented them, all acted as reference points in the construction of his public and social identity. As long as a courtesan's clients were all men of similar social status there was no conflict of interests. But if a man of a certain social group (whether determined by ethnicity, profession or rank) visited a courtesan who was normally frequented by men of a different social

---

[97] See Montaigne for an account of a meal shared with a cardinal. Michel de Montaigne, *The Diary of Montaigne's Journey to Italy in 1580 and 1581*, ed. and trans. E. J. Trechmann (London: Hogarth Press, 1929), 158.

[98] Cohen and Cohen, 'Open and Shut', 61.

[99] For a fuller discussion of this practice, which she has termed 'house-scorning', see Elizabeth S. Cohen, 'Honour and Gender'.

group, the honour of the apartment could be 'tainted'. By implication so might that of her clientele. It was therefore also in the clients' interests to keep a watchful eye on who was being admitted to the house.

CROWNING A QUEEN: EUGENIA'S PARTY

A case from January 1605 brings together a description of a party held by courtesans, whilst illustrating the sensitivities over territory and status associated with a courtesan's apartment. The dispute centred on the attempts by a group of Corsicans to enter a flat where some Roman prostitutes were holding a party.[100] The party had required considerable organisation, possibly including bribing the police to allow it to take place.[101] Each woman had contributed a *scudo*, two married women had cleaned the flat beforehand, and two musicians had been invited to provide the music for dancing for the eight courtesans present.[102] Only one man, one of the women's friends, was present, 'serving at table'.[103] Once the women had all arrived and eaten, Eugenia was 'crowned queen'. Neighbours and onlookers heard the women shouting '*Viva la regina, viva la regina.*' Then confetti (olives, fennel and an apple) was thrown from the window of the first-floor apartment.[104] Dianora Ferrarese, a courtesan who had not been invited, knew what to expect. She was sitting outside 'so as to see who was going in and who was coming out', as well as keeping an eye on her two-year-old daughter, so she would not run into the road when the confetti was thrown.[105] There was also a large group of Corsicans waiting in the piazza below to gather it up.[106] Upstairs in the apartment the women began dancing, but trouble was brewing down in the street and in the *osteria* below. One of the courtesans, Jan Sabbatina, had recently taken a Corsican soldier as a client. When he had asked her earlier that day to lunch with him she had declined, explaining that she was invited to the 'queen's dinner' as the 'lady-in–waiting'.[107] Presumably annoyed by her rejection he arrived in the street below during the party and called up for her. She ran down, thinking it was a Roman friend of hers,

---

[100] The party mentioned at the close of chapter 7. ASR, TCG, Processi, sec. XVII, vol. 44, c108r–131r.

[101] One of the witnesses is asked whether the police were bribed. Ibid., 130v.

[102] Ibid., c112v–113v, Eugenia De Orvieto, 25 January 1605. And c124r, Honofria ux. Clementi Florentini, 26 January 1605.

[103] Ibid., c128r, Palma di Tagliacozzo, 26 January 1605. And c126r–v, Joanna Napolitana, 26 January 1605.

[104] This moment is recounted by several witnesses, including Joanna Napolitana, c126r and Palma di Tagliacozzo, c128r.

[105] Ibid., c115r, Dianora de Rubeis Ferrarese, 25 January 1605.

[106] Ibid., c126, Joanna Napolitana, 26 January 1605.

[107] Ibid., c117r , Jan Sabbatina de Orvieto, 25 January 1605.

bringing 'something for the table'. When she found it was the Corsican with seven or eight others wanting to come upstairs, she refused to let them in. They then tried to gain entry by trickery, pretending they were *birri*, and, becoming abusive and violent, they tried to break the door down. The *birri* soon heard what was going on and came to a vigorous defence of the courtesans. (This may not have been an entirely disinterested act: there is a suggestion that some of them were their 'friends', and that they had permitted this illegal party.) When they arrived on the scene they found fifteen Corsicans with drawn swords. A battle ensued in the defence of the women's territory and one man was killed.

All the evidence suggests that this was not a casual, nor a common kind of party. It seems to have functioned as an attempt to establish a higher status for the group of courtesans and to communicate this to those in the streets below. Its hallmarks were gestures associated with liberality, magnificence, courtly carnival traditions and parlour games, all of which point to associations with the elite. There was a lover waiting at table to whom a gift of fennel was presented; there was the public throwing of confetti and the crowning of a 'queen', who had a 'lady-in-waiting'.[108] Given the nature of the party, it is not surprising that the women wanted to keep the Corsicans out. They were lowly soldiers, seen as 'outsiders' in the community, and from Eugenia's description of them, not the kind of men any self-respecting courtesan would want around her house.

I don't know any of them and have no friends amongst them, indeed, when I see them I hide in the house . . . and as far as I know none of the women in my house is friends with Corsicans: everyone runs away from them because they are insolent and to some they give and to others they [only] make promises.[109]

She was wrong, of course, because Jan Sabbatina had made 'friends' with a Corsican. This, perhaps predictably, was the result. The status quo was questioned, boundaries were threatened and honour was avenged.

The party at Eugenia's was a rare one. Parties in the *luoghi* were usually predominantly male gatherings, reflecting the demographic imbalance in the city, which increased the likelihood of outbreaks of jealousy and

---

[108] Montaigne observed that on *giovedì grasso*, a great dinner was held at which the ladies 'were served by their husbands'. Montaigne, *Journey to Italy*, 174. In parlour games a king or queen was elected master of ceremonies. This in itself was a vestige of antique culture (the King of Revels, or *rex convivii*) which had remained as part of the city's popular culture. See Thomas F. Crane, *Italian Social Customs of the Sixteenth Century and their Influence on the Literatures of Europe* (New Haven: Yale University Press, 1920), 263, 266 and chapter 8.

[109] ASR, TCG, Processi, sec. XVII, vol. 44, c112v–113v, Eugenia q. JoMaria de Orvieto, 25 January 1605.

rivalry between men. As observed earlier, men were prohibited from carrying weapons in the *luoghi* and in the company of prostitutes, and prostitutes from holding parties. As a result there was no shortage of charges on which to arrest both prostitutes and their clients. Of the prostitutes noted in the *Relazioni dei Birri* between 1594 and 1606, 14 per cent had been arrested at parties, some of which would have been authorised to take place with a special licence.[110] The sounds of guitars, singing, laughing or fighting rang through the streets catching the attention of the police spies or the patrols on their nightly rounds of the city. As one of these noted, 'because there are nearly always people at Anna's place, and parties, and this has been referred to me, I went along and knocked'.[111] It was common for the *birri* to find 'a great multitude of people at the door of a woman who is a courtesan', and if they were lucky they found the door open so they could catch the revellers unawares, singing and dancing.[112] 'Having gone upstairs I found the door open in the room where they were having a party and they were playing music and dancing, and there were nine men and a whore called Julia, and they were saying "whoever doesn't dance has to pay for a half (of wine)".'[113] At other times, the *birri* knocked in vain at the door and could hear the sound of the party-goers fleeing along staircases and making off across the roofs. Finally they would break the door down. They might find swords or 'a pair of French cards' thrown on top of the canopy above the bed or tossed out in the courtyard below, evidence that illegal weapons had been carried, or that gambling had been taking place.[114]

Musical gatherings were a common feature in the homes of prostitutes and courtesans and were often raided by the *birri*. The night after Christmas in 1605, Caterina and Julia, who lived at the foot of Trinità dei Monti, received a visit from a group of Frenchmen 'who come every Christmas to visit'. They had brought along two musicians with them 'because they wanted to start playing some music'.[115] The next evening the police interrupted a musical evening in an apartment near the church of SS Apostoli, held by Antonia.

---

[110] For example, Rosa Fortunati di Narni, who claimed 'I held the above party or *recreazione* in my house with a licence from Mon. Governatore.' ASR, TCG, Costituti, vol. 551, c132, 14 February 1605.

[111] ASR, TCG, RB, vol. 99, c110v, 5 October 1597.

[112] ASR, TCG, RB, vol. 104, c1r, 16 January 1611.

[113] ASR, TCG, RB, vol. 99, c175v, 3 April 1598.

[114] ASR, TCG, RB, vol. 97, c133r, 26 December 1594. And RB, vol. 99, cnn, 10 December 1598. Angela d'Orvieto, near Trinità dei Monti, Osteria del Turchetto.

[115] ASR, TCG, Costituti, Julia de Rubeis Ferrarese and Caterina Malacarne, vol. 557, c187, 26 December 1605.

I live near SS. Apostoli and I am a whore. I was at home and Donna Annunccia and Portia my neighbours came over and we were around the fire when a certain Spanish Maria came . . . and behind her finally came Martio, my neighbour with a Spanish guitar and he was playing and then the police arrived.[116]

One night in August 1597 as the *birri* passed through Piazza Capranica they heard the sound of music drifting down through the street: 'I heard a cembalo being played and there was singing and a guitar playing so I knocked and went in and found that there were three men and a whore and [a poor woman?] with three children.'[117]

Accounts of the activities of elite courtesans and their clients are less common, because their clients' wealth and status automatically afforded them protection. Just occasionally the court extended its net to include such men and women, especially when there had been a murder. In 1603 a well-known doctor, Albertus Brecatius Lucrentis, was interrogated about his friendships with courtesans and with the infamous Bargello, Captain Valerio. He and his friends, other gentlemen and noblemen, typically spent their evenings in the company of courtesans, enjoying the musical entertainment they provided. 'I have been alone and in the company of my friends and countrymen to hear Settimia play . . .'[118] Another witness from amongst this group of friends, Cavaliere Cesare from Cremona, stated: 'I remember that Clementia wanted to meet Settimia because she had heard that she could sing, and so one evening Alberto and I took Clementia to meet Settimia.'[119] Questioned about his movements and Clementia's illegal use of carriages, Albertus described a typical evening out.

I have certainly been out and about Rome by night with her [Clementia] and when I have been out it was by carriage, and once Cavaliere Arsilio da Fermo came, and a certain Horatio . . . and the Illustrious Annibale Cortese and the Illustrious Francesco Patrizio and others whose names I don't recall . . . We went to collect Clementia and we took her to Settimia's house and we stayed there *a veglia* for a while, then we took her home in the same carriage, and another time I went in Captain Valerio's carriage with Cavaliere Cesare who had come to collect me at my house and there was a woman I didn't know and we went together *a spasso* through Rome.[120]

The doctor mentioned two kinds of entertainment to be found in a courtesan's home. One he called *conversatione*, the other a *veglia*. The

[116] ASR, TCG, Costituti, vol. 557, c191v, Antonia Petri di Palermo, 27 December 1605.
[117] ASR, TCG, RB, vol. 99, c92r, 19 August 1597.
[118] ASR, TCG, TD, vol. 190, 17 March 1603, c10r–17r, c11v, Duns Albertus Brecatius Lucrentis.
[119] ASR, TCG, TD, vol. 190, 20 March 1603, c34r, Cesare Armen [. . .] di Cremona.
[120] ASR, TCG, TD, vol. 190, 17 March 1603, c11v, Duns Albertus Brecatius Lucrentis.

former was a formal gathering in which acquaintances talked, made music and played games. The latter was more like an intimate party, a gathering of friends which involved singing and musical entertainment as well. Testimonies from another murder inquiry, this time in the city of Orvieto, about a hundred kilometres from Rome, give an account of what was evidently a routine evening's entertainment for a well-to-do courtesan and her *amici*.[121] It began at about nine in the evening when Hieronimo and Cesare went to their friend Tiberio's house in order to read the *gazzetta*, and there met up with Cavaliere Scipione Sensati. They then left and called on Orsola Rosatini. She came down and joined the group of friends which had by now increased to seven, and they strolled about the city, calling in on a friend from whom she collected a necklace. Then Antonio tuned his guitar and started playing, and they returned to Orsola's house. She left the door open 'as I usually do when I have people around for a veglia', so that friends could come and go freely in the course of the evening. Once in her house they had gathered round the fire, 'and we stayed a while *a veglia* in Orsola's house, playing and singing and after a while Cesare returned and we all stayed there and had a merry evening'.[122] After this the group dispersed, leaving Cesare to sleep with Orsola whilst the others went home.

The home was central to the prostitute's and courtesan's professional life and although its importance undoubtedly increased with their social aspirations, in terms of function there is no clear dividing line between the homes of the richer and poorer prostitutes. Both were key venues for entertainment for the city's men, as well as places for sex, if not seduction. It was in every prostitute's interests to create a space which was comfortable and could enable the required sociability, according to her clientele and aspirations. There are some puzzling facts, however. Contemporary imagery and verse might incline us to think of the courtesan's domestic interior as a particularly female space: enchanting, seductive, full of luxurious drapes and furnished with objects specifically articulating her professional persona. While we do find some evidence of this in their erotic paintings, musical instruments and attention to bed-linen, the courtesans' apartments do not otherwise seem to have been particularly 'feminine'. They had walnut furniture rather than the white woods predominantly found in honest women's inventories; they owned paintings of a kind normally favoured by men; and we have seen that elite men frequently bought their furnishings

---

[121] Archivio di Stato, Sezione Orvieto, Archivio del Governatore, Processi, vol. 121a: 1600–1602: cnn, 17 January 1601, Ursolina Faustina Rosatini di Monte Testis, Hieronimo Gualtieri, Antonio Morabottino, Cesare Megalotti.

[122] Ibid., cnn, Antonio Morabottino, 17 January 1601.

from courtesans, suggesting an overlap in their taste for interior decor. All this suggests that the courtesans' apartments were much more ambiguously gendered than we might have expected; indeed, they seem ultimately to have been very much a negotiated space, one created by both prostitute and client.

The key to understanding the courtesans' apartments lies in the relationship between the courtesan, her domestic goods and her clients. Objects circulated between courtesan and client, moving in both directions: sometimes clients gave courtesans objects, sometimes they seem to have seconded their choices, and sometimes it was they who bought from courtesans. It appears as though, in the context of sociability, the courtesan's home was not exclusively her territory but was seen as shared ground. Just as her clients had a stake in who went there, so they were concerned about how it was furnished. This was partly because the decor advertised their own wealth, status and taste to their friends and associates, but this was not the most important reason. Contemporary literature and imagery point us towards another issue which was at stake, in their portrayals of the courtesans' apartments as 'traps' or cages: dangerous places for men. This links closely with widespread fears that men were effeminised by frequenting spaces which were too obviously a female domain. This is reflected in the way in which boys were taken from their mothers at a critical age, around six, and breeched. They were then symbolically and literally transferred to the male sphere. Likewise, the courtesan's *casa* seems to have been perceived as being dangerously female, associated with the loss of male reason, self-control, dignity and social status through his submission to sensuality.[123] By paying for or influencing the furnishing of a courtesan's rooms with more 'masculine' objects, men may have been unconsciously seeking to appropriate this space: making it more 'male', assuming control over it and thereby hoping to neutralise the dangers of prostitution.

This would have been particularly pertinent for those men who had nowhere else to entertain courtesans. Dependent youths, students living with their relatives, or courtiers living in the palace of an ambassador, cardinal or nobleman were restricted in whom they could bring home. A contemporary guide for courtiers living *in Palazzo*, for example, advises against taking prostitutes to their rooms. Even if the prince apparently tolerated it, it was deemed inappropriate for reasons of modesty, 'honesty'

---

[123] On the dangers of 'feminine' spaces to men's masculinity, see Michèle Cohen, 'Manliness, Effeminacy and the French: Gender and the Construction of National Character in Eighteenth-Century England', in Tim Hitchcock and Michèle Cohen, eds., *English Masculinities, 1660–1800* (London and New York: Longman, 1999), 44–62.

and respect. It also warns men to allow only the very closest of friends into their room, on the grounds that otherwise people might find something to criticise: 'Even if it is as tidy as a King's . . . there will always be someone who . . . will sing out if he has found any defect.'[124] This advice, given in the context of seeking to minimise the intrigues, rivalries and dangers involved in court life, reminds us of the importance of maintaining appearances, and the weakness of boundaries between the private and public sphere. The courtesan's apartments may therefore have come to function rather as an extension of men's homes, a more neutral space where they could meet and entertain friends and acquaintances, as well as frequenting their courtesans, without the risk of compromising their own personal space and reputation.

[124] Woodhouse, '*La Cortegiania* di Niccolo Strozzi', 184.

CHAPTER 9

'Because we are all made of flesh and blood': prostitutes and their clients

As the courtesan Maddalena Santini from Florence pointed out during an interrogation, brief relationships were a characteristic of prostitution: 'You know how it is with us "other" women, that one leaves today, another comes tomorrow and there are many friends but few stay around for long.'[1] This transience was particularly marked at the lower levels of the professional hierarchy, amongst the kind of prostitutes who, to use the words of another woman, took 'one man one day, and another the next'.[2] One such client was Emilio the barber who described himself as frequenting prostitutes in a very casual manner:

I have no firm friendships with any women and when I want to have a quick screw I go here and there . . . Sometimes one goes walking around the streets, as you do in Rome, and you see some woman who opens to you . . . these days I don't go for a screw because business is bad and it's not a time to waste money.[3]

Giving testimony, men and women engaged in such casual relationships (or seeking to convey that impression) spoke about the other in terms which indicated distance: women might call a client 'a youth', or 'a gentleman', 'a Spaniard'; men would refer to the woman as a *puttana* (whore), or simply *meretrice*, or as 'a women'; and both parties would say that they had 'had dealings' with the other, or had 'had something to do with' him or her (*ho trattato, ho avuto prattica, ho avuto a che fare*). Yet we have also seen that prostitution in Rome was structured around longer-term relationships which benefited both parties. These mitigated the economic and physical vulnerability of the profession for women, as well as compensating for the emotional instability. There were benefits for the clients too. For the men it was a way of keeping a prostitute within their sphere of influence;

---

[1] ASR, TCG, Processi, sec. XVII, vol. 46, c719r, 6 May 1605. This phrase has also been cited by Elizabeth S. Cohen in 'Camilla la Magra, prostituta romana', 183.
[2] 'Although I am a courtesan, I am not the kind who admits one man one day, and another the next.' ASR, TCG, Costituti, vol. 519, c113r, Vincentia Sinna Romana, 3 December 1602.
[3] ASR, TCG, Processi, sec. XVII. vol. 154, c120r, 21 February 1619.

of keeping them available for when they wanted to see them; it reduced the likelihood of her taking 'undesirable' clients; it lessened the danger of violent and unseemly disputes over women; and it was seen as a way of guarding against venereal disease.[4] It is therefore not surprising that an analysis of twenty-five women's responses to questions about the duration of their friendships shows a tendency towards relationships which lasted months, rather than days. In only seven cases did the women claim that they had known the client for fewer than fifteen days. Nine stated they had known them for between one and two months, three estimated between three and five months, whilst six had been with a client for between nine months and five years. A similar pattern has been found in Bologna, where, of eighty relationships, all had lasted for more than a couple of months, and thirty had lasted for a year or more.[5]

'UNO BELLO, UNO BRAVO ET L'ALTRO CURRINO'
(A HANDSOME ONE, A STRONG ONE AND A GENEROUS ONE)

When Camilla de Francesco from Siena was asked how many '*amici*' she had, she replied: 'I only have three, who see to my domestic needs, although we do not resemble that proverb which says, "a handsome one, a strong one and a kind one".'[6] The fact that there was a proverb summing up this kind of arrangement suggests that it was a practice of some standing, which is confirmed by another reference to it which crops up in an English verse account of a famous Roman courtesan, printed in 1609, called 'The Famous Whore or Noble Curtizan' by Gervase Markham.[7]

There is no curtezan of account but hath three sorts of men belonging unto her, the first is called her *curso*, and he is the man that keepeth her *alaposta* . . . by the month or by the yeare as he pleaseth giving her according to the price they agree upon. The second is her *bravo* and this is he which is her champion, swaggereth everywhere on her behalf and in all her quarrels, seeking to defend her small honour with his no little shame. The third and last is her *bello* and that is some neat spruce and well-favoured youth, on whom she commonly doteth.

Although it seems unlikely that many courtesans were lucky enough to have such well-defined roles allotted to their *amici*, a group of friends could

---

[4] Ferrante, 'Pro mercede carnali', 50.   [5] Ibid.
[6] ASR, TCG, Costituti, vol. 50, c119v, 18 August 1555.
[7] Gervase Markham, *The Famous Whore or Noble Curtizan: Containing the Lamentable Complaint of Pauline the Famous Roman Curtizan, sometimes Mistress unto the Great Cardinall Hypolito of Este* (London, 1609), 27. (This is a comment printed in the margins, by way of explanation. In the British Library it is clearer in the nineteenth-century reprinted edition.)

share the costs of maintaining a courtesan. In the course of a trial which took place in the city of Orvieto, a gentleman named Cesare Megalotti explained how it worked: 'I am not the only one who goes to Sig. Orsola, and I alone do not keep her. There is a group of us. Until now Mr Curzio Butio, Mr Alessandro Saracinello, Mr Gerolamo Gualtieri and myself have kept her, but at present only Sig. Gerolamo and myself frequent her'.[8] This was apparently not an unusual practice, as travellers to Venice made clear in their reports. In the late seventeenth century Amelot de la Houssaie wrote: 'They (the noble Venetians) have something marvellous, which is that they come to an agreement over a prostitute whom they share amongst themselves, so that which is a subject of dispute elsewhere produces union and friendship amongst themselves.'[9]

Alexandre Toussaint Limojon de Saint-Disdier commented on similar cases, noting that hard-up noblemen tended to 'associate in four so that the expense should not be too onerous', adding, however, that this also happened amongst the richest nobles 'as if in these shared pleasures there was greater enjoyment than in exclusive ones'.[10] Although there are hints that this system facilitated illicit erotic pleasures,[11] apart from the reduced expenditure, the emphasis was placed on the way the system enhanced male friendships. François Maximilien Misson echoed Disdier and Houssaie when he wrote that 'this promiscuity [i.e. clubbing together to keep a prostitute in common] which elsewhere would be intolerable, here just tightens the bonds of friendship amongst these *compagni d'avventura*.'[12]

These comments suggest that Renaissance ideals of friendship which probably underlay the initial development of courtesan culture in the late fifteenth century still had a strong influence on men's attitudes towards prostitution. Drawing on classical paradigms, 'true friendship' was taken to imply a bond between 'virtuous men' who were like 'a single soul in two bodies'. Ideally friends held their possessions in common, their affection was reciprocal, their character, taste and opinions were in complete agreement, and through this friendship their wisdom, goodness and virtue would be

---

[8] Archivio di Stato, Sezione Orvieto, Archivio del Governatore, Processi vol. 121A, 1600–1602, cnn, 17 January 1601. Ursola Faustina Rosatini de M Testis and Cesare Megalotti (cnn).
[9] Bruno Alfieri, ed., *Il gioco dell'amore: le cortigiane di Venezia dal trecento al settecento* (Milan: Berenice Art Books, 1990), 75.
[10] Ibid., 76.
[11] 'It isn't difficult to believe that which is murmured: that the courtesans are used in such infamous abuses that . . . one can't but be horrified.' Ibid.
[12] Ibid., 77.

increased.[13] It is easy to see how the sharing of a courtesan might fit into this paradigm: not only did such a formal agreement prevent the jealousies and rivalries associated with exclusive sexual relationships, but they were making a statement about their friendship by sharing a woman's body.

Whether or not there was normally such a formal agreement amongst the men who visited a courtesan in seventeenth-century Rome, it was none the less true that men introduced their friends to the women they had met and they frequented the same woman or women in the company of their friends. As a well-off goldsmith, arrested in 1601, explained to the police, 'I have been to these women's house before, because the notary Panizza brought me here.'[14] This, plus the imperatives of male honour, contributed to the creation of a socially homogeneous clientele for many women. Elizabeth Cohen has commented on the apparent anomaly of a situation in which men and women from the social periphery, generally thought to be without honour (people such as prostitutes and stable-boys), sought to dishonour one another and to defend their own honour. She suggests that they were none the less 'shaped by, and used the precepts of, honour, but they had to adapt and adjust them to their own situations'.[15] The logic behind the honourability of prostitutes and courtesans was not just something they 'claimed' or 'invented' for themselves, but was both based on their public 'persona' and, above all, directly related to the honourability of their clientele. The courtesan's body and sexual honour were linked to the honour of her clients just as a respectable woman's honour was linked to that of her husband or father. As the Chevalier de Saint-Disdier remarked of Venetian courtesans: 'It is a great untruth that the title of courtesan counts as a dishonour to those women who declare themselves as such amongst the people, since on the contrary it confers upon them a consideration and respect which are proportional to the status of those who frequent them.'[16]

Courtesans who aspired to cultivate a clientele of gentlemen were generally expected to behave with decorum, but above all had to respect their client's honour. This meant in particular that they were not to frequent men of inferior status, since the courtesan was herself implicitly constitutive

[13] Reginald Hyatte, *The Arts of Friendship: the Idealization of Friendship in Medieval and Early Renaissance Literature* (Leiden: Brill, 1994), 1, 4–5. See also David Wootton, 'Friendship Portrayed: a New Account of Utopia', *History Workshop Journal* 45 (1998), 29–47.

[14] ASR, TCG, Costituti, vol. 508, c 24r, Natalins Ricci de Acquasparta, 29 October 1601.

[15] Cohen, 'Honour and Gender', 610, 619.

[16] Alexander T. L. de Saint-Disdier, *La ville et la République de Venise* (La Haye: 1685), cited in Alfieri, *Il gioco dell'amore*, 75.

to her client's identity.[17] If she damaged her reputation by associating with lower-class men, this stain would be transferred to her high-status clients. Likewise, men had to be careful about whom they frequented. Trial documents from 1616 show peer pressure being exerted on a man to avoid a low-class prostitute, as if his friends also feared being affected by his dishonour. Apart from a printer, the men involved in the trial all held important positions in the households of senior cardinals. Francesco Severus, the principal witness, was a *castrato* in the employ of Cardinal Borghese, the Cardinal *Padrone* and musician to the Pope. Geronimo was secretary of the ambassador of Ferrara, Thomaso was in the Camera Apostolica and treasurer for Cardinal Montalto.[18] The friends had been out serenading a woman with whom 'Francesco Castrato' was in love, but later in the evening Francesco had wanted to go and talk to 'a certain Madalena who lived in Campo Marzio'. She must have been a prostitute, certainly unattractive and presumably low class. Thomas admonished him by saying, 'What do you want to do with her, she looks like a portrait of death.'[19] Hieronimo Floretto added: 'I heard Sig. Thomaso reply to him that it was shameful that a man like him, who was with [i.e. in the household of] an important person, should go to such a place and he [Francesco] said that he wasn't interested in sinning but had important business to do with her.'[20]

As for courtesans, although a discreet tryst with a lower-status man may have gone unheeded, an ongoing relationship across social boundaries would be a cause for serious concern. A courtesan who transgressed this rule risked losing her reputation or her clientele, whilst the offending lower-status client also had to watch out, as emerges from the investigation into the murder of Pietro the Florentine, stable-hand, in 1605.

PIETRO THE STABLE-HAND AND THE FRENCH GENTLEMAN

One morning in May 1605 the body of Pietro Fiorentino was found in Piazza Trinità. As the court sought to unravel the murder they focused on two courtesans he had frequented, Maddalena from Florence and Donna Menica from Rome.[21] Judging from the lines of inquiry, one suspicion was that he had been murdered to avenge the honour of one of the gentlemen who frequented Menica. As the police spy who supplied the opening

---

[17] See Cohen, 'Camilla la Magra, prostituta romana', 181.
[18] ASR, TCG, Processi, sec. XVII, vol. 132, c393r, Jacobo Ribera and Antonio Valerio, 21 June 1616.
[19] Ibid., 401r, 21 June 1616, Thomas Mattei de Bertis Romanus.
[20] Ibid., 404v, 22 June 1616, Hieronimus Florettus q. Ridolphi, c405v.
[21] ASR, TCG, Processi, sec. XVII, vol. 46, 710r–v, 6 May 1605, Teste Secretus.

testimony pointed out, Pietro had frequented Menica not openly but secretly, and this was clearly an important clue to understanding why he had been killed.

You should know that Pietro Fiorentino, stable-hand in the house of Signor Marquise Peretti, found dead in the morning in Piazza Trinità practised in the house of a Florentine woman courtesan who lives in that piazza, called Maddalena . . . Pietro also frequents the house of a Donna Menica who lives behind Piazza San Silvestro, *and he goes there secretly, because Menica is friends with certain gentlemen who don't like Pietro to go to her*, and when he goes there, he goes secretly.[22]

Why had Menica hidden her friendship with Pietro? Menica, according to local public knowledge, worked 'as a famous courtesan'.[23] In accordance with the requirements of this social identity she was not seen out and about in the streets, but 'stayed inside', like honourable women,[24] and according to her mother, she only had friendships with gentlemen.[25] Her relationship with Pietro was obviously something of an anomaly and to have acknowledged it publicly would have damaged her reputation and cost her her clientele. Even in court Menica sought to maintain this reputation, underplaying her liaison with Pietro and claiming she had been tricked about his identity: 'He had carnal relations with me two or three times but when (I knew?) that he was a stable-hand I didn't want him to frequent me any more . . . Lilla had implied that he was a gentleman and not a stable-hand.'[26] Her mother also stressed that he saw her rarely, clearly hoping to mitigate any possible dishonour. 'He had carnal relations with my daughter a few times, but only that, because he didn't have a firm-friendship with her and only came secretly . . . because my daughter doesn't take men like him, . . . staff-bearers.'[27]

In the first instance this secrecy meant admitting him to her house as rarely as possible and only by night, as well as resorting to the expedient of meeting elsewhere at friends' homes.[28] Despite her caution, such indiscreet trysts compromised Menica. Slipping in and out of other people's houses was in itself an indication that she was behaving dishonourably. 'I didn't say I had a relationship with him because I didn't want people to know that I was going to other people's houses in that way.'[29] Meanwhile Pietro was

---

[22] Ibid., 710v (italics added).
[23] Ibid., c713r, Margarita Francisi de Cortona, 7 May 1605, c713r–v.
[24] Ibid., 714r, Camilla filia di . . . de Faenza, 6 May 1605. [25] Ibid.
[26] Ibid., c720r, Menica Pauli Remedi Romana, 6 May 1605.
[27] Ibid., c714v, Camilla filia di . . . . de Faenza, 6 May 1605.
[28] Ibid., c713r, Margarita Francisi, 7 May 1605.
[29] Ibid., Menica Pauli Remedi Romana, 7 May 1605.

tiring of this secrecy: 'He seemed to want to do something to upset her and this he said because Menica didn't want him to go to her house openly.'[30] Menica had clearly got out of her depth trying to manage the situation, which culminated in Pietro being turned away by her mother one evening, because Menica was with the French gentleman. Pietro's reaction had been violent and uncontrolled.

He began to vent his anger on the door, beating on it very loudly and shouting. I was forced to get up from the table and go downstairs to the door and beg him not to be so insolent and not damage me, telling him that I had a French Gentleman in the house who was going to do me some good, and that I didn't want him to disturb him, and that anyway he could come another evening and I said so much that he agreed to leave.[31]

Menica then took great pains to insist that Gerolamo, the gentleman, had barely reacted to this incident, presumably trying to forestall any suspicion that Gerolamo was responsible for the fact that Pietro was found dead in the piazza early next morning.

Maddalena Fiorentina was another courtesan called as a witness in the case, and she too sought to present herself as a 'high-class' courtesan, stressing her exclusivity and higher-status clientele. When asked whether she knew Pietro, she initially denied it vehemently: 'I neither know, nor have ever heard mention of any Pietro Fiorentino, groom to the Marchese Peretti, because I do not have any friends among such people as stable-hands.'[32] She then burst into tears, protesting that she would rather 'die of hunger than take people like stable-hands as clients', a point she reiterated in her final interrogation. 'Although I am a poor woman, and I am who I am, I do not allow stable-hands to come, nor do I have practise with them',[33] emphasising how uncouth they were: 'Because I know that they are all insolent, and . . . all of them when they pass by where some of us poor women live, they insult us with a thousand abuses.'[34] Like Menica she was playing a double game. Finally confronted with the testimony of other witnesses, she admitted that she not only knew Pietro, who often brought letters to her house for her from her 'friend' in Florence, but knew that rumour had it that 'this Pietro was in love with me (*innamorato*) and came to my house'.[35] Indeed, another courtesan named Virginia had described Pietro's affection for Maddalena in her deposition.

[30] Ibid., c723v, Laura filia Sartis . . . Anconitana, 9 May 1605.
[31] Ibid., c738r, Menica, 11 May 1605.
[32] Ibid., c718r, 763r, Maddalena Landina, 6–7 May 1605.
[33] Ibid., 762r–764v, 21 May 1605.   [34] Ibid., c718v.
[35] Ibid., c765v, Maddalena Landina Fiorentina, 23 May 1605.

I had known Pietro for about ten years in Florence and here in Rome, and he always stopped by at my house and greeted me and whilst we came to the subject of love he told me that he was friends with a certain Maddalena . . . who lives in Piazza della Trinità and when he left my house he always said that he wanted to go to Maddalena's . . . and he told me that Maddalena had a child.[36]

It is hard to explain why both Menica and Maddalena frequented Pietro, unless they were in love with him, very good friends, or at least flattered by his attentions. Otherwise why would they have risked their reputation and clientele to see him? His behaviour towards Menica seems to have been chivalrous and kind. On one occasion when he was passing by, he had learnt from Menica's mother that she was ill and Menica recalled that 'He came to my house and asked whether I needed anything, offering to send me whatever I needed. I thanked him without accepting anything, but he, out of courtesy, sent me a chicken, a little bit of beefsteak and some small birds.'[37]

Perhaps as the proverb cited earlier suggests, while the gentlemen were paying the bills and furnishing Menica's and Maddalena's homes, Pietro was the 'love interest', the '*bello*', or to use Markham's words, 'some neat spruce and well-favoured youth, on whom she commonly doteth'. This would explain why they were prepared to run the risks of frequenting a mere stable-hand in the closely packed community in which they lived.

'I HAVE NEVER HAD COMMERCE WITH WHORES': DENIALS, EXPLANATIONS AND JUSTIFICATIONS

Whilst we come across brief references to love, friendships and honourable behaviour in the criminal archives, most men were reluctant to admit to anything more than a casual acquaintance with courtesans. Marcello and his friends from Brescia are typical examples of the kind of well-born young men who, sent to Rome to receive an education and to learn the arts of the courtier, passed much of their time in the company of prostitutes. They evidently enjoyed a very casual kind of sociability around these women, which fitted easily into their daily routines.[38]

In the morning I usually get up at six and study physics and philosophy and medicine and then I go out, and go to mass, and then I walk until lunch time

---

[36] Ibid., c744r, Virginia Nicola Fiorentina, 13 May 1605.   [37] Ibid., c733r, Menica, 11 May 1605.

[38] TCG, Processi, sec. XVII, vol. 36, c211–248v, Marcellum, Jo Baptistam, Marinum et . . . ad numero dodecem incogniti Bresciani, 29 June 1604.

when either alone or in company I go home and I stay there until nine p.m. and then I go out again and go walking, sometimes alone, sometimes in company.[39]

There were also days when he had to spend the whole day at the ambassador's house or was involved in processions,[40] but on one evening in particular they had gone to the Fontana di Trevi and were 'making music, as S. Giobattista was playing the Spanish guitar, and S. Girolamo and S. Giselli were playing the theorbo'.[41] It was only on his second interrogation that Jo Antonio Marino admitted to frequenting four courtesans, amongst whom were Alteria, whom he'd known 'for two years and I've had dealings with her as I have with Aurelia'.[42] Jo Antonio Giselli was less reticent about his connections with prostitutes. 'I know many *puttane* in Rome, some of whose names I know and others not,' his casual indifference indicating his lack of interest in them.[43] Asked about the kind of relationships he and his friends had with them, he replied: 'Yes I do usually frequent Aurelia and Hieronima's house and I call Hieronima a great beast, but I haven't had sex with her, but with Aurelia I have had sex . . . On many occasions we have passed the time there together, chatting and discussing things with those *puttane*.'[44] Jo Antonio Marino described his relationships with these courtesans in the following manner: 'I went to her house and teased her, without screwing her and I was courteous, and when I passed by them in the streets I greeted them saying how are you, (?) good evening, and they reply "good evening" and "happy new year" and in Hieronima's house I have only been once.'[45]

These accounts of the everyday sociability of rich and well-born young men must be seen in the context in which they were given. In fact, Marcello and his friends were accused of behaviour which was far from gentlemanly: breaking into Aurelia's apartment, taunting and insulting her, and demanding anal sex. They had an interest therefore in stressing their links with the courts of ambassadors, their studious and courteous behaviour, their musical skills and referring to the women as 'courtesans' in a gentlemanly fashion.[46] But apart from this they present these relationships as an entirely blameless and routine part of their social life.

---

[39] Ibid., c218r, Jo Antonio Marino Bresciano, 2 July 1604.   [40] Ibid., c219r.
[41] Ibid., c220v. The theorbo was a long-necked, big-bellied string instrument, somewhat like a lute.
[42] Ibid., c236, Jo Antonio Marino, 4 July 1604.
[43] Ibid., c229, Jo Antonio Giselli, 4 July 1604.
[44] Ibid., c229v, Jo Antonio Giselli, 4 July 1604.
[45] Ibid., c236v, Jo Antonio Marino, 4 July 1604.
[46] Stefano Lorenzetti, 'Per animare agli esercizi nobili: esperienza musicale e identità nobiliare nei collegi di educazione', *Quaderni Storici* 95:2 (1997), 435–59.

One young man, when questioned about whether he frequented prostitutes, suggested that it was a physical necessity. 'I don't usually go to the houses of bad women because I am poor, but it is true that I have sometimes gone to women, because we are all made of flesh and blood (*perche tutti siamo di carne*), although it must be one or two months since I have been.'[47]

When Emilio the barber was questioned about his relationships his reply suggested that there were two ways of frequenting prostitutes: he went alone if he was going to satisfy his sexual needs and otherwise he went with friends. 'When I've gone to women's houses on my own account I've gone alone, and sometimes I have gone to some woman's house for fun and entertainment . . . and sometimes I've hung out at Felicia Cortigiana's house in Strada delli Condotti with Ludovio de Quarti her friend, and I can't remember the others' names.'[48] A similar distinction was employed by Alberto Brecatius Lucrentis, a doctor called as a witness in a murder investigation. Alberto had a reputation to uphold in court, given the social and professional circles in which he moved. 'I am a doctor', he declared, 'and I am the one who has the secrets of the flesh relating to the ailments of the urinary tract and I have treated Cardinal Colonna, Cardinal Terranuova and Cardinal Desti.'[49] In his account of his social life he named five noblemen as his principal friends. When asked whether he had any friendships with women or courtesans, he replied, 'I have not had any friendships with any women.'[50] As often happened, it emerged that the court was better informed about his social life than he expected, and he was forced to qualify this statement: 'Although I have had dealings with women, *since I am a man like any other*, I have not had close friendship, *neither alone nor in company*.'[51]

Alberto's reply is intriguing for two reasons. Firstly he verbalised the belief that having sex with prostitutes was an 'integral' aspect of manhood. It was something he reiterated later on when asked about his relationship to Settimia. 'I have had dealings with a woman prostitute called Settimia several times, *like the man that I am.*' It is almost as if he felt the question were an affront to his manhood. Was Alberto just articulating a 'medical' point of view, referring to the 'need' to expel semen for the sake of maintaining the balance of his humours, or did this affirmation link him to the intellectual circles of the so-called '*libertini*'? Libertines refuted

[47] ASR, TCG, Processi, sec. XVII, vol. 154, c136v, Vincenzo Matthia Caldorossi, 28 February 1619.
[48] ASR, TCG, Processi, sec. XVII, vol. 154, c120r, Emilio Barbiere, 21 February 1619.
[49] ASR, TCG, TD, vol. 190, c10v, Duns Albertus Brecatius Lucrentis, 17 March 1603.
[50] Ibid.   [51] Ibid., c11r (italics added).

Christian ethics on sexual matters, stressing the importance of the power of nature and accepting the essential naturalness of sexual desire. Alberto may well have frequented such circles.[52] In his testimony he mentions a friend, 'Giulio Manchio' [?], and this may well have been Giulio Mancini, doctor, art critic, writer and later physician to Pope Urban VIII. Mancini, who has tentatively been linked to the libertines, was also a friend of the infamous Captain Valerio and was godfather to his illegitimate son with the courtesan Antonia Segnoverde.[53]

Alberto's reply is also interesting because of the way he initially denies having 'friendships' with women. The court was using the term generically, meaning 'did he have sex with women?', but he may have misunderstood this and thought that they were asking whether he had *close* friendships with them – which he most emphatically did not want to admit to. This suggests that the distinction between having casual sex with a prostitute and having a close friendship with one was of some significance. When asked about his relationship with Settimia and Clementia Fortunata he was deliberately 'casual', saying that he had had sex with Settimia only 'a few times' and that he couldn't 'remember having ever taken her anywhere except to [his] house'.[54] He also stressed that his behaviour was absolutely normal practice in the city: 'When I saw Clementia as I said above, Cav. Cesari took me there . . . in his company, and he took me there so we could go out, *in the way that people go to women's houses for conversation*.'[55]

This denial of emotional ties to prostitutes in criminal depositions may have been a strategy to avoid being implicated in any crimes, but may also have been shaped by an awareness that there was something problematic – be it dishonourable or unmanly – in admitting to having a close relationship with a prostitute, although it was acceptable to have sex with one. Certainly the description Menica gave of her French gentleman's reactions to Pietro battering on the door portrayed a man of reason, a self-disciplined, detached man, who dominated his passions and impulses.[56] 'Sig. Gerolamo is a gentleman . . . a quiet person as they say, cold, he didn't show anything,

[52] Libertinism has been described as 'a generic rebellion, an irritation with dogma and moral rules, an enjoyment of scandal and impertinence'. Giorgio Spini, *La ricerca dei libertini* (Florence: La Nuova Italia, 1983), 12–13.

[53] ASR, TCG, Processi, sec. XVII, vol. 23, c104r–107, Giulio Mancini Senese Medico, 29 April 1603. Roberto Zapperi suggests that Mancini may have been a *libertino* in *Eros e controriforma* (Turin: Bollati Boringhieri, 1994), 58. He also wrote a treatise on painting which discusses the placings and uses of erotic paintings in the home. *Considerazioni sulla pittura*, ed. Luigi Salerno (Rome: Marucchi, 1957).

[54] ASR, TCG, Processi, sec. XVII, vol. 23, 11v.   [55] Ibid., c111r (italics added).

[56] Renata Ago, 'Farsi uomini: giovani nobili nella Roma barocca', *Memoria* 27: 3 (1989), 7–21, 17.

nor did he say anything . . . not even when I went back upstairs to S. Gerolamo did he say anything, nor did he complain in anyway while the other was knocking on the door, he didn't even ask who he was.'[57] We will see later that it is not unlike the model of gentlemanly behaviour to which another courtesan, Aurelia, referred when her client behaved indecently. Whether or not this was a 'true' account of Gerolamo's response to discovering that his courtesan also frequented a stable-hand, it was a portrayal of an 'ideal' seventeenth-century Italian gentleman. It was, it appears, no longer fashionable to wear one's heart on one's sleeve as far as courtesans were concerned. In Counter-Reformation Rome, sexual 'release' was one thing, but being dominated by emotions and desire, like their Renaissance forebears, was quite another.

LOVE, FRIENDSHIP AND JEALOUSY

Despite the instances in which men expressed indifference to the prostitutes they frequented, we also find the language of friendship, love and affection embedded alongside the more curt and dismissive language of carnal commerce, suggesting quite high levels of emotional engagement. Whether this emotion derived principally from issues pertaining to damaged honour or to damaged 'hearts' is unclear. Sometimes such emotions emerge from very brief comments. A coachman described how some French gentlemen he used to drive often said to him: 'Drive in front of *la specchiarina*'s house [the little mirror girl], *because she is our friend and our beloved* . . . and seeing her at the window . . . they waved to her and she bowed, saluting them, and I heard that she was friends with those Frenchmen.'[58]

Of course, what 'beloved' might have meant in each of these contexts is impossible to define, except when the speakers themselves attach an explanation. When Antonia Angelis Senese spoke about her friend Antonio the sailor, she used her hope of marriage to indicate the intensity of the relationship.[59] 'I have been his friend for two years . . . I loved him . . . and now I love Antonio because he said that this Easter he wanted to marry me.'[60] In another case 'love' was used to explain a young woman's departure

---

[57] ASR, TCG, Processi, sec. XVII, vol. 23, c738v.

[58] ASR, TCG, Processi, sec. XVII, vol. 145, c516r–517r, Lorenzo Barocculo Ludovico Romano, 4 July 1618 (italics added).

[59] See Lucia Ferrante's discussion of prostitutes who had hoped that long-term clients would marry them. 'Pro mercede carnali', esp. 51–7.

[60] ASR, TCG, Costituti, vol. 457, c225v, 4 April 1596.

from her home town and her descent into prostitution. Blasio, a policeman from Albano, a town about twenty kilometres south of Rome, was suspected of having lured a young orphan named Joanna into prostitution, helping her to leave Albano and bringing her to Rome to work as a prostitute.[61] Whilst Joanna denied that Blasio had played any part in her move to Rome, he presented their relationship as a love story. He explained that they had met two years earlier, at one of her neighbours' homes, where 'we began to know each other, looking at one another, and I was told that she loved me'. He also stated, 'we fell in love with one another, that is, she said that she loved me and that she wanted to marry me'. This is an interesting moment in the narrative, as if he was aware of making a 'slip' by making their love sound as if it were reciprocal. He continued by saying, 'that is, she said that she loved me and that she wanted to marry me', putting the onus for these feelings on to Joanna and extricating himself from the implication of emotional involvement. Since Blasio already had a wife, marriage was out of the question, but according to his account Joanna was so in love that she had backed out of a prearranged marriage with another man and followed him to Rome. He portrayed her as a woman in the grip of her passions, ungovernable and lusty, careless of her honour, very much in keeping with the characterisation of prostitutes in moralising narratives. It was the obvious way to exonerate himself from blame in her downfall.

One woman who claimed she felt strong feelings for her client was Delia Angeli Romana, led into prostitution by her mistress and interrogated in connection with the trial of Captain Valerio. The Captain had frequented Delia occasionally for nearly a year, and she was asked to account for her movements on the night she heard of his arrest. She explained that when she had heard Captain Valerio had been arrested and might die, she had 'left the house at about six or seven p.m., because the moon was already up . . . to go to Captain Valerio's house to get news of him'. Asked why she had wanted news of him, she replied, 'I wanted to know and it was my right to know how Captain Valerio was, because I loved him (*lo amavo*) and was fond of him (*gli volevo bene*).' Asked why she loved him she said, 'I loved him because we had known one another as lovers (*concubinatione*) and had spent time together.'[62]

---

[61] ASR, TCG, Costituti, vol. 456, c181r–182r, Joanna Andrei Molinari di Albano, 19 April 1596, and c175v–177r, Blasio Lucentis de Monte Rinaldo, 17 April 1596. He uses both '*innamorarsi*' and '*volere bene*' interchangeably.

[62] ASR, TCG, Processi, sec. XVII, vol. 23, c172–179, Delia q. Angeli ('*Havevo havuto concubinatione et pratica*').

This is a very strong emotional statement, unusually so for these documents. Of course, one could argue that Delia was saying this to protect Valerio in some way, as if by declaring her love he might be exonerated from his numerous crimes, although given the accusations and weight of evidence against him such a statement would probably have counted for little. Indeed, she was actually reinforcing the fact that as a married man he had been committing long-term adultery. Rather than dismiss it outright, we can let it take us into another dimension of relationships between prostitutes and their clients, where powerful emotional bonds might well develop over time. Whether Delia's feelings were reciprocated is a different matter, but judging from several accounts of Valerio's relationships with women he was an extremely sexually jealous and possessive man, and their relationship was certainly passionate. Delia described how one evening he had stayed with herself and her mistress Sueca at her home when they heard a knock at the door. Delia had gone to the window to see who it was and Valerio had heard a man call her name and ask her to let him in. The Captain had gone downstairs, summoned his men and chased the stranger. When he came back he was angry, remonstrating that she knew very well who the man was, and then left:

And didn't come back until the Wednesday evening at which when I went to open the door he showed that he was very angry with me, because when I tried to take his hand he pulled it back behind him saying, 'Get out of my way, I don't care for you anymore', and he went upstairs to talk to Sueca. I withdrew to one side crying and Sueca said, 'How can you speak like that, with her there crying and you saying nothing at all to her', and he replied, 'She shouldn't have wronged me as she did.'[63]

Given the broader context of Valerio's association with several women as prostitutes, plus accusations that he was essentially controlling them, it is easy for us to assume that Valerio was a heartless, calculating pimp, as he may have been. But it is interesting that Sueca chided him for not taking responsibility for the emotional distress he had caused Delia, as if she none the less expected him to be kinder and more considerate of her feelings.

'UNA DONNA LIBERA' (A FREE WOMAN)[64]

Although 'freedom' is not a term which we would instinctively associate with prostitution, it was certainly a concept which belonged to the mental

[63] ASR, TCG, Processi, sec. XVII, vol. 23, c181r–183r, Delia q. Angeli, 5 December 1602.
[64] ASR, TCG, Processi, sec. XVII, vol. 23, c130v, Valerio Armenzano, 18 October 1602.

world of prostitutes and courtesans. We see it used when they claimed before the court that they were '*donne libere*', free to dispose of their bodies as they saw fit, when defending their right to prostitute themselves given that they had no marital ties. But it was also used to explain and justify women's desire for release from certain relationships.

Antonia Segnoverde Napolitana was another of the prostitutes called to testify about her relationship with Captain Valerio, with whom she had lived for four years and to whom she had borne a son.[65] Subsequently she had left him to set up on her own, and, asked why she had done so, she replied simply that 'I just really wanted to leave.'[66] Antonia's account of why she had left Valerio was crucial. Had she left of her own accord, or had Valerio's rival, Giacomo Francese, 'taken' her away from the Captain by acting as her *ruffiano* and finding her clients? If she had left him on account of her acquaintance with Giacomo this may have given Valerio a motive for killing him.[67]

Antonia's claims that it was she who had taken the decision to leave him were supported by other witnesses, whose portrayals of her are remarkably consistent in showing her as the protagonist of events: determined, strong willed and utterly independent. She was, according to all accounts, a woman who wanted her 'freedom' and asserted it, despite Captain Valerio's attempts to bend her to his will. As her friend Marcilla pointed out, leaving Valerio was not the obvious thing to do, since she had a young boy by him and he was an important and relatively wealthy man. How could she possibly find 'a better match'?[68] But Antonia had replied that 'she did not care about her things nor her son and that she wanted more *libertà*. The Captain 'had done everything to try and make her stay in his house, even putting her in prison, but she simply didn't want to stay anymore'.[69]

When asked by the court why he had imprisoned her, she explained, 'He did not want me to have sex with any other men.'[70] But she was not daunted and she had told him 'that I wanted to do things my way, and that I no longer wanted to feel myself controlled by him (*sottoposta da esso*)'.[71] She had also told him that 'I wanted to be a woman on my own', and this 'upset him greatly'.[72] When he had claimed that she was casting shame on him and that people would call their child 'son of a whore', she told the court: 'I replied that I am a free woman and I wanted to do things my own

[65] Ibid., c42v–43r, Antonia Segnoverde Panormitana.   [66] Ibid., c43r.
[67] Ibid., Antonia, c100r, 14 October 1602.
[68] Ibid., c47v, Marcilla Adriani Montis Leonis, 9 October 1602.
[69] Ibid., c47v.   [70] Ibid., c100r, Antonia, 14 October 1602.   [71] Ibid.   [72] Ibid.

way if he did not want to marry me.'[73] Since Valerio himself was already married with three children, she must have been referring to the fact that he could have given her a dowry and found her a husband if he had really wanted to make her respectable.

Antonia's situation may have been unusual, and Valerio an exceptionally jealous man. None the less, the language used in the case suggests that there was a vocabulary of freedom upon which women could draw, as well as an idea of a life which was not governed entirely by a single man, giving the impression that women did feel that they had a 'choice' and some 'agency' to live as they chose. Another courtesan gave a very similar account of trying to leave a long-term relationship with a man and set up on her own (claiming, however, that she intended to live as an honest woman). She too employed the language of subjection and liberty to describe her relationship and her decision to leave it. This woman was Dianora Hieronima Pisana who had lived as a courtesan in Rome prior to 1592, and had then lived with Filippo Lucchese in Pisa for four years. From allusions in her testimony he had probably been supported by her earnings.[74] The case came to court because she had gone to stay with a client named Cesare whom she had met four years earlier. This had led to a fight between Filippo and Cesare, resulting in their arrest. Filippo had apparently asked Dianora to marry him but she insisted to the court that she had no intention of doing so. 'I wouldn't marry him for anything, he is a good-time man, not a man to look after a house, and he leaves in the morning and doesn't return until seven or eight at night.'[75] Like Antonia, she asserted that she wanted 'to be free', or at least free of Filippo. 'And I didn't want to [marry him] for anything, I wanted to be free, and I didn't want to be in his hands (*nelle sue mani*) any longer.'[76]

REJECTION AND RETALIATION

Having the 'freedom' to reject a client seems to have been taken for granted by prostitutes in the city. Even though the word 'power' – or a simile – was never adopted in court, what was at stake when women turned away a client was the issue of who was in control; some men tolerated being seen to be in a weaker position better than others. It was not only common to

---

[73] Ibid., c44v, Testimony of Antonia.
[74] ASR, TCG, Costituti, vol. 464, c15v–16v, c21v–23v, Dianora Hieronima Pisana, 19–20 October 1596; c16v–17r, Cesare Passamontis di Bari, 19 October 1596; c18r–21v, Cesare Petri Pisano, 20 October 1596.
[75] Ibid., 22r.   [76] Ibid., 22v.

refuse clients, but this underpinned the whole system of elite prostitution. Even so, women put themselves in physical danger by refusing clients on whatever grounds. Elizabeth Cohen has coined the term 'house-scorning' to describe the 'ritualised revenge' attacks made on a person's honour through an attack on their dwelling, a standard response made by disgruntled clients of prostitutes who had been rejected in some way.[77] She has emphasised the importance of honour in understanding the dynamics of these attacks: the man was insulted, his honour damaged by the rejection, so he sought redress. Along with honour I suggest we also consider some of the other dynamics present, in particular the role played by the linked notions of 'power' or control, and 'freedom' within relationships of prostitution.

Lucretia Anconitana, who lived at Monte Citorio in November 1621, gave no reason as to why she had refused to receive a certain Jo Antonio in her house, but she obviously had strong feelings about it, having put him off on many occasions. He was more articulate about his reasons for being angry at this rejection:

You should know that many times the accused has asked whether he could have dealings with me but I have always told him to mind his own business. Around the twenty-fifth of October he came one evening at about ten o'clock, there was a knock on my door which I thought was one of my friends, so I went downstairs and when I opened the door I found that it was Jo Antonio who said to me: 'I am an honourable young man and my money is as good as that of all the others.' Finally, since I hadn't wanted to give him what he desired he drew his sword and began to swear at me.[78]

The reasons for another youth's problems with prostitutes are a little clearer. GioPietro Lambertino was probably a very young man, since he and his friends were described as being 'youths without beards . . . some just beginning to grow a beard' by Diamante, a '*donna di partito*', the kind of prostitute who received 'all kinds of people'.[79] GioPietro had been one of these until some fifteen or twenty days prior to the events which took them to court. Diamante claimed that she had stopped seeing GioPietro then because he had started to frequent another woman nearby called Madalena, 'and so I didn't want to be his friend anymore'. Even more so 'because he had *la scolatione*', or gonorrhoea. 'Although GioPietro has not had anything more to do with me carnally for about fifteen or twenty days, despite this he has come into my house several times, by night and by day,

[77] Cohen, 'Honour and Gender', 597–8, 613–15.
[78] ASR, TCG, Processi, sec. XVII, vol. 175, c48r, 19 November 1621.
[79] ASR, TCG, Processi, sec. XVII, vol. 154, c111v–113v, 18 February 1619, Diamante fil Gabrielis Neapolitana.

but has done nothing but kiss me, although he wanted to have sex with me, but I didn't want to because of the *scolatione*, as I said earlier.' The fact that she had continued to see him for several weeks, limiting him just to kisses, suggests that she was in control of the relationship. Eventually, on the last day of *Carnevale* after lunch he visited her and asked for sex. She must have felt she could fend him off no longer, for after about two hours with her he had left, 'because I forced him to go away'. Later that night he had returned, battering on the door which he threatened to break down, although finally he left. GioPietro was evidently out of luck as far as prostitutes went. Perhaps knowledge that he was diseased had spread, for the rival prostitute Madalena, who lived in Piazza del Popolo, had also told him that 'she didn't want him in her house anymore'.[80] Still, on that last day of *Carnevale* he had passed by her house with his friends and asked whether he could go up. Madalena was upstairs with Gerolamo Bonfatti whom she had hoped would stay the night with her. Emilio the barber had also dropped by. She had asked Emilio not to mount the stairs because she was '*impedita*' (already busy), with Gerolamo. Emilio was just leaving when GioPietro passed by. Madalena heard GioPietro speaking to Emilio and she called down to GioPietro, 'Insolent . . . and you dare to come to my door!'[81] He and his friends had thrown some stones on the ground, perhaps as a warning, and gone away.

One witness said that GioPietro had given the *scolatione* to Madalena (or perhaps it was vice versa, it is not clear) ten days before *Carnevale*, and that ever since then they had not seen one another. Whatever it was that had taken place between Madalena and GioPietro had certainly generated great animosity, and he returned later that night and attacked her door and window, throwing a bottle of ink from the street – the classic signs of 'house-scorning'. Despite his confident assertion to his friends, who had expressed anxiety about carrying out this illegal attack, that nothing would come of it because the *birri* would be enjoying that last evening of *Carnevale*, they were all arrested, interrogated and imprisoned. Indeed, very unusually the verdict of the case is recorded in the same volume.

GioPietro Lambertini has been tried and interrogated because having had a friendship for a long time with Donna Madalena, courtesan at Piazza del Popolo, and her not having wanted to receive him in her house anymore etc . . . Four of his companions were imprisoned and all were tortured . . . GioPietro was given a warning (*monitorio*) and a suspended fine of two hundred *scudi* and ten years on the galleys, but was not sentenced.

In its precise legalistic prose, this draws attention to the fact that this had been a long-term relationship brought to a close by Madalena, and that GioPietro had hoped to make her pay for this act of autonomy with his attack. The court obviously did not favour these arrogant youths, and saw it as their duty to protect an otherwise unremarkable prostitute from the aggression of her rejected suitor.

Finally, let us turn to an attack which took place on the house of a courtesan named Aurelia in 1604, carried out by the 'courtly' young men discussed earlier, Marcello, Aurelio and their friends from Brescia. According to the courtesan Aurelia, she had been attacked by Marcello and Aurelio because she had rejected Marcello's request for anal sex. In retaliation they had broken into the courtyard, 'serenaded' her with an obscene song, and mocked her for having no man at home.[82] In order to defend her damaged reputation Aurelia took the men to court, and was asked to explain why this offence had occurred. Aurelia explained that she had known Marcello, the ringleader of the group, for some time, and some days earlier he had had sex with her without paying. He had had the effrontery to return a few days later with his friend Marini, saying that he wanted sex with her again. This she had refused, replying, presumably ironically: 'Why not; I can't believe that you would treat me as you treated me the last time.'[83] She was not only taking back control over her body, but humiliating him by openly reprimanding him for his behaviour in front of his friend. He had then replied that he would pay her in good time, but that he wanted to sodomise her, a proposal which she also rejected. This accusation was no small matter. 'Unnatural sex' (*contra-natura*) was viewed severely by the courts and punishment for both parties ranged from whipping, to exile or burning at the stake. Calling a prostitute a *bugiarona* – a bugger – was also a serious insult and a mark of infamy. Merely asking Aurelia for anal sex was implicitly offensive to a prostitute who valued her 'honour' and reputation. It is not surprising therefore that Aurelia refused. 'I told him that that was not the way a gentleman would behave but the behaviour of a papier mâché gentleman,' yet again humiliating him in front of his friends.[84] He had gone away, only to come back some time later with his friends in order

---

[82] For a detailed description of the nature of the attack see Cohen, 'Honour and Gender', 613–15.

[83] TCG, Processi, sec. XVII, vol. 36, 211v, Aurelia q. Alexandri de Ripa, 29 June 1604. (I read this remark as having been ironic, intended to point out his poor behaviour on the previous occasion. Elizabeth Cohen reads it as having been a genuine acceptance. See 'Honour and Gender', 614.)

[84] TCG, Processi, sec. XVII, vol. 36, 211.

to dishonour her by singing an abusive serenade, after which she filed her complaint against him.[85] Insults continued to be traded in the court room where Marcello claimed that he had refused to have sex with Hieronima, a friend of Aurelia's who had also been present. He claimed that she was diseased, thus turning the tables on the women's narrations of being in control of the relationship. 'She dislikes me because once I went to screw her and I found a scab on her cunt and didn't want to have sex with her, and for this reason she has always secretly hated me, and for this reason she has made this deposition against me.'[86]

The song, the taunts, the obscene language and the accusation were clearly a verbal attempt to reassert male domination over the women, both in the threatened act of buggery and in his references to his being 'too big', implying that he would cause her pain. Furthermore the references to scabs implied not just syphilis, but taking too many clients, denoting her as a public whore. The battle between Aurelia and Marcello was a battle for control and a battle over identities, in the insults traded both in the street and in court. What is particularly striking is that Aurelia trusted that the courts would believe her version and help her to restore her damaged honour, much as Madalena did fifteen years later.

The nature of criminal sources means that the majority of the relationships for which we have evidence are those which had 'gone wrong' in some way or involved the lower-status street prostitutes who were engaged in casual encounters with strangers that left them vulnerable to abuse. These must be set against the background of the thousands of commercial carnal transactions which took place each week in the city, the majority of which have left no trace behind, and which presumably proceeded fairly amicably.

Judging from the cases considered here two broad dynamics governed relationships between prostitutes and clients in the city. On the one hand were relationships founded on an ideal of sociability, friendship and trust. Both parties understood that their honour rested upon the correct behaviour of the other, and the day-to-day maintenance of these relationships depended on mutual respect and civility. These ideals underlay the practice of the *amico fermo* and the sharing of courtesans amongst friends. The system had evolved to prevent jealousies and rivalries, but inevitably these did sometimes arise, particularly when – despite all the

[85] Ibid., c213r, Hieronima Blanchi d'Orvieto, 29 June 1604.
[86] Ibid., c235r, Jo Baptista, 4 July 1604.

precautions – love found a way to disrupt the otherwise orderly management of carnal commerce.

On the other hand were those relationships in which this mutuality had broken down. These were relationships which had been running smoothly, as described above, and then suffered a rupture, or they may have failed to observe the traditional 'model' from the start. Problems then arose when the prostitute asserted her wishes over those of a current or prospective client, or when men refused to recognise the prostitute's right to determine her clientele or to set her own terms. Furthermore, this state of potential conflict is reflected in the insulting and dismissive language often used by men when referring to prostitutes in court. Even when long-term, apparently amicable relationships were brought under the scrutiny of the court there seems to have been a marked disinclination for men to admit to having anything more than a very casual acquaintance with prostitutes and courtesans and fervent denial of any feelings of 'love'. It seems unlikely that this was entirely a result of the fraught circumstances in which they were speaking and the need to disassociate themselves from criminal activities. This reluctance of men to admit to emotional entanglements with courtesans must surely be attributed to the impact of Counter-Reformation morality and ideals of manhood, as men were increasingly aware of the church's disapproval of prostitutes in general and of special 'relationships' with them in particular. Whether it was art mirroring life, or life mirroring art, there was certainly a strong correlation between the portrayals of prostitute–client relationships presented in Counter-Reformation moralising texts and the narrative accounts of their relationships given by men in the court room. Women's accounts of the same relationships, however, undermine these appearances of detached and purely casual liaisons, reminding us of the intense emotional ties and needs which often co-existed with carnal commerce.

Conclusion: Continuity and change: prostitution after the Reformations

The control of sexuality was crucial to both Protestant and Catholic visions of a renewed and disciplined society. In a culture in which reason, discipline and self-control were associated with the male, the body, sexuality and disorder were associated with the female. Sexuality – particularly that of women – had to be governed at all cost. Prostitutes were the embodiment of this unfettered female sexuality, of disorderliness and of the immorality of women lacking male governance. Their presence was considered to set a dangerous example to decent women, as well as inciting lusts in men, fomenting gambling, drinking and fighting. Therefore controlling prostitution played a central role in the disciplinary ambitions of both confessional areas.[1] Yet despite the similarity of the underlying rhetoric on prostitution, Protestant and Catholic areas tailored their approaches differently, with widely varying results, depending on the local political and social context.

I

Lutherans saw sexual desire as so powerful that it could not be denied or resisted by men or women. Celibacy consequently lost its status, considered as an impossible state to maintain, whilst monks and nuns were encouraged to leave their cloisters and marry and priests to take a wife. Many monastic houses were closed down and marriage and family life were elevated to a position of supreme importance in the civic arena, the only context in which sexuality could be legitimately expressed.[2] As was to happen under Tridentine Catholicism, marriage was made subject to much closer control by the authorities, and great emphasis was placed on its public nature, so that without parental consent, a public ceremony and the presence of a

---

[1] See James Farr's discussion of this, *Authority and Sexuality in Early Modern Burgundy (1550–1730)* (Oxford and New York: Oxford University Press, 1995), 7–8.
[2] Wiesner-Hanks, *Christianity and Sexuality*, 63–4.

pastor a marriage was not valid.[3] Marriage was also the symbol of a man's incorporation into the world of civic responsibilities and adult masculinity. In Augsburg masters had to be married men, only married men could elect guild representatives and hold office, making a wife 'thus guarantor of her husband's achieved adult masculinity: she proved his masterhood'.[4] Within the family husbands were expected to rule and wives to submit and obey, with the domestic household unit envisaged as a model of public order and discipline in miniature. Discord and disagreement between spouses was viewed as 'wilful' and courts and consistories sought to impose peace between them.[5]

One of the consequences of reform in Protestant areas was that extra-marital sexuality was seen as deeply transgressive, and this had a profound effect on prostitution. Brothels were closed and prostitutes were execrated and demonised.[6] Indeed, as a class of women they no longer 'existed', as in Augsburg, where by 1537 their crimes were dealt with under the categories of fornication or adultery.[7] Even male sexuality was targeted and in Germany, where unmarried men and youths had once tended to socialise openly around prostitutes in brothels, by the 1550s such behaviour was being actively discouraged and indeed, forbidden to journeymen.[8] None the less, prostitution continued illicitly, and it has been pointed out that in the obsessive focus on their sexuality the campaign against prostitutes 'may have made the prostitute . . . far more sexually compelling . . . than she would otherwise have been'.[9] Furthermore, in some ways the women were at greater liberty than they had been before, although they were now at the mercy of illicit brothel keepers who could exploit them ruthlessly, and were always in danger of discovery and severe punishment.[10] Ulinka Rublack paints an extremely grim picture of the consequences of this 'criminalisation of extra-marital sexual behaviour' in Protestant areas of Germany. Women known to have had extra-marital sex, particularly with soldiers, and those who bore illegitimate children had become 'the main target of moral reform' by the mid-seventeenth century. Punishments were harsh: the women were banished and no one was allowed to offer to raise the children. Rublack concludes that the chances of survival for these women – and their offspring – were remote.[11]

---

[3] Ibid., 74.   [4] Lyndal Roper, *Holy Household* (Oxford: Oxford University Press, 1989), 31.
[5] Ibid., 163–205. And Wiesner-Hanks, *Christianity and Sexuality*, 67–8.
[6] Ibid., 63–4.   [7] Roper, 'Discipline and Respectability', 19, 21.
[8] Wiesner-Hanks, *Christianity and Sexuality*, 85.
[9] Roper, *Oedipus and the Devil*, 150.   [10] Wiesner-Hanks, *Christianity and Sexuality*, 85.
[11] Ulinka Rublack, *The Crimes of Women in Early Modern Germany* (Oxford: Clarendon Press, 1999), 124, 145.

In England sexual morality does not appear to have been as sharply re-drawn. Laura Gowing does not find a 'consistent, homogeneous (sexual) morality' in the early seventeenth century, but a 'range of moral structures', some rooted in popular practice rather than church teaching.[12] Perhaps as a reflection of this, prostitution, although illegal, was dealt with less severely than in Germany, and 'nautie houses', pimps and street prosti-tution flourished.[13] However, as a result of the trade being made illegal, eighteenth-century prostitutes became vulnerable, were heavily policed, and the women had to pay a cut of their earnings to the owners of the lodging houses they used.[14] Despite this, Henderson argues that they were not a 'despised community', and were 'as much an accepted part of plebeian London as any other identifiable group'.[15]

The conditions in which prostitutes lived and worked in seventeenth- and eighteenth-century Protestant Amsterdam were harsh. Although a much bigger city than Rome, it had about the same numbers of prostitutes (800–1,000), in a population with a huge surplus of lower-class women. Not only was there intense competition for clients, but the male population was largely composed of passing sailors, not a particularly wealthy group.[16] The criminalisation of prostitution meant that prostitutes rarely worked independently, surrendering their freedom in exchange for their board, lodgings and the clientele supplied by the brothel owner. The system made them extremely dependent on the brothel keeper, who took about half their earnings, and this dependence favoured the accumulation of debts with the result that prostitutes were bought and sold on by brothels like slaves, even guarded to prevent their escaping before they had paid off their dues.[17] In addition to this the very high levels of policing, averaging at about 900 arrests per year (compared with the 30 per annum in Rome), surely indicate that the lives of prostitutes must have been utterly miserable.[18]

Although reforms were not consistent across Protestant Europe, the ten-dency was for male power over prostitutes to be sharply increased, as pimps,

---

[12] Laura Gowing, *Domestic Dangers: Women, Words and Sex in Early Modern London* (Oxford: Claren-don Press, 1996), 10–11.

[13] For the sixteenth century see Paul Griffiths, 'The Structure of Prostitution in Elizabethan London', *Continuity and Change* 8:1 (1993), 39–63.

[14] Henderson, *Disorderly Women*, 29, 33–4.

[15] For example 1,407 women were charged for immoral conduct by a single central London parish, between 1773 and 1779. Ibid., esp. 14, 43–4, 90, 128.

[16] Van de Pol, *Het Amsterdams hoerdom*, from an unpublished translation of chapter 7, 'Sex for Money and Money for Sex: Prostitution as a Pre-Industrial Trade', 22, 31.

[17] Ibid., 34–5, 37–8.

[18] As I stress in chapter 4, this refers to the numbers of prostitutes arrested by the Governor's *sbirri* as noted down in their own records.

bawds and lodging-house owners become structural elements of an illegal trade, limiting the women's freedom to operate and above all damaging their earning potential. As a result prostitutes were more exposed to harassment by officials and this harsh regime stripped them of the vestiges of respect they once commanded in their communities, making their social position far more vulnerable than prior to the Reformation.

II

Post-Tridentine Catholicism, in complete contrast to Protestantism, reaffirmed celibacy and virginity as the ideal state. The greatest honour was accorded to those who renounced their sexuality, and for women this meant entering a convent. The chastity, self-discipline and obedience of nuns stood as a symbol not only of perfect womanhood, but of the ideal state and the purity of its ruling classes.[19] Yet in order to protect this purity radical change was envisaged for women's religious orders by the Tridentine Reforms. Motivated by fears that the boundaries between convents and the outside world were too porous, endangering the honour and chastity of nuns, and by extension their families, after 1566 all convents were to be enclosed. This meant that professed nuns had to stay within the convent, communication with the outside world was strictly limited, and when it took place women could speak only through grilles, or meet family members in the convent parlour.[20] As a result the active roles they had played in helping the sick, as well as in the ritual and ceremonial life of the community, were to be ended, whilst the convent as a whole was to be brought under the close supervision of a male religious order and male confessors. The heightened status and importance accorded to convent life went hand in hand with changing marital and economic strategies amongst the elite. Spiralling dowry payments, a limited pool of acceptable husbands and a determination not to divide family patrimonies led patrician families to offer their daughters up as brides of Christ, rather than to leave them unwed, so their bodies and hence family honour would be shielded from disrepute. As a result the late sixteenth century saw a dramatic increase in the numbers of young women entering holy orders. In Venice in 1581, for example, about 54 per cent of patrician women were in convents.[21] Nuns

---

[19] Ulrike Strasser, *State of Virginity: Gender, Religion and Politics in an Early Modern Catholic State* (Ann Arbor: University of Michigan Press, 2004).

[20] The council decree was reaffirmed by Pope Pius V's bull *Circa pastoralis* in 1566. Mary Laven, *Virgins of Venice: Enclosed Lives and Broken Vows in the Renaissance Convent* (London; Penguin, 2002), xxiv.

[21] Jutta Gisela Sperling, *Convents and the Body Politic in Late Renaissance Venice* (Chicago and London: University of Chicago Press, 1999), 18.

comprised 1 per cent of the population of Naples in 1623, 5.5 per cent in Florence in 1622, 9.3 per cent in Prato, and 13 per cent in Gubbio.[22]

Despite the rhetoric, virginity was not intended to be an option for the majority of women, for convents also required a dowry which was well beyond the reach of most.[23] Although rhetorically speaking marriage was a second-class option, in practice it was a lauded state for all other women, one which enabled them to perform their duty as mothers and as educators of children. Both confessions saw the married couple and the domestic household which developed around it as the primary 'building block' of the state. It provided social stability by harnessing sexuality and procreation into a safe, controlled sphere and it acted as a reflection in miniature of the state.[24] It was a place in which the husband and father was judge, and ruler over his wife or daughter, his obedient servant.

In order to gain greater control over marriage and sexuality, the Tametsi decree of the Council of Trent sought to create clearer distinctions between the married and unmarried, between those who could legitimately have sexual intercourse, and those for whom it was forbidden. Pre-marital sex had previously been the norm across wide swathes of Europe, often as an accepted prelude to marriage. Concubinage had also been quite common, a state in which the boundaries between marriage, adultery, fornication and prostitution were blurred.[25] It had also been easy for people to marry in secret, without the knowledge or permission of their parents, and the rite had been more a secular than a religious pact. Tametsi addressed this issue by declaring marriage a sacrament, thereby bringing it fully under the church's jurisdiction. As a result concubinage was to be rooted out, pre-marital sexuality was discouraged and women who became pregnant out of wedlock would find it harder and harder to force the child's father to marry them, since the verbal 'marriage promise' once accepted by secular courts was no longer valid.[26]

---

[22] Helen Hills, *Invisible City: the Architecture of Devotion in Seventeenth Century Neapolitan Convents* (Oxford: Oxford University Press, 2004), 186–7.

[23] Silvia Evangelisti points out that only the families of the aristocracy and financial and mercantile bourgeoisie could afford them, in 'Wives, Widows and Brides of Christ', 241.

[24] See Strasser's discussion of this theme in *State of Virginity*, 8–10.

[25] Nor were these ambiguities wiped out that easily, as Sherrill Cohen shows from debates conducted in mid-seventeenth-century Florence as to which women should be registered as prostitutes, and which defined as adulteresses. *The Evolution of Women's Asylums*, 49–51.

[26] See Wiesner-Hanks, *Christianity and Sexuality*. Also Sandra Cavallo and Simona Cerutti, 'Female Honor and the Social Control of Reproduction in Piedmont between 1600 and 1800', in Edward Muir and Guido Ruggiero, eds., *Sex and Gender in Historical Perspective* (Baltimore and London: The Johns Hopkins University Press, 1990), 73–109.

Finally, a flood of didactic and moralising literature aimed at women was disseminated throughout society. Prints, books, tracts and images urged them to adopt behavioural models which were based on codes derived from monastic discipline, and to take as their models the Virgin Mary and the female saints. Zarri has summarised this aesthetic with the phrase 'with downcast eyes and head bowed'– capturing the spirit of chastity, modesty, obedience, docility and calm acceptance which was proposed as the ideal of womanhood.[27]

Whilst convent life and marriage were proposed as the most perfect state for women, there were always those who became neither nuns nor wives, or who did marry but were widowed or abandoned; such women accounted for up to 25 per cent of adult females in the Italian states.[28] These were the women who, in the eyes of moralists, occupied a dangerous no-man's-land between chastity and whoredom. If they had left their father's home they were beyond the direct control of men, and it was they who were considered most likely to fall into prostitution. Unlike Protestantism, however, post-Tridentine Catholicism did not outlaw prostitutes, and its approach to prostitution remained fundamentally the same as it had been before the Reformation. Male sexuality continued to be seen as irrepressible and in this sense prostitution continued to work alongside the institution of marriage, protecting married women from the lusts of men by providing a 'safe outlet' for them. Prostitutes were women who had fallen, *donne di malavita* ('women of evil life'), but they were women to be converted and saved, rather than persecuted, providing others with an opportunity to perform 'good works' in the process. Preaching, religious education, the confessional and other devotional practices were aimed at inducing inner change in prostitutes, and there was a renewed vigour in the impetus to found and improve the provision of institutions for vulnerable girls or fallen women. This demonstrated a recognition of the economic vulnerability which led to and sustained prostitution. From the mid-sixteenth century in Rome the Jesuits had provided a unique approach to helping 'fallen women' which permitted them an unusual degree of choice and which underscores the ways in which marriage, convent life and prostitution were interlinked. Casa Santa Marta, Santa Maria Felice and Casa Pia were institutions which offered women a refuge from prostitution and from failed or troubled

[27] See Gabriella Zarri, ed., *Donna, disciplina, creanza cristiana dal XV al XVII secolo: studi e testi a stampa* (Rome: Edizioni di Storia e Letteratura, 1996), Introductory essay 'Donna, disciplina, creanza cristiana: un percorso di ricerca', 5–19, 5–7. See also her extensive bibliography of such texts printed in Italian and the linked essays.

[28] See Bennett and Froide, *Singlewomen in the European Past*, 43–5.

marriages. They could stay there whilst they decided whether to be reconciled with a husband, to be placed as a domestic servant, to marry, or to become a nun in the confines of the Convertite.[29] For those women who continued living as prostitutes, the strategies to contain and reduce visible prostitution in the streets were also a continuation and extension of former practices. In terms of their day-to-day life prostitutes in Counter-Reformation Rome were not indiscriminately stigmatised, whether by the community or by institutions, as is demonstrated by the fact that even lowly prostitutes were afforded protection by the courts and could obtain judgments in their favour against well-born men.

III

The impact of the Catholic and Protestant Reformations on women's lives, and their significance as watersheds in gender history, is currently a topic of scholarly debate.[30] On the one hand, the emphasis in the historical 'master narrative' on the Renaissance and Reformations as periods of major social transition and rupture is seen as being unhelpful to the study of gender, obscuring the profound continuities which had dominated women's lives in the past.[31] On the other hand, there are those who see the later sixteenth and the seventeenth century as a period in which there were marked shifts in gender relations, characterised by an increase in patriarchal control and authority over women.[32] Olwen Hufton suggests a way forward, in a sense a compromise between the two, adopting a Braudelian approach when looking at women's history. She argues that thinking about change over time in terms of the long, medium and short term 'promotes a consideration of how the experience of certain generations might differ while the framework of reference remains largely unchanged'.[33] This advice seems particularly pertinent when trying to sum up the effects of the Counter-Reformation on prostitution in Rome.

The first thirty years after the Council of Trent can be taken as the short term. It represents the period in which the Counter-Reformation ideal of

[29] Lazar, *In the Vineyard of the Lord*, 32, 50, 69.

[30] Lyndal Roper, 'Gender and the Reformation', *Archive for Reformation History* 92 (2001), 290–302.

[31] Judith Bennett, 'Medieval Women, Modern Women: Across the Great Divide', in David Aers, ed., *Culture and History, 1350–1600: Essays on English Communities, Identities and Writing* (London: Harvester Wheatsheaf, 1992), 147–75. Bridget Hill, 'Women's History: a Study in Change, Continuity or Standing Still?', *Women's History Review* 2:1 (1993), 5–22. For examples of histories influenced more by continuities than ruptures see Hufton, *The Prospect Before Her*. G. Duby and M. Perrot, gen. eds., *A History of Women in the West: Renaissance and Enlightenment Paradoxes* (Cambridge, Mass.: The Belknap Press of Harvard University Press, 1993).

[32] Wiesner-Hanks, *Christianity and Sexuality*.   [33] Hufton, *The Prospect Before Her*, 488.

social discipline was pursued with greatest determination. Undoubtedly the three or four generations of women involved in prostitution after 1566 bore the brunt of religious and institutional zeal. They and their clientele were suddenly subjected to an ever-increasing battery of laws, and when punishments were meted out they were often ferocious. The repeated decisions to move, expel, segregate and confine prostitutes to different streets or areas, even if only temporarily successful, caused insecurity, great inconvenience, loss of revenue and savings.

Taking as the 'medium term' the period running from 1590 to the 1650s, which has formed the central focus of this study, the results are more mixed. Tridentine policies had no effect on the overall presence of prostitutes as their numbers climbed steadily from 1600 to 1639 – despite some annual drops – both as a total and as a percentage of the female population. By 1639 3.5 out of every 100 adult women were noted as prostitutes in the *Stati delle Anime*.[34] The severity of the long-term economic situation, the ongoing demand for prostitutes in a population heavily dominated by men and the unusual socio-economic profile of men in Rome must explain the continuing attractions of the profession. Police activity was characterised by intermittent low-level harassment of prostitutes and their clients: raiding their parties, stopping their carriages and interrupting their evening perambulations about the city. However, the numbers of arrests compared with the overall population of prostitutes was small and probably not a deterrent.[35] The initially ambitious quest to drive all wealthy prostitutes out of the city or to encourage them to convert had also failed and wealthy courtesans continued to be a visible presence in the city, certainly until the mid-century. Their homes were important meeting places, their company was openly sought out by elite men, and there were significant numbers of 'comfortably off' prostitutes.

In the longer term the drive to control prostitution seems to have relaxed, since the numbers of women recorded as prostitutes started to decrease after 1650 until, in 1700, only 400 women were registered.[36] It is unlikely that prostitution itself had diminished, since as long as women's wages were low and jobs scarce, prostitution would thrive. It has been suggested that the drive to control and regulate their presence had petered out, as a reflection of increasingly tolerant attitudes amongst the clergy, manifested particularly

---

[34] Sonnino, 'Le anime dei romani', 354–6.
[35] The missing records of the Vicariato might have painted a slightly different picture, particularly of the control of married prostitutes.
[36] Sonnino, 'Le anime dei romani', 248.

by the abandonment of the requirement to note their presence in the *Stati delle Anime* in 1750.[37]

Alongside the economic and demographic explanations for these continuities were social and cultural factors. One important element in the failure of the post-Tridentine papacies to reform prostitution was the resistance offered by the men of the lay elite. For although not a cohesive social group, without their support the papacy could not hope to effect change, and the majority did not share the papacy's convictions about the necessity of transforming practices of prostitution in the city.[38] Financial concerns, issues related to honour and the need for alternative forms of sexual and social relationships with women seem to have underlain this resistance to a change in the status quo. This was a society in which as many as 45 per cent of male aristocrats never married, and those who did had to wait until their late twenties.[39] In Rome frequenting an 'honest courtesan' had become a crucial aspect of elite men's lives: it was a way in which such men could 'perform' their masculinity, setting themselves apart from 'vulgar' men.[40] It was in their interests to keep courtesan culture alive, and to protect those things which conferred distinction upon the women: luxury clothing, travel by carriages and residence in honourable streets.

Research into prostitution across Italy for the seventeenth century is patchy, but suggests that the situation in Rome was not unusual. In the principal cities, Milan, Naples, Florence and particularly Venice, the profession was similarly characterised by the wealth and ostentation of its prostitutes and the persistence of their highly visible forms of social life. As a reflection of this the main thrust of regulations was to prevent prostitutes from being mistaken for honest gentlewomen, to prohibit them from living in high-class areas, curbing their ownership of luxury goods and restricting their presence in the streets at the most popular times of day or night. From the repeatedly reiterated legislation it would appear that a kind of 'stalemate' had been reached everywhere, with city authorities managing at

---

[37] M. Porri and C. Schiavoni, 'Aspetti della condizione femminile e del lavoro della donna a Roma fra XVII e XVIII secolo', *Genus* 3–4 (1988), 245–63, 247. And Sonnino, 'Le anime dei romani', 358–61. Between 1694 and 1698, although the official number of prostitutes was about 528, curates only notified their superiors of 294 women 'amongst the most scandalous and disorderly'. Porri and Schiavoni, 'Aspetti della condizione femminile', 248–9.

[38] Some were representatives of ancient feudal landholding families, some were members of more recently ennobled papal families, some merchants, some bankers, some professionals.

[39] These data are for Venice and Milan. Gianna Pomata, 'Family and Gender', in John A. Marino, ed., *Early Modern Italy, 1550–1796* (Oxford and New York: Oxford University Press, 2002), 69–81, 79.

[40] John Tosh, 'What Should Historians Do with Masculinity?', *History Workshop Journal* 38 (1994), 179–202, esp. 184–92.

best to tax and police the poorest and most vulnerable, whilst the better-off carried on as usual.[41]

In other Catholic areas of Europe a less tolerant picture emerges, though to some extent this may be due to studies which have relied heavily on legislative sources, which tend to reveal intentions rather than practices. Elizabeth Perry's study of Seville portrays a heavily regulated and repressive system in which prostitutes were forced to live in brothels, supervised by men. When these were finally closed down in 1623, prostitution became clandestine.[42] In the Pays Basque, on the other hand, brothels had never been set up. Instead, prostitutes were rejected by their own communities, but tacitly accepted on the edges of towns, and along main roads.[43] In France a combination of Protestantism, Calvinism and Jesuit influences led to the closure of brothels in the 1560s, followed in the late seventeenth century by increasingly repressive legislation. Women found guilty of sexual crimes were supposed to be sent to reform institutions, whose character shifted towards a harsher, disciplinary regime. In Montpellier, considered to be a southern 'Mecca' for prostitution, 630 women are known to have been admitted to the Bon Pasteur, the reformatory for fallen women, between 1594 and 1729.[44] In Paris, a well-organised police force issued a battery of laws during the eighteenth century, resulting in the arrests of between 700 and 800 women for prostitution annually. Benabou has argued that this police activity was largely directed at keeping the poor, occasional prostitutes under constant pressure, ignoring those who worked from brothels and the upper-class courtesans.[45]

In spite of the flood of moralising literature, the preaching and the proselytising of missionaries, Counter-Reformation Catholicism also appears to have struggled to impose its views on prostitution and to transform ordinary people's consciousness of sin and morality.[46] Judging from the criminal records, the rigid and stigmatised identities proposed for prostitutes were widely rejected, in particular the notion that occasional acts of prostitution made them 'prostitutes'. Indeed, what is striking is women's articulate defiance of moral norms on the grounds that they were 'free' to act as they wished and that they had no reasonable economic alternative. This is echoed by studies of sixteenth-century Augsburg and eighteenth-century Paris and Montpellier, which suggest that women did not employ

---

[41] See Canosa and Colonnello, *La prostituzione*, for chapters on several Italian cities.
[42] Perry, *Gender and Disorder*, 151–2. [43] Bazán Díaz et al., 'La prostitution au Pays Basque'.
[44] Jones, 'Prostitution and the Ruling Class', 23.
[45] For Paris see Benabou, *La prostitution*, and also A. Mericskay's discussion of the book, 'La prostitution à Paris (dans les marges d'un grand livre)', *Histoire, Economie et Société* 4 (1987), 495–508, esp. 501–3.
[46] See, for example, De Boer, *The Conquest of the Soul*, 44.

moralising terms to describe their activities, nor did they see prostitution as altering their basic social identity. They considered it as work, and if they had another job as well, they continued to define themselves by their primary *métier*.[47] Likewise, as we saw in chapter 9, the Roman criminal records show that carnal commerce remained an unexceptional event for most men, in terms of their conscience. Having sex with prostitutes was still an unquestioned facet of manhood, indeed, almost its proof. This said, men's testimonies reveal an awareness of the church's position on prostitution, leading them to pay at least lip-service to the idea that it was preferable to avoid prostitutes during Lent, that it was praiseworthy to help a prostitute 'convert' or marry, and that it was best to appear to be emotionally uninvolved with prostitutes, to give the impression that contacts with such women were fleeting, casual and occasional.

IV

The reforms of prostitution also need to be considered in the broader context of sexual mores and practices across Catholic Europe which changed very slowly, with much regional variation.[48] For example, despite Tridentine rulings to the contrary, until the eighteenth century pre-marital fornication was still widely practised in Italy as long as there was a 'promise' of marriage.[49] To illustrate the regional variation in mores, in Salzburg the illegitimacy rate in the late seventeenth century was 30 per cent, while in France it was only 1 per cent.[50] In Mediona in rural Catalonia between 1575 and 1630 only an estimated 28 per cent of marriages were performed in church and people lived together for two or three years and had children before marriage.[51] In the Pays Basque in the early seventeenth century bigamy, incest and concubinage were common, canonical marriage 'weakly rooted' and promiscuous sexual behaviour only of concern if patrimonial issues were at risk.[52]

Indeed, all over Europe Tridentine reforms clashed with tradition. Local communities had established rules and informal procedures which governed sexual behaviour and, as Cavallo and Cerutti point out, were rarely

---

[47] Roper, 'Discipline and Respectability', 19. Mericskay, 'La prostitution à Paris', 502. Benabou, *La prostitution*, 307. Hébert, 'Les "femmes de mauvaise vie"', 504–5.
[48] Wiesner-Hanks, *Christianity and Sexuality*, 121.
[49] See Cavallo and Cerutti's discussion of this for Piedmont in 'Female Honor and the Social Control of Reproduction'.
[50] Wiesner-Hanks, *Christianity and Sexuality*, 121.
[51] Henry Kamen *The Phoenix and the Flame* (Yale: Yale University Press, 1993), 283.
[52] Bazán Díaz et al. 'La prostitution au Pays Basque', 1296.

as 'black and white as the morality fashioned by the church'. Indeed, they find that community judgements were subtle and elastic, easily adapted to individual circumstances.[53] Particularly important was the distinction between 'private' and 'public' sin. Although each community set its own limits, sexual transgressions were widely accepted provided they were kept within the 'private' sphere. Much was tolerated as long as people did not impinge on the honour of others or disrupt the community, as did adultery, the bearing of illegitimate children and publicly lewd behaviour. Neighbours and families observed one another, used gossip to control behaviour and preferred to 'discipline' infringements of moral codes amongst themselves, turning to institutions only when this failed.[54] It was only with the strengthening of ecclesiastical control over marriage and increasing urbanisation that the community lost its ability to control sexual behaviours.[55]

V

One explanation for the grudging and incomplete reformation of sexual morality must lie with the difficulties encountered by the clergy. Studies from southern Italy, Lombardy and south-west Germany show that when faced with the immense task of educating hundreds of thousands of barely literate people, priests sought to keep things simple. Expectations were kept to a minimum as they sought to develop a religion 'which was accessible and comprehensible to all'.[56] Some set their sights on teaching the ten commandments and the Lord's prayer, others hoped to teach the catechism and impress the importance of confession on their flock. Wherever they were, in order to be accepted by the community, priests had to conform to local beliefs and adapt notions of piety to suit their flock.[57] Their authority was not accepted unquestioningly: adjustment and negotiation were the key to success.[58] Under these circumstances criticism of sexual behaviours

---

[53] Cavallo and Cerutti, 'Female Honor', 87–8.
[54] See, for example, Rublack, *The Crimes of Women*. Cavallo and Cerutti, 'Female Honor'. And Hébert, 'Les "femme de mauvaise vie"', 509–13.
[55] Cavallo and Cerutti, 'Female Honor', 87.
[56] David Gentilcore, '"Adapt Yourselves to the People's Capabilities": Missionary Strategies, Methods and Impact in the Kingdom of Naples, 1600–1800', *The Journal of Ecclesiastical History* 45:2 (1994), 269–96, 270.
[57] Ibid. And Ulinka Rublack, *Reformation Europe* (Cambridge: Cambridge University Press, 2005), 184–5.
[58] Selwyn, *A Paradise*, 50. Marc R. Forster, *Catholic Revival in the Age of the Baroque: Religious Identity in Southwest Germany, 1550–1750* (Cambridge: Cambridge University Press, 2001), chapters 2 and 3 especially.

was not always politic. In Milan under Carlo Borromeo's zealous reform programme, community notions of honour collided with what was initially a harsh policy on sexual sin. As a result, when it came to the busy period of Lenten confessions, sexual sins were routinely absolved unless they had been committed in a sacred place.[59]

This is not to suggest that prostitutes and their clients were unaffected by the religious fervour of the Counter-Reformation. Prostitutes as a group were specifically targeted by the Jesuits and it is likely that many prostitutes in Rome had come into contact with Jesuit 'missionaries'. Testamentary practices, notarial records and depositions show that prostitutes in Rome did not shun religion and that they were aware of the peril to their souls, attending mass, making their confessions, asking for masses to be said at their death in chapels across the city and leaving pious legacies to numerous religious institutions.[60] Evidently they did not see their sexual behaviour, or the magical practices they commonly practised and with which they were associated, as being incompatible with their beliefs as Catholics. Viewed in this light the religious objects they owned – paintings, kneelers and rosaries – were not necessarily placed for show or to fabricate an 'honest' persona for themselves, as is often implied in discussions of the religious paraphernalia belonging to prostitutes. It is more likely that they were part of the 'material culture' of religion, an essential aspect of their religious iden-tity.[61] Recent scholarship on conversion and missionary work has pointed out that there can be a wide gap between what is taught and what is under-stood, that different sets of beliefs are not mutually exclusive, and that people did not passively accept elite understandings about religion.[62] So when prostitutes attended mass, made confession or went on pilgrimages (and I find examples of all these), they were acting out 'their own ideas about the place of religion in their lives, their own way of expressing their iden-tity as Catholics, rooted in popular practice and tradition'.[63] This was not necessarily seen as being incompatible with the fact that they prostituted themselves. It also appears as though these ritual practices were considered

---

[59] De Boer, *The Conquest of the Soul*, 228–30, 250–5.

[60] For their accounts of attending mass, see chapter 4. Antonia Segnoverde Palermitana went to her confessor after having been urged to commit perjury by a judge. ASR TCG, Processi, vol. 23, sec. XVII, 1602, c340. I have studied fifty wills: 75 per cent of these women requested that additional masses (other than those associated with burial) be said for their soul.

[61] I am prompted by Ulinka Rublack's discussion of the material culture of Protestantism in *Reformation Europe*, 151, 158.

[62] Forster, *Catholic Revival*, 12–29. Kenneth Mills and Anthony Grafton, eds., *Conversion: Old Worlds and New* (Rochester, N.Y.: University of Rochester Press, 2003), Introduction: Peter Gose, 'Con-verting the Ancestors', 140–74, 140, and Allan Greer, 'Conversion and Identity', 175–98, 177–87.

[63] Mills and Grafton, *Conversion*, 12.

sufficient as signs of belief by the clergy who ministered to them. Demographic historians have pointed to the discrepancy between the relatively few adults registered in the parish records in the late seventeenth century as not being fit to take communion, and the many hundreds of prostitutes in the city, all of whom in theory should have been disqualified from the sacrament.[64] They have explained this with the hypothesis that prostitutes were being permitted to take the sacrament, provided their behaviour was outwardly decent and that they observed the ritual life of the church, an illustration of what Greer describes as the importance of 'performance rather than belief', in religious practice in specific social contexts.[65]

VI

Recent research into the study of the effects of the Counter-Reformation on women's lives has acknowledged the intensification of patriarchal hegemony over women, yet chosen to focus on women's resistance to and defiance of the norms and legislation through which the encroachment on women's freedoms was implemented. This approach stresses the importance of female agency against the backdrop of an increasingly intolerant and repressive gendered social order, whilst implicitly calling into question the efficacy of both the legislation and the moralising and didactic literature which sought to govern and condition women's behaviour.

One area in which this is particularly striking is that of histories of female religious orders in the period which suggest that, far from accepting models of pious, obedient and submissive behaviour, nuns could be extremely assertive, defiant and active when it came to defending their access to the public sphere, their autonomy and their privileges. They show that well into the seventeenth century nuns across Catholic Europe were fighting the strict enforcement of Tridentine decrees on convents. One study of Venetian convents has stressed the ways in which the women routinely ignored, circumvented or overcame many of the restrictions theoretically placed on them.[66] In Bologna the nuns in one convent went to extreme measures to resist the imposition of a bishop's authority over them: refusing to take the sacrament for twenty-two months; declining to elect a new abbess; and showering stones and tiles down on the builders sent to seal them off from the outside world as part of the implementation of more rigorous enclosure. It was only after being threatened with excommunication that they finally

---

[64] Sonnino, 'Le anime dei romani', 361. And Porri and Schiavoni, 'Aspetti della condizione femminile', 249.
[65] Greer, 'Conversion and Identity', 178.   [66] Laven, *Virgins of Venice.*

submitted, in deed, but not in spirit, to the changes imposed on them by the ecclesiastic authorities.[67] In another long drawn-out battle which took place in the 1660s in Bavaria, a convent of Franciscan nuns sought to circumvent the general constraints placed on their autonomy and agency, by buying and seeking to display relics without the permission of the male convent administrator. This was just one in a catalogue of actions over the years which had seen nuns from this convent resisting attempts to restrict their autonomy and access to the public domain.[68]

Nuns were not alone in their resistance to the strengthening of patriarchy. Married women also attempted to set limits on the exercise of patriarchal power within the home, as two analyses of marital disputes in Venice have shown. Wives of all social classes sought redress through the courts when their husbands took their authority too far, thereby protecting their financial interests, challenging abusive behaviour and criticising men who fell short of their domestic responsibilities.[69] And although not contextualising her research in terms of the Counter-Reformation, Chojnacka shows the agency and autonomy which characterised the daily lives of plebeian women in early modern Venice as they headed households, managed property, moved about the local community, conducted business, worked and socialised in their own right.[70]

Women involved in prostitution were no different to these nuns or wives when it came to challenging the encroachment of patriarchal power over their lives. In Rome, Bologna, Paris or Montpellier there were many who resisted being labelled as 'prostitutes' and identified themselves primarily as working women forced to supplement their income with prostitution. Prostitutes in Italian cities ignored attempts to move them out of their homes and communities, whilst in Rome they went even further, actively complaining about new statutes, causing them to be modified, in one case demanding (and receiving) compensation for the enforced moves. Nor did Italian prostitutes who were attacked or slandered by clients take the insults

---

[67] Craig A. Monson, *Disembodied Voices: Music and Culture in an Early Modern Italian Convent* (Berkeley, Los Angeles and London: University of California Press, 1995), esp. 151–66.

[68] Ulrike Strasser, 'Bones of Contention: Cloistered Nuns, Decorated Relics, and the Contest over Women's Place in the Public Sphere of Counter-Reformation Munich', *Archive for Reformation History* 90 (1999), 254–88. See also Silvia Evangelisti, '"We Do Not Have It, and We Do Not Want It": Women, Power and Convent Reform in Florence', *Sixteenth Century Journal* 34:3 (2003), 677–700.

[69] Daniela Hacke, *Women, Sex and Marriage in Early Modern Venice* (Aldershot: Ashgate, 2004) and Joanne M. Ferraro, *Marriage Wars in Late Renaissance Venice* (Oxford: Oxford University Press, 2001).

[70] Monica Chojnacka, *Working Women of Early Modern Venice* (Baltimore and London: The Johns Hopkins University Press, 2001), xvi.

meekly. They fought back, taking men to courts to re-establish their honour, whilst the alternatives to prostitution, such as the opportunity to take shelter in an institution and 'convert', were not always willingly embraced. Camerano observes that in Rome many single women and professional prostitutes 'fought to keep their daughters with them and obstinately refused the intervention of the *Conservatorio*'.[71] Sherrill Cohen concludes that in Tuscany 'the refuges for *convertite* were faced, in the sixteenth and seventeenth centuries, with women's determined claims to greater liberty in the ordering of their own lives . . . [pitting] themselves against attempts to keep them enclosed'.[72]

EPILOGUE

Little is known about the history of prostitution in Rome in the longer term, or when it was that the convergence of those social, cultural, economic and demographic factors which had contributed to forge the character of prostitution in the city finally came to an end. The *amico fermo*, the huge pool of well-off clients, the premise that sex with prostitutes was a sign of manhood, and the importance of the courtesan in constructions and practices of masculinity had all been integral to Roman prostitution over a period of about 150 years. But the impression is that by the end of the seventeenth century important shifts had occurred in the sphere of elite prostitution. Judging from *avvisi*, diaries and commentaries, courtesans appear to have gradually lost their pre-eminence on the social scene. Increasingly, men from the upper ranks of society are described as seeking the favours of 'singers', '*cantarine*' or '*virtuose*' rather than those of courtesans, whilst princes and noblemen vied to employ the most gifted and famous of these women, searching out talent and paying huge fees to add them to their entourage, while *virtuose* ran musical *soirées* from their homes.[73] Without tarring all such women with the same brush (since differences between 'honest' and 'dishonest' would always have pertained), there is evidence that the *cantarina* or *virtuosa* could be a courtesan by another name. Fashioned for a new cultural context they were allied firmly with the theatrical and musical

---

[71] Camerano, 'Assistenza richiesta', 234.

[72] Cohen, *The Evolution of Women's Asylums*, 113. Likewise see Alessandra Camerano's discussion of the reactions of young women enclosed in Santa Caterina dei Funari. 'Assistenza richiesta'.

[73] See, for example, Alessandro Ademollo, *La Bell'Adriana ed altre virtuose del suo tempo alla corte di Mantova* (Citta di Castello: Lapi, 1888), esp. 36–7. And Elena Tamburini, 'La lira, la poesia, la voce, e il teatro musicale del seicento. Note su alcune vicende biografiche e artistiche della baronessa Anna Rosalia Carusi', in B. M. Antolini, A. Morelli and V. Vita Spagnuolo, eds., *La musica a Roma attraverso le fonti d'archivio* (Lucca: Libreria Musicale Italiana, 1994), 419–31.

entertainment so characteristic of Baroque sociability, which had perhaps enabled them to shed the association with prostitution. Even so, according to a Dutch traveller in 1655, some of them offered both musical and sexual services.

There are some ladies in Rome who are called *virtuose*, who know how to sing, dance, play instruments and who converse reasonably well. One goes to them sometimes in company, as many as ten or twelve, and one can have a serious discussion or just a chat. When you want to go, you pay a *scudo* or two each . . . and leave . . . and if someone wants to stay the night, he will be satisfied. Such houses are not infamous, on the contrary, they are honourable.[74]

It may just have been a case of the leopard changing its spots: of changing fashions, and a new sense of propriety which dictated that upper-class 'courtesans' were simply known by another name. Yet it seems more likely that amongst the elite, attitudes and mores had shifted and that the 'golden age' of the elite Italian courtesan, usually posited as having ended in 1527, finally came to a close some time after 1650.[75] Overall, the spaces and context of much elite sociability had changed, as men and women mingled in the '*conversazione*' (known in France as the *salon*), which dominated later seventeenth-century Roman society. No longer associated with courtesans, these events were presided over by ladies of the nobility, intellectuals and cardinals, and were governed by quite a different set of values.[76] Likewise, there are numerous descriptions of a new kind of sociability which saw married women of the elite escorted in society not by their husbands but by a *cicisbeo*, a man often reputed to have been also her lover.[77] Such developments must have signalled changes in the social imperatives and cultural assumptions which had underlain the structure of prostitution in the Italian states. In particular, given the evidence of men's and women's awareness of moralising discourse on prostitution, it seems probable that the shifts in attitudes promoted by the Counter-Reformation eventually affected the way in which prostitutes and courtesans were viewed within their communities and by their clients.

Yet for most women whose lives were touched by prostitution, in all likelihood, much remained unchanged. There would have been no improvement

---

[74] Tamburini, 'La lira', 426.

[75] The term 'golden age' has been widely used to describe the first appearance of the courtesans in the early *cinquecento*. The term now has acquired particular resonance in view of the debates on continuity and change in women's history. See especially Hill, 'Women's History'.

[76] Mirabelle Madignier, 'Sociabilité informelle et pratiques sociales en Italie: les salons romains et florentins au XVIIIème siècle', PhD thesis, European University Institute, Florence, 1999.

[77] P. G. Battista Labat, *Un Monaco francese nell'Italia del settecento* (Tivoli: Aldo Chicca, 1951), 67. And Pomata, 'Family and Gender', 84.

in the meagre wages available to those women who had to manage without men, or to supplement their husband's or parents' incomes. There would still have been a substantial pool of 'singlewomen', eking out a living at the margins of destitution, the majority of whom would have been extremely vulnerable to life-cycle changes such as illness, widowhood and abandonment which could lead even 'decent' women into prostitution. And for those who became prostitutes, for however brief a spell, there would always be the dangers of random violence, the shouted insults, the hazards of police harassment, arrest and prison.

Donna Menica Romana was one such woman, arrested in the Ortaccio one night in January 1602 in the company of a man. Taken before the court she described how her husband had 'gone to war' in 'June or July' of the previous year, leaving her to manage alone, so she had begun 'living the life of a courtesan'. The news of his death had been brought to her only a few nights earlier by a returning soldier. Despite these circumstances, Menica did not claim that she had no alternative (though this may have been the case). Instead she justified her actions on the grounds that 'I don't want to go around dressed like a scarecrow, because I have no other way of getting clothes.'[78] With these words Menica was adding another strand to the thread which ran through so many women's accounts of their recourse to prostitution. Some stressed their freedom to act as they wished; some pointed to the starkness of the choices available – starvation or commercial sex – challenging their interrogators to find fault with them. Some women blamed their inept husbands and others pointed to the material benefits of prostitution. What Menica conveyed in her brief statement was a reminder that there was more at stake than just survival. Carnal commerce had also offered her the means to dress decently, so that despite her desperate circumstances she was able to maintain her dignity and self-esteem, even as she hurried furtively through the cold, dark, winter streets.

---

[78] ASR, TCG, Costituti, vol. 511, c8v, Donna Menica Jo Baptista Romana, 16 January 1602.

Origins of prostitutes living in Rome

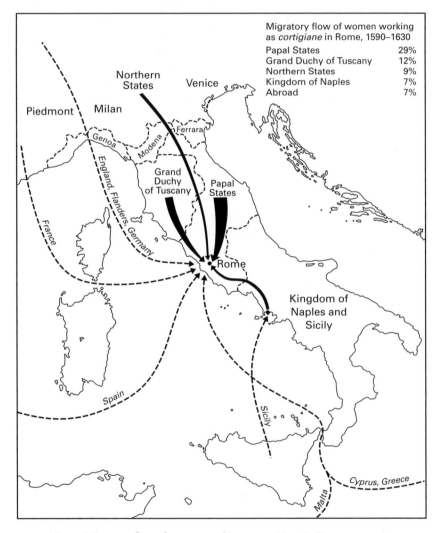

Map 2 Migratory flow of women working as *cortigiane* in Rome, 1590–1630

Table A1 *Origins of 1,198 prostitutes living in Rome between 1590 and 1630, by nearest large town, region or country*

Town	Totals	Town	Totals
Rome	192	Fabriano	5
Florence	86	Cortona	5
Siena	49	Toscanella	5
Naples	45	Civita Castellana	5
Perugia	45	Pisa	5
Orvieto	36	Montepulciano	5
Viterbo	35	Bergamo	5
France	27	Campagna	5
Spain	25	Sermoneta	5
Bologna	25	Parma	4
Milan	24	Padua	4
Ancona	22	Tagliacozzo	4
Todi	21	Fermo	4
Sicily	21	Rieti	4
Venice	20	Matrice	4
Ferrara	18	Bari	4
Foligno	17	Orte	3
Arezzo	16	Morlupo	3
Velletri	16	Malta	3
Romagna	14	Marche	3
Città Castello	14	Albano	3
Piedmonte	14	Pistoia	3
Macerata	11	Trevi	3
Urbino	11	Flanders	3
Spoleto	11	Savoia	3
Narni	10	Gaeta	3
Tivoli	9	Terni	3
Montefiascone	9	Jesi	2
Borgogne	9	Messina	2
Fano	9	Abruzzo	2
Pesaro	8	Borgo di San Sepolcro	2
Veneto	8		
Assisi	8	Camerano	2
Camerino	7	Castro	2
Faenza	7	Cesena	2
Ascoli	7	Cisterna	2
Aquila	6	Lucca	2
Palestrina	6	Agnagni	2
Germany	6	Fornello	2
Genoa	6	Lubriano	2
Palermo	5	Greece	2
Toscana	5	Cyprus	2
Rimini	5	Esio	2

(cont.)

Table A1 (*cont.*)

Town	Totals	Town	Totals
Frisolone	2	Bracciano	1
Gradole	2	Arpino	1
Cori	2	Capistillio	1
Nepi	2	Bassano	1
Sutri	2	Taranto	1
Piacenza	2	Biella	1
Pezzuolo	2	Supino	1
Recanati	2	Subiaco	1
Salerno	2	Sinigallia	1
Barcelona	2	Spello	1
Sulmona	2	Valencia	1
Tollentino	2	Arnara	1
Piediluco	2	Lombardia	1
Segno	2	Collevecchio	1
Tiburtino	2	Gardescia (Lago di	1
Montopoli	2	Garda prob.)	
Trento	2	Pescara	1
Segni	2	Graffignano	1
Monte S. Giovanni	2	Olmi	1
Volterra	2	Hercolano	1
Melia	2	Holland	1
Poli	2	Pitigliano	1
Castel dell Pieve	1	Nettuno	1
Carpeneta	1	Pogibonsi	1
Carita	1	Monterotondo	1
Capua	1	Magliano in Sabina	1
Castel Bolognese	1	Mantua	1
Castelnovo Cananese	1	Monte Santostefano	1
Castelvetro	1	Marengo	1
Castilione	1	Marino	1
Soriano	1	Monte Giorgio	1
Cavignano (Cavigliano)	1	Molise	1
Sora	1	Imola	1
Chieti	1	Provence	1
Castel Fiorentino	1	Sermoneta?	1
Tirol	1	Civitanova	1
Acquapendente	1	Civitello	1
Voglina	1	Comachio	1
Vicomero	1	Cremona	1
Verona	1	Savona	1
Anerzano	1	England	1
Apulia	1	Pietra santa	1
Valle Diana Regni	1	Ragusa	1

Table A1 (*cont.*)

Town	Totals	Town	Totals
Sessa	1	Prato	1
Prisciano (SS)	1	Formio	1
Fiumata	1	Foro pompilij (Pompei)	1
Prenestina	1	Fossombrone	1
Prattica	1	Sancasciano	1
		Total	1,198

Note: For the names of towns and villages, a modern atlas has been used to work out the nearest big town and province. For states the boundaries which existed at the beginning of the seventeenth century have been observed. If the place name referred to several places, all in roughly the same area of Italy, the largest of these was chosen. If there were many small villages of the same name distributed across the peninsula, the data were discounted. Many of the women are identified in such a way as to make it unclear whether the region or city was meant, in which cases I have plumped for the region (for example, Caterina Veneta I would assume referred to the province, whereas Caterina Veneziana seems to refer to the city)

Notes on the registers consulted from the Archivio del Vicariato di Roma

1. Santa Maria del Popolo, *Stati delle Anime*, 1604–21
   I have used data from the following years:
   1601, 1602, 1603, 1605, 1606, 1607, 1610, 1613, 1615.
2. Santa Maria del Popolo, *Matrimoni*, 1596–1620
3. Santa Maria in Via, *Stati delle Anime*, 1610
   At the end of the volume the number of *meretrici* in the parish is given as thirty-four although I counted sixty. I cannot explain this discrepancy.
4. Sant' Andrea delle Fratte, *Stati delle Anime*, 1607–11
   Very few women are noted as *meretrici*, especially in the earlier decades.
5. San Lorenzo in Lucina, *Stati delle Anime*, 1607
   The records for this year are extremely clear. A large 'c' in the left-hand column indicates *cortigiana*. Some of these single women have two 'c's, indicating that they are *cortigiane* who have taken communion. The page numbering is very confused. Up until Strada Vittoria I have counted from the beginning to identify the page number. Afterwards I use the number given on the top right hand of the page.
6. Santissimi Dodici Apostoli, *Stati delle Anime*, 1601–2
   As with Santa Maria in Via this was just outside the official boundaries of the Ortaccio. At the end is an interesting list of *concubines* (male and female) and *meretrici* (c116v–c117r), and where they live, which reveals the haziness about distinctions between them.

Bibliography

ARCHIVAL SOURCES

ARCHIVIO DI STATO DI ROMA (ASR)

Fondo Santa Croce, Filza 188. Lettera scritta da incerto a Papa Pio Quinto acciò che gli ebrei e le meretrici non si scaccino da Roma con le ragioni allegati per il medemo effetto da Romani. (Letter written by an unknown hand to Pope Pius V so the Jews and prostitutes are not expelled from Rome, with the reasons for this given by the Romans).

Camerale 1, Fabbriche b.1514 Tassa fatta alle cortegiane (1548) (also available on microfilm).

Camerale II,° Sanità, Busta 4/5, Contagio di Roma. Descrittione del rione di Campo Martio, fatta il mese di luglio 1656. (Contagion in Rome. Description of the Rione of Campo Marzio, made in July 1656.)

Relazione dei Birri, Buste 1–8.

Tribunale Criminale del Governatore di Roma (TCG) *Costituti* Vols. 47, 49, 50, 52, 55, 58, 174, 175, 176, 177, 179, 180, 181, 183, 184, 442, 443, 450, 452, 453, 457, 454, 456, 458, 459, 461, 464, 508, 513, 515, 517, 518, 519, 520, 521, 523, 547, 548, 551, 553, 554, 715, 716, 721, 733.

Tribunale Criminale del Governatore, *Processi*, vol. 20 (sec. XVII), c1246r–1348r. Sigismondo Attavanti Bernardinus, Dianora sua moglie. 4 July 1602.

Tribunale Criminale del Governatore, *Processi*, vol. 23 (1602) sec. XVII. fols. 1–340. Valerio Armenzano and Jacobi Landi Galli and Aquilante Abatiuns de Mte Cas[. . .]illo.

Tribunale Criminale del Governatore, *Processi*, vol. 36 (sec. XVII), fols. 1–89v. Gaspare Tronsarelli, Livia, sua moglie, and others, 2 June 1604.

Tribunale Criminale del Governatore, *Processi*, vol. 36 (sec. XVII), fols. 211–48v. Marcello, Jo Baptista, Marino et . . . dodecem incogniti Bresciani. 29 June 1604.

Tribunale Criminale del Governatore, *Processi*, vol. 44 (sec. XVII), c102–41. Marco de Porchia sbirro, con Antonio Jacobum Massarom. 1605.

Tribunale Criminale del Governatore, *Processi*, vol. 46 (sec. XVII), fol. 709. Pietro Staffieri, Menica Curiale and others. 1605.

Tribunale Criminale del Governatore, *Processi*, vol. 63 (sec. XVII) fols. 1–101r. Tarquinio di Lucca, Artemetia moglie e Giulia figlia di lei. 1607.

Tribunale Criminale del Governatore, *Testimoni per la difesa*, vol. 190 (re the trial of Captain Valerio).

Trenta Notaii Capitolini, Ufficio 19, late 1590s to 1620s. Vols. 27, 28, 33, 34, 35, 36, 37, 38, 39, 43, 45, 52, 56, 57, 63, 64, 66, 67, 68, 69, 70, 71, 72, 74.

Tribunale Criminale del Governatore, Atti di Cancelleria, Busta 105, Fasc. 158, 'Cortegiane'.

Archivio Sforza Cesarini, SFZ II, S1, Giu. Ovale. V498.

Sezione Orvieto.

Archivio del Governatore, Cancelleria Criminale B.121A 1600–2: Processum Diversorum. 1600 8 January 1601 and 13 January 1601 (D Alrinic Gentilis de Castro Lubriano).

ARCHIVIO DI STATO DI FIRENZE

Carte Strozziane, (Part 1) *Summarium Animarum Romae Existentium Anno*, c139. *Ufficiali dell'Onestà*, b4 (Libro di Condemnazione).

ARCHIVIO DI SANTA MARIA IN ACQUIRO

The original *collocazione* was Sez. H Eredità e Carteggi del XVI –XVII secoli. Eredità Sebastiano Caccini. The archive was being reorganised when I consulted it, and the markings may have changed. I found this information in a volume entitled *Libro Mastro, 1598–1603*.

ARCHIVIO CAPITOLINO

Cred. I vol. XXIII, Decreti di Consigli Magistrati, Cittadini Romani.

ARCHIVIO SEGRETO VATICANO (ASV)

Armadio VII, no. 36. Sacre Congregazioni: Visitazionis Aplic. pro Monialibus, c355 (498 new numbering).

Miscellanea. Armadio IV–V.

Diversi Camera, vol. 108, f47, 30 August 1537.

BIBLIOTECA APOSTOLICA VATICANA (BAV)

Barberini Latini, 4975, Racconto delle cose più considerabili che sono occorse nel governo di Roma in tempo di Mons. Giov. Battista Spada. 18 January 1635.

Fondo Capponi, v189, c17r. Relazione della Roma di Sisto Quinto. Relazione della morte di Agata Pignacci moglie di Ferdinando Allegrini di Napoli con le notizie più veridiche che mosero Sisto V a condannarla a morte. (An account of Rome made during the pontificate of Sixtus V. An account of the death of Agata Pignacci, wife of Ferdinando Allegrini of Naples, with the most accurate explanation of why Sixtus V condemned her to death.)

Urbinati Latini (Urb. Lat.), vols. 1038–73.

Vaticani Latini v9729. Tributo di Miscellanee di Roma sacre politiche erudite istoriche in prosa ed in verso offerto da Francesco Cancellieri a sua ecellenza Milord Francis Henry Egerton nel mese di Aprile dell'anno MDCCCVIII, c104r–107r, *Lettera sulla tolleranza delle meretrici in Roma.* (A miscellaneous collection of sacred, political, erudite and historical texts about Rome in prose and verse offered by Francesco Cancellieri to his excellency Lord Francis Henry Egerton in April 1808. *Letter on the tolleration of Prostitutes in Rome.*)

ARCHIVUM ROMANUM SOCIETATIS IESU (ARSI)

Rom 128, 2. C599–602: Rilationi dilla Missione fatta alle Diocesi Tusculane et Albanese.

BIBLIOTECA VALLICELLIANA

Codice Corvisieri, Busta 3, fasc. A, c9r–11r: Cortigiane.

ACCADEMIA DEI LINCEI

Codice Corsini, 34.E.f10. Relazione di casi diversi succeduti in Roma sotto il Governo di Monsignore Spada.

PRINTED VERSES

The popular songs listed here represent only a fragment of those kept in Italian libraries and are simply those which discuss *cortigiane* to be found in the catalogues of the BNF and in the Fondo Capponi Stampati of the BAV. They have been ordered chronologically.

Purgatorio delle cortigiane. Sonnetti sopra el detto purgatorio, Canzona sopra el detto purgatorio. Bologna: Joan Maria lirico Venitiano, 1529. (BNF, Palatino, E.6.6.153.ii.)

Il lamento di una cortigiana ferrarese quale per aver il mal franzese si condussi andare in carretta. Mastro Andrea Veneziano. Siena, 1540.

Il vanto e lamento della cortigiana Ferrarese, per esempio a tutte le donne di mala vita. Con il lamento d'una villanella, che desiderava maritarsi. Siena: Gio. Batista Verini Fiorentino, 1540. (BNF Coll. Landau Finaly. 535. 7.)

Lamento della ferrarese cortigiana. Composto per Maestro Andrea Pittore Venitiano, et da lui recitato in Roma nelle feste del carnevale, in habito di donna in una carretta che cosi si condusse detta cortigiana ferrarese. (Composed by Maestro Andrea, a Venetian painter, and recited by him in Rome during carnival, dressed up as a woman and standing in a cart, just like the courtesan from Ferrara in the song.) Siena: presso San Viglio, ad istantia di Giovanni di Alisandro Libraio, 1546. (BAV, Capponi Stampati, vol. 681, 336.)

Purgatorio delle cortigiane, recitato in Roma per Andrea Pittore, nella festa di carnovale, vestito di povero con le croccie et uno campanello in mano. Siena, 1546.

Nuova canzonetta. Di giovani impoveriti per le meretrici (c.1530s–1550s). In Carlo Verzone, ed., *Le rime burlesche di A. F. Antonfrancesco Grazzini, detto il Lasca, Le rime burlesche. Edite e inedite* (Florence: Sansoni, 1882).

Opera nova dove si contiene un esordio che da una donna a una sua figliuola, nella quale l'insegna con quante sorte di gente ha da fare l'amore, cosa ridiculosa e bella. Con un lamento che fa una figliuola con la madre che è mal maritata. (A new work which contains an exhortation by a woman to her daughter, in which she teaches her about the kinds of men she will make love to, something funny and lovely. With a lament made by an unhappily married girl to her mother.) Perugia, 1584. (BAV, Capponi Stampati, vol. 684.)

Nove mila novecento novanta nove malitie delle donne . . . Cioè che usano le false e scelerate cortegiane per gabbare i semplicetti giovani, che di loro s'innamorano, si come la signor Lesina gli discopre, sopra il corpo d'una femina. (The 9,999 malices of women. Those used by the false and wicked courtesans to trap simple youths, who fall in love with them, etc.) Composto per Antonio de Santi fiorentino, In Venice: appresso il Bonsadino, con licenza, 1614. (BAV, Capponi Stampati, vol. 683, 240.)

Risposta sotterranea della Signora Margarita Francese, famosissima cortegiana di Venetia, uccisa a tradimento da un suo amante. Contro quelli i quali cantano l'horrendo suo caso. Venice: Gio Battisata Bosadino, con licentia, 1614. (BAV, Capponi Stampati, vol. 684.)

La Veronese. Caso compassionevole: dove s'intende la inusitata morte data da un giovane parmesano ad Elisabetta cortegiana veronese. La quale sotto colore di benevolenza è stata condotta da lui fuori di Verona nella bassa di Caldiero, dove l'hà uccisa, rubbata, e sepolta il di 18 del mese di Luglio 1605. (The girl from Verona. A compassionate case, in which we learn of the unusual death of Elisabeth, the courtesan from Verona, by the hand of a young man from Parma. She was tricked by his friendly approach into being led out of Verona, to Caldiero, where he killed her, robbed her and buried her, on 18 July 1605.) Stampato, Francesco Fratanchini Veronese, Macerata, 1619. Con licentia. (BAV, Capponi Stampati, vol. 683, c106.)

Caso lacrimoso e lamentevole. Di Cecilia Bruni Muranese cortegiana in Venetia à San Paterniano. Occisa nella propria sua casa, dal suo amante, portandogli via Ori, e Gioie alli 8 Agosto, 1618. (The tearful and lamentable case of Cecilia Bruni Muranese, a courtesan in Venice who was killed in her own house by her lover, who took away all her jewels and gold on 8 August 1618 etc.) Composta in ottava rima da Valentino Detio detto Colloredo, Macerata and Ronciglione, 1621. (BAV, Capponi Stampati, vol. 683.)

Ridicolosa canzonetta nella qual s'intende un soggetto occorso sopra d'un contadino gabato da una meretrice, comme leggendo intenderete il tutto. Paolo Britti, Macerata, 162?. Con licentia. (BAV, Capponi Stampati, vol. 684.)

Il discorso di Lena cortiggiana con il suo maritaggio con Zan Scarsella. Opera nova in forma di Zingaresca. Di Gasparre Angeli da Viterbo, Ronciglione, 1622. Con licentia. (BAV, Capponi Stampati, vol. 682; also vol. 683.)

Lamento che fa una meretrice dolendosi della sua cattiva fortuna essortando le altre a lassar la pessima vita. Lucchesino sopradetto il Scacciarogna. Venice, 1626. Con licentia. (BAV, Capponi Stampati, vol. 684.)

Canzonetta nuova nella quale s'intende un giovane caduto in precipitio, per amare una meretrice. Ole Bricci, Cieco da Venetia. Macerata: Pietro Salvioni, 1627. (BAV, Capponi Stampati, vol. 684(49).)

Il lamento che fa una cortesana per esser li mancato il suo bon tempo. Paolo Britti, Macerata, 1632. Con licentia. (BAV, Capponi Stampati, vol. 684(93).)

Opera nova sententiosa. Nella quale s'intende il lamento fatto da una cortegiana, quale contiene la sua sciagurata vita, sue disgratie, pericoli, tormenti, travagli, patimenti che patiscono tutte insieme col suo pericoloso fine. Qual'è di grandissimo essempio alle istesse cortigiane nel quale dismostrar che debbono lasciar la trista vita, e ritirarsi al ben fare. (A new sententious work in which we learn of the lament made by a courtesan, which contains her wicked life, her misfortunes, the dangers, torments and sufferings and her dangerous end. Which is of great example to courtesans showing them they should leave their evil ways, withdraw and turn to good works.) Marino Sarenza Venetiano, ad istantia della Pecunia. Treviso: Girolamo Righetti, 1637. Con licentia. (BNF, Palatino, E.6.6.153.ii.)

La fortunata cortegiana sfortunata: dove s'intende Principio, Mezo e fine della vita Cortigianesca. Composta in otta rima, In Lingua veneziana, Da Pietro de Piccoli da Venetia, Venice and Treviso: Francesco Righettini, 1668, con licentia. (BNF, Palatino, E.6.6.153.i.)

La putta che diventa corteggiana, per il mal governo di sua madre, per volerghe far metter troppo presto il para sù. Opera molto ridicolosa, composta da un capriccio bizaro, sopra l'Aria di Ruggiero. Venice: appresso A. Z. 1668, con licentia. (BNF, Palatino, E.6.6.153.ii.)

Bandito in questo luoco solitario, tramutato per un giovine che haveva il mal francese. Con capitolo in lingua Venetiana contra una cortigiana molto bello, ne più stampato. (No date). (BAV, Capponi Stampati, vol. 681, c296.)

Nuova canzonetta: nella quale s'intende il lamento che fa un povero giovane con un suo compagno per esser stato gabbato da una cortegiana. Sopra l'aria della Nave. Treviso, con licentia: seventeenth century. (BNF, Palatino, E.6.6.153.i.)

Quattro bellissimi avertimenti. Necessarie per schivarsi da molti pericoli. Padua and Bassano: Gio Antonio Remondini, con licentia. (BNF E.6.6.153.ii, n.II.)

PUBLISHED PRIMARY SOURCES

[Anon.] *Ragionamento del Zoppino: Fatto frate, e Lodovico, puttaniere, dove contiensi la vita e genealogia di tutte le cortigiane di Roma*, attributed to Francisco Delicado. Milan: Longanesi, 1969. (orig. 1539, Venice).

Alberi, Eugenio. *Le relazioni degli ambasciatori veneti al Senato.* Vol. X, Serie 2, Tomo IV. Florence: Società Editrice Fiorentina, 1857.

Aretino, Pietro. 'Dialogo di Messer Pietro Aretino.' *Ragionamento, dialogo* (orig. 1534) Milan: Garzanti, 1984.

Il piacevol ragionamento de l'Aretino: dialogo di Giulia e di Madalena, ed. Claudio Galderisi. Rome: Salerno Editrice, 1987.

Sei giornate, ed. Giovanni Aquilecchia (Rome and Bari: Laterza, 1975).

Biondi, Michelangelo. *Angittia cortigiana. De natura de cortigiano*. Venice, 1540.

Burchardi, Joannis. *Diarium sive rerum urbanarum commentarii, 1483–1506*. Italian edition, *Diario del Burchardo,* April 1498, vol. ii (orig. 1498), ed. L. Thuasne, 3 vols. Paris: Ernest Leroux, 1884.

Codogno, Ottavio. *Compendio delle poste*. Milan: Giovanni Battista Bidelli, 1623.

Coryat, Thomas. *Crudities, vol. I* (orig. 1611) Glasgow: James MacLehose and Sons, 1905.

Delicado, Francisco. *La lozana andalusa*, ed. Luisa Orioli. Milan: Adelphi, 1970.

Fanucci, Camillo. *Trattato di tutte l'opere pie dell'alma città di Roma*. Rome, 1601.

Grazzini, Antonfrancesco. *Le rime burlesche. Edite e inedite*, ed. Carlo Verzone. Florence: Sansoni, 1882.

Landi, Ortensio. *Commentario delle più notabili et mostruose cose d'Italia, e altri luoghi*. Venice, 1548.

Lucian. *Chattering Courtesans and Other Sardonic Sketches*, ed. and trans. Keith Sidwell. London: Penguin, 2004.

Mancini, Giulio. *Considerazioni sulla Pittura*, ed. Luigi Salerno. Rome: Marucchi, 1957.

Markham, Gervase. *The Famous Whore or Noble Curtizan: Containing the Lamentable Complaint of Pauline the Famous Roman Curtizan, sometimes Mistress unto the Great Cardinall Hypolito of Este*. London, 1609.

Martin, Gregory. *Roma Sancta* (1581), ed. George Bruner Parks. Rome: Edizioni di Storia e Letteratura, 1969.

Montaigne, Michel de. *The Diary of Montaigne's Journey to Italy in 1580 and 1581*, ed. and trans. E. J. Trechmann. London: Hogarth Press, 1929.

Petronio, M. Alessandro da Città Castellana. *Del viver delli romani et di conservar la sanità*. Rome, 1592.

Saint-Disdier, Limojon de. *La ville et la République de Venise*. Amsterdam: Daniel Elsevier, 1680.

Scanaroli, JoBaptista. *De visitatione carceratorum, Libri Tres*. Rome, 1655.

Thomas, William. *A History of Italy*, 1549, ed. G. B. Parks. Ithaca: Cornell University Press, 1963.

Veniero, Lorenzo. *La Zaffetta* (orig. 1531, Venice; reprint Paris, 1861).

SECONDARY SOURCES

Ackerman, James S. 'The Planning of Renaissance Rome, 1450–1580.' In P. A. Ramsey (ed.), *Rome in the Renaissance: the City and the Myth* (Binghamton, N.Y.: Medieval and Early Modern Texts and Studies, 1982), 3–19.

Ademollo, Alessandro. *La Bell'Adriana ed altre virtuose del suo tempo alla corte di Mantova* (Citta di Castello: Lapi, 1888).

Ago, Renata. *Carriere e clientele nella Roma barocca* (Rome and Bari: Laterza, 1990).
'Di cosa si può fare commercio: mercato e norme sociali nella Roma barocca.' *Quaderni Storici* 91:1 (1996), 113–33.
Economia barocca. Mercato e istituzioni nella Roma del seicento. Rome: Donzelli, 1998.
'Farsi uomini: giovani nobili nella Roma barocca.' *Memoria* 27:3 (1989), 7–21.
'Gerarchia delle merci e meccanismi dello scambio a Roma nel primo seicento.' *Quaderni Storici* 96 (1997), 663–83.
'Il linguaggio del corpo.' In Carlo Marco Belfanti and Fabio Giusberti, eds., *Storia d'Italia, annali 19: La moda.* Turin: Einaudi, 2003, 117–48.
'Maria Spada Veralli, la buona moglie.' In Giulia Calvi, ed., *Barocco al femminile.* Rome and Bari: Laterza, 1992, 51–70.
'Middling Sort Domestic Interiors in Seventeenth-Century Rome', unpublished paper given at 'Domestic and Institutional Interiors in Early Modern Europe', held at the Victoria and Albert Museum, London, 19–20 November 2004.
'Quadri e libri a Roma tra XVI e XVII secolo.' *Quaderni Storici* 110:2 (2002), 380–4.
'Young Nobles in the Age of Absolutism: Paternal Authority and Freedom of Choice in Seventeenth Century Italy.' In Giovanni Levi and Jean Claude Schmitt, eds., *A History of Young People in the West*, trans. Camille Naish. London: The Belknap Press of Harvard University Press, 1997, 283–324.
Alberti, Giuseppe. 'Le cortegiane, le stufe e la lue nella Roma del primo cinquecento.' *Il Vasari* 19:3 (1941), 67–73.
Alfieri, Bruno, ed. *Il gioco dell'amore: le cortigiane di Venezia dal trecento al settecento.* Milan: Berenice Art Books, 1990.
Allegra, Luciano. 'Oltre le fonti criminali: Chieri nel '500.' *Quaderni Storici* 49:1 (1982), 265–74.
Allerston, Patricia. 'Clothing and Early Modern Venetian Society.' *Continuity and Change* 15:3 (2000), 367–90.
'Reconstructing the Second-Hand Clothes Trade in Sixteenth- and Seventeenth-Century Venice.' *Costume* 33 (1999), 46–56.
Amelang, James S. *Honored Citizens of Barcelona: Patrician Culture and Class Relations, 1490–1714.* Princeton: Princeton University Press, 1986.
Amussen, Susan Dwyer. 'Gender, family and the social order, 1560–1725.' In John Stevenson and Anthony Fletcher, eds., *Order and Disorder in Early Modern England.* Cambridge: Cambridge University Press, 1985, 196–217.
Angeleri, Carlo. 'Bibliografia delle stampe popolari a carattere profano dei secoli XVI e XVII conservate nella Biblioteca Nazionale di Firenze.' In Marco Parenti, ed., *Contributi alla biblioteca bibliografica italica.* Florence: Sansoni Antiquariato, 1953.
Appadurai, Arjun. 'Introduction: Commodities and the Politics of Value.' In Appadurai, ed., *The Social Life of Things: Commodities in Cultural Perspective.* Cambridge: Cambridge University Press, 1986, 3–63.

Aquilecchia, G. 'Pasquinate romane del cinquecento.' In A. Marzo, A. Romano and V. Marucci, eds., *Pasquinate romane del Cinquecento*, vol. I. Rome: Salerno Editrice, 1983.

'Per l'attribuzione e il testo del "Lamento d'una cortigiana ferrarese".' In *Tra latino e volgare per Carlo Dionisotti*. Padua: Antenore, 1974, 3–25.

Ariès, Philippe. *Amour et sexualité en Occident*. Paris: Editions du Seuil, 1991.

Armellini, M. 'Un censimento della città di Roma sotto il pontificato di Leone X. Tratto da un codice inedito dell'Archivio Vaticano.' *Gli Studi in Italia* I (1881), 890–909, 2 (1882), 69–84, 136–92, 323–55, 481–518.

Arru, Angiolina. *Il servo: storia di una carriera nel settecento*. Bologna: Il Mulino, 1995.

Askew, Pamela. *Caravaggio's Death of the Virgin*. Oxford: Princeton University Press, 1990.

Austern, Linda Phyllis. ' "Sing Againe Syren": the Female Musician and Sexual Enchantment in Elizabethan Life and Literature.' *Renaissance Quarterly* 42 (1989), 420–48.

Aymard, Maurice. 'La fragilità di un'economia avanzata.' In Ruggiero Romano, ed., *Storia dell'economia italiana, vol. II: L'età moderna: verso la crisi*. Turin: Einaudi, 1991, 5–137.

Bailey, Victor. 'Reato, giustizia penale e autorità in Inghilterra. Un decennio di studi storici, 1969–1979.' *Quaderni Storici* 44 (1980), 581–602.

Bakhtin, Mikhail. *Rabelais and his World*, trans. Hélène Iswolsky. Bloomington: Indiana University Press, 1984.

Baldacci, L. *Il petrarchismo italiano nel cinquecento*. Milan and Naples: Ricciardi, 1957.

Baldini, Enzo. *Puntigli spagnoleschi e intrighi politici nella Roma di Clemente VIII: Girolamo Frachetta e la sua relazione del 1603 sui cardinali*. Milan: Franco Angeli, 1981.

Bandello. *Novelle*, ed. G. Ferrero. Turin: UTET, 1974.

Barbagli, Marzio. *Sotto lo stesso tetto. Mutamenti della famiglia in Italia dal XV al XX secolo*. Bologna: Il Mulino, 1984.

Barberis, Walter. 'Uomini e corte nel cinquecento. Tra il primato della famiglia e il governo dello stato.' In C. Vivanti and R. Romano, eds., *Storia d'Italia. Annali, vol. 4: Intellettuali e potere*. Turin: Einaudi, 1981.

Barbone, Roberto and Antonio Stäuble. 'Proposte per una tipologia dei personaggi femminili nella commedia rinascimentale.' In M. Chiabo and F. Doglio, eds., *Origini della commedia nell'Europa del cinquecento*. Lausanne: Centro Studi sul Teatro Medioevale e Rinascimentale, 1993.

Barzman, Karen-Edis. 'Gender, Religious Representation and Cultural Production in Early Modern Italy.' In Robert C. Davis and Judith C. Brown, eds., *Gender and Society in Renaissance Italy*. London and New York: Longman, 1998.

Bassani, Riccardo and Fiora Bellini. *Caravaggio assassino: La carriera di un 'valenthuomo' fazioso nella Roma della Controriforma*. Rome: Donzelli, 1994.

Bassermann, Lujo. *The Oldest Profession: a History of Prostitution*, trans. J. Cleugh. London: Arthur Barker, 1967.

Battista Labat, P. G. *Un Monaco francese nell'Italia del settecento*. Tivoli: Aldo Chicca, 1951.

Bazán Díaz, Iñaki, Francisco Vázquez García and Andrés Moreno Mengibar, 'La prostitution au Pays Basque entre XIVe et XVIIIe siècles.' *Annales HSS* 55:6 (2000), 1283–302.

Belfanti, Carlo Marco. 'Rural Manufactures and Rural Proto-industries in the "Italy of the Cities" from the Sixteenth through the Eighteenth Century.' *Continuity and Change* 8:2 (1993), 253–80.

Belk, Russell W. 'Studies in the New Consumer Behaviour.' In Daniel Miller, ed., *Acknowledging Consumption: a Review of New Studies*. London and New York: Routledge, 1995.

Bell, Shannon. *Reading, Writing and Rewriting the Prostitute Body* (Bloomington and Indianapolis: Indiana University Press, 1994).

Bellettini, Athos. *La popolazione italiana*. Turin: Einaudi, 1987.
   'La popolazione italiana dall'inizio dell'età volgare ai giorni nostri. Valutazioni e tendenze.' In C. Vivanti and C. Romano, eds., *Storia d'Italia. Dalla caduta dell'impero romano al secolo XVIII, vol. II*. Turin: Einaudi, 1974, 489–532.

Benabou, Erica Marie. *La prostitution et la police des moeurs au XVIIIe siècle*. Paris: Perrin, 1987.

Bennett, Judith. 'Medieval Women, Modern Women: Across the Great Divide.' In D. Aers, ed., *Culture and History, 1350–1600: Essays on English Communities, Identities and Writing*. London: Harvester Wheatsheaf, 1992, 147–76.
   'Women's History: a Study in Continuity and Change.' *Women's History Review* 2:2 (1993), 173–84.

Bennett, Judith and Amy Froide, eds., *Singlewomen in the European Past, 1250–1800* (Philadelphia: University of Pennsylvania Press, 1999).

Berengo, Marino. 'Lo studio degli atti notarili dal XIV al XVI secolo.' *Fonti medio-evali e problematica storiografica* 1 (1976), 1–161.

Bernos, Marcel. 'Le Concile de Trente et la sexualité: la doctrine et sa postérité.' In Bernos, ed., *Sexualité et Religion* (Paris: Cerf, 1988), 217–39.

Bertarelli, Achille. *Le stampe popolari italiane*. Milan: Rizzoli, 1974.

Bertolotti, Antonio. *Le prigioni di Roma nei secoli XVI, XVII, e XVII*. Rome, 1890.
   Repressioni straordinarie alla prostituzione in Roma nel secolo XVI. Rome: Tipografia delle Mantellate, 1887.

Bertone Pannain, Alberta, Sandro Bulgarelli and Ludovica Mazzola. *Il giornalismo romano, delle origini, sec. XVI–XVII*. Mostra Bibliografica. Rome: Biblioteca Nazionale Centrale, 1979.

Bettarini, M. T. and Roberto Ciapetti. 'L'arte della seta a Firenze: un censimento del 1633.' *Ricerche Storiche* 12:1 (1982), 35–49.

Biagi, Guido. *Un'etera romana: Tullia D'Aragona*. Florence: Roberto Paggi, 1897.

Biondi, Albano. 'Aspetti della cultura cattolica post-Tridentina.' In C. Vivanti and R. Romano, eds., *Storia d'Italia: Intellettuali e Potere: Annali 4*. Turin: Einaudi, 1981, 225–302.

Blastenbrei, Peter. 'La quadratura del cerchio. Il Bargello di Roma nella crisi sociale tardocinquecentesca.' *Dimensioni e Problemi della Ricerca Storica* 1 (1994), 5–37.

'I romani tra violenza e giustizia nel tardo cinquecento.' *Roma Moderna e Contemporanea* 5:1 (1997), 67–79.

Blockmans, Wim. 'Circumscribing the Concept of Poverty.' In Thomas Riis, ed., *Aspects of Poverty in Early Modern Europe*. Florence: EUI, 1981, 39–45.

Bober, Phyllis Pray. 'The Coryciana and the Nymph Corycia.' *Journal of the Warburg and Courtauld Institutes* 40 (1977), 223–39.

Bodart, Didier. 'La descrizione del rione di Campo Marzio di Roma: artistes à Rome durant la peste de 1656.' *Bulletin de l'Institut Historique Belge de Rome* 38 (1967), 475–531.

Bonghi, Salvatore. *Il Velo Giallo di Tullia D'Aragona*. Florence: G. Carnesecchi e Figli, 1886.

Borsi, Stefano. *Roma di Sisto V. La pianta di Antonio Tempesta 1593*. Roma: Officina, 1986.

Boschi, Daniele. 'I reati contro la persona a Roma alla metà del Settecento.' *ARSRSP* 112 (1989), 453–80.

Bossy, John. 'The Counter Reformation and the People of Catholic Europe.' *Past and Present* 47 (1970), 51–70.

'The Mass as a Social Institution, 1200–1700.' *Past and Present* 100 (1983), 29–61.

'The Social History of Confession.' *Transactions of the Royal Historical Society* 25 (1975), 21–38.

Bourdieu, Pierre. *Distinction: a Social Critique of the Judgement of Taste*, trans. Richard Nice. London: Routledge and Kegan Paul, 1984.

Brackett, John. 'The Florentine Onestà and the Control of Prostitution, 1403–1680.' *Sixteenth Century Journal* 24:2 (1993), 273–300.

Brewer, John and Roy Porter. *Consumption and the World of Goods*. London and New York: Routledge, 1993.

Brezzi, Paolo and Maristella de Panizza Lorch, eds. *Umanesimo a Roma nel quattrocento*. Rome and New York: Istituto di Studi Romani and Barnard College, Columbia University, 1981.

Briggs, Robin. *Communities of Belief: Cultural and Social Tension in Early Modern France*. Oxford: Clarendon Press, 1989.

Brilli, Attilio. *Il viaggio in Italia*. Milan: Banca Popolare di Milano, 1987.

Brown, Judith C. and Robert C. Davis. *Gender and Society in Renaissance Italy*. London and New York: Longman, 1998.

Brown, Judith C. and Jordan Goodman. 'Women and Industry in Florence.' *The Journal of Economic History* 40:1 (1980), 73–80.

Brucker, Gene. *Giovanni and Lusanna: Love and Marriage in Renaissance Florence*. London: Weidenfeld and Nicolson, 1986.

Brundage, James. *Law, Sex and Christian Society in Medieval Europe*. Chicago: University of Chicago Press, 1987.

'Prostitution in the Medieval Canon Law.' *Signs* 1 (1976), 825–45.

Sex, Law and Marriage in the Middle Ages (Aldershot: Variorum, 1993)

'Sumptuary Laws and Prostitution in Medieval Italy.' *Journal of Medieval History* 13 (1987), 343–55.

Bryson, Norman. 'Semiology and Visual Interpretation.' In Michael Ann Holly, Keith Moxey and Norman Bryson, eds., *Visual Theory: Painting and Interpretation*. Oxford: Polity Press, 1991, 61–73.

Bulgarelli, Tullio. *Gli avvisi a stampa in Roma nel cinquecento*. Rome: Istituto di Studi Romani, 1967.

Bullough, Vern and Bonnie. *Women and Prostitution: a Social History*. New York: Prometheus Books, 1987.

Burckhardt, Jacob. *The Civilization of the Renaissance in Italy*, trans. S. G. C. Middlemore. St. Ives: Penguin, 1990.

Burke, Peter. *The Historical Anthropology of Early Modern Italy: Essays on Perception and Communication*. Cambridge: Cambridge University Press, 1987.

Popular Culture in Early Modern Europe. London: Temple Smith, 1978.

ed. *New Perspectives on Historical Writing*. Oxford: Polity Press, 1991.

Bush, M. L., ed. *Social Orders and Social Classes in Europe since 1500: Studies in Social Stratification*. London: Longman, 1992.

Cadden, Joan. 'Medieval Scientific and Medical Views of Sexuality: Questions of Propriety.' *Medievalia et Humanistica*, new series, 14 (1986), 157–71.

'Western Medicine and Natural Philosophy.' In Vern L. Bullough and James A. Brundage, *Handbook of Medieval Sexuality*. New York and London: Garland, 1996, 51–80.

Camerano, Alessandra. 'Assistenza richiesta ed assistenza imposta: il Conservatorio di S. Caterina della Rosa di Roma.' *Quaderni Storici* 82 (1993), 227–60.

'Donne oneste o meretrici? Incertezza dell'identità fra testamenti e diritto di proprietà a Roma.' *Quaderni Storici* 99:3 (1998), 637–75.

Campana, L. 'Monsignor Giovanni della Casa e i suoi tempi.' *Studi Storici* 16 (1907), 1–84.

Campbell, Colin. 'Understanding Traditional and Modern Patterns of Consumption in Eighteenth Century England: a Character-Action Approach.' In John Brewer and Roy Porter, eds., *Consumption and the World of Goods*. London and New York: Routledge, 1993.

Canosa, Romano. *La restaurazione sessuale: per una storia della sessualità tra cinquecento e settecento*. Milan: Feltrinelli, 1993.

Canosa, R. and I. Colonnello. *Storia della prostituzione in Italia*. Rome: Sapere 2000, 1989.

Caravale, Giorgio. 'Censura e pauperismo tra cinque e seicento.' *Rivista di Storia e Letteratura Religiosa* 38:1 (2002), 39–77.

Caravale, Mario and Alberto Caracciolo. *Lo stato pontificio da Martino V a Pio IX*. Turin: UTET, 1978.

Carroll, Linda L. 'Who's on Top? Gender as Societal Power Configuration in Italian Renaissance Drama.' *Sixteenth Century Journal* 20:4 (1989), 531–58.

Caselli, Virgilio. *Il Vicariato di Roma: note storico-giuridiche*. Rome: Foro Traiano, 1957.

Cavallo, Sandra. 'Assistenza femminile e tutela dell'onore nella Torino del XVIII secolo.' *Annali della Fondazione Luigi Einaudi* 14 (1980), 127–55.

Charity and Power in Early Modern Italy: Benefactors and their Motives in Turin, 1541–1789. Cambridge: Cambridge University Press, 1995.

'Donne, famiglie e istituzioni nella Roma del sette–ottocento.' *Quaderni Storici* 92 (1996), 429–39.

Cavallo, Sandra and Simona Cerutti. 'Female Honor and the Social Control of Reproduction in Piedmont between 1600 and 1800.' In Edward Muir and Guido Ruggiero, eds., *Sex and Gender in Historical Perspective.* Baltimore and London: The Johns Hopkins University Press, 1990, 73–109.

Cavazzini, Patrizia. 'La diffusione della pittura nella Roma di primo seicento: collezionisti ordinari e mercanti.' *Quaderni Storici* 2 (2004), 353–74.

Ceen, Allan. *The Quartiere de'Banchi: Urban Planning in Rome in the First Half of the Sixteenth Century.* New York and London: Garland, 1986.

Cerasoli, F. 'Censimento della popolazione di Roma dall' anno 1600 al 1739.' *Studi e documenti di Storia e di Diritto dell'Accademia Storico-Giuridica Rome* 12 (1891), 169–99.

Chabot, Isabelle. 'La reconnaissance du travail des femmes dans la Florence du bas Moyen Age: contexte idéologique et réalité.' In S. Cavaciocchi, ed., *La donna nell'economia secc. XIII–XVIII.* Prato: Istituto Internazionale di Storia Economica F. Datini, 1990, 563–76.

Chartier, Roger. *The Cultural Uses of Print in Early Modern France*, trans. Lydia G. Cochrane. Princeton: Princeton University Press, 1987.

'Culture as Appropriation: Popular Cultural Uses in Early Modern France.' In Steven Kaplan, ed., *Understanding Popular Culture: Europe from the Middle Ages to the Nineteenth Century.* Berlin: Modern Publishers, 1984, 229–54.

Chauvin, Charles. 'Ignace et les courtisanes. La Maison Sante Marthe (1542–1548).' In Juan Plazaola, ed., *Ignacio de Loyola y suo tiempo.* Bilbao: Ediciones Mensajero, 1992, 551–62.

'La Maison Sainte-Marthe: Ignace et les prostituées de Rome,' *Christus* 149 (1991), 117–26.

Chojnacka, Monica. *Working Women of Early Modern Venice.* Baltimore and London: The Johns Hopkins University Press, 2001.

Chojnacki, Stanley. 'The Most Serious Duty: Motherhood, Gender and Patrician Culture in Renaissance Venice.' In M. Migiel and J. Schiesari, eds., *Refiguring Woman: Perspectives on Gender and the Italian Renaissance.* New York: Cornell University Press, 1991, 133–54.

'Subaltern Patriarchs: Patrician Bachelors.' In Chojnacki, *Women and Men in Renaissance Venice.* Baltimore: The Johns Hopkins University Press, 2000, 244–56.

Ciammitti, Luisa. 'Quanto costa essere normali. La dote nel conservatorio femminile di Santa Maria del Baraccano (1630–1680).' *Quaderni Storici* 53 (1983), 469–97.

Ciampi, I. 'Un periodo di cultura in Roma nel secolo XVII.' *ARSRSP* 1:13 (1877), 257–389, 393–458.

Cian, Vittorio. *Galanterie italiane del secolo XVI*. Turin: La Letteratura, 1888.

Cibin, Patrizia. 'Meretrici e cortegiane a Venezia nel '500.' *Donnawomanfemme: Quaderni di Studi Internazionali sulla Donna* 25–26 (1985), 79–102.

Cipolla, Carlo. 'Economic Fluctuations: the Poor and Public Policy, Italy, 16th and 17th Centuries.' In Thomas Riis, ed., *Aspects of Poverty in Early Modern Europe*. Florence: EUI, 1981, 65–77.

Cirinei, A. 'Bandi e giustizia criminale a Roma nel cinque e seicento.' *Roma Moderna e Contemporanea* 5:1 (1997), 81–95.

Clementi, F. *Il carnevale romano. Nelle cronache contemporanee*. Citta di Castello: Edizioni Rore/Niruf, 1939.

Cohen, Elizabeth S. 'Camilla the Go-Between: the Politics of Gender in a Roman Household (1559).' *Continuity and Change* 4 (1989), 53–77.

'Camilla la Magra, prostituta romana.' In Ottavia Niccoli, ed., *Rinascimento al femminile*. Bari: Economica Laterza, 1998. 163–96.

'Honour and Gender in the Streets of Early Modern Rome.' *Journal of Interdisciplinary History* 22:4 (1992), 597–625.

'Open and Shut: the Social Meanings of the Cinquecento Roman House.' *Studies in the Decorative Arts*, Fall–Winter (2001–2), 61–84.

'Seen and Known: Prostitutes in the Cityscape of Late-Sixteenth-Century Rome.' *Renaissance Studies* 12:3 (1998), 392–409.

Cohen, Michèle. 'Manliness, Effeminacy and the French: Gender and the Construction of National Character in Eighteenth-Century England.' In Tim Hitchcock and Michèle Cohen, eds., *English Masculinities, 1660–1800*. London and New York: Longman, 1999, 44–62.

Cohen, Sherrill. 'Convertite e malmaritate: donne "irregolari" e ordini religiosi nella Firenze rinascimentale.' *Memoria* 5 (1982), 46–63.

The Evolution of Women's Asylums since 1500: From Refuges for Ex-Prostitutes to Shelters for Battered Women. New York: Oxford University Press, 1992.

Cohen, Thomas V., *Love and Death in Renaissance Italy*. Chicago and London: University of Chicago Press, 2004.

Cohen, Thomas V. and Elizabeth S. *Words and Deeds in Renaissance Rome: Trials before the Papal Magistrates*. Toronto: University of Toronto Press, 1993.

Cohn, Samuel K. Jr. 'Donne e Controriforma a Siena. Autorità e proprietà nella famiglia.' *Studi Storici* 30 (1989), 203–24.

Women in the Streets: Essays on Sex and Power in Renaissance Italy. Baltimore and London: The Johns Hopkins University Press, 1996.

Comba, Rinaldo. '"Apetitus libidinis coherceatur": Strutture demografiche, reati sessuali e disciplina dei comportamenti nel Piemonte tardo medievale.' *Studi Storici* 27:3 (1986), 529–76.

Comune di Roma. *Regesti di bandi, editti, notificazioni, e provvedimenti diversi relativi alla città di Roma ed allo Stato Pontificio*, 5 vols. Rome: Società Tipografica Castaldi, 1920.

Connors, Joseph. 'Alliance and Enmity in Roman Baroque Urbanism.' *Römisches Jahrbuch für Kunstgeschichte* 25 (1989), 209–94.

Corbin, Alain. *Les filles de noce*. Paris: Flammarion, 1982.

Corradi, A. *Nuovi documenti per la storia delle malattie veneree in Italia dalla fine del quattrocento alla metà del cinquecento*. Milan, 1884.

Cox, Virginia. *The Renaissance Dialogue: Literary Dialogue in its Social and Political Contexts, Castiglione to Galileo*. Cambridge: Cambridge University Press, 1992.

Crane, Thomas F. *Italian Social Customs of the Sixteenth Century and their Influence on the Literatures of Europe*. New Haven: Yale University Press, 1920.

Crescenzi, Lucio, ed. *Roma Capitale*. Rome: Editalia, 1988.

Creytens, Raimondo. *Il Concilio di Trento e la Riforma Tridentina*. Rome: Herder, 1965.

Cropper, Elizabeth. 'On Beautiful Women: Parmigianino, Petrarchismo and the Vernacular Style.' *Art Bulletin* 58:3 (1976), 374–94.

Cruciani, Fabrizio. *Il teatro del campidoglio e le feste romane del 1513*. Milan: Il Polifilio, 1969.

Cruciani, Fabrizio and Daniele Seragnoli. *Il teatro a Roma nel Rinascimento*. Rome: Bulzoni, 1969.

Curtius, Ernst Robert. *European Literature and the Latin Middle Ages*. London: Routledge and Kegan Paul, 1953.

Dabhoiwala, Faramerz. 'The Pattern of Sexual Immorality in Seventeenth and Eighteenth Century London.' In Paul Griffiths and Mark S. R. Jenner, eds., *Londinopolis: Essays in the Cultural and Social History of Early Modern London*. Manchester and New York: Manchester University Press, 2000, 86–106.

D'Amelia, Marina. 'Economia familiare e sussidi dotali. La politica della Confraternità dell'Annunziata a Roma.' In Simona Cavaciocchi, ed., *La donna nell'economia. Secc. XIII–XVI*. Prato: Istituto Internazionale di Storia Economica F. Datini, 1990.

'La conquista di una dote. Regole del gioco e scambi femminili alla Confraternità dell'Annunziata a Roma (secc. XVII–XVIII).' In G. Pomata, L. Ferrante and M. Palazzi, eds., *Ragnatele di rapporti. Patronage e reti di relazione nella storia delle donne*. Turin: Rosenberg and Sellier, 1988, 305–43.

'La peste del 1656–57 a Roma nel carteggio del Prefetto dell'Annona.' *Dimensioni e Problemi della Ricerca Storica* 2 (1990), 135–51.

'La presenza delle madri nell'Italia medievale e moderna.' In Marina d'Amelia, ed., *Storia delle donne in Italia: storia della maternità* (Rome and Bari: Laterza, 1997), 3–52.

'Scatole cinesi: vedove e donne sole in una società d'ancien régime.' *Memoria* 18 (1986), 58–79.

D'Amico, John. *Renaissance Humanism in Papal Rome: Humanists and Churchmen on the Eve of the Reformation*. Baltimore: The Johns Hopkins University Press, 1983.

D'Amico, Stefano. 'Shameful Mother: Poverty and Prostitution in Seventeenth-Century Milan.' *Journal of Family History* 30:1 (2005), 109–20.

Dandelet, Thomas J. 'Politics and the State System after the Habsburg–Valois Wars.' In John A. Marino, ed., *Early Modern Italy, 1550–1796*. Oxford: Oxford University Press, 2002, 11–23.

Davis, Natalie Zemon. 'Boundaries and the Sense of Self in Sixteenth Century France.' In Morton Sosna, David E. Wellbery and Thomas C. Heller, eds., *Reconstructing Individualism: Autonomy, Individuality, and the Self in Western Thought*. Stanford: Stanford University Press, 1986, 55–9.

Fiction in the Archives: Pardon Tales and their Tellers in Sixteenth-Century France. Stanford: Stanford University Press, 1987.

Day, John. 'Strade e vie di comunicazione.' In Ruggiero Romano and Corrado Vivanti, eds., *Storia d'Italia, vol. V(1): I documenti (I)*. Turin: Einaudi, 1973, 89–116.

De Boer, Wietse. *The Conquest of the Soul: Confession, Discipline and Public Order in Counter-Reformation Milan*. Leiden: Brill, 2001.

De Caprio, Vincenzo. 'I cenacoli umanistici.' In Asor Rosa, ed., *Letteratura italiana. Il letterato e le istituzioni*. Turin: Einaudi, 1982, 799–822.

'Intellettuali e mercato del lavoro nella Roma medicea.' *Studi Romani* 29:1 (1981), 26–46.

Del Re, Niccolò. *Monsignor Governatore di Roma*. Rome: Istituto di Studi Romani, 1972.

Delumeau, Jean. *Catholicism between Luther and Voltaire: a New View of the Counter-Reformation*, trans. J. Moiser, intro. John Bossy. London: Burns and Oates, 1977.

Vie économique et sociale de Rome dans la seconde moitié du XVIe siècle, 2 vols. Paris: De Boccard, 1957.

Del Vita, Alessandro. *Galanteria e lussuria nel Rinascimento*. Arezzo: Edizioni Rinascimento, 1952.

Di Giacomo, Salvatore. *La prostituzione in Napoli nei secoli XVe, XVIe e XVIe I: Documenti inediti*. Naples: R. Marghieri, 1899.

Di Sivo, Michele. 'Le costituzioni e i bandi di Sisto V: l'amministrazione della giustizia tra accentramento e crisi dello stato pontificio.' *Archivi per la Storia* 1–2 (1991), 137–48.

'Il tribunale criminale capitolino nei secoli XVI–XVI: note da un lavoro in corso.' *Roma Moderna e Contemporanea* 3:1 (1995), 201–15.

Ditchfield, Simon. 'Of Dancing Cardinals and Mestizo Madonnas: Reconfiguring the History of Roman Catholicism in the Early Modern Period.' *Journal of Early Modern History* 8:3–4 (2004), 387–408.

Dizionario del dialetto veneziano di Giuseppe Boerio. Venice: Giovanni Cecchini Editori, 1856.

D'Onofrio, C. *La via del corso*. Rome: Cassa di Risparmio di Roma, 1961.

Duby, G. and M. Perrot, gen. eds. *A History of Women in the West: Renaissance and Enlightenment Paradoxes*, eds. Natalie Zemon Davis and Arlette Farge. Cambridge, Mass.: The Belknap Press of Harvard University Press, 1993.

du Fresne, Charles, Seigneur du Cange. *Glossarium ad scriptores mediae et infimae latinitatis*, vol. II (orig. 1678) Graz: Akademische Druck-U. Verlagsanstalt, 1954.

Earle, Peter. 'The Female Labour Market in London in the Late Seventeenth and Early Eighteenth Centuries.' *Economic History Review* 3 (1989), 328–53.

Ehrle, Francesco. *Roma prima di Sisto V: la pianta di Roma du Perac-Lafrery.* Rome: Danesi, 1908.

Eisenach, Emlyn. *Husbands, Wives and Concubines.* Kirksville, Mo.: Truman State University Press, 2004.

Eleventh International Economic History Congress 1994. *Material Culture: Consumption, Life-Style, Standard of Living, 1500–1900,* vol. B4, eds. J. Anton, Lorena Walsh, and S. Schuurman. Milan: Università Bocconi, 1994.

Elias, Norbert. *The Civilizing Process, vol. I: the History of Manners* ed. and trans. Edmund Jephcott. New York: Urizen, 1978. (Orig. *Über den Prozess der Zivilisation,* vol. I, Basel, 1939.)

The Civilizing Process, vol. II: Power and Civility, ed. and trans. Edmund Jephcott. New York: Pantheon Books, 1982. (Orig. *Über den Prozess der Zivilisation,* vol. II, Basel, 1939).

Enriques, Fernando. *Storia generale della prostituzione, vol. II: Il medioevo e l'età moderna.* Milan: Suger Editore, 1965.

Erikson, Amy Louise. *Women and Property in Early Modern England.* London: Routledge, 1993.

Esch, Arnold. 'Roman Customs Registers, 1470–80: Items of Interest to Historians of Art and Material Culture.' *Journal of the Warburg and Courtauld Institutes* 58 (1995), 72–87.

Esposito, Anna. 'Ad dotandum puellas virgines, pauperes et honestas: Social Needs and Confraternal Charities in Rome in the Fifteenth and Sixteenth Centuries.' *Renaissance and Reformation* 30:2 (1994), 5–19.

' "Li nobili huomini di Roma": strategie familiari tra città, curia e municipio'. In S. Gensini, ed., *Roma capitale, 1447–1527* (Rome: Ministero per i Beni Culturali e Ambientali, 1994), 373–88.

'La parrochia "agostiniana" di S. Trifone nella Roma di Leone X.' *Mélanges de l'École française de Rome. Moyen Age, Temps modernes. (Mefrm)* 93:2 (1981), 495–523.

Evangelisti, Silvia. ' "We Do Not Have It, and We Do Not Want It": Women, Power and Convent Reform in Florence.' *Sixteenth Century Journal,* 34:3 (2003), 677–700.

'Wives, Widows and Brides of Christ: Marriage and the Convent in the Historiography of Early Modern Italy,' *The Historical Journal* 43:1 (2000), 233–47.

Fabretti, A. *La prostituzione in Perugia.* Turin, 1890.

Fairchilds, Cissie. 'Consumption in Early Modern Europe: a Review Article.' *Comparative Studies in Society and History* 35 (1993), 850–8.

Fantham, Elaine, Helene Peet Foley, Natalie Boymel Kampen, Sarah B. Pomeroy and H. A. Shapiro. *Women in the Classical World: Image and Text.* Oxford: Oxford University Press, 1995.

Fantini, Maria Pia. 'La circolazione clandestina dell'orazione di Santa Marta: un episodio modenese.' In Gabriella Zarri, ed., *Donna disciplina, creanza cristiana dal XV al XVII secolo. Studi e testi a stampa.* Rome: Edizioni di Storia e Letteratura, 1996, 45–65.

'Les mots secrets des prostituées (Modène, 1580–1620).' *Clio: Histoire, Femmes, et Sociétés (Parler, Chanter, Lire, Écrire)* 11 (2000), 21–47.

Farr, James R. *Authority and Sexuality in Early Modern Burgundy (1550–1730)*. New York: Oxford University Press, 1995.

'Crimine nel vicinato: ingiurie, matrimonio e onore nella digione del XVI–XVII secolo.' *Quaderni Storici* 66:3 (1987), 839–54.

'The Pure and Disciplined Body: Hierarchy, Morality, and Symbolism in France during the Catholic Reformation.' *Journal of Interdisciplinary History* 21:3 (1991), 391–414.

Fauve-Chamoux, Antoinette. 'La femme seule.' *Annales de démographie historique* (1981), 207–13.

Ferrajoli, Alessandro. *Il ruolo della corte di Leone X*, ed. Vincenzo de Caprio. Rome: Bulzoni, 1984.

Ferrante, Lucia. 'L'onore ritrovato: donne nella casa di soccorso di S. Paolo a Bologna (sec. XVI–XVII).' *Quaderni Storici* 53 (1983), 499–528.

'Pro mercede carnali. Il giusto prezzo rivendicato in tribunale.' *Memoria* 17 (1986), 42–58.

'La sessualità come risorsa. Donne davanti al foro archivescovile di Bologna (sec. XVII)', *Mélanges de l'École française de Rome* 99 (1987), 989–1016.

'Il valore del corpo: ovvero la gestione economica della sessualità femminile.' In Angela Groppi, ed., *Il lavoro delle donne*. Rome and Bari: Laterza, 1996, 206–28.

Ferraro, Joanne M. *Marriage Wars in Late Renaissance Venice*. Oxford: Oxford University Press, 2001.

Ferroni, Giulio. *Le voci dell'istrione. Pietro Aretino e la dissoluzione del teatro*. Naples: Liguori, 1977.

Findlen, Paula. 'Humanism, Politics and Pornography in Renaissance Italy.' In Lynn Hunt, ed., *The Invention of Pornography: Obscenity and the Origins of Modernity, 1500–1800*. New York: Zone Books, 1993.

Finnegan, Frances. *Poverty and Prostitution: a Study of Victorian Prostitutes in York*. Cambridge: Cambridge University Press, 1979.

'Missioni della Compagnia di Gesu nell'agro romano nel XVII secolo.' *Dimensioni e Problemi della Ricerca Storica* 2 (1994), 216–34.

Foa, Anna. 'The New and the Old: the Spread of Syphilis (1494–1530).' In Edward Muir and Guido Ruggiero, eds., *Sex and Gender in Historical Perspective*: Selections from *Quaderni Storici*, trans. M. A. Gallucci, M. M. Gallucci and C. C. Gallucci. London: The Johns Hopkins University Press, 1990, 26–45.

Fontaine, Laurence. 'Gli studi sulla mobilità in Europa nell'età moderna.' *Quaderni Storici* 93 (1996), 739–56.

History of Pedlars in Europe, trans. Vicki Whittaker. Oxford: Polity Press, 1996.

'Solidarités familiales et logiques migratoires en pays de montagne.' *Annales ESC* 45:6 (1990), 1433–47.

Fornili, Carlo Cirillo. *Delinquenti e carcerati a Roma alla metà del '600: opera dei papi nella riforma carceraria.* Rome: Editrice Pontificia Università Gregoriana, 1991.

Forster, Marc R. *Catholic Revival in the Age of the Baroque: Religious Identity in Southwest Germany, 1550–1750.* Cambridge: Cambridge University Press, 2001.

Fortini Brown, Patricia. *Private Lives in Renaissance Venice: Art, Architecture and the Family.* New Haven and London: Yale University Press, 2004.

Fosi, Irene. 'Introduzione.' *Roma Moderna e Contemporanea* 5:1 (1997), 7–17.

'Sudditi, tribunali e giudici nella Roma barocca.' *Roma Moderna e Contemporanea* 5:1 (1997), 19–40.

Foucault, Michel. *History of Sexuality, vol. I,* trans. Robert Hurley. New York: Random House, 1990.

Frantz, David O. *Festum Voluptatis: a Study of Renaissance Erotica.* Columbus: Ohio State University Press, 1989.

Freccero, Carla. 'Acts, Identities and Sexuality's (Pre)Modern Regimes.' *Journal of Women's History* 11:2 (1999), 186–91.

Freedberg, David. *The Power of Images: Studies in the History and Theory of Response.* Chicago: University of Chicago Press, 1989.

Frick, Carole Collier. *Dressing Renaissance Florence: Families, Fortunes and Fine Clothing.* Baltimore and London: The Johns Hopkins University Press, 2002.

Frommel, Christopher. 'Papal Policy: the Planning of Papal Rome.' *Journal of Interdisciplinary History* 17:1 (1986), 39–65.

Fuchs, Rachel G. and Leslie Page Moch. 'Pregnant, Single, and Far from Home: Migrant Women in Nineteenth-Century Paris.' *American Historical Review* 95 (1990), 1007–31.

Gamrath, Helge. *Roma sancta renovata: studi sull'urbanistica di Roma nel XVI secolo.* Rome: L'Erma, 1987.

Gemini, Fiorenza. 'Interventi di politica sociale nel campo dell'assistenza femminile: tre conservatori romani tra sei e settecento.' *La Demografia Storica delle Città Italiane,* ed. Società Italiana di Demografia Storica. Bologna: Clueb, 1982.

Gensini, S., ed. *Roma capitale (1447–1527).* Pisa: Centro di studi sulla civiltà del tardo medioevo di San Miniato, 1994.

Gentilcore, David. '"Adapt Yourselves to the People's Capabilities": Missionary Strategies, Methods and Impact in the Kingdom of Naples, 1600–1800.' *The Journal of Ecclesiastical History* 45:2 (1994), 269–96.

Giedion, Siegfried. 'Sixtus V and the Planning of Baroque Rome.' *Architectural Review* no. 664 (1952), 217–26.

Gigli, Giacinto. *Diario romano, 1608–1670 a cura di G. Ricciotti.* Rome: Tumminelli, 1958.

Ginzburg, Carlo. *The Cheese and the Worms: the Cosmos of a Sixteenth Century Miller,* trans. John and Anne Tedeschi. London: Penguin, 1992.

'High and Low: the Theme of Forbidden Knowledge in the Sixteenth and Seventeenth Centuries.' *Past and Present* 73 (1976), 28–41.

Myths, Emblems, Clues. London: Hutchinson Radius, 1990.

'Ovid and Sixteenth Century Codes for Erotic Illustrations.' In Ginzburg *Myths, Emblems, Clues*. London: Hutchinson Radius, 1990, 77–95.

Ginzburg, Carlo and Carlo Poni. 'Il nome e il come. Mercato storiografico e scambio disuguale.' *Quaderni Storici* 40 (1979), 181–90.

Il gioco dell'amore: Le cortegiane di Venezia dal trecento al settecento: catalogo della mostra. Venice: Berenice, 1990.

Glennie, Paul. 'Consumption within Historical Studies.' In Daniel Miller, ed., *Acknowledging Consumption: a Review of New Studies*. London and New York: Routledge, 1995.

Gnoli, Domenico. 'Censimento di Roma sotto Clemente VII.' *ARSRSP* 17: 2–4 (1894), 375–520.

Gnoli, Umberto. *Cortigiane romane*. Arezzo: Il Vasari, 1941.

Goffman, Erving. *The Presentation of Self in Everyday life*. Harmondsworth: Penguin, 1984.

Goldberg, Jonathan. 'Fatherly Authority: the Politics of Stuart Family Images.' In M. Quilligan, N. J. Vickers and M. W. Ferguson, eds., *Rewriting the Renaissance: the Discourses of Sexual Difference in Early Modern Europe*. Chicago and London: University of Chicago Press, 1986, 3–32.

Goldthwaite, Richard A. 'The Empire of Things: Consumer Demand in Renaissance Italy.' In F. W. Kent and P. Simons, eds., *Patronage, Art and Society in Renaissance Italy*. Oxford: Clarendon Press, 1987.

Wealth and the Demand for Art in Italy 1300–1600. Baltimore and London, The Johns Hopkins University Press, 1993.

Gose, Peter. 'Converting the Ancestors.' In Kenneth Mills and Anthony Grafton, eds., *Conversion: Old Worlds and New*. Rochester, N.Y.: University of Rochester Press, 2003, 140–74.

Gowing, Laura. *Domestic Dangers: Women, Words and Sex in Early Modern London*. Oxford: Clarendon Press, 1996.

Graf, A. *Attraverso il cinquecento*. Turin: Ermanno Loescher, 1888.

Grande dizionario della lingua italiana, ed. Salvatore Battaglia. Turin: UTET, 1981.

Greer, Allan. 'Conversion and Identity.' In Kenneth Mills and Anthony Grafton, eds., *Conversion: Old Worlds and New*. Rochester, N.Y.: University of Rochester Press, 2003, 175–98.

Grendi, Eduardo. 'Premessa', *Quaderni Storici* 66 (1987), 695–700.

'Ripensare la microstoria.' *Quaderni Storici* 86 (1994), 539–48.

Grendler, Paul F. *Critics of the Italian World, 1530–1560*. Madison and London: University of Wisconsin Press, 1969.

Griffiths, Paul. 'The Structure of Prostitution in Elizabethan London.' *Continuity and Change* 8:1 (1993), 39–63.

Groppi, Angela. *I conservatori della virtù, donne recluse nella Roma dei Papi*. Rome and Bari: Laterza, 1994.

'Lavoro e proprietà delle donne in età moderna', in Angela Groppi, ed., *Storia delle donne in Italia: Il lavoro delle donne* (Bari: Editori Laterza, 1996), 131.

Guasco, Luigi. *L'archivio storico capitolino*. Rome: Reale Istituto di Studi Romani, 1946.

Guasco, Maurilio and Angelo Torre, eds. *Pio V nella società e nella politica del suo tempo*. Bologna: Il Mulino, 2005.

Hacke, Daniela. *Women, Sex and Marriage in Early Modern Venice*. Aldershot: Ashgate, 2004.

Hanawalt, Barbara A. *Women and Work in Pre-Industrial Europe*. Bloomington: Indiana University Press, 1986.

Härter, Karl. 'Disciplinamento sociale e ordinanze di polizia nella prima età moderna.' In Paolo Prodi, ed. *Disciplina dell'anima, disciplina del corpo, disciplina della società tra medioevo ed età moderna*. Bologna: Il Mulino, 1994, 635–58.

Hébert, Geneviève. 'Les "femmes de mauvaise vie" dans la communauté (Montpellier, 1713–1742).' *Histoire Sociale* 36:72 (2003), 497–517.

Henderson, Tony. *Disorderly Women in Eighteenth-Century London: Prostitution and Control in the Metropolis, 1730–1830*. London and New York: Longman, 1999.

Hill, Bridget. 'Women's History: a Study in Change, Continuity or Standing Still?', *Women's History Review* 2:1 (1993), 5–22.

Hills, Helen. *Invisible City: the Architecture of Devotion in Seventeenth Century Neapolitan Convents*. Oxford: Oxford University Press, 2004.

Honeyman, Katrina and Jordan Goodman. 'Women's Work, Gender Conflict and Labour Markets in Europe, 1500–1900.' *Economic History Review* 4 (1991), 608–28.

Hufton, Olwen. *The Poor of Eighteenth Century France, 1750–1789*. Oxford: Clarendon Press, 1974.

   The Prospect Before Her: a History of Women in Western Europe, vol. I: 1500–1800 London: Harper Collins, 1995.

   'Women and the Family Economy in Eighteenth Century France.' *French Historical Studies* 1 (1975), 1–22.

   'Women without Men: Widows and Spinsters in Britain and France in the Eighteenth Century.' *Journal of Family History* 9:4 (1984), 355–76.

Hughes, Steven C. 'Fear and Loathing in Bologna and Rome: the Papal Police in Perspective.' *Journal of Social History* 21:1 (1987), 97–116.

Hyatte, Reginald. *The Arts of Friendship: the Idealization of Friendship in Medieval and Early Renaissance Literature*. Leiden: Brill, 1994.

Jardine, Lisa. *Worldly Goods: a New History of the Renaissance*. London: Macmillan, 1996.

Johnson, Geraldine A. and Sara F. Matthews Grieco, eds. *Picturing Women in Renaissance and Baroque Italy*. Cambridge: Cambridge University Press, 1997.

Johnson, P. 'Conspicuous Consumption amongst Working Class Consumers in Victorian England.' *Transactions of the Royal Historical Society* 5th series, 38 (1988), 27–42.

Jones, Ann Rosalind. 'City Women and their Audiences: Louise Labé and Veronica Franco.' In Maureen Quilligan, Nancy J. Vickers and Margaret W. Ferguson, eds., *Rewriting the Renaissance: the Discourses of Sexual Difference in Early Modern Europe*. Chicago: University of Chicago Press, 1986, 299–317.

Jones, A. R. and Peter Stallybrass. *Renaissance Clothing and the Materials of Memory*. Cambridge: Cambridge University Press, 2000.

Jones, Colin. 'Prostitution and the Ruling Class in Eighteenth-Century Montpellier.' *History Workshop Journal* 6 (1978), 7–28.

Jütte, Robert. 'Poor Relief and Social Discipline in Sixteenth Century Europe.' *European Studies Review* 11 (1981), 25–52.

Poverty and Deviance in Early Modern Europe. Cambridge: Cambridge University Press, 1994.

Kamen, Henry. *The Phoenix and the Flame*. New Haven: Yale University Press, 1993.

Kaplan, Steven Laurence, ed. *Understanding Popular Culture: Europe from the Middle Ages to the Nineteenth Century*. Berlin: Mouton, 1984.

King, Margaret L. *Women of the Renaissance*. Chicago and London: University of Chicago Press, 1991.

Klapisch-Zuber, Christiane. *Women, Family and Ritual in Renaissance Italy*. Chicago and London: University of Chicago Press, 1985.

Kopytoff, Igor. 'The Cultural Biography of Things: Commoditization as a Process.' In A. Appadurai, ed., *The Social Life of Things: Commodities in Cultural Perspective*. Cambridge: Cambridge University Press, 1983, 3–63.

Kowaleski, Maryanne. 'Singlewomen in Medieval and Early Modern Europe: the Demographic Perspective.' In Judith Bennett and Amy Froide, eds., *Singlewomen in the European Past, 1250–1800*. Philadelphia: University of Pennsylvania Press, 1999, 38–81.

Kuehn, Thomas. *Law, Family and Women: Towards a Legal Anthropology of Renaissance Italy*. Chicago: Chicago University Press, 1993.

Kunzle, David. *The Early Comic Strip: Narrative Strips and Picture Stories in the European Broadsheet from c.1450 to 1825*. Berkeley: University of California Press, 1973.

Kurz, Hilde. 'Italian Models of Hogarth's Picture Stories.' *Journal of the Warburg and Courtauld Institutes* 15 (1952), 136–68.

Kurzel-Runtscheiner, Monica. *Töchter der Venus: Die Kurtisanen Roms im 16. Jahrhundert*. Munich: Beck, 1995.

Labrot, Gérard. *L'image de Rome: une arme pour la Contre-réforme, 1534–1677*. Seyssel: Champ Vallon, 1987.

Lafage, Valérie. 'Le gîte, le couvert et l'habit. Aspects de la culture matérielle à Montpellier dans le premier tiers du XVII siècle.' *Annales du Midi: la culture matérielle dans le midi de la France à l'époque moderne* 115 (2003), 2–41.

Langdon, Helen. *Caravaggio: a Life*. London: Chatto & Windus, 1998.

Lansing, Carol, 'Gender and Civic Authority: Sexual Control in a Medieval Italian Town.' *Journal of Social History* 31:1 (1997), 33–59.

Laqueur, Thomas. *Making Sex: Body and Gender from the Greeks to Freud*. Cambridge, Mass.: Harvard University Press, 1990.

Larivaille, Paul. 'L'Orazia de l'Aretin, tragédie des ambitions déçues.' In *Les écrivains et le pouvoir en Italie á l'époque de la Renaissance, vol. II*. Centre de Recherche sur la Renaissance Italienne. Paris: Université de la Sorbonne Nouvelle, 1973, 279–360.

La vita quotidiana delle cortigiane nell'Italia del Rinascimento. Milan: Rizzoli, 1975.

Laven, Mary. *Virgins of Venice: Enclosed Lives and Broken Vows in the Renaissance Convent*. London: Penguin, 2002.

Lawner, Lynn. *Lives of the Courtesans*. New York: Rizzoli, 1986.

ed., *I Modi nell'opera di Giulio Romano, Marcantonio Raimondi, Pietro Aretino e Jean-Frédéric-Maximilien de Waldeck*. Milan: Longanesi, 1984.

Lazar, Lance Gabriel. *Working in the Vineyard of the Lord: Jesuit Confraternities in Early Modern Italy*. Toronto: University of Toronto Press, 2005.

Lee, Egmont. 'Foreigners in Quattrocento Rome.' *Renaissance and Reformation*, new series, 7:2 (1983), 135–46.

'Notaries, Immigrants and Computers: the Roman Rione Ponte, 1450–1480.' In Paolo Brezzi and Egmont Lee, eds., *Sources of Social History: Private Acts of the Late Middle Ages*. Papers in Mediaeval Studies 5. Toronto: Pontifical Institute of Mediaeval Studies, 1984, 239–49.

'The Two Romes of the Renaissance.' *Canadian Journal of History* 19:1 (1984), 71–4.

Lehoux, Françoise. *Le cadre de vie des médecins parisiens aux XVIe et XVIIe siècles*. Paris: Editions Picard, 1976.

Levi, Giovanni. 'On Microhistory.' In Peter Burke, ed., *New Perspectives on Historical Writing*. Cambridge: Polity Press, 1991, 93–113.

'Un problema di scala.' In Sergio Bologna et al., eds., *Dieci interventi sulla storia sociale*. Turin: Rosenberg and Sellier, 1981, 75–81.

Lindberg, Carter. *The European Reformations*. Oxford: Blackwell, 1996.

Linde, Charlotte. 'Explanatory Systems in Oral Life Stories.' In D. Holland and N. Quinn, eds., *Cultural Models in Language and Thought*. New York: Cambridge University Press, 1987.

Life Stories: the Creation of Coherence. New York and Oxford: Oxford University Press, 1993.

Lombardi, Daniela. *Povertà maschile, povertà femminile. L'ospedale dei mendicanti nella Firenze dei Medici*. Bologna: Il Mulino, 1988.

Londei, Luigi. 'La funzione giudiziaria nello stato pontificio di antico regime.' *Archivi per la Storia* 1–2 (1991), 13–31.

Lorenzetti, Stefano. 'Per animare agli esercizi nobili: esperienza musicale e identità nobiliare nei collegi di educazione.' *Quaderni Storici* 95:2 (1997), 435–59.

Lotz, Wolfgang. 'Gli 883 cocchi della Roma del 1594.' *ARSRSP* 23 (1973), 247–66.

Luzio, A. and R. Renier. 'Contributo alla storia del malfrancese ne'costumi e nella letteratura italiana del sec. XVI.' *Giornale Storico della Letteratura Italiana* 5 (1885), 430.

McClure, Peter. 'Patterns of Migration in the Late Middle Ages: the Evidence of English Placename Surnames.' *Economic History Review* 32:2 (1970), 167–82.

McGinness, Frederick. 'The Rhetoric of Praise and the New Rome of the Counter-Reformation.' In P. A Ramsey, ed., *Rome in the Renaissance: the City and the Myth*. Binghamton, N.Y.: Medieval and Renaissance Texts and Studies, 1982, 355–70.

McLaren, Angus. *A History of Contraception: From Antiquity to the Present Day*. Oxford: Basil Blackwell, 1990.

McPherson, David. 'Roman Comedy in Renaissance Education: the Moral Question.' *Sixteenth Century Journal* 12:1 (1981), 19–30.

Madignier, Mirabelle. 'Sociabilité informelle et pratiques sociales en Italie: les salons romains et florentins au XVIIIème siècle', PhD thesis, European University Institute, Florence, 1999.

Maffesoli, Michel. 'La prostitution comme "forme de socialité"'. *Cahiers Internationaux de Sociologie* 76 (1984), 119–33.

Maidment, B. E. *Reading Popular Prints, 1790–1870*. Manchester and New York: Manchester University Press, 1996.

Malanima, Paolo. *Il lusso dei contadini: consumi e industrie nelle compagne toscane del sei e settecento*. Bologna: Il Mulino, 1990.

Maravall, J. A. *La cultura del barocco. Analisi di una struttura storica*. Bologna: Il Mulino, 1985.

Martin, John Jeffries. 'Religion, Renewal and Reform in the Sixteenth Century.' In John A. Marino, ed., *Early Modern Italy, 1550–1796*. Oxford: Oxford University Press, 2002, 30–45.

Masson, G. *Courtesans of the Italian Renaissance*. London: Secker and Warburg, 1975.

Matthews Grieco, Sara F. *Ange ou diablesse: la représentation de la femme au XVIe siècle*. Paris: Flammarion, 1991.

'The Body, Appearance and Sexuality.' In G. Duby and M. Perrot, eds., *A History of Women in the West: Renaissance and Enlightenment Paradoxes*. Cambridge, Mass.: The Belknap Press of Harvard University Press, 1993, 66–85.

'Matrimonio e vita coniugale nell'arte dell'Italia moderna.' In Michela de Giorgio and Christiane Klapisch-Zuber, eds., *Storia delle donne in Italia. Storia del matrimonio*. Rome and Bari: Laterza, 1996, 251–82.

'Pedagogical Prints: Moralizing Broadsheets and Wayward Women in Counter Reformation Italy.' In Geraldine A. Johnson and Sara F. Matthews Grieco, eds., *Picturing Women in Renaissance and Baroque Italy*. Cambridge: Cambridge University Press, 1997, 61–88.

Mauss, Marcel. *The Gift: the Form and Reason of Exchange in Archaic Societies*, trans. W. D. Halls. London: Routledge, 1990.

Mazo Karras, Ruth. *Common Women: Prostitution and Sexuality in Medieval England*: Oxford and New York: Oxford University Press, 1996.

'Prostitution and the Question of Sexual Identity in Medieval Europe.' *Journal of Women's History* 11:2 (1999), 159–77, 193–7.

Mazzi, Maria Serena. *Prostitute e lenoni nella Firenza del quattrocento*. Milan: Mondadori, 1991.

Medin, A. and C. Frati. *Lamenti storici dei secoli XIV, XV, XVI*. Bologna: Romagnoli-Dall Acqua, 1887.

Menjot, Denis. 'Prostitution et ruffianage dans les villes de Castille à la fin du Moyen Age.' *IAHCCJ Bulletin* 19 (1994), 21–38.

Mennell, S. *Norbert Elias: Civilization and the Human Self-Image*. Oxford: Blackwell, 1989.

Mericskay, A. 'La prostitution à Paris (dans les marges d'un grand livre).' *Histoire, Economie et Société* 4 (1987), 495–508.

Merzario, Raul. *Anastasia, ovvero la malizia degli uomini. Relazioni sociali e controlo delle nascite in un villaggio ticinese, 1650–1750*. Rome and Bari: Laterza, 1992.

Migiel, M. and J. Schiesari, eds., *Refiguring Woman: Perspectives on Gender and the Italian Renaissance*. New York: Cornell University Press, 1991.

Milano, Alberto. 'Stampe e stampatori nel fondo di stampe P. P. della raccolta Bertarelli.' In A. Amitrano Savarese and A. Rigoli, eds., *Stampe popolari profane della civica raccolta Achille Bertarelli*. Vigevano: Diakronia, 1995.

Miller, Daniel, ed. *Acknowledging Consumption: a Review of New Studies*. London and New York: Routledge, 1995.

Mills, Kenneth and Anthony Grafton, eds. *Conversion: Old Worlds and New*. Rochester, N.Y. University of Rochester Press, 2003.

Mollat, Michel. *The Poor in the Middle Ages*. New Haven: Yale University Press, 1978.

'The Poor in the Middle Ages: the Experience of a Research Project.' In Thomas Riis, ed., *Aspects of Poverty in Early Modern Europe*. Florence: EUI, 1981, 29–37.

Monson, Craig A. *Disembodied Voices: Music and Culture in an Early Modern Italian Convent*. Berkeley, Los Angeles and London: University of California Press, 1995.

Montalto, L. *Un mecenate in Roma barocca. Il Cardinale Benedetto Pamphilij*. Florence: Sansoni, 1955.

Mori, Elisabetta. 'Cittadinanza e nobiltà a Roma tra cinque e seicento.' *Roma Moderna e Contemporanea* 4:2 (1996), 379–403.

Muir, Edward and Guido Ruggiero. *History from Crime*, trans. Corrada Biazzo Curry, Margaret A. Gallucci and Mary M. Gallucci (Baltimore: The Johns Hopkins University Press, 1994).

Mutinelli, Fabio. *Storia arcana e anedottica d'Italia raccontata dei Veneti ambasciatori, vol*. I. Venice, 1865.

Muzzarelli, Maria Giuseppina. *Guardaroba medievale: vesti e società dal XII al XVI secolo*. Bologna: Il Mulino, 1999.

Niccoli, Ottavia. 'Lotte per le brache: la donna indisciplinata nelle stampe popolari d'ancien regime.' *Memoria* 2 (1981): 49–63.

Profeti e popolo nell'Italia del Rinascimento. Rome: Laterza, 1987.

Norberg, Kathryn. 'Prostitutes.' In G. Duby and M. Perrot, eds., *A History of Women in the West: Renaissance and Enlightenment Paradoxes*. Cambridge, Mass.: The Belknap Press of Harvard University Press, 1993, 458–74.

Novati, Francesco. *Intorno alle origini e la diffusione delle stampe popolari*. Palermo: Il Vespro, 1880.

La poesia popolare italiana. Livorno: Giusti, 1906.

La storia e la stampa nella produzione popolare italiana, con un elenco topografico di tipografi e calcografi italiani che dal sec. XV al XVII impressero storie e stampe popolari. Bergamo: Istitute Italiano d'Arti Grafiche, 1907.

Novi Chiavarria, Elisa. 'Ideologia e comportamenti familiari nei predicatori italiani tra cinque e settecento. Tematiche e modelli.' *Rivista Storica Italiana* 100:3 (1988), 679–723.

Nussdorfer, L. *Civic Politics in the Rome of Urban VIII.* Princeton and Oxford: Princeton University Press, 1992.

'Il popolo romano e i papi: la vita politica della capitale religiosa.' In Luigi Fiorani and Adriano Prosperi, eds., *Storia d'Italia, annali 16, Roma, la città del papa.* Turin: Einaudi, 2000, 241–62.

Nye, Robert. 'Crime in Modern Societies: Some Research Strategies for Historians.' *Journal of Social History* 11:4 (1978), 491–507.

Olivieri, Achille. 'Eroticism and Social Groups in 16th Century Venice: the Courtesan.' In P. Ariès and A. Béjin, eds., *Western Sexuality.* Oxford: Basil Blackwell, 1985.

Immaginario e gerarchie sociali nella cultura del '500. Verona: Libreria Universitaria, 1986.

O'Malley, John. *The First Jesuits.* Cambridge, Mass.: Harvard University Press, 1993.

Rome and the Renaissance. London: Variorum Reprints, 1981.

Orbaan, J. A. F. *Documenti sul Barocco in Roma.* Rome: Miscellanea della R. Società Romana di Storia Patria, 1920.

Otis, Linda L. *Prostitution in Medieval Society: the History of an Urban Institution in Languedoc.* London: University of Chicago Press, 1985.

Outram Evennett, H. *The Spirit of the Counter-Reformation.* Notre Dame: University of Notre Dame Press, 1970.

Owen Hughes, Diane. 'Le mode femminili e il loro controllo.' In Georges Duby, Michelle Perrot and Christiane Klapisch-Zuber, eds., *Storia delle donne in occidente. Il medioevo.* Rome and Bari: Laterza, 1998, 166–93.

Page Moch, Leslie. *Moving Europeans: Migration in Western Europe since 1650.* Bloomington and Indianapolis: Indiana University Press, 1992.

Paglia, Vincenzo. *La pietà dei carcerati: confraternite e società a Roma nei secoli XVI–XVIII,* introd. Gabriele De Rosa. Rome: Edizioni di storia e letteratura, 1980.

Palermo, Luciano. 'Espansione demografica e sviluppo economico a Roma nel Rinascimento.' *Studi Romani* 44:1–2 (1996), 21–47.

Panizza, Letizia, ed. *Women in Italian Renaissance Culture and Society.* Oxford: Legenda, 2000.

Partner, Peter. *All the Pope's Men: the Papal Civil Service in the Renaissance.* New York: Oxford University Press, 1990.

Renaissance Rome, 1500–1559: a Portrait of a Society. Berkeley and Los Angeles: University of California Press, 1979.

Passigli, Susanna. 'Gli stati delle anime: un contributo allo studio del tessuto urbano di Roma.' *ARSRSP* 112 (1989), 293–340.

Pastor, Ludovico Barone von. *Storia dei papi dalla fine del medioevo*, trans. and ed. Mons. Prof. Angelo Mercati. Reprint, Rome: Desclée, 1958.

Pavan, Elizabeth. 'Police des moeurs, société et politique à Venise à la fin du Moyen Age.' *Revue Historique* 5:36 (1980), 241–88.

Pediconi, Angelica. 'The Art and Culture of Bathing in Renaissance Rome', MA dissertation, History of Design, Victoria and Albert Museum/Royal College of Art, London, 2004.

Pelaja, Margherita. 'Relazioni personali e vincoli di gruppo. Il lavoro delle donne nella Roma dell'ottocento', *Memoria* 30:3 (1990), 45–54.

Pelliccia, Guerrino. 'Scuole di catechismo e scuole rionali per fanciulle nella Roma del seicento.' *Ricerche per la storia religiosa di Roma* 4 (1980), 237–68.

Pennell, Sara. 'Consumption and Consumerism in Early Modern England.' *The Historical Journal* 42:2 (1999), 549–64.

Percopo, E. 'Di Anton Lelio Romano.' *Giornale Storico Della Letteratura Italiana* 28 (1896), 45–91.

Perry, Mary Elizabeth. 'Deviant Insiders: Legalised Prostitutes and a Consciousness of Women in Early Modern Seville.' *Comparative Studies in Society and History* 27 (1985), 138–58.

Gender and Disorder in Early Modern Seville. Princeton: Princeton University Press, 1990.

Petrocchi, Massimo. *Roma nel seicento*. Bologna: Cappelli, 1970.

Pfister, Max. *Lessico etimologico italiano*. Wiesbaden: Dr. Ludwig Reichert Verlag, 1979.

Pisano, Giulio. 'I birri a Roma nel '600 ed un progetto di riforma del loro ordinamento sotto il pontificato d'Innocenzo XI.' *Roma* 10 (1932), 543–56.

Polverini Fosi, Irene. 'I Fiorentini a Roma nel cinquecento: storia di una presenza.' In Sergio Gensini, ed., *Roma Capitale (1447–1527)*. Rome: Ministero per i Beni Culturali, 1995, 389–414.

'Fonti giudiziarie e tribunali nella Roma del cinquecento. Problemi metodologici per una ricerca di demografia storica.' In Eugenio Sonnino, ed., *Popolazione e società a Roma dal medioevo all'età contemporanea*. Rome: Il Calamo, 1998, 591–6.

'Signori e tribunali. Criminalità nobiliare e giustizia pontificia nella Roma del cinquecento.' In M. A. Visceglia, ed., *Signori, patrizi, cavalieri nell'età moderna*. Roma and Bari: Laterza, 1992, 214–30.

La società violenta. Il banditismo nello stato pontificio nella seconda metà del cinquecento. Rome: Edizioni dell'Ateneo, 1985.

Pomata, Gianna. 'Family and Gender.' In John A. Marino, ed., *Early Modern Italy, 1550–1796*. Oxford and New York: Oxford University Press, 2002, 69–81.

Pomeroy, Sarah B. *Goddesses, Whores, Wives, Slaves. Women in Classical Antiquity*. New York: Schocken Books, 1975.

Pompeo, Augusto. 'Procedure usuali e "iura specialia in criminalibus" nei tribunali romani di antico regime.' *Archivi per la Storia* 1–2 (1991), 111–24.

Porri, M. and C. Schiavoni. 'Aspetti della condizione femminile e del lavoro della donna a Roma fra XVII e XVIII secolo.' *Genus* 3–4 (1988), 245–63.

Porter, Roy. 'Seeing the Past.' *Past and Present* 118 (1988), 186–205.

Prodi, Paolo. *Il sovrano pontefice.* Bologna: Il Mulino, 1982.

Ed. *Disciplina dell'anima, disciplina del corpo, disciplina della società tra medioevo ed età moderna.* Bologna: Il Mulino, 1994.

Prosperi, Adriano. 'Intellettuali e chiesa all'inizio dell'età moderna.' *Storia d'Italia: annali 4, intellettuali e potere.* Turin: Einaudi, 1981, 161–252.

Pullan, Brian. 'Poveri, mendicanti e vagabondi (secoli XIV–XVII).' In C. Vivanti and R. Romano, eds., *Storia d'Italia. Dal feudalismo al capitalismo. Annali I.* Turin: Einaudi, 1978, 981–1048.

'Support and Redeem: Charity and Poor Relief in Italian Cities from the Fourteenth to the Seventeenth Century.' *Continuity and Change* 3:2 (1988), 177–208.

Quétel, C. *A History of Syphilis.* Baltimore: The Johns Hopkins University Press, 1990.

Ramsey, P. A., ed. *Rome in the Renaissance: the City and the Myth.* Binghamton, N.Y.: Medieval and Renaissance Texts and Studies, 1982.

Randolph, Adrian. 'Regarding Women in Sacred Space.' In Geraldine A. Johnson and Sara F. Matthews Grieco, eds., *Picturing Women in Renaissance and Baroque Italy.* Cambridge: Cambridge University Press, 1997, 17–41.

Reinhard, Wolfgang. 'Disciplinamento sociale, confessionalizzazione, modernizzazione. Un discorso storiografico.' In Paolo Prodi, ed., *Disciplina dell'anima, disciplina del corpo, e disciplina della società tra medioevo ed età moderna.* Bologna: Il Mulino, 1994.

Revel, Jacques. 'Micro-analyse et construction du social.' In Jacques Revel, ed., *Jeux d'echelles.* Paris: Gallimard-Le Seuil, 1996, 15–36.

Richardson, Catherine, ed. *Clothing Culture, 1350–1650.* Aldershot: Ashgate, 2004.

Riddle, John M. 'Oral Contraceptives and Early Term Abortifacients during Classical Antiquity and the Middle Ages.' *Past and Present* 132 (1991), 3–32.

Rigoli, Aurelio and Annamaria Amitrano Savarese, eds. *Stampe popolari profani della civica raccolta Achille Bertarelli.* Vigevano: Diakronia, 1995.

Riis, Thomas. *Aspects of Poverty in Early Modern Europe.* Florence: EUI, 1981.

Roche, Daniel. *Le peuple de Paris. Essai sur la culture populaire au XVIIIe siècle.* Paris: Fayard, 1998.

Rocke, Michael. *Forbidden Friendships: Homosexuality and Male Culture in Renaissance Florence.* Oxford: Oxford University Press, 1998.

Rodocanachi, Emmanuel. *Cortigiane e buffoni di Roma: studio dei costumi romani del XVI secolo.* Milan: Edizioni Pervinca, 1927.

La femme italienne à l'époque de la Renaissance. (Sa vie privée et mondaine et son influence sociale). Paris: Hachette, 1907.

Les institutions communales de Rome sous la papauté. Paris: Alphonse Picard, 1901.

Romani, Mario. *Pellegrini e viaggiatori nell'economia di Roma dal XIV al XVII secolo.* Milan: Vita e Pensiero, 1948.

Romano, Ruggiero. 'La storia economica dal secolo XIV al settecento. I meccanismi.' In R. Romano and C. Vivanti, eds., *Storia d'Italia. Dalla caduta dell'impero romano al secolo XVIII, vol. II.* Turin: Einaudi, 1974, 1841–904.

Roper, Lyndal. 'Discipline and Respectability: Prostitution and the Reformation in Augsburg.' *History Workshop Journal* 19 (1985), 3–28.

'Gender and the Reformation.' *Archive for Reformation History* 92 (2001), 290–302.

The Holy Household (Oxford: Oxford University Press, 1989).

'Madri di depravazione: le mezzane nel cinquecento.' *Memoria* 2 (1986), 7–23.

Oedipus and the Devil: Witchcraft, Sexuality and Religion in Early Modern Europe. London and New York: Routledge, 1994.

Rosenthal, Margaret F. *The Honest Courtesan: Veronica Franco, Citizen and Writer in Sixteenth-Century Venice*. Chicago and London: University of Chicago Press, 1992.

Rossi, Ermete. 'Un curioso incidente diplomatico tra Vienna e Roma.' *ARSRSP* 60 (1937), 243–55.

Rossiaud, Jacques. *Medieval Prostitution*. Oxford: Basil Blackwell, 1988.

'Prostitution, jeunesse et société dans les villes du sud-est au XVe siècle.' *Annales ESC* 31:2 (1976), 289–325.

Rublack, Ulinka. *The Crimes of Women in Early Modern Germany*. Oxford: Clarendon Press, 1999.

Reformation Europe. Cambridge: Cambridge University Press, 2005.

Ruggiero, Guido. *Binding Passions: Tales of Magic, Marriage and Power at the End of the Renaissance*. Oxford: Oxford University Press, 1993.

The Boundaries of Eros: Sex, Crime and Sexuality in Renaissance Venice. London and New York: Oxford University Press, 1995.

'Re-reading the Renaissance: Civic Morality and the World of Marriage, Love and Sex.' In J. G. Turner, ed., *Sexuality and Gender in Early Modern Europe: Institutions, Texts, Images*. Cambridge: Cambridge University Press, 1993, 10–30.

Russell, Diane H., with Bernadine A. Barnes, *Eva/Ave: Woman in Renaissance and Baroque Prints*. Washington, D.C.: National Gallery of Art; New York: The Feminist Press at the City University of New York, 1990.

Salerno, Luigi and Gianfranco Spagnesi. *La chiesa di San Rocco all'Augusteo*. Rome: Desclée e C. Editori, 1962.

Salles, Catherine. 'Les prostituées de Rome.' In Philippe Ariès, ed., *Amour et sexualité en occident*. Paris: Editions du Seuil, 1991.

San Martini, Barovecchio M. L. *Il tribunale criminale del governatore di Roma (1512–1809)*. Rome: Pubblicazioni degli Archivi di Stato, 1981.

Santini, Antonio. 'Le strutture socio-demografiche della popolazione urbana.' In *La demografia storica delle città italiane: relazioni e comunicazioni presentate al convegno tenuto ad Assisi*. Bologna: Clueb, 1982, 125–47.

Santore, Cathy. 'Julia Lombardo "sontuosa meretrize": a Portrait by Property.' *Renaissance Quarterly* 41:1 (1988), 44–83.

'The Tools of Venus.' *The Society for Renaissance Studies* 11:3 (1997), 179–208.

Sarti, Raffaella. *Europe at Home: Family and Material Culture, 1500–1800*. New Haven and London: Yale University Press, 2002.

Sbriccoli, Mario. 'Fonti giudiziarie e fonti giuridiche. Riflessioni sulla fase attuale degli studi di storia del crimine e della giustizia criminale.' *Studi Storici* 29 (1988), 491–501.

Schiavoni, Claudio. 'Brevi cenni sullo sviluppo della popolazione romana dal 1700 al 1824.' In *Demografia storica delle città italiane: relazioni e comunicazioni presentate al convegno tenuto ad Assisi.* Bologna: Clueb, 1982, 401–31.

'Gli infanti esposti del Santo Spirito in Saxia di Roma tra '500 e '800: numero, ricevimento, allevamento e destino.' In *Enfance abandonnée et société en Europe, XIVe–XXe siècle.* Collection de l'École Française de Rome. Rome: École Française de Rome, 1991, 1017–64.

Schiavoni, C. and E. Sonnino. 'Aspects généraux de l'évolution démographique à Rome, 1598–1824.' *Annales de Démographie Historique* (1982), 91–109.

Schilling, Heinz. 'Chiese confessionali e disciplinamento sociale. Un bilancio provvisorio della ricerca storica.' In Paolo Prodi, ed., *Disciplina dell'anima, disciplina del corpo e disciplina della società tra medioevo ed età moderna.* Bologna: Il Mulino, 1994, 125–61.

Scribner, Robert W. *For the Sake of Simple Folk: Popular Propaganda for the German Reformation.* Cambridge: Cambridge University Press, 1981.

Sekora, John. *Luxury: the Concept in Western Thought, Eden to Smollett.* Baltimore: The Johns Hopkins University Press, 1977.

Selwyn, Jennifer. *A Paradise Inhabited by Devils: the Jesuits' Civilizing Mission in Early Modern Naples.* Aldershot: Ashgate, 2004.

Serra, Armando. 'Viaggiatori e servizi di posta o a vettura nel bacino tiberino preferroviario.' In Enzo Mattesini, ed., *Vie di pellegrinaggio medievale attraverso l'alta valle del Tevere.* Citta di Castello: Petruzzi Editore, 1998, 152–91.

Sharpe, Jim. 'History from Below.' In Peter Burke, ed., *New Perspectives on Historical Writing.* Oxford: Polity Press, 1991, 24–41.

'Human Relations and the History of Crime.' *IAHCCJ Bulletin* 14 (1991), 10–32.

Shesgreen, Sean. *Images of the Outcast: the Urban Poor in the Cries of London.* Manchester: Manchester University Press, 2002.

Simons, Patricia. 'Portraiture, Portrayal and Idealization: Ambiguous Individualism in Representations of Renaissance Women.' In Alison Brown, ed., *Languages and Images of Renaissance Italy.* Oxford: Clarendon Press, 1995, 271–85.

Singleton, C. *Canti carnascialeschi del Rinascimento.* Bari: Laterza, 1936.

Sogner, Solvi. 'Introduction', in *Socio-Economic Consequences of Sex-ratios in Historical Perspective, 1500–1900.* Proceedings of the Eleventh International Economic History Congress, Milan, Sept. 1994. Milan: Università Bocconi, 1994, 9–16.

Somers, Margaret. 'The Narrative Constitution of Identity: a Relational and Network Approach.' *Theory and Society* 23 (1994), 605–49.

Sonnino, Eugenio. 'Le anime dei romani: fonti religiose e demografia storica.' In Luigi Fiorani and Adriano Prosperi, eds., *Storia d'Italia, annali 16, Roma la città del papa.* Turin: Einaudi, 2000, 329–366.

'Gli stati delle anime a Roma nella prima metà del secolo XVII: entità e qualità delle registrazioni.' In Rosa Traino, Eugenio Sonnino and Carla Sbrana, eds., *Gli stati delle anime a Roma dalle origini al secolo XVII*. Rome: La Goliardica, 1977, 19–38.

'Intorno alla "Sapienza". Popolazione e famiglie, collegiali e studenti a Roma nel seicento.' *Roma e lo studium urbis: spazio urbano e cultura dal quattro al seicento*. Atti del Convegno, Rome: Ministero per i Beni Culturali e Ambientali, 1992, 341–68.

'In the Male City: the *Status Animarum* of Rome in the Seventeenth Century.' In Antoinette Fauve-Chamoux and Solvi Sogner, eds., *Socio-economic Consequences of Sex-Ratios in Historical Perspective, 1500–1900*. Proceedings of the Eleventh International Economic History Congress, Milan, 1994, vol. B5. Milan: Università Bocconi, 1994.

'From the Home to the Hospice: The Plight and Fate of Girl Orphans in Seventeenth and Eighteenth Century Rome.' In Richard Wall and John Henderson, eds., *Poor Women and Children in the European Past*. London and New York: Routledge, 1994, 94–116.

'Problèmes de recherche dans une grande ville: le cas de Rome (XVIIe siècle).' *Annales de démographie historique* (1972), 221–3.

Sonnino, Eugenio and Rosa Traina, 'La peste del 1656–57 a Roma. Organizzazione sanitaria e mortalità', in *Demografia Storica delle Città Italiane: Relazioni e comunicazioni presentate al convegno tenuto ad Assisi, 1980*. Bologna: Clueb, 1982, 433–52.

Spagnuolo, Vera Vita, 'Gli atti notarili dell'Archivio di Stato di Roma: saggio di spoglio sistematico: l'anno 1590,' in B. Antolini, A. Morelli and V. V. Spagnuolo, eds., *La musica a Roma attraverso le fonti d'archivio* (Lucca: Libreria Musicale Italiana, 1994), 19–65.

Sperling, Jutta Gisela. *Convents and the Body Politic in Late Renaissance Venice*. Chicago and London: University of Chicago Press, 1999.

Spierenberg, Pieter. 'Justice and the Mental World: Ten Years of Research and Interpretation of Criminal Justice Data from the Perspective of the History of Mentalities.' *IAHCCJ Bulletin* 14 (1991), 38–77.

Spini, Giorgio. *La ricerca dei libertini. La teoria dell'impostura delle religioni nel seicento italiano*. Florence: La Nuova Italia, 1983.

Storey, Tessa 'The Clothing of Courtesans in Seventeenth Century Rome.' In Catherine Richardson, ed., *Clothing Culture, 1350–1650*. Aldershot: Ashgate, 2004, 95–108.

'Fragments from the "Life Histories" of Jewellery Belonging to Prostitutes in Early Modern Rome.' *Renaissance Quarterly* 19:5 (2005), 647–57.

'Prostitution and the Circulation of Second-Hand Goods in Seventeenth Century Rome.' In Laurence Fontaine, ed., *Alternative Exchanges: Second-Hand Circulations from the Sixteenth Century to the Present*. Oxford: Berghahn, 2007.

'Storie di prostituzione nella Roma della Controriforma,' *Quaderni Storici* 106:1 (2001), 261–95.

Strasser, Ulrike. 'Bones of Contention: Cloistered Nuns, Decorated Relics, and the Contest over Women's Place in the Public Sphere of Counter-Reformation Munich.' *Archive for Reformation History* 90 (1999), 254–88.

State of Virginity: Gender, Religion and Politics in an Early Modern Catholic State. Ann Arbor: University of Michigan Press, 2004.

Tacchi-Venturi, Pietro. *Storia della Compagnia di Gesù in Italia: narrata col sussidio di fonti inedite.* Rome: La Civiltà Cattolica, 1950.

Talvacchia, Bette. *Taking Positions: On the Erotic in Renaissance Culture.* Princeton: Princeton University Press, 1999.

Tamburini, Elena. 'La lira, la poesia, la voce, e il teatro musicale del seicento. Note su alcune vicende biografiche e artistiche della baronessa Anna Rosalia Carusi,' In B. M. Antolini, A. Morelli and V. Vita Spagnuolo, eds., *La musica a Roma attraverso le fonti d'archivio.* Lucca: Libreria Musicale Italiana, 1994, 419–31.

Tateo, Francesco. *Umanesimo etico di Giovanni Pontano.* Lecce: Milella, 1972.

Thornton, Peter. *The Italian Renaissance Interior, 1400–1600.* London: Weidenfeld and Nicolson, 1991.

Tinagli, Paola. *Women in Italian Renaissance Art: Gender, Representation, Identity.* Manchester and New York: Manchester University Press, 1997.

Toschi, P. 'La letteratura popolare e la stampa nel quattrocento.' *In Studi e ricerche sulla storia della stampa del quattrocento,* introd. Giuseppe Bottai. Milan: Hoepli, 1942.

Tosh, John. 'What Should Historians Do with Masculinity?' *History Workshop Journal* 38 (1994), 179–202.

Tosi, Mario. *Il Sacro Monte di Pietà di Roma e le sue amministrazioni (1539–1874).* Rome: Cassa di Risparmio di Roma, Libreria dello Stato, 1937.

Traina, Rosa. 'Caratteristiche di registrazione dello stato delle anime a Roma.' In Carla Sbrana, Rosa Traina and Eugenio Sonnino, eds., *Gli stati delle anime a Roma dalle origini al secolo XVII.* Rome: La Goliardica, 1977, 345–75.

Travaglini, Carlo. 'Rigattieri e società romana nel settecento.' *Quaderni Storici* 80:2 (1992), 415–47.

Trexler, Richard. 'La prostitution florentine au XVe siècle: patronages et clientèles.' *Annales ESC* 36 (1981), 983–1015.

Public Life in Renaissance Florence. New York: Cornell University Press, 1991.

Turchini, Angelo. 'Dalla disciplina alla "creanza" del matrimonio all'indomani del Concilio di Trento.' In Gabriella Zarri, eds., *Donna, disciplina, creanza cristiana dal XV al XVII secolo: studi e testi a stampa.* Rome: Edizioni di Storia e Letteratura, 1996, 205–14.

Van der Meer, Theo. 'Medieval Prostitution and the Case of a (Mistaken?) Sexual Identity.' *Journal of Women's History* 11:2 (1999), 178–91.

Van de Pol, Lotte. *Het Amsterdams Hoerdom. Prostitutie in de Zeventiende en Achtiende Eeuw.* Amsterdam; Wereldbibliotheek, 1996.

'The Lure of the Big City. Female Migration to Amsterdam.' In Els Kloek, Nicole Teeuwen, and Marijke Huisman, eds., *Women of the Golden Age: an*

International Debate on Women in the Seventeenth Century: Holland, England and Italy (Hilversum: Uitgeverij Verloren, 1994), 73–83.

Vasaio, Maria Elena. 'Il tessuto della virtù: le zitelle di S. Eufemia e di S. Caterina dei Funari nella controriforma.' *Memoria* 11–12:2–3 (1984), 53–64.

Veblen, Thorstein. *The Theory of the Leisure Class: an Economic Study of Institutions.* New York: Macmillan, 1912.

Verzone, Carlo, ed. *Le rime burlesche di A. F. Antonfrancesco Grazzini, detto il Lasca, Le rime burlesche. Edite e inedite* (Florence: Sansoni, 1882).

Vickery, Amanda. 'Women and the World of Goods: a Lancashire Consumer and her Possessions.' In John Brewer and Roy Porter, eds., *Consumption and the World of Goods.* London and New York: Routledge, 1993, 206–27.

Villari, Renzo. 'Sullo studio della devianza. Note su alcuni aspetti storiografici e metodologici.' *Società e Storia* 13 (1981), 639–70.

Visceglia, Maria Antonietta, 'I consumi in Italia in età moderna.' In Ruggiero Romano, ed., *Storia dell'economia italiana. L'età moderna. Verso la crisi.* Turin: Giulio Einaudi, 1991, 212–42.

Vocabulario degli Accademici della Crusca. Verona, 1806.

Walkowitz, Judith. *Prostitution and Victorian Society: Women, Class and the State.* Cambridge: Cambridge University Press, 1980.

Weatherill, Lorna. 'The Meaning of Consumer Behaviour in Late Seventeenth and Early Eighteenth Century England.' In John Brewer and Roy Porter, eds., *Consumption and the World of Goods.* London and New York: Routledge, 1993.

 'A Possession of One's Own: Women and Consumer Behaviour in England, 1660–1740.' *Journal of British Studies* 25 (1986), 131–56.

Wiesner, Merry. *Women and Gender in Early Modern Europe.* Cambridge: Cambridge University Press, 1993.

Wiesner-Hanks, Merry E. *Christianity and Sexuality in the Early Modern World: Regulating Desire, Reforming Practice.* London: Routledge, 2000.

Wijsenbeek Olthuis, Thera. 'A Matter of Taste: Lifestyle in Holland in the Seventeenth and Eighteenth Century.' In Anton J. Shuurman and Larena S. Walsh eds., *Material Culture: Consumption, Life-Style, Standard of Living, 1500–1900.* Proceedings of the Eleventh International History Congress, Milan, 1994, vol. B4 Milan: Università Bocconi, 1994.

Woodhouse, John, 'La cortigiania di Niccolo Strozzi', *Studi Secenteschi* 23 (1982), 141–93.

Woolf, Stuart. *Domestic Strategies, Work and Family in France and Italy, 1600–1800.* Cambridge: Cambridge University Press, 1991.

 The Poor in Western Europe in the 18th and 19th Centuries. London: Methuen, 1986.

Wootton, David. 'Friendship Portrayed: a New Account of Utopia.' *History Workshop Journal* 45 (1998), 29–47.

Wright, A. D. *The Counter Reformation: Catholic Europe and the Non-Christian World.* London: Weidenfeld and Nicolson, 1982.

The Early Modern Papacy: From the Council of Trent to the French Revolution. Harlow: Longman, 2000.

Zapperi, Roberto. *Eros e Controriforma*. Turin: Bollati Boringhieri, 1994.

Zarri, Gabriella, ed. *Donna, disciplina, creanza cristiana dal XV al XVII secolo: studi e testi a stampa*. Rome: Edizioni di Storia e Letteratura, 1996.

Zatz, Noah D. 'Sex Work/Sex Act: Law, Labor, and Desire in Constructions of Prostitution.' *Signs* 22:2 (1997), 227–308.

Zorzi, Andrea. 'Giustizia criminale e criminalità nell'Italia del tardo medioevo. Studi e prospettive di ricerca.' *Società e Storia* 11 (1989), 923–66.

Index

NEW STUDIES IN EUROPEAN HISTORY